Lecture Notes in Computer Science 601

D. Dolev Z. Galil M. Rodeh (Eds.)

Theory of Computing and Systems

ISTCS '92, Israel Symposium
Haifa, Israel, May 27-28, 1992
Proceedings

Springer-Verlag
Berlin Heidelberg New York
London Paris Tokyo
Hong Kong Barcelona
Budapest

Series Editors

Gerhard Goos
Universität Karlsruhe
Postfach 69 80
Vincenz-Priessnitz-Straße 1
W-7500 Karlsruhe, FRG

Juris Hartmanis
Department of Computer Science
Cornell University
5149 Upson Hall
Ithaca, NY 14853, USA

Volume Editors

Danny Dolev
Hebrew University
Givat Ram, Jerusalem, Israel

Zvi Galil
Columbia University, New York, NY 10027, USA
and
Tel Aviv University
Ramat Aviv, Tel Aviv, Israel

Michael Rodeh
IBM Israel Ltd., Science and Technology, Technion City
Haifa 32000, Israel

CR Subject Classification (1991): F.1-4, B.3, C.2, G.1-2, I.1, E.4, D.2-3

ISBN 3-540-55553-6 Springer-Verlag Berlin Heidelberg New York
ISBN 0-387-55553-6 Springer-Verlag New York Berlin Heidelberg

Printed in Germany

Typesetting: Camera ready by author/editor
Printing and binding: Druckhaus Beltz, Hemsbach/Bergstr.
45/3140-543210 - Printed on acid-free paper

Foreword

ISTCS'92 — The Israel Symposium on the Theory of Computing and Systems, came about spontaneously as a result of informal interaction between a group of people who viewed the conference as an appropriate expression of Israeli strength in theoretical aspects of computing and systems. These people then created the following organizational structure:

Symposium Chairs
Zvi Galil, Columbia and Tel-Aviv U.
Michael Rodeh, IBM Israel

Program Committee
Catriel Beeri, Hebrew U.
Danny Dolev (Chair), Hebrew U.
Nissim Francez, Technion
Shafi Goldwasser, MIT
Alon Itai, Technion
Shmuel Katz, Technion
Nimrod Megiddo, IBM Almaden Research Center
Yoram Moses, Weizmann Institute
Ehud Shapiro, Weizmann Institute
Amiram Yehudai, Tel Aviv U.

Local Arrangements
Shmuel Katz, Technion

The enthusiasm that the symposium created took three major forms: submission of high quality papers which led to strict acceptance criteria; acceptance of the symposium invitation to deliver an invited talk by Richard M. Karp and Michael O. Rabin, and positive response to requests for sponsorship/cooperation by non-profit professional organizations, computer-related industrial organizations, and academic institutions:

Sponsorship. The Israel Academy of Sciences and Humanities, Israel Association of Electronic Industries, the Leibniz Center for Research in Computer Science, the Hebrew University of Jerusalem, and U.S. National Science Foundation.

Cooperation. The ACM Special Interest Group for Automata and Computability Theory (SIGACT), IEEE Computer Society, IEEE Israeli Chapter, and ILA - Information Processing Association of Israel.

Industrial Sponsors. Digital (Israel) Ltd., IBM (Israel) Ltd., Intel Ltd., Motorola Communications Ltd., and National Semiconductors.

We thank all the organizations that have helped make this symposium successful. Thanks are also due to the Technion for helping in organizing the symposium, and to Springer Verlag, Heidelberg, for accepting the task of getting this volume into press in a very brief time interval.

April 1992

Danny Dolev
Zvi Galil
Michael Rodeh

This article was processed using the LaTeX macro package with LLNCS style

Table of Contents

This article was processed using the LaTeX macro package with LLNCS style

Merging and Splitting Priority Queues and Deques in Parallel

Jingsen Chen

Department of Computer Science, Lund University, Box 118, S-221 00 Lund, Sweden

Abstract. We investigate the parallel complexity of merging priority queues and double-ended priority queues (priority deques, for short). The implicit data structures that implement the queues studied in this paper are the heap, the twin-heap, the min-max heap, and the deap. It is known that heaps can be merged sequentially in sublinear time whereas merging min-max heaps requires linear sequential time. In this paper, we design efficient $O(\log n)$-time parallel algorithms to merge two priority queue or deque structures of the same type on n and k elements ($n \geq k$), respectively, which achieves the optimal speed-up. More precisely, two heaps of sizes n and k can be merged in $O(\log n)$ time with $\log k$ processors. Moreover, a related problem of splitting a heap on n elements into two heaps of sizes k and $n-k$ is solved in $O(\log n)$ parallel time with $\log n$ processors, which also achieves the optimal speed-up. For the merge operation on priority deques, we show that the problem of merging twin-heaps can be solved in the same complexity as that for heaps both sequential and in parallel. Algorithms for merging two min-max heaps or two deaps of sizes n and k are demonstrated, which achieves a parallel time of $O(\log n)$ with $\frac{k}{\log n} + \log k$ processors. The study of parallel solution to the problem of merging deaps also provides us with the first serial deap merging algorithm of time complexity $O(k + \log n \cdot \log k)$. The parallel computation model used in this paper is the EREW PRAM (Exclusive-Read Exclusive-Write Parallel Random Access Machine).

1 Introduction

One of the fundamental data types in computer science is the priority queue. It has been useful in many applications [1, 14]. A *priority queue* is a set of elements on which two basic operations are defined: insert a new element into the set; and retrieve and delete the minimum element of the set. Several data structures have been proposed for implementing priority queues. The probably most elegant one is the heap, which was introduced by Williams [21].

The problems of constructing, merging, and splitting heaps have received considerable attention in the literature [7, 10, 11, 12, 14, 15, 19, 20] and sequential constructing algorithms of linear time and sublinear time heap merging and splitting algorithms have been developed. However, designing optimal heap construction and heap merging and splitting algorithms in parallel models of computation has not been so deeply studied. Recently, Rao and Zhang [18] presented a $\Theta(\log n)$ worst case time EREW parallel algorithm for building a heap on n elements and Carlsson and Chen [6] reduced the time for the construction to $\Theta((\log\log n)^2)$ on the parallel comparison tree model.

Another abstract data type that has appeared in the literature is the *double-ended priority queue* (*priority deque*, for short), which provides insert access and remove access to both the minimum and the maximum element efficiently at the same time. It can be found useful in some applications, for example in external quicksort. Several implicit data structures have been developed for implementing priority deques, namely the twin-heap (Williams [14], p. 159), the min-max heap (Atkinson et al. [3]), and the deap (Carlsson [5]). The sequential complexities of building the data structures above for priority deques are of $\Theta(n)$ time and have been studied thoroughly [3, 5, 7, 10, 12, 15, 17] and their parallel solutions have been given in [6]. The problem of sequential merging min-max heaps has also been investigated [13].

In this paper, we will study the parallel complexities of merging and splitting priority queue and priority deque structures, and design parallel algorithms for the tasks. The model of parallel computation used in this paper is the Exclusive-Read Exclusive-Write Parallel Random Access Machine (EREW PRAM) [2]. If P and T is the processor and the time complexity of a parallel algorithm, respectively, and if the product $P \cdot T$ equals, up to a constant factor, the time complexity of the fastest known sequential algorithm for the problem under consideration, then we say that the algorithm achieves the *optimal speed-up*.

The rest of this paper is organized as follows. In Section 2, we review some terminology and definitions. Section 3 describes an $O(\log n)$-time, $\log k$-processor solution to the problem of merging heaps on the EREW PRAM model, which has the optimal speed-up. We also present an optimal speed-up algorithm for solving the related problem of splitting a heap of size n into two heaps on k and $n-k$ elements in $O(\log n)$ time on $\log n$ EREW-PRAM processors. Section 4 is devoted to designing parallel algorithms for merging min-max heaps, deaps, and twin-heaps. We show that the parallel complexity of merging twin-heaps is the same as that for heaps. Efficient EREW-PRAM merging algorithms for min-max heaps and deaps are presented, which take $O(\log n)$ time by using $\frac{k}{\log n} + \log k$ processors and achieve the optimal speed-up. The parallel complexity of deap merging also provides us with the first sequential deap merging algorithm of time complexity $O(k + \log n \cdot \log k)$. Some concluding remarks are given in Section 5.

2 The Data Structures

A (min-)heap is a binary tree with *heap-ordering*: (*i*) It has the *heap shape*; i.e., all leaves lie on at most two adjacent levels and all leaves on the last level occupy the leftmost positions; all other levels are complete; (*ii*) It is *min-ordered*: the key value associated with each node is not smaller than that of its parent. The minimum element is then at the root. A heap of n elements can be stored level by level from left to right in an array with the property that the element at position i has its parent at $\lfloor \frac{i}{2} \rfloor$ and its children at $2i$ and $2i+1$. We refer to the number of elements in a heap as its *size*. The *height* of the heap is thus $\lfloor \log(size+1) \rfloor$. A (max-)heap is defined similarly.

The worst-case upper bound of $O(\log n \cdot \log k)$ comparisons for merging two heaps of sizes n and k is due to Sack and Strothotte [19, 20]. A heap of size n can be split into two heaps on k and $n-k$ elements with $O(\log^2 n)$ comparisons [19]. We shall present parallel heap merging and splitting algorithms by making use of the structural view of heaps posed in [19].

A min-max heap [3] is a binary tree having the following properties: (*i*) It has the *heap shape*; (*ii*) It is *min-max ordered*: elements on even(resp. odd) levels are less(resp. greater) than or equal to their descendants, where the *level* of an element at location i is $\lceil \log i \rceil$. The minimum element is then at the root, whereas the maximum element is one of the children of the root. See Fig. 1, for example, a min-max heap with an even number of levels. A max-min heap is similarly defined. In the worst case, a min-max heap of size n can be constructed in $\Theta(n)$ comparisons sequentially [3]. Hasham and Sack [13] established a lower bound of $\Omega(\min\{n, k\})$ comparisons for merging two min-max heaps of sizes n and k.

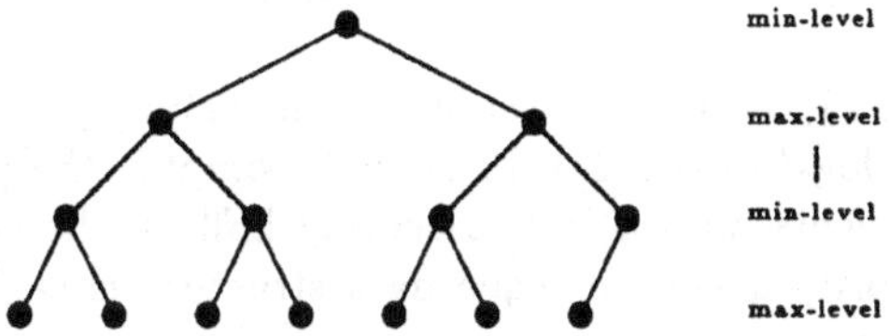

Fig. 1. A min-max heap with an even number of levels

A deap is also a variation of the heap and was proposed as an alternative to the min-max heap [5]. This symmetrical data structure for implementing priority deques implicitly is a heap-like tree with a hole at the position of the root. The left subtree of the root is a min-heap, whereas the right subtree is a max-heap. Moreover, any node i in the left subtree of the root of the deap is smaller than its corresponding element in the right subtree, $i+a$, if it exists, and $\lfloor \frac{i+a}{2} \rfloor$ otherwise, where a is $2^{\lfloor \log i \rfloor - 1}$. So the minimum element in a deap is stored in the position 2 and the maximum in position 3. Notice that a deap is actually a structure with two separate heaps, the min-heap (the left subtree of the "hole" root of the deap) and the max-heap (the right one).

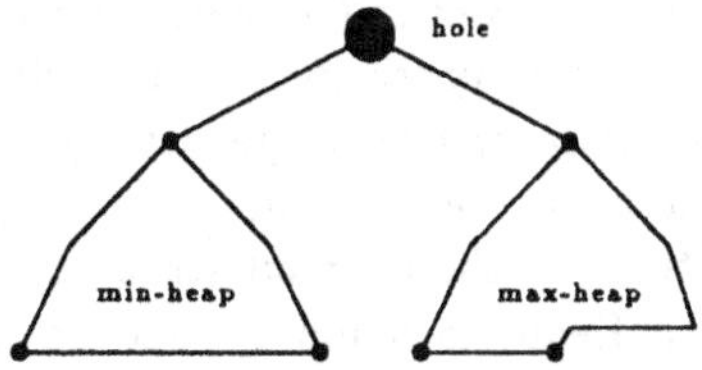

Fig. 2. A symmetric view of a deap as two separate heaps

The third structure for implementing priority deque implicitly is the twin-heaps, proposed by Williams ([14] p. 619). This structure keeps two heaps in a suitable way (see Fig. 3). The difference between a deap and a twin-heap is that the latter has two separate heaps of the same size (see Fig. 2 and Fig. 3). Both of the deap and the twin-heap can be constructed optimally in linear sequential time in the worst case [5, 14]. By modifying and parallelizing the serial heap merging algorithm [19], we show that the problem of merging priority deque structures can be solved in a parallel time $O(\log n)$. All these parallel merging algorithms achieve the optimal speed-up, and the serial version of the parallel deap merging algorithm is also the first sequential algorithm for solving the same problem.

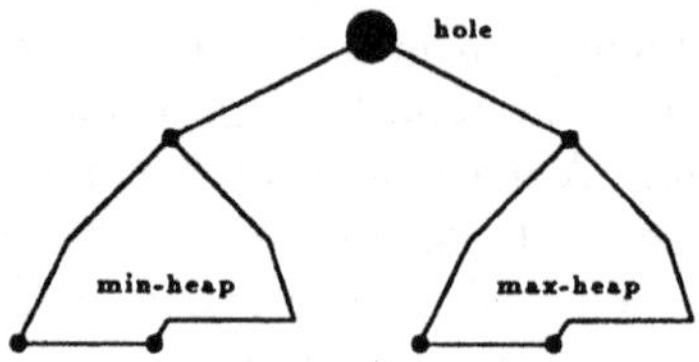

Fig. 3. A twin-heap

Let $X = \{x_1, x_2, \cdots, x_n\}$ be a set of n elements from a totally ordered domain and let $\log x$ denote $\log_2(\max\{x, 2\})$. In order to simplify the presentation, we assume that all the elements are distinct. Denoting $\|S\|$ by the cardinality of a set S of elements. A priority queue or deque data structure is said to be *perfect* if all its leaves are on the same level.

3 Parallel Heap Merging and Splitting Algorithms

In this section, we consider the problems of merging and splitting heaps on the EREW PRAM model. An efficient $O(\log n)$ time algorithm for merging two heaps of sizes n and k with $\log k$ processors is presented. The *time*$\times$*processor* product of the algorithm achieves the best $O(\log n \cdot \log k)$ sequential upper bound [19, 20]. We also demonstrate that a heap on n elements can be split into two heaps of sizes k and $n - k$ in $O(\log n)$ time with $\log n$ processors, which achieves the optimal speed-up as well. In what follows, we shall always assume that $n \geq k$.

For merging two heaps of sizes n and k into one heap on $n+k$ elements, we can, of course, neglect the order structure in the heaps and build a heap directly from $n+k$ "unrelated" elements. Using the parallel heap construction algorithm in [18], the problem of heap merging can be solved in $O(\log n)$ time with $\frac{n}{\log n}$ EREW-PRAM processors. To reduce the number of processors needed without any increase in the parallel time, we shall use a sublinear time sequential heap merging algorithm [19] for developing parallel solutions for the problem.

We now recall the definitions on the pennant structures of heaps in [19]. A *pennant SH* (Substructure of a Heap) is a binary tree on 2^k elements whose root contains the minimum element and has exactly one child which is a perfect (min-)heap (see Fig. 4). A *pennant forest* $(SH_m, \cdots, SH_0)$ is an ordered collection of pennants such that $\text{root}(SH_i) \leq \text{root}(SH_{i-1})$ (which is called the heap-ordering among the pennants) and $size(SH_i) \geq size(SH_{i-1})$ for $0 < i \leq m$. For every pennant forest $(SH_m, \cdots, SH_0)$, we associate it with a *descriptor* $(d_{m'}, \cdots, d_0)$, where d_i $(i = 0, \cdots, m')$ is the number of pennants of size 2^i in the forest. (This descriptor is also called the descriptor for the integer n.) We say that a pennant forest *corresponds* to a heap if it contains the same elements as the heap and if all the ordering relations between elements in the forest hold in the heap as well. A pennant forest is *valid* if and only if the number of pennants of the same sizes in the forest is at most 2 and the number of pennants of sizes smaller than or equal to 2^j is either $j+1$ or $j+2$.

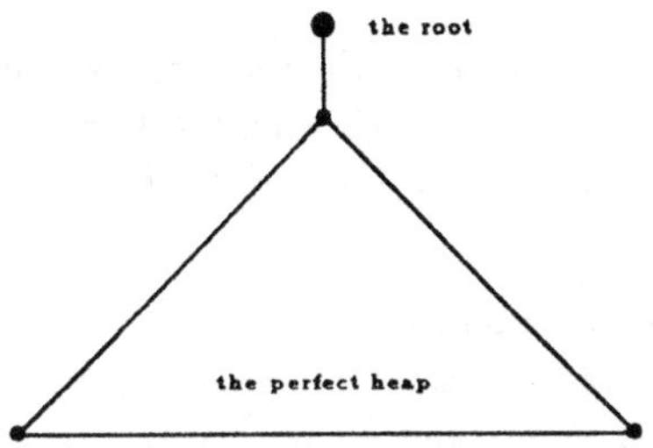

Fig. 4. The pennant structure

It has been shown in [19] that heaps and valid pennant forests are in one-to-one correspondence. In particular, any heap of size n can be viewed as a unique ordered collection of $\lceil \log(n+1) \rceil$ pennants rooted at the nodes on the path from the root to the last leaf in the heap. Therefore, we can regard the valid pennant forest as its corresponding heap and two heaps can be merged by constructing a valid pennant forest corresponding to the merged heap. We shall utilize repeatedly the fact that two pennants of equal sizes can be merged efficiently.

3.1 Merging Heaps in Parallel

The main idea of the heap merging algorithm in [19] is that: for two heaps of sizes n and k to be merged together (called n-heap and k-heap, respectively), construct first their corresponding valid pennant forests (called n-forest and k-forest, respectively) by removing all edges on the path from the root to the last leaf in the heaps and then merge the forests (see [19] for details). The parallel heap merging procedure can be stated as follows.

Algorithm 1 *Suppose the number of EREW-PRAM processors available is* $\lceil \log k \rceil$.

1. *Compute the valid pennant forests of the n-heap and k-heap, respectively;*
2. *For all pennants of height larger than or equal to* $\log \frac{n}{k} - 1$, *ensure that their roots are smaller than the minimum element of the k-heap in parallel;*
3. *Rearrange the pennants of height smaller than or equal to* $\log k$ *such that they appear in decreasing order of size and in increasing order of the roots among pennants of the same sizes in parallel; establish the heap-ordering among the pennants in parallel;*
4. *Merge equal-sized pennants in parallel and restore the heap-ordering in the pennant forests obtained to make it valided;*
5. *Construct a heap on* $n+k$ *elements corresponding to the valid pennant forest output above.*

Analogous to the proof in [19], the correctness of Algorithm 1 follows. We now show that this algorithm runs in $O(\log n)$ parallel time with $\lceil \log k \rceil$ EREW-PRAM processors.

Notice that no comparison is needed to construct a valid pennant forest from a given heap and vice versa [19], Steps 1 and 5 can be done in at most $O(\log n)$ parallel time.

Step 2 can be done by comparing the roots of the pennants (of height $\geq \log \frac{n}{k} - 1$) in turn with the root of the k-heap, swapping these two comparands if necessary, and restoring the heap-ordering in the k-heap. In fact, this step is a special case of the lemma below.

Lemma 1. *Given a data structure containing a sorted list of l elements and a heap of size m (called m-heap), we want to construct a new structure that composes a (new) sorted list of l elements and a (new) heap of size m, where every element in the (new) list is smaller than every element in the (new) heap. With* $\min\{l, \lceil \log m \rceil\}$ *EREW-PRAM processors, we can complete the task in* $O(\max\{l, \lceil \log m \rceil\})$ *time.*

Proof. Assume without loss of generality that $l \leq \lceil \log m \rceil$. Suppose the list is $L = \{a_1, \cdots, a_l\}$ and the processors available are $P_1, \cdots, P_l$. For $1 \leq i \leq l$, we associate each processor P_i a list element a_i. (For $l > \lceil \log m \rceil$, we can assign one processor to each level of the m-heap).

Every processor P_i compares a_i with the present root r of the m-heap. If $a_i < r$, then P_i stops. If $a_i > r$, then P_i swaps a_i and r, compares a_i with two sons of r, and assigns the smallest to be the new root of the m-heap. Then, P_i continues to insert a_i into the m-heap by linear search in a top-down fashion. To avoid the simultaneous access to the same location of the memory, the processor P_{i+1} starts its work five unit-time steps after that the processor P_i has begun its work (i.e., after P_i has assigned the new root of the heap and begins to insert a_i into the heap). In the worst case, this pipelined procedure takes $O(l + \log m) = O(\log m)$ time.

By letting $l = \log \frac{n}{k} - 1$ and $m = k$, we know that Step 2 can be done in at most $O(\max\{\log \frac{n}{k} - 1, \log k\}) = O(\log n)$ time with $\min\{\log \frac{n}{k}, \log k\} \leq \log k$ processors.

In Step 3 we need to sort $O(\log k)$ roots of the pennants for the roots' rearrangement and to perform one top-down insertion in each of the $O(\log k)$ pennants of height $\leq \log k$ for the heap-ordering establishment in the worst case. With $\log k$ processors, we can complete this step in $O(\log k) = O(\log n)$ time.

The task required to be done during Step 4 is the pair-wise merges of $O(\log k)$ pennants of sizes $O(\frac{k}{2^i})$, $i = 0, 1, \cdots, O(\log k)$. Notice that two pennants each of size m can be merged into one larger pennant in $O(\log m)$ sequential time by performing a top-down insertion in the pennants [19]. We know immediately from Lemma 1 and its proof that:

Lemma 2. *There is an EREW PRAM algorithm for merging l pairs of equal-sized pennants of height $\leq O(\log m)$ in at most $O(l + \log m)$ time with l processors.*

Taking $l = O(\log k)$ and $m = k$, we know that Step 4 is completed after $O(\log n)$ parallel time with $O(\log k)$ processors. The time complexity of Algorithm 1 is thus $O(\log n)$. To sum up, we have successful implementing the serial heap merging algorithm [19] in parallel.

Theorem 3. *There is an EREW-PRAM algorithm that merges two heaps of sizes n and k in $O(\log n)$ time with $\log k$ processors, which achieves the optimal speed-up.*

Notice that if we modify slightly the five steps above for merging heaps to priority deque structures, mainly on the procedure of top-down insertions in Lemma 1, we can obtain efficient parallel implementations of the priority deque structure merges.

3.2 Splitting Heaps in Parallel

To split a given heap on n elements into two heaps of sizes k and $n-k$, one trivial method is to remove the last $\min\{k, n-k\}$ nodes from the heap of size n and build a new heap on these elements. This method can be completed in $O(\min\{k, n-k\})$ sequential time. An efficient $O(\log^2 n)$-time serial algorithm has been presented in [19], which utilizes a fact that a pennant can be split into two pennants of equal size without using any further comparisons between the elements. We describe below a paralle version of this algorithm in this subsection.

Algorithm 2 *Suppose the number of EREW-PRAM processors available is $\lceil \log n \rceil$.*

1. *Compute the valid descriptors $\{d_i^{(n)}\}$, $\{d_i^{(k)}\}$, and $\{d_i^{(n-k)}\}$ for the integers n, k, and $n-k$, respectively;*
2. *For each $i = 0, 1, \cdots, \lfloor \log n \rfloor$, if the n-heap does not have enough pennants of height i $\left(i.e., d_i^{(k)} + d_i^{(n-k)} > d_i^{(n)}\right)$, then we split larger pennants and restore the heap-ordering among the pennants in the n-heap in parallel;*
3. *Construct a heap on k elements from its valid descriptor by removing it from the new descriptor of the n-heap obtained above, and a heap on $n-k$ remaining elements.*

The correctness of the algorithm is from its serial version [19]. Steps 1 and 3 can be done in at most $O(\log n)$ parallel time since no comparison is required. For Step 2, at most one split of some pennant is needed for each $0 \le i \le \lfloor \log n \rfloor$ and thus at most one heap-ordering restoration is required. The worst case of this step is that we need to perform $\lceil \log n \rceil$ splittings. The following lemma shows how to complete this step in due time.

Lemma 4. *Suppose that a data structure DS contains a collection of $m+1$ pennants each of size at most s. To establish the heap-ordering among the pennants in DS while maintaining its shape, at most m EREW-PRAM processors are needed to complete the task in $O(m + \log s)$ time.*

Proof. Assume that the data structure $DS = \{SH_0, SH_1, \cdots, SH_m\}$ and the root of the pennant SH_i is denoted by r_i for $i = 0, 1, \cdots, m$. Let $s = \max_{1 \le i \le m} \{size(SH_i)\}$. Our goal is to construct a new data structure $\widetilde{DS} = \{\widetilde{SH}_0, \widetilde{SH}_1, \cdots, \widetilde{SH}_m\}$ such that $\widetilde{SH}_i$ is a pennant of $size(\widetilde{SH}_i) = size(SH_i)$ for $i = 0, 1, \cdots, m$ and the root $\widetilde{r}_i$ of $\widetilde{SH}_i$ is greater than $\widetilde{r}_{i+1}$.

We associate with the root r_i of SH_i one processor P_i, $1 \le i \le m$. Every processor P_i compares its associated root r_i with r_{i-1}. If $r_i < r_{i-1}$, then P_i stops. Otherwise,

P_i swaps r_i and r_{i-1} (i.e., r_{i-1} is now the new root of SH_i), compares r_i with the root r_{i-2} of SH_{i-2}. If $r_i < r_{i-2}$, then P_i compares r_i with the root of the perfect heap that is the child of r_{i-1}, and assigns the smaller one to be the new root of SH_{i-1} and inserts the larger one into this perfect heap. If $r_i > r_{i-2}$, then P_i swaps r_i and r_{i-2} and performs a similar task. To avoid the simultaneous memory accesses, the processor P_{i+1} starts its work six unit-time steps after that the processor P_i has begun its work (i.e., after the processor P_i has assigned the new roots of SH_i and SH_{i-1} and begins to insert r_i into the corresponding perfect heap). This pipelined procedure of heap-ordering restoration will be completed in at most $O(m + \log s)$ time.

Notice that the pennant forest corresponding to a heap of size n is an ordered collection of $\lceil \log(n+1) \rceil$ pennants of sizes 2^i with $i = 0, 1, \cdots, \lfloor \log n \rfloor$. By letting $s = O(n)$ and $m = \lceil \log(n+1) \rceil$, we know from Lemma 4 that Step 2 in Algorithm 2 can be done in $O(m + \log s) = O(\log n)$ time. Therefore:

Theorem 5. *There is an EREW-PRAM algorithm that splits a heap of size n into two heaps of sizes k and $n-k$ in $O(\log n)$ time with* $\log n$ *processors, which achieves the optimal speed-up.*

4 Parallel Merging of Priority Deques

We now show how to adapt the heap merging algorithm to handle the problem of merging priority deque structures (the min-max heap, the deap, and the twin-heap) and achieve the same parallel time complexity as that of heap.

In applying the pennant structural view of heaps in [19] to implement the priority deque merge operations in parallel, we shall use the *HEAP* to denote one of the following structures: the min-max heap, the deap, or the twin-heap; and the *HEAP-ordering* means the corresponding ordering-property of the HEAP structure. *PENNANTs* here will denote the pennant's structure corresponding to the different priority deque structures. For example, a min-max pennant is a pennant-shaped structure where the root is the minimum element and its unique child is a perfect max-min heap. The max-min pennant is defined similarly. For deaps and twin-heaps, such a PENNANT composes one pennant of the min-heap and its corresponding pennant in the max-heap.

To merge together two HEAPs of sizes n and k, we can just simply use cost optimal $\Theta(\log n)$-time, $\frac{n}{\log n}$-processor EREW-PRAM algorithms for constructing HEAPs (min-max heaps, deaps, or twin-heaps) [8] to do the merge job. However, with the help of the pennant-like structures, we can design more efficient parallel algorithms for solving the problem of merging HEAPs. Analogous to the proof of pennant structures of heaps in [19], we can show that there is a one-to-one correspondence between HEAPs and valid PENNANT forests. Therefore, merging two HEAPs can be completed by constructing a valid PENNANT forest corresponding to the merged HEAP. We shall present a uniform scheme for merging two HEAPs of sizes n and k, which is similar to Algorithm 1 of merging heaps.

Algorithm 3 *The input is two HEAPs of the same type on n and k elements, respectively. Suppose the number of EREW-PRAM processors available is* $\lceil \frac{k}{\log n} + \log k \rceil$.

1. *Compute the valid PENNANT forests of the n-HEAP and the k-HEAP, respectively;*
2. *Ensure the HEAP-ordering among all PENNANTs of height* $\geq \log \frac{n}{k} - 1$ *and the k-HEAP in parallel;*
3. *Rearrange the PENNANTs of height* $\leq \log k$ *such that they appear in decreasing order of size and in increasing order of the roots among PENNANTs of the same sizes in parallel; establish the HEAP-ordering among the PENNANTs in parallel;*
4. *Merge in pair equal-sized PENNANTs of sizes* $O(\frac{k}{2^i})$, $i = 0, 1, \cdots, O(\log k)$ *in parallel and make the PENNANT forest obtained valided;*
5. *Construct a HEAP on* $n + k$ *elements from the valid PENNANT forest obtained above.*

The correctness of this algorithm can be established with a similar argument to that for heaps in [19]. Moreover, Steps 1 and 5 can be done in at most $O(\log n)$ time. In the following, we shall derive the parallel complexity of this scheme for merging min-max heaps, deaps, and twin-heaps.

4.1 Merging Min-Max Heaps in Parallel

The valid PENNANT forest corresponding to a min-max heap is an ordered collection of the min-max pennants and the max-min pennants rooted at the nodes on the path from the root to the last leaf in the min-max heap. Suppose $(SH_m, \cdots, SH_0)$ is such a PENNANT forest, where SH_i is either a min-max pennant or a max-min pennant and $size(SH_i) \geq size(SH_{i-1})$ for $0 < i \leq m$. Notice that now the HEAP-ordering means that $\text{root}(SH_i) \leq \text{root}(SH_{i-2}) \leq \text{root}(SH_{i-1})$ if $m - i$ is even and $\text{root}(SH_i) \geq \text{root}(SH_{i-2}) \geq \text{root}(SH_{i-1})$ otherwise. Therefore, Step 2 (in Algorithm 3) of maintaining HEAP-ordering for all PENNANTs of height $\geq \log \frac{n}{k} - 1$ can be done by ensuring that all the roots of the min-max pennants are smaller than the minimum element in the k-min-max heap and that all the roots of the max-min pennants are larger than the maximum element in the k-min-max heap. Since every insertion in the k-min-max heap can be done by at most two separating insertions in a k-heap, we can complete Step 2 in a similar pipelined fashion to that of Lemma 1 in $O(\max\{\log \frac{n}{k} - 1, \log k\}) = O(\log n)$ time with $\min\{\log \frac{n}{k}, \log k\} \leq \log k$ processors.

Step 3 will now sort $O(\log k)$ minimum elements and $O(\log k)$ maximum elements in the PENNANTs of height $\leq \log k$, and do one trickle-down in each of the $O(\log k)$ PENNANTs. It can easily be shown that Step 3 is done in at most $O(\log k)$ time with $\log k$ processors.

Analogous to Lemma 2, the procedure of merging PENNANTs in Step 4 can be performed in $O(\log n)$ parallel time with $\log k$ processors. However, to make the PENNANT forest obtained valid, we need to convert $O(\log k)$ min-max pennants of sizes $O(\frac{k}{2^i})$ $(i = 0, 1, \cdots, O(\log k))$ into max-min pennants and vice versa in the worst case. We can convert all of these PENNANTs in parallel. For each PENNANT SH of size $\frac{k}{2^j}$ for some $0 \leq j \leq O(\log k)$, we have $1+\frac{(\frac{k}{2^j})}{\log n}$ processors available. If $\frac{k}{2^j} \leq \log n$, then we do the conversion of SH sequentially, which takes $O(\frac{k}{2^j}) = O(\log n)$ time. If $\frac{k}{2^j} > \log n$, then we do the conversion by constructing some min-max heap of size $\frac{k}{2^j}$ with $1+\frac{(\frac{k}{2^j})}{\log n}$ processors, which takes $O(\log n)$ time as well. Therefore, Step 4 can be done in $O(\log n)$ time with $\frac{k}{\log n} + \log k$ processors.

Recall that an $\Omega(n)$ sequential lower bound on the number of comparisons required to merge two min-max heaps each of size n has been proved in [13], we have then:

Theorem 6. *There is an EREW-PRAM algorithm that merges two min-max heaps of sizes n and k in $O(\log n)$ time with $\frac{k}{\log n} + \log k$ processors, which achieves the optimal speed-up. Moreover, the algorithm is cost optimal when $k = O(n)$.*

4.2 Merging Twin-Heaps and Deaps in Parallel

The symmetrical property of twin-heaps allows us to merging twin-heaps efficiently, namely the merging complexity of twin-heaps is the same as that for heaps. Assume without loss of generality that the number of elements in a twin-heap is even. The PENNANT forest corresponding to a twin-heap is the ordered collection of the pennants rooted at nodes on the path from the root to the last leaf of the min-heap of the twin-heap, together with their corresponding pennants in the max-heap of the twin-heap. Notice that the situation here is similar to that of min-max heaps except in Step 4 of Algorithm 3. For merging twin-heaps, there is no need for converting operations as that in min-max heap merges. Furthermore, every insertion operation during the merge of twin-heaps can be regarded as four separated heap-insertions. Therefore:

Theorem 7. *There is an EREW-PRAM algorithm that merges two twin-heaps of sizes n and k in $O(\log n)$ time with $\log k$ processors, which achieves the optimal speed-up.*

The similarity between twin-heaps and deaps guarantees that the merge operation on perfect deaps can be performed analogously to that for twin-heaps plus a simultaneous insertions of $O(k)$ elements into a heap of size $O(k)$. With $\frac{k}{\log n} + \log k$ processors, we can complete the merging task in $O(\log n)$ time. For merging two deaps of arbitrary sizes n and k, we first view the n-deap as a twin-heap, where the min-heaps respective in the deap and in the twin-heap are the same. Moreover, the leaf node in the max-heap of the twin-heap is the same as that in the n-deap if it exists and is an "empty node" otherwise. A similar view is on the k-deap as well. Merging in parallel these two twin-heaps of sizes n' and k' ($n \leq n' \leq 1.5n$ and $k \leq k' \leq 1.5k$) and then transforming the merged twin-heap into a deap by deleting the empty nodes and simultaneous insertions of $O(k)$ elements. Thus, we have:

Theorem 8. *There is an EREW-PRAM algorithm that merges two deaps of sizes n and k in $O(\log n)$ time with $\frac{k}{\log n} + \log k$ processors, which achieves the optimal speed-up.*

5 Concluding Remarks

In this paper, we have designed parallel algorithms for merging and splitting priority queue and priority deque data structures on the EREW PRAM model. We show that the merge and the split operation can be implemented efficiently in $O(\log n)$ parallel time. It would be interesting to develop more fast parallel algorithms for merging and splitting the structures.

References

1. A. V. Aho, J. E. Hopocroft, and J. D. Ullman: *The Design and Analysis of Computer Algorithms*. Addison-Wesley, Reading, MA, 1974.
2. S. G. Akl: *The Design and Analysis of Parallel Algorithms*. Prentice-Hall International, Inc., 1989.
3. M. D. Atkinson, J.-R. Sack, N. Santoro, and Th. Strothotte: Min-max heaps and generalized priority queues. *Communications of the ACM* **29** (1986), 996-1000.
4. B. Bollobás and I. Simon: Repeated random insertion into a priority queue. *Journal of Algorithms* **6** (1985), 466-477.
5. S. Carlsson: The deap - A double-ended heap to implement double-ended priority queues. *Information Processing Letters* **26** (1987), 33-36.
6. S. Carlsson and J. Chen: Parallel complexity of heaps and min-max heaps. To appear in: *International Symposium in Theoretical Computer Science* (1992).
7. S. Carlsson and J. Chen: The complexity of heaps. *Proceedings of the Third Annual ACM-SIAM Symposium on Discrete Algorithms* (1992), 393-402.
8. J. Chen: Constructing priority queues and deques optimally in parallel. To appear in: *The Twelfth World Computer Congress* (1992).
9. R. Cole: Parallel merge sort. *SIAM Journal on Computing* **17** (1988), 770-785.
10. E. E. Doberkat: An average case analysis of Floyd's algorithm to construct heaps. *Information and Control* **61** (1984), 114-131.
11. R. W. Floyd: Algorithm 245 - Treesort 3. *Comm. ACM* **7** (1964), p. 701.
12. G. H. Gonnet and J. I. Munro: Heaps on heaps. *SIAM Journal on Computing* **15** (1986), 964-971.
13. A. Hasham and J.-R. Sack: Bounds for min-max heaps. *BIT* **27** (1987), 315-323.
14. D. E. Knuth: *The Art of Computer Programming. Vol. 3: Sorting and Searching.* Addison-Wesley, Reading, MA, 1973.
15. C. J. H. McDiarmid and B. A. Reed: Building heaps fast. *Journal of Algorithms* **10** (1989), 352-365.
16. N. Megiddo: Applying parallel computation algorithms in the design of serial algorithms. *Journal of the Association for Computing Machinery* **30** (1983), 852-865.
17. T. Porter and I. Simon: Random insertion into a priority queue structure. *IEEE Transactions on Software Engineering* **SE-1** (1975), 292-298.
18. N. S. V. Rao and W. Zhang: Building heaps in parallel. *Information Processing Letters* **37** (1991), 355-358.
19. J.-R. Sack and Th. Strothotte: A characterization of heaps and its applications. *Information and Computation* **86** (1990), 69-86.
20. J.-R. Sack and Th. Strothotte: An algorithm for merging heaps. *Acta Informatica* **22** (1985), 171-186.
21. J. W. J. Williams: Algorithm 232: Heapsort. *Comm. ACM* **7** (1964), 347-348.

This article was processed using the LaTeX macro package with LLNCS style

Lower Bounds for the Complexity of Functions in a Realistic RAM model

- Extended Abstract -

Nader H. Bshouty[1]
Department of Computer Science, The University of Calgary
Calgary, Alberta, Canada T2N 1N4
e-mail: bshouty@cpsc.ucalgary.ca

Abstract

From the literature, many lower bounds are known for the complexity of computing (or approximating) functions in random access machines (RAMs) that use arithmetic operations, comparisons and indirect addressing. However, no nontrivial lower bound is known when the RAM model also uses bitwise boolean operations or bit shift operations.

This paper develops a new technique that finds lower bounds for the complexity of programs that compute or approximate functions in a *realistic RAM model*. The realistic RAM model is a model that uses the arithmetic operations $\{+,-,\times\}$, the standard bit operations *Shift, Rotate, AND, OR, XOR, NOT* (bitwise), comparisons and indirect addressing.

In particular, for computing the integer division $DIV(x,y) = \lfloor x/y \rfloor$ of two integers of size n in this model, we prove

- A lower bound $\Omega(\frac{n}{\log n})$ for the complexity. The upper bound is $O(n)$.
- A lower bound $\Omega(\frac{\log(1/\alpha)}{\log\log(1/\alpha)})$ for the $2^{\alpha n}$-approximation. The upper bound is $O(\log(1/\alpha))$. In particular, A lower bound $\Omega(\frac{\log n}{\log\log n})$ for the complexity of the λ-approximation , for any constant λ.

This paper proves general results that give bounds for the complexity of computing and approximating integer division, modulo, square root, gcd and logarithms.

We also show that if we add the integer division to the realistic RAM model, then no nontrivial lower bound can be proven. This follows because we were able to prove that

- In the realistic RAM model with the integer division operation, any integer functions $f_1, f_2, \cdots, f_k$ with j inputs of size n can be computed with complexity $O(k+j)$.
- In the realistic RAM model, with the integer division operation, any finite language (subset of 0-1-strings) can be recognized with complexity $O(1)$.

Our results can be also generalized to probabilistic, nondeterministic and parallel RAM models.

1 Introduction

Our computation model is the random access machine (RAM) with some fixed operations $F \subseteq \{+, -, \times, \text{DIV}, \cdots\}$. An F–RAM, M, has an unbounded memory $M[0], M[1], \cdots$, where each location can store an integer. The computation is directed by a finite program that consists of instructions of the following type: direct and indirect addressing storage accesses, conditional branching (IF-THEN-ELSE) and operations from F. Each of them can be executed at unit cost. For a function $f : \mathcal{N}^n \to \mathcal{N}^m$ ($\mathcal{N}$ is the set of nonnegative integers), the complexity of f in the F–RAM, $C_F(f, n)$, is the maximal number of steps taken over all inputs of size n and over all programs that computes f. We also define $C_F(f, \lambda, n)$ to be the complexity of λ–approximating f, i.e., the program outputs f^* where $\frac{1}{\lambda} \leq \frac{f^*}{f} \leq \lambda$.

The set of operations F considered in the literature are either the arithmetic operations or the arithmetic operations with addition of integer division. The first known lower bound is $\Omega(n \log n)$ for sorting n elements using only comparisons ($F = \emptyset$). Ben Or [B] gave tight lower bounds for decision problems in the $\{+, -, \times, /\}$–RAM model without indirect addressing. Yao [Y] generalizes Ben Or's result by restricting the inputs to be integers. Both papers, [B] and [Y], give tight bounds for the complexity of computing the functions modulo, integer division and greatest common divisor (gcd) of two integers in the $\{+, -, \times, /\}$–RAM model without indirect addressing. Paul and Simon [PS] developed a new technique that handles RAM models with indirect addressing. The technique they used can be applied to prove tight bounds for the complexity of computing the functions modulo, integer division and gcd in the $\{+, -, \times, /\}$–RAM with indirect addressing. Bshouty [BS2,BS3] and Mansour, Shieber and Tiwary [MST2,MST3] gave other techniques that handle $\{+, -, \times, /\}$–RAM models with indirect addressing when the domain of the input is finite. Mansour, Shieber and Tiwary found a new technique that establishes lower bounds when the RAM model also contains the integer division DIV. They proved that there does not exist a program with complexity $O(1)$ that computes the gcd function in the $\{+, -, \times, /, \text{DIV}\}$-RAM model. Mansour, Shieber and Tiwari [MST*], and Bshouty, Mansour, Shieber and Tiwari [BMST], also apply these new techniques for computing the square root. Other results for this model can be found in [Bs0,Bs4,BJM,H,JM,S].

In this paper we develop a new technique that handles RAM models of computation that contain the bitwise boolean operations and the bit shift and rotate operations. Our techniques find lower bounds for the complexity of computing and approximating functions in a realistic RAM model. The realistic RAM model is an R–RAM where (R- and L- stand for Right and Left):

$$R = \{+, -, \times, \text{R-Shift}, \text{L-Shift}, \text{R-Rotate}, \text{L-Rotate}, \text{AND}, \text{OR}, \text{XOR}, \text{NOT}\}.$$

Our model also has indirect addressing and comparisons. (We will see that all the lower bounds are true even if the RAM model has unlimited power for answering YES/NO questions). The boolean operations in the R-RAM can be executed on any consecutive bits. E.g, L-Shift$(M[k], i, j)$ is an operation that shift the bits $i, i+1, \ldots, j$ in the content of $M[k]$ to the left. Therefore, if

$M[k] = \cdots m_{i+1}m_im_{i-1}\cdots m_{j+1}m_jm_{j-1}\cdots m_1m_0$, (the binary representation) then

L-Shift$(M[k], i, j) = \cdots m_{i+1}m_{i-1}m_{i-2}\cdots m_{j+1}m_j0m_{j-1}\cdots m_1m_0$. To the best of our knowledge, prior to this work, no lower bound was known on the complexity of functions using the operations in R.

It is true that the model will be more realistic if we also add the integer division operation to the set of operation R, but it has been proven by Bshouty, Mansour, Shieber and Tiwary [BMST] that all functions with one variable can be computed with complexity $O(1)$ if the integer division DIV is added to the model. This implies that no nontrivial lower bound can be proven for functions with one variable in the model $R \cup \{DIV\}$–RAM. In this paper we push this result further. We prove that no nontrivial lower bound can be proven for any function (or any language, in the sense of decision problems) in the $R \cup \{DIV\}$–RAM model.

The following table summarizes our results. (Here $\tilde{\Omega}(k) = \Omega(k/\log k)$)

	Complexity	λ-approximation any constant λ	α-approximation
$x \times y$	$\Omega(\frac{n}{\log n})$	$\Omega(\frac{\log n}{\log\log n})$	$\tilde{\Omega}(\log n - \log\log\alpha)$
$R\backslash\{\times\}$-RAM	$O(n)$	$O(n)$	$O(n)$
DIV(x, y)	$\Omega(\frac{n}{\log n})$	$\Omega(\frac{\log n}{\log\log n})$	$\tilde{\Omega}(\log n - \log\log\alpha)$
R–RAM	$O(n)$	$O(\log n)$	$O(\log n - \log\log\alpha)$
$x \bmod y$	$\Omega(\frac{n}{\log n})$	$\Omega(\frac{\log n}{\log\log n})$	$\tilde{\Omega}(\log n - \log\log\alpha)$
R–RAM	$O(n)$	$O(n)$	$O(n)$
$\lfloor\sqrt{x}\rfloor$	$\Omega(\frac{n}{\log n})$	$\Omega(\frac{\log n}{\log\log n})$	$\tilde{\Omega}(\log n - \log\log\alpha)$
R–RAM	$O(n)$	$O(\log n)$	$O(\log n - \log\log\alpha)$
gcd(x, y)	$\Omega(\frac{n}{\log n})$	$\Omega(\frac{\log n}{\log\log n})$	$\tilde{\Omega}(\log n - \log\log\alpha)$
R–RAM	$O(n)$	$O(n)$	$O(n)$
$\lfloor\log x\rfloor$	$\Omega(\frac{\log n}{\log\log n})$	$\Omega(\frac{\log\log n}{\log\log\log n})$	$\tilde{\Omega}(\log\log n - \log\log\alpha)$
R–RAM	$O(\log n)$	$O(\log\log n)$	$O(\log\log n - \log\log\alpha)$
$\lfloor\log\log x\rfloor$	$\Omega(\frac{\log\log n}{\log\log\log n})$	$\Omega(\frac{\log\log\log n}{\log\log\log\log n})$	$\tilde{\Omega}(\log\log\log n - \log\log\alpha)$
R–RAM	$O(\log\log n)$	$O(\log\log\log n)$	$O(\log\log\log n - \log\log\alpha)$
$\log^* x$	$\Omega(\frac{\log^* n}{\log\log^* n})$	$\Omega(\frac{\log\log^* n}{\log\log\log^* n})$	$\tilde{\Omega}(\log\log^* n - \log\log\alpha)$
R–RAM	$O(\log^* n)$	$O(\log\log^* n)$	$O(\log\log^* n - \log\log\alpha)$
$F(x_1, \ldots, x_k)$ k constant $R \cup \{DIV\}$–RAM	$\Theta(1)$	$\Theta(1)$	$\Theta(1)$
$F(x_1, \ldots, x_r)$ Any r $R \cup \{DIV\}$-RAM	$\Theta(r)$	$\Theta(r)$	$\Theta(r)$
Is $x \in L$ Finite $L \subset \mathcal{N}^r$ $R \cup \{DIV\}$-RAM	$\Theta(r)$	$\Theta(r)$	$\Theta(r)$

Notice that all the lower bounds in this paper are for the nonuniform R–RAM model and therefore they also apply for the uniform R–RAM model. Unfortunately, the upper bounds do not necessarily apply for the uniform RAM model (otherwise, the result in the previous paragraph proves P=NP and solves the integer factoring problem). The upper bounds we have in this paper are important in the sense that they show that it is impossible to prove certain lower bounds.

In the full paper we also define two models. The first is the extended realistic RAM model, R_e−RAM, that is, the R−RAM model where we also allow shifting of a certain number of bits in one operation (all we need is shifting of upto polylog(m) bits where m is the size of the output). The second is the restricted RAM model, R_r−RAM, that is, the R−RAM model with finite memory.

We show that in the R_e−RAM most of the lower bounds in the above table are tight and in the R_r−RAM model most of the upper bounds in the table are tight.

2 Definitions

Any F-RAM program, P, can be regarded as a computation tree T_P with labeled vertices. The label of vertex v is denoted by l_v. The tree has five types of vertices:

- *Input vertex*: The root of the tree T_P is the input vertex that assigns the input of the program to $M[1], \ldots, M[n]$.
- *Computation vertices*: Each computation vertex v has one child and is labeled with a binary operation $M[i] \leftarrow M[j] \circ M[k]$ where $\circ \in F$.
- *Assignment vertices*: Each assignment vertex v has one child and is labeled with one of $M[i] \leftarrow a$ for some constant a, $M[i] \leftarrow M[j]$ or $M[i] \leftarrow M[M[j]]$.
- *Comparison vertices*: Each comparison vertex v has two children and is labeled with $M[i] > 0$?.
- *Halt vertices*: The halt vertices are the leaves of T_P. Each leaf is labeled with *Halt*.

The computation in T_P begins at the root of the tree. We always execute the command in the vertex and go to its child. In the comparison vertex we go to the left child if $M[i] > 0$ and to the right child otherwise. The computation in T_P terminates when we arrive at a leaf. The outputs of the function are in $M[1], \ldots, M[s]$, where s is the number of outputs. It is obvious that the complexity of computing f in a program P is the height of the tree T_P.

When the program P does not contain IF-THEN-ELSE commands, then we say that P is a *straight line program*.

Let A and B be sets of integers. A *generator program* that generates B from A with the operations in F is a straight line program that uses only the constants in A and generates the constants in B using the operations in F. The complexity of a generator program is the number of operations used in the generator. We define $\Delta_F(A, B)$ to be the minimal number of operations needed to generate the integers in B using only the integers in A and the operations in F. We also define $\Delta_F^{(\lambda)}(A, t)$

to be the minimal number of operations needed to generate a constant c such that $t/\lambda \le c \le \lambda t$.

The set of operations we shall consider in this paper is

$$R = \{+, -, \times, \text{R-Shift}, \text{L-Shift}, \text{R-Rotate}, \text{L-Rotate}, \text{AND}, \text{OR}, \text{XOR}, \text{NOT}\}.$$

Here R-Shift and L-Shift are as defined in the introduction and

$$\text{AND}(a, b, i, j) = \cdots a_l \cdots a_{i+1}(a_i \wedge b_i) \cdots (a_j \wedge b_j) a_{j-1} \cdots a_0$$

where $\cdots a_l a_{l-1} \cdots a_0$ and $\cdots b_l b_{l-1} \cdots b_0$ are the binary representations of a and b, respectively. The operations in R can be simulated in $O(1)$ using the operations

$$\{+, -, \times, \text{R-Shift}(a, i, 0), \text{NAND}(a, b, i, 0)\},$$

(e.g. L-Shift(a, i, j) can be simulated in $O(1)$ steps using NAND, multiplication by 2 and the constants $2^i - 1$ and $2^j - 1$.) We will also assume that when the RAM uses the substraction $a - b$ then $a \ge b$. Therefore, without loss of generality, we assume that

$$R = \{+, -, \times, \text{R-Shift}(a, i, 0), \text{NAND}(a, b, i, 0)\}.$$

All the lower bounds in this paper are true even if the model has unlimited power for answering YES/NO questions.

Other notation that will be frequently used in this paper is the following: For a set, H, the number of elements in H will be denoted by $|H|$. log will always mean $\log_2$. The set of integers is $\mathcal{N}$ and $\mathcal{N}_j = \{0, 1, \ldots, j\}$. For an integer a we will write $a = \cdots a_i a_{i-1} \cdots a_1 a_0$ for the binary representation of a where a_0 is the least significant bit of a. The number $[a]_{i,j}$ is $a_i a_{i-1} \ldots a_j$. For a vector $\bar{a} = (a_1, \ldots, a_n) \in \mathcal{N}^n$, $[\bar{a}]_{i,j} = ([a_1]_{i,j}, \cdots, [a_n]_{i,j})$ and for a set of vectors S we write $[S]_{i,j}$ for $\{[s]_{i,j} | s \in S\}$.

3 Complexity of exactly computing functions

3.1 The main theorem

In this subsection we will give a general theorem that implies all the lower bounds for the complexity of exactly computing functions.

Lemma 1 *Let W be a set of constants and F be a set of operations. Let $H \subseteq \mathcal{N}^s$ be a set of constants such that $|F| + |W| \le (\log |H|)^{O(1)}$. Then, there exists $(t_1, \ldots, t_s) \in H$ such that*

$$\Delta_F(W, (t_1, \ldots, t_s)) \ge \Omega\left(\frac{\log |H|}{\log\log |H|}\right).$$

(Here, $s = O(1)$ with respect to $|H|$)

Sketch of Proof . The proof follows from a simple counting argument. The number of generator programs with at most h steps is less than or equal to

$$|F|^h(|W|)^2(|W|+1)^2\cdots(|W|+h)^2 \le |F|^h(|W|+h)^{2h}.$$

Since the number of programs is greater than or equal to the number of elements in H (modulo the order, i.e. $|H|/s!$) the result follows.□

It is easy to see that when $F=\{+,\times\}$, $W=\{1\}$ and $H=\{1,\cdots,t\}$, the above bound is tight.

We remind the reader that $\mathcal{N}$ is the set of integers and $\mathcal{N}_j=\{0,1,\ldots,j\}$. The number $[a]_{i,j}$ is $a_ia_{i-1}\ldots a_j$ where $\cdots a_ia_{i-1}\cdots a_0$ is the binary representation of a. For a vector $\bar{a}=(a_1,\ldots,a_n)\in\mathcal{N}^n$, $[\bar{a}]_{i,j}=([a_1]_{i,j},\cdots,[a_n]_{i,j})$ and for a set of vectors S we write $[S]_{i,j}$ for $\{[s]_{i,j}|s\in S\}$.

The main theorem in this section is:

Theorem 2 *Let $f:\mathcal{N}^r\to\mathcal{N}^s$ be an integer function. Suppose for every integer n there exist integers τ, ξ, a vector $\bar{c}\in\mathcal{N}_{2^n}^r$ and a subset $M\subseteq\mathcal{N}_{2^n}^r$ such that*

$$[M]_{\tau,\xi}=\{\bar{c}\}. \qquad (\star)$$

Then, the complexity of computing f for inputs of size n in the $R\backslash\{\times\}$-RAM model is

$$C_{R\backslash\{\times\}}(f,n)\ge\Omega\left(\frac{\log|[f(M)]_{\tau,\xi}|}{\log\log|[f(M)]_{\tau,\xi}|}\right).$$

If $\xi=0$, then the complexity of computing f for inputs of size n in the R-RAM model is

$$C_R(f,n)\ge\Omega\left(\frac{\log|[f(M)]_{\tau,0}|}{\log\log|[f(M)]_{\tau,0}|}\right).$$

Sketch of Proof . We prove the second statment (the proof of the first is similar). The proof will be for the set of operations

$$R=\{+,-,\times,\text{R-Shift}(a,i,0),\text{NAND}(a,b,i,0)\}.$$

All the other operations in the realistic RAM model can be simulated using the operations of R in $O(1)$ steps. Let $H=[f(M)]_{\tau,0}$. Let P be a program that computes f for inputs of size n with complexity $C_R(f,n)$. We change the program to a computation tree T_P as described in section 2. If the number of leaves in T_P is greater than $|H|^{1/2}$, then the height of T_P, which is the complexity $C_R(f,n)$, is greater than $\Omega(\log|H|)=\Omega(\log|[f(M)]_{\tau,0}|)$ and the result follows. Therefore the number of leaves in the tree T_P is less than $|H|^{1/2}$. Since $|[f(M)]_{\tau,0}|=|H|$, and each input $x\in M$ terminate in the computation at some leaf of the tree, there exists a leaf v in the tree such that the set of inputs $M'\subset M$ that arrive in the computation at this leaf satisfies $|[f(M')]_{\tau,0}|\ge|H|^{1/2}$ (Pigeon-hole principle). Let $H'=[f(M')]_{\tau,0}$. Then

$$h=|H'|\ge|H|^{1/2}.$$

The path from the root to the leaf v computes f for the inputs in M'. We now take this path and delete all the comparison vertices in it. We will be left with a straight line program that computes f for the inputs in M'. (Here we can see that the model can have unlimited power for answering YES/NO questions.) Let $P' \equiv P_1, P_2, \ldots, P_\eta$ be the instructions in this straight line program. If $\eta \geq \log |H|$ then the result follows (because the height of the tree is at least η). Therefore,

$$\eta \leq \log |H|.$$

Let $W_{P'}$ and $R_{P'}$ be the set of constants and the set of operations, respectively, that are used in the straight line program P'. Define the set of constants

$$\tilde{W} = (W_{P'} \bmod 2^{\tau+1}) \cup \{2^\tau\} \cup C,$$

where C is the set of entries of the vector $\bar{c}$ in $(\star)$. We now define a new set of operations $\bar{R}$. The set $\bar{R}$ contains the operations $\{+_{2^{\tau+1}}, -_{2^{\tau+1}}, \times_{2^{\tau+1}}\}$, the arithmetic operations modulo $2^{\tau+1}$, i.e., $a +_{2^{\tau+1}} b = (a+b) \bmod 2^{\tau+1}$. It also contains $\mathrm{NAND}(a, b, i, 0)$ for $0 \leq i \leq \tau$ and $\text{R-Shift}(a, i, 0)$ for $0 \leq i \leq \tau$. Let $R_{P'}$ be the set of operations that are used in the straight line program P'. We define

$$\tilde{R} = (\bar{R} \cap \Lambda(R_{P'})) \cup \{+_{2^{\tau+1}}\}$$

where $\Lambda(R_{P'}) = \{\Lambda(z) | z \in R_{P'}\}$ and for $z \in R_{P'}$, we have

$$\Lambda(z) = \begin{cases} -_{2^{\tau+1}} & z = - \\ +_{2^{\tau+1}} & z = + \\ \times_{2^{\tau+1}} & z = \times \\ \mathrm{NAND}(\star,\star,\tau,0) & z = \mathrm{NAND}(M[a], M[b], i, 0) \text{ and } i > \tau \\ \mathrm{NAND}(\star,\star,i,0) & z = \mathrm{NAND}(M[a], M[b], i, 0) \text{ and } i \leq \tau \\ \text{R-Shift}(\star,\tau,0) & z = \text{R-Shift}(M[a], i, 0) \text{ and } i > \tau \\ \text{R-Shift}(\star,i,0) & z = \text{R-Shift}(M[a], i, 0) \text{ and } i \leq \tau \end{cases}.$$

Since

$$|\tilde{W}| \leq |W_{P'}| + r + 1 \leq \eta + r + 1 \leq O(\log |H|)$$

and

$$|\tilde{R}| \leq |R_{P'}| + 1 \leq \eta + 2 \leq O(\log |H|),$$

by lemma 1, there exists $\bar{t} \in H'$ such that

$$\Delta_{\tilde{R}}(\tilde{W}, \bar{t}) \geq \Omega\left(\frac{\log |H'|}{\log\log |H'|}\right) = \Omega\left(\frac{\log |H|}{\log\log |H|}\right). \tag{1}$$

Now, we will show that

$$C_R(f, n) \geq \frac{1}{2} \Delta_{\tilde{R}}(\tilde{W}, \bar{t}) \tag{2}$$

and then combining this with (1) the result follows.

To prove (2) we will show how to change the straight line program P' to a generator program that generates $\bar{t}$ from $\tilde{W}$ using the operations in $\tilde{R}$. By the condition ($\star$) in the theorem and since $\bar{t} \in H' = [f(M')]_{\tau,0}$ and $[M']_{\tau,0} \subseteq [M]_{\tau,0} = \{\bar{c}\}$, there exists $\bar{a} \in M'$ such that

$$[\bar{a}]_{\tau,0} = \bar{c} \quad , \quad [f(\bar{a})]_{\tau,0} = \bar{t}.$$

We now substitute $\bar{a}$ in the algorithm P' as an input. Since the input in P' is a fixed integer, all indirect addressing can be changed to direct addressing and then $M[i]$ in the algorithm can be replaced by its content. The resulting program $\tilde{P} = P'(a)$ is a generator program that generates $f(\bar{a})$ from the entries of $\bar{a}$ and the constants in $W_{P'}$ using the operations in $R_{P'}$. We now change the generator algorithm to a new generator algorithm that generates $\bar{t}$ from the constants in $\tilde{W}$ using only the operations in $\tilde{R}$. Step P_i in algorithm $\tilde{P}$ will be changed to step $\Gamma(P_i)$, defined as follows:

(1) We change all the constants a in the algorithm $\tilde{P}$ to $a' = a \bmod 2^{\tau+1}$.

(2) If $P_i \equiv a \leftarrow b \circ c$ where $\circ \in \{+, -, \times\}$, then we change the step to $\Gamma(P_i) \equiv a' \leftarrow b' \circ_{2^{\tau+1}} c'$.

(3) If $P_i \equiv \text{NAND}(a, b, i, 0)$, then

$$\Gamma(P_i) \equiv \begin{cases} \text{NAND}(a', b', \tau, 0) & i > \tau, \\ \text{NAND}(a', b', i, 0) & i \leq \tau. \end{cases}$$

(4) If $P_i \equiv \text{R-Shift}(a, i, 0)$, then

$$\Gamma(P_i) \equiv \begin{cases} \text{R-Shift}(a', \tau, 0) & i > \tau, a_{\tau+1} = 0, \\ \text{R-Shift}(a', \tau, 0);\ a' \leftarrow a' + 2^\tau & i > \tau, a_{\tau+1} = 1, \\ \text{R-Shift}(a', i, 0) & i \leq \tau. \end{cases}$$

It can be shown that the new generator generates $\bar{t}$ from $\tilde{W}$ using the operations in $\tilde{R}$. Since the number of steps in the new generator algorithm $\Gamma(\tilde{P})$ is less than or equal to 2 times the number of steps in $\tilde{P}$, the result (2) follows.□

3.2 Lower bounds

In this subsection we show how to use Theorem 2 to prove lower bounds for the complexity of (exactly) computing functions. We give the proofs for the functions gcd and logarithm. The proof for the other functions is similar

Corollary 1 . *Let $gcd : \mathcal{N}_{2^n}^2 \to \mathcal{N}_{2^n}$ be the integer function that computes the greatest common divisor of two integers. Then*

$$O(n) \geq C_R(gcd, n) \geq \Omega\left(\frac{n}{\log n}\right).$$

Sketch of proof . Let

$$M = \{(b_A 2^m - 1, A2^m) \mid m = \lfloor n/2 \rfloor, b_A 2^m \equiv 1 \bmod A, b_A < A, A = 1, 3, 5, \ldots, 2^{\lfloor n/4 \rfloor} + 1\},$$

and $\tau = \lfloor n/3 \rfloor$. It can be easily shown that $M \subseteq \mathcal{N}^2_{2^n}$ and $[M]_{\tau,0} = \{(2^{\tau+1}-1,0)\}$. Now, since

$$gcd(b_A 2^m - 1, A2^m) = gcd(b_A 2^m - 1, A) = A,$$

$$[f(M)]_{\tau,0} = \{1,3,5,\ldots,2^{\lfloor n/4 \rfloor} - 1\} \quad \text{and} \quad |[f(M)]_{\tau,0}| \geq 2^{\lfloor n/4 \rfloor - 1},$$

by Theorem 2,

$$C_R(gcd,n) \geq \Omega\left(\frac{\log |[f(M)]_{\tau,0}|}{\log\log |[f(M)]_{\tau,0}|}\right) = \Omega\left(\frac{n}{\log n}\right).$$

The upper bound follows from Stein's algorithm [Knu81].□

Corollary 2 .

$$C_R(\log,n) \geq \Omega\left(\frac{\log n}{\log\log n}\right).$$

Sketch of Proof . We take $M = 2^{n/2}\mathcal{N}_{2^{n/2}}$ and $\tau = \log n$. It can be shown that $[M]_{\tau,0} = \{0\}$ and $|[f(M)]_{\tau,0}| = n$, so by Theorem 2 the result follows.□

4 Complexity of λ-approximating functions

4.1 Lower bound

In this section we prove lower bounds for λ-approximating functions. To prove the main result we first prove a lemma similar to lemma 1.

Lemma 3 *Let C be a set of constants and F be a set of operations. Let H be a set of constants such than $|F| + |W| \leq (\log\log |H|)^{O(1)}$. Then, there exist $t \in H$ such that*

$$\Delta_F^{(\lambda)}(W,t) \geq \Omega\left(\frac{\log\log |H| - \log \lambda}{\log\log\log |H|}\right).$$

Sketch of Proof . The number of generator programs with $\leq h$ steps is less that or equal to

$$c \leq |F|^h(|W|)^2 \cdots (|W|+h)^2.$$

Let $G_1,\cdots,G_c$ be those generator programs and let $t_1,\ldots,t_c$ be the integers that they generate, respectively. Then G_i is a generator program that λ-approximates all the integers in $[t_i/\lambda, \lambda t_i]$. If $c \leq \log |H| / \log \lambda$ then

$$\bigcup_{i=1}^{c} [t_i/\lambda, \lambda t_i] \neq T.$$

Therefore, c must be greater than or equal to $\log |H| / \log \lambda$ and the result follows.□

The proof of the main Theorem is similar to the proof of Theorem 2 and will be omitted from this abstract.

Theorem 4 *Let $f : \mathcal{N}^r \to \mathcal{N}$ be an integer function. Suppose that for every integer n there exist integers τ, ξ, a vector $\bar{c} \in \mathcal{N}_{2^n}^r$ and a subset $M \subseteq \mathcal{N}_{2^n}^r$ such that*

$$[M]_{\tau,\xi} = \{\bar{c}\}.$$

Then

$$C_{R\setminus\{\times\}}(f, \lambda, n) \geq \Omega\left(\frac{\log\log|[f(M)]_{\tau,\xi}| - \log\lambda}{\log(\log\log|[f(M)]_{\tau,\xi}| - \log\lambda)}\right).$$

If $\xi = 0$, then

$$C_R(f, \lambda, n) \geq \Omega\left(\frac{\log\log|[f(M)]_{\tau,0}| - \log\lambda}{\log(\log\log|[f(M)]_{\tau,0}| - \log\lambda)}\right).$$

4.2 Upper bounds

In this subsection we prove two upper bounds. The first upper bound proves the bounds for the square root, $\log n$, $\log\log n$ and $\log^* n$ in the table. The second result shows that adding integer division to the model solves all the problems in computer science (in the nonuniform model which allow one unit cost for exponential size of integers, unbounded memory and distinct programs for different input size).

Theorem 5 *Let $f : \mathcal{N} \to \mathcal{N}$ be any monotone function. Then*

$$C_R(f, n) \leq O(\log f(2^n))$$

and

$$C_R(f, \lambda, n) \leq O(\log\log f(2^n) - \log\log\lambda).$$

Sketch of Proof . We prove the second statement. Consider the list $1, \lambda, \lambda^2, \cdots, \lambda^{\lceil\frac{\log f(2^n)}{\log\lambda}\rceil}$ with the list of $f^{-1}(\lambda^i)$. The program simply does a binary search for the input x in the second list. If $f^{-1}(\lambda^{i-1}) \leq x \leq f^{-1}(\lambda^i)$, then λ^i is a λ-approximation for $f(x)$. The binary search takes

$$\log(\lceil\log f(2^n)/\log(\lambda)\rceil) = \log\log f(2^n) - \log\log\lambda$$

operations.□

Obviously, the above proof gives a nonuniform program for computing $f(x)$. In the full paper, we show that some of the functions in the table can be computed in a uniform RAM model with the same complexity.

Theorem 6 *For any function $(f_1, \ldots, f_k)(x_1, \ldots, x_j)$, we have*

$$C_{R\cup\{DIV\}}((f_1, \ldots, f_k), n) = \Theta(k + j).$$

Sketch of Proof . Since the domain of the inputs is finite ($\mathcal{N}_{2^n}^j$), we may assume that $f_1, \ldots, f_k$ are polynomials (interpolation of a finite number of points). For $k = 1$ and $j = 1$ the proof can be found in [BMST]. The idea of the proof for any k and any j is the following: We pack the inputs $x_1, \ldots, x_j$ in one input (e.g. $X = x_1 + x_2 2^{n+1} + \cdots + x_j 2^{(j-1)(n+1)}$). We pack the $f_1, \cdots, f_k$ in one integer output. We use the Bshouty, Mansour, Shieber and Tiwary result [BMST] to compute a polynomial with one variable in $O(1)$ operations and then unpack the output. The cost of the pack and unpack are $O(k)$ and $O(j)$, respectively.□

References

[B] M. Ben-Or, Lower bound for algebraic computation trees, in *STOC* 1983, pp. 80-86.

[Bs0] Nader H. Bshouty, Euclid's GCD algorithm is not optimal. Manuscript, 1990.

[Bs1] N. H. Bshouty, On the extended direct sum conjecture, *STOC* 1989, pp. 177-185.

[Bs2] N. H. Bshouty, Lower bounds for algebraic computation trees of functions with finite domains, TR-576, Technion, Israel, July 1989.

[Bs3] N. H. Bshouty, On the complexity of functions for random access machines. (To appear in Journal of ACM).

[Bs4] N. H. Bshouty, $\Omega(\log\log(1/\epsilon))$ lower bound for approximating the square root. TR No. 89/367/29, University of Calgary.

[BG] A. M. Ben-Amram, Z. Galil, Lower bounds for data structure problems on RAMs, *FOCS* 1991, pp. 622-631.

[BJM] L. Babai, B. Just, F Meyer auf der Heide, On the limits of computations with the floor function. *Information and Computation* 78,4, 99-107, (1988).

[BMST] N. H. Bshouty, Y. Mansour, B. Schieber, P. Tiwari, The complexity of approximating with the floor operation.

[H] J. Hong, On lower bounds of time complexity of some algorithms, *Scientia Sinica*, **22**, 890-900, (1979).

[IMR83] O. H. Ibarra, S. Moran, L. E. Rosier. On the control power of integer division. *Theoretical Computer Science*, 24:35–52, 1983.

[JM] B. Just, F. Meyer auf der Heide, A. Wigderson. On computation with integer division. In *Proc. 5th STACS, Lecture Notes in Computer Science*. 294,pp. 29-37. Springer-Verlage, February 1988.

[Knu81] D.E. Knuth. *The Art of Computer Programming*, volume 3. Addison-Wesley, Reading, Ma, second edition, 1981.

[MSM] S. Moran, M. Snir, U. Manber, Applications of Ramsey's theorem to decision tree complexity, *J. of ACM*, **32**, 938-949, (1985).

[MST1] Y. Mansour, B. Schieber, P. Tiwari, Lower bounds for integer greatest common divisor computation, In *FOCS* 1988, pp. 54-63.

[MST2] Y. Mansour, B. Schieber, P. Tiwari, Lower bounds for computations with the floor operations, In *Proceeding of ICALP*, 1989.

[MST2] Y. Mansour, B. Schieber, and P. Tiwari, The complexity of approximating the square root. *FOCS* 1989, pp. 325-330.

[PS] W. Paul, J. Simon, Decision trees and random access machines, in *Monographie 30, L'Enseignement Mathematique, Logic and Algorithmic — An International Symposium Held in Honor of Ernst Specker. Univ. Geneva Press,* 331-340, (1982).

[S] A. Schönhage, On the power of random access machines, 6th ICALP, 520-529, 1979

[Y] A. Yao, Lower bounds for Algebraic Computation Trees with Integer Inputs, *FOCS*, 1989.

On Boolean Decision Trees with Faulty Nodes

Claire Kenyon[1] and Valerie King[2]

[1] LIP-IMAG, Ecole Normale Supérieure de Lyon, 46, allée d'Italie, 69364 Lyon Cedex 07, France.
[2] NECI, 4 Independance Way, Princeton, NJ 08540, USA.

Abstract. We consider the problem of computing with faulty components in the context of the Boolean decision tree model, in which cost is measured by the number of input bits queried and the responses to queries are faulty with a fixed probabilty. We show that if f can be represented in $k-DNF$ form and in $j-CNF$ form, then $O(n\log(min\{j,k\}/q))$ queries suffice to compute f with probability of error less than q. This work uses a new approach to extend results of Feige, Raghavan, Peleg and Upfal, who proved the same bound for a narrower class of functions.

1 Introduction

In this paper, we describe a method for performing reliable computation despite the presence of faulty components. This problem has been well studied in various contexts; in particular, Pippinger and others have looked at the amount of redundancy required for circuits whose gates are "noisy", see [7], [5], [8]. The model we consider here is the noisy Boolean decision tree.

In a Boolean decision tree, the value of a function on n bits is computed as follows: Each step consists of a query of an input bit, where the choice of the query may depend on the outcome of the previous queries. The cost of the algorithm is the number of queries required for the worst case input. The algorithm may be represented as a tree in which each node is a query, and the computation ends when a leaf labelled with an output is reached. The cost is the depth of the tree.

In the noisy version, each response to a query is correct with probability p, where p is a fixed constant greater than 1/2. This induces a probability distribution on the computation paths followed for an input. We specify a tolerance parameter q, $0 < q < 1/2$ and require that for every input, the probability that the correct answer is reached is at least $1-q$. The cost of the algorithm is, as before, the depth of the tree.

It is not difficult to see that if the noiseless Boolean decision tree depth is d, one can construct a noisy decison tree by repeating each query $O(\log d/q)$ times and using the majority of the responses to determine the next step.

In 1990, Feige, Peleg, Raghavan and Upfal [1] showed that this logarithmic blowup was necessary for some problems while unnecessary for others. Thus, they introduced the question of how one might characterize the noisy Boolean decision complexity of a function. Their paper gives tight bounds on the complexity of computing threshold functions. A second paper [2] extends these results to all symmetric functions. In 1991, Reischuk and Schmeltz [8] proved that almost all Boolean functions require $\Omega(n\log n)$ queries.

In this paper we use a very different approach to design an algorithm whose cost matches the [1], [2] bounds for symmetric functions and generalizes that result as follows:

Theorem 1. *Let f be a Boolean function on n bits such that f can be represented in CNF form by clauses of size no greater than N_0 and in DNF form by clauses of size no greater than N_1. Then there is a noisy Boolean decision tree with tolerance q of depth $O(n \log(min\{N_0, N_1\}/q)$.*

For example, our algorithm shows that determining whether a graph contains a triangle can be decided with $O(n\log(1/q))$ noisy queries where n is the total number of possible edges, since $N_1 = 3$. This resolves an open question suggested by Feige, and is optimal to within a constant factor, when q is a constant, since n queries are required in the noiseless case.

We observe that an upper bound of $O(n\log(\max\{N_0, N_1\}/q))$ follows immediately from the trivial $O(d\log(d/q))$ algorithm mentioned above and Blum's observation (see [6]) that $d < N_0N_1$ for any function f, where d is the noiseless Boolean decision tree depth of f and N_0 and N_1 are any numbers that satisfy the conditions of our theorem.

Other variants of the Boolean decision tree model, with error, have been studied. Our approach was inspired by a 1989 work [3] by Kenyon and A. Yao on the complexity of computing on Boolean decison trees where no more than a fixed number of queries were answered incorrectly. Feige, Peleg, Raghavan, and Upfal and Reiscuk and Schmeltz also look at lower bounds for probabilistic noisy Boolean decision trees, in which coin-tossing is permitted in the algorithms. They also consider a static model in which the sequence of queries may not depend on the answers given. Feige, Peleg, Raghavan and Upfal also consider faulty computation in comparison decision trees and in parallel models of computation [8], [1], [2].

2 Definitions and the Algorithm

2.1 Definitions

Following the standard definitions, we say that a pair $M = (T, F)$, where T and F are disjoint subsets of $\{x_1, ..., x_n\}$, is called a *minterm* of f (resp. a *maxterm* of f) if the following holds:
1• if x is such that for all x_j in T, $x_j = 1$, and for all x_j in F, $x_j = 0$, then $f(x) = 1$ (resp. $f(x) = 0$) regardless of the values of the other coordinates of x.
2• no other pair (T', F') with $T' \subset T$ and $F' \subset F$ satisfies condition 1.

If f can be represented in CNF and DNF form with clauses of size no greater than N_0 and N_1, respectively, then there is a set of minimal clauses, each of size no greater than by N_0, which are maxterms and a set of minimal clauses, each of size no greater than N_1 which are minterms. Moreover, every input in $f^{-1}(0)$ is consistent with at least one of these maxterms. and every input in $f^{-1}(1)$ is consistent with at least one of these minterms.

A function may have large minterms for example, yet have a DNF representation does not require large clauses (minterms). For example, the storage access function is defined to be 1 iff in a string of $n = m + \log n$ bits, there is a 1 in the ith position, where i is the value of the last $\log m$ bits. This function can be represented by an $O(\log n)$-DNF form even though f has a minterm of size $\Theta(n)$. We note that the minimal K such that f can be represented in DNF form *and* CNF form with clauses of size no greater than K is called the *non-deterministic* or *certificate complexity* of f (see [6]).

From this point on in the paper, we fix a representation of f in N_1-DNF form and another in N_0-CNF form, and use the terms "minterm" and "maxterm" to refer to the minterms and maxterms given by those representations.

2.2 Notations

Let f be a Boolean function on $\mathbf{x} = x_1, x_2, \ldots, x_n$. At each step, the algorithm must choose a variable to query. The decision is based on the current "label" of the variables, where the *label $v(x_j)$ of variable x_j* is the difference between the number of queries on x_j which were answered by a 1, and the number of queries on x_j which were answered by a 0, from the beginning of the algorithm until the current step:

$$v(x_j) = \#\text{1-answers on } x_j - \#\text{0-answers on } x_j \ .$$

Thus, the larger $v(x_j)$ is, the more confident we feel that $x_j = 1$.

To satisfy a minterm or maxterm $M = (T, F)$, we want every x_j in T to be 1 and every x_j in F to be 0. Thus we define the label of x_j within minterm or maxterm M:

$$v_M(x_j) = \begin{cases} v(x_j) & \text{if } x_j \in T \\ -v(x_j) & \text{if } x_j \in F \\ \text{is undefined otherwise} & \end{cases} \ .$$

Then the label of a minterm or maxterm M is defined as follows:

$$v(M) = \min_{x_j \in T \cup F} v_M(x_j) \ .$$

Thus if $v(M)$ is large we can feel confident that M is satisfied by the input vector.

We can now describe the algorithm.

2.3 Algorithm

The basic idea is to look, at each step, for a likely minterm or maxterm, and try to make it more likely, before $cn \log(\min\{N_0, N_1\}/q)$ queries are used up, where c is a constant dependent on p.

At each step, we do not know the underlying input vector $\mathbf{x}$, but we know what it looks like: x_j "looks like" a 1 if $v(x_j) > 0$ and like a 0 if $v(x_j) < 0$, and it could be either if $v(x_j) = 0$. It is easy to see that at each step, there is at least one minterm or maxterm M with a non-negative label. Moreover, it is impossible to have simultaneously $v(M_1) > 0$ and $v(M_0) > 0$ for a minterm M_1 and a maxterm M_0.

The algorithm is now very simple. Formally, it goes as follows:

Initialization: *Choose a minterm* $M = (T, F)$.
Repeat:

- *Query* $x_i \in T \cup F$ *such that* $v_M(x_i)$ *is minimum*
- *if* $v(M) < 0$, *replace* M *by another minterm or maxterm with a non-negative label.*

Until:

(1) $\exists M_1$ *minterm such that* $v(M_1) \geq c\log(N_0/q)$, or
(2) $\exists M_0$ *maxterm such that* $v(M_0) \geq c\log(N_1/q)$. or
(3) *the total number of queries has exceeded* $cn\log(\min\{N_0, N_1\}/q)$.
In Case (1), output "$f = 1$", else output "$f = 0$".

3 Correctness

What is the probability that the algorithm outputs the wrong answer? In the first subsection, we show that the probability that the algorithm outputs the wrong answer when it terminates by condition (1) or (2) is less than $q/2$. In the second subsection we show that the probability that the algorithm terminates by condition (1) or (2) is at least $1 - q/2$. Thus the probabililty of failure is less than q.

Our analysis uses facts about random walks in $\mathbb{Z}$. For a given input I to f, and a variable x_i which has been queried exactly k times,

let

$$h_{x_i}(k) = \begin{cases} v(x_i) & \text{if } x_i = 1 \text{ in } I \\ -v(x_i) & \text{if } x_i = 0 \text{ in I} . \end{cases}$$

Then for any x_i, $h_{x_i}(k) = 0$ initially, and $h_{x_i}(k+1) = h_{x_i}(k)+1$ with probability p and $h_{x_i}(k+1) = h_{x_i}(k) - 1$ with probability $(1-p)$. The function h descibes a weighted random walk on a line. (Since the behavior of h_{x_i} is the same for all x_i, we will drop the x_i from the notation where there is no ambiguity.)

See Feller's book [4] for proof techniques for the following lemmas.

Lemma 2. *The probability that* $h(n)$ *ever reaches level* $-l$, *where* $l \geq 0$, *is*

$$\left(\frac{1-p}{p}\right)^l .$$

Lemma 3. *Let* $l \geq 0$. *The expected value of the last* n *such that* $h(n) = l$ *is* $al + b$, *and the variance is* cl, *where* a, b, c *are constants which depend on* p.

Lemma 4. *Given* n *random, independent, identically distributed variables with variance* $(\sigma)^2$ *and expectation* E, *the probability that the sum of the variables exceeds* $n(t + E)$ *is less than* σ^2/nt^2.

Lemma 3 implies that at some point in the random walk, since p is a constant greater than 1/2, h will not fall below 0 again and will instead approach infinity. We say that the value of the variable x_j is "decided" after h_{x_j} has crossed 0 for the last time.

3.1 Termination Conditions (1) and (2)

Let us suppose that the input I is such that $f(I) = 1$ (the other case is similar). Then there is at least one minterm M_1 satisfied by I. What is the probability that the algorithm terminates by condition (2) and outputs "$f(I) = 0$"? This occurs only if it finds a maxterm M_0 which seems to be satisfied, i.e. which has a high label.

Since M_0 and M_1 are incompatible, there is some variable x_i in $T_0 \cap F_1$ or $T_1 \cap F_0$ whose label is misleading, i.e., at the termination point,

$$v_{M_0}(x_i) \geq c \log(N_1/q) \ ,$$

and

$$h_{x_i} \leq -c \log(N_1/q) \ .$$

The probability of a wrong output given input I is the probability that some variable in M_1 has $h \leq -c\log(N_1/q)$:

$$\begin{aligned} &\Pr\{\text{wrong output}\} \leq \\ &\leq \Pr\{\exists x_i \in M_1, h_{x_i} \leq -c\log(N_1/q)\} \\ &\leq |T_1 \cup F_1| \Pr\{h \leq -c\log(N_1/q)\}. \end{aligned}$$

By Lemma 2 the probability that h ever reaches level $-c \log N_1/q$ is

$$\left(\frac{1-p}{p}\right)^{c\log(N_1/q)} < \frac{q}{2N_1}$$

if we choose $c = 2/\log(p/1-p)$.

Then $\Pr\{$ wrong output $\} < N_1 q/2N_1 = q/2$,

4 Termination Condition (3)–Limits on the Number of Queries

We show that the probability that condition (3) is reached before condition (1) or (2) is satisfied is less than $q/2$.

Let us assume that $N_1 < N_0$ (the other case is similar).

We note that we may assume that $N_1 < n/\log n$ and $q > 16/n$ for otherwise, the trivial algorithm of querying each variable $\log n/q$ times and taking the majority does as well as our algorithm.

We partition the queries into the following classes:

Case 1: Queries made on any variable before its value is decided, that is, before h remains positive.

Claim: The probability that $O(n)$ queries do not suffice is less than $1/n$.

Proof. Let Y_i = the number of queries made on variable x_i before $h_x = 0$ for the last time. Then let $Y = \sum_{j=1}^{j=n} Y_i$. ¿From Lemma 3 we have that for each i, $E[Y_i] = O(1)$ and $var(Y_i) = O(1)$. By Lemma 4, we have that the probability that $O(n)$ queries do not suffice is less than $1/n$. □

Case 2: Queries made during a test of a maxterm which were made on a variable after its value is decided.

Claim: The probability that $O(n\log(N_1/q))$ queries do not suffice is less than $1/n$.

Proof. Let Y_i be the number of queries made on variable x_i after $h = 0$ for the last time and until h reaches $\log(N_1/q)$ or x_i is no longer queried. By Lemma 3, we have that $E[Y_i] = O(\log(N_1/q))$ and $var(Y_i) = O(\log(N_1/q))$. By Lemma 4, the probability that the sum of Y_i exceeds $O(n\log(N_1/q))$ is less than $1/n$. □

Case 3: Queries done on variables in the test of the final minterm m (if the algorithm ends up deciding that f must be 1), after its value is decided.

Claim: The probability that $O(n)$ queries do not suffice is less than $1/n$, when $N_1 < n/\log n$.

Proof. Let Y_i be the number of queries made on variable x_i after $h = 0$ for the last time and until h reaches $\log(N_0/q)$. Let $Y = \sum_{i|x_i\in m} Y_i$. By Lemma 3, we have that $E[Y_i] = O(\log(N_0/q))$ and $var(Y_i) = O(\log(N_0/q))$. By Lemma 4, we have that the probability that Y is not $O(n)$ is less than $(N_1\log(N_0/q))/n^2 \leq 1/n$ when $N_1 < n/\log n$. □

Case 4: Queries done on variables after their values are decided and during the test of a non-final minterm.

This is the only somewhat complicated case. The ideas is to show that for each variable x_j, there is a bound b_j such that x_j is only queried during the test of a non-final minterm when $h_{x_j} < b_j$ and with probability $1 - q/8$, $B = \sum_{j=1}^{n} b_j = O(n\log N_1)$. It follows from Lemmas 3 and 4 that with probability at least $1 - q/4$, $O(n\log N_1)$ queries suffice.

For each test of a non-final minterm m, there is a "spoiling" variable $x_s \in m$ such that $v_m(x_s) \geq 0$ at the beginning of the minterm test and $v_m(x_s) = -1$ at the end of the minterm test. In between, $v_m(x_s)$ wanders in the non-negative range. Let l be the maximum level reached by $v_m(x_s)$ during the minterm test.

Claim: Every $x_j \in m$ which is queried during that minterm test has $v_m(x_j) \leq l + 1$.

Proof. At each step, the algorithm queries a variable x_j only if $v_m(x_j)$ is minimal over all labels of variables in the same minterm. Thus $v_m(x_j) \leq v_m(x_s) \leq l$ just before the query, and $v_m(x_j) \leq l + 1$ □

It follows from the claim that the maximum value that h_{x_j} can attain during a test of a non-final minterm is $l' + 1$ where l' is the maximum, over all non-final minterm tests involving x_j, of the highest label attained by the spoiling variable during that minterm test.

Let $l_{i,t}$ denote the maximum height that $|v_{x_i}|$ attains between the tth and $(t+1)^{st}$ times it crosses 0. Let $L = \{l_{i,t}|i = 1,\ldots,n; t = 0,1,\ldots\}$. In the worst case, the largest n/N_1 numbers in L are heights of labels of spoiling variables. Also in the worst case, the largest number in L "affects" $N_1 - 1$ variables, the second largest affects a disjoint set of $N_1 - 1$ variables, etc. Let $L' \subset L$ denote the n/N_1 largest numbers in l. We have

$$\sum_{j=1}^{n} \max\{h_{x_j}| \text{ attained during tests of a non-final minterm}\}$$

$$\leq \sum_{l \in L'} (l+1)N_1 \ .$$

Claim: The probability is at least $1 - 1/8q$ *that:*

$$\sum_{l \in L'} (l+1)N_1 = O(n \log N_1) \ .$$

Proof. The expected number of passes through 0 by any variable is a constant, as is the variance, where the constant depends on p, by Lemma 3. Thus, by Lemma 4, the probability is less than $1/n$ that the number of consecutive passes through 0 over all variables is greater than cn where c is a constant depending on p, i.e., $|L| > cn$ with probability $< 1/n$.

The probability that there are n/N_1 elements of L which sum to more that B, given that $|L| \leq cn$, is bounded by the following:

$$\sum_{M=B+1}^{\infty} \binom{cn}{n/N_1} \binom{M + n/N_1 - 1}{n/N_1 - 1} d^M \ ,$$

where the first factor in each term of the summation is the number of ways of choosing n/N_1 elements of L, the second factor is the number of ways to partition M over these elements, the third factor is

$$\prod_{j} Pr[\text{element } l \in L \text{ attains level } i_j \text{ assigned by the partition}] \ ,$$

and d is a constant less than 1, depending on p. There is a constant b depending on p, such that for $B = b(-\log q + (n/N_1)\log N_1)$, this expression is less than $q/8$. Hence, with probability at least $1 - q/8$,

$$\sum_{j=1}^{n} \max h_{x_j} \text{ attained during the testing of a nonfinal minterm}$$

$$< N_1 B$$

$$= O(n \log N_1)$$

since we assume $q > 1/n$ and $N_1 < n/\log n$. □

This completes the analysis of Case 4.

Finally we conclude that the probability that $O(n \log(N_1/q))$ queries do not suffice is no greater than the sum of the probabilities that $O(n \log(N/q_1))$ queries do not suffice in of Cases (1)-(4), which is no greater than $q/2$, for $q > 16/n$.

References

1. Uriel Feige, David Peleg, Prabhakar Raghavan and Eli Upfal. *Computing with Noisy Information*, 22nd Annual ACM Symposium on Theory of Computing, 1990, 128-137.
2. Uriel Feige, David Peleg, Prabhakar Raghavan and Eli Upfal. *Computing with Noisy Information*, unpublished manuscript (1991).
3. Claire Kenyon and Andrew C. Yao. *On evaluating boolean functions with unreliable tests*, International Journal of Foundations of Computer Science, 1, 1(1990), 1-10.
4. William Feller. *An Introduction to Probability Theory and its Applications*, Volume 1, Wiley and Sons 1957.
5. Anna Gal *Lower Bounds for the Complexity for Reliable Boolean Circuits with Noisy Gates*, FOCS '91.
6. N. Nisan *CREW PRAMs and Decision Trees* STOC '89.
7. N. Pippenger *On Networks of Noisy Gates* FOCS '85.
8. R. Reischuk and B. Schmeltz. *Reliable Computation with Noisy Circuits and Decision Trees – A General* $n \log n$ *Lower Bound*, FOCS '91.

This article was processed using the LaTeX macro package with LLNCS style

Interval Graphs, Interval Orders and the Consistency of Temporal Events (extended abstract)

Martin Charles Golumbic[1] and Ron Shamir[2]

[1] IBM Israel Scientific Center, Technion City, Haifa, Israel, and Bar Ilan University, Ramat Gan, Israel. email: golumbic@israearn.bitnet

[2] Department of Computer Science, Sackler Faculty of Exact Sciences, Tel Aviv University, Tel-Aviv 69978, Israel. email: shamir@math.tau.ac.il

Abstract. Temporal events are regarded here as intervals on a time line. This paper deals with problems in reasoning about such intervals when the precise topological relationship between them is unknown or only partially specified. This work unifies notions of interval algebras in artificial intelligence with those of interval orders and interval graphs in combinatorics.
The *satisfiability, minimum labeling* and *all consistent solutions* problems are considered for temporal (interval) data. Several versions are investigated by restricting the possible interval relationships yielding different complexity results. We show that even when the temporal data comprises of subsets of relations based on intersection and precedence only, the satisfiability question is NP-Complete. On the positive side, we have obtained efficient algorithms for several restrictions of the problem. In the process, the *interval graph sandwich problem* is introduced, and is shown to be NP-complete. This problem is also important in molecular biology, where it arises in physical mapping of DNA material.

1 Introduction

Interval consistency problems deal with events, each of which is assumed to be an interval on the real line or on any other linearly ordered set. Given certain explicit topological relationships between pairs of events, we would like to infer additional relationships which are implicit in those given. For example, the transitivity of "before" and "contains" may allow us to infer information regarding the sequence of events. Such inferences are essential in story understanding, planning and causal reasoning. There are a great number of practical problems in which one is interested in constructing a time line where each particular event or phenomenon corresponds to an interval representing its duration. These include seriation in archeology [20, 21], behavioral psychology [9], temporal reasoning [1], scheduling [27], and combinatorics [28]. Other applications arise in non-temporal contexts: For example, in molecular biology, arrangement of DNA segments along a linear chain involves similar problems [6].

In this paper, we relate the two notions of interval algebra from the temporal reasoning community and interval graphs from the combinatorics community, obtaining new algorithmic and complexity results of interest to both disciplines. Allen [1] defined a fundamental model for temporal reasoning where the relative position of two time intervals is expressed by the relations (less than, equal or greater than) of their four endpoints, generating thirteen primitive relations (see Figure 1). We call this *13-valued interval algebra* $\mathcal{A}_{13}$.

RELATION	NOTATION	INTERPRETATION
x before y y after x	$\prec$ $\succ$	
x meets y y met-by x	m m^{-1}	
x overlaps y y overlapped-by x	o o^{-1}	
x starts y y started-by x	s s^{-1}	
x during y y includes x	d d^{-1}	
x finishes y y finished-by x	f f^{-1}	
x equals y	$\equiv$	

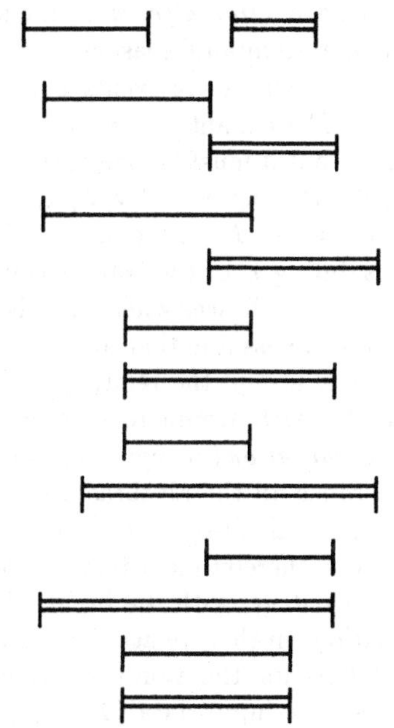

Fig. 1. The 13-valued interval algebra $\mathcal{A}_{13}$. (Single line: x interval. Double line: y interval.)

Our approach has been to simplify Allen's model in order to study its complexity using graph theoretic techniques. The first of the two lines of specialization which we study in this paper is macro relations. Macro relations refers to partitioning the 13 primitive relations into more coarse relations by regarding a subset of primitive relations as a new basic relation. We let

$$\cap = \{m, m^{-1}, o, o^{-1}, s, s^{-1}, f, f^{-1}, d, d^{-1}, \equiv\}$$

$$\alpha = \{m, o\}, \quad \alpha^{-1} = \{m^{-1}, o^{-1}\}$$

$$\subset = \{s, f, d\}, \quad \subset^{-1} = \{s^{-1}, f^{-1}, d^{-1}\}$$

From these we define the 3-valued and 7-valued interval algebras $\mathcal{A}_3$ and $\mathcal{A}_7$ whose elements are called its *atomic relations*, respectively,

$$\mathcal{A}_3 : \{\prec, \succ, \cap\} \qquad \mathcal{A}_7 : \{\prec, \succ, \alpha, \alpha^{-1}, \subset, \subset^{-1}, \equiv\}$$

For certain applications it is convenient to assume that all interval endpoints are distinct. This simplification generates the 6-valued algebra

$$\mathcal{A}_6 \ : \ \{\prec, \succ, o, o^{-1}, d, d^{-1}\}$$

The choice of which of these algebras $\mathcal{A}_i$ to use depends on the nature of the application, data, constraints and on the type of complexity result being proved.

We use the term "algebra" here since the set of atomic relations in each $\mathcal{A}_i$ forms a Boolean algebra, and in certain cases, together with an additional composition operation, forms a *relation algebra*, in the sense defined by Tarski [30], see [23].

The input to all temporal reasoning problems which will be studied here is a set of events, and for each pair of events x and y, a set $D(x,y)$ of atomic relations in a fixed algebra A_i. The semantics here is that we do not know precisely the relationship between x and y, but it must be one of those in the set $D(x,y)$. For example, we read $D(x,y) = \{\prec, \subset\}$ (or, equivalently, $x\{\prec, \subset\}y$) as "x is either before or contained in y"; and $D(x,y) = \{\prec, d^{-1}, \equiv\}$ and $x\{\prec, d^{-1}, \equiv\}y$ both mean "either x ends before y starts, or y is during x, or the two are equal". We also call a set of atomic relations a *relation set*. We omit braces when there is no ambiguity, e.g., $x{\prec}y$ or $x{\cap}y$. Without loss of generality, we assume that all relation sets are non-empty, and that for each pair of elements x and y, the relation sets $D(x,y)$ and $D(y,x)$ given as input are consistent, i.e., for each atomic relation R, $R \in D(x,y) \Leftrightarrow R^{-1} \in D(y,x)$.

An *interval realization* (or *representation*) is an assignment of intervals on the real line to events. Since all the algebras discussed here are concerned with topological properties only, a realization can be viewed also as a complete weak order of the interval endpoints, thereby identifying all realizations which differ in metric only. A realization is *consistent* with the input $\{D(x,y)\}$ if for each pair of events, one of the atomic relations in their relation set holds. Two realizations are *distinct* if for at least one pair of events, the atomic relations which hold between them differ in the two realizations. The input data $\{D(x,y)\}$ is *consistent* (or *satisfiable*) if it admits a consistent realization.

The *interval satisfiability problem* (ISAT), is to determine if the input data $\{D(x,y)\}$ is consistent, and to find one consistent realization in case it is. The *minimal labeling problem* (MLP) is to determine the minimal sets $D'(x,y) \subseteq D(x,y)$ such that the set of consistent interval realizations is unchanged, and every remaining atomic relation holds in some realization.

Example: For the input $x\{\prec, m, o\}y$, $y\{\prec, \equiv, \succ\}z$, $z\{f, s\}x$, two consistent realizations are shown in Figure 2. The relations $y{\prec}z$ and $z \equiv y$ are impossible. The minimal labeling for this problem is $x\{\prec, m, o\}y$, $y{\succ}z$, $z\{f, s\}x$.

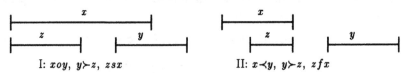

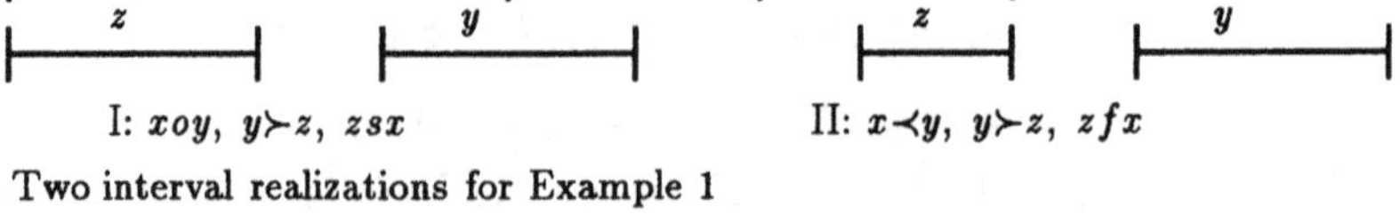

I: $xoy,\ y{\succ}z,\ zsx$ II: $x{\prec}y,\ y{\succ}z,\ zfx$

Fig. 2. Two interval realizations for Example 1

The *all consistent solutions problem* (ACSP) is that of enumerating all the combinations of atomic relations which are consistent with the given data. This problem arises since not all tuples of the cross product of a minimal labeling are consistent. The number of combinations may, of course, be exponential, and the goal here is to construct a ***polynomial representation structure*** Σ requiring $O(p(n))$ space and from which k distinct solutions can be produced in $O(q(n,k))$ time, where n is the number of variables, p and q are polynomial functions, and k is any number less than or equal to the number of solutions. The closely related ***endpoint sequence problem*** (ESP), is that of enumerating all the distinct interval realizations which are consistent with the given data. For $\mathcal{A}_{13}$, the last two problems are equivalent, but in the smaller algebras there may be several (or many) distinct endpoint sequences which realize the same combination of atomic relations. Previous to the work of Belfer and Golumbic [3, 5, 4], we do not know of any study which has investigated the ESP.

Allen [1] originally provided a heuristic approach for solving the MLP in $\mathcal{A}_{13}$. That algorithm is polynomial but does not always provide a minimal solution, and may give a false positive answer to ISAT. Vilian and Kautz [33] have shown that MLP is in fact NP-complete for $\mathcal{A}_{13}$. We obtain a stronger result using macro relations to reduce the number of atomic relations from thirteen to three. Our first main result is to show that even in $\mathcal{A}_3$, the interval satisfiability problem in NP-complete. Consequently, all four problems ISAT, MLP, ACSP and ESP are intractable for all four interval algebras $\mathcal{A}_i$, $i = 3, 6, 7, 13$.

To prove that ISAT is NP-complete for $\mathcal{A}_3$, we introduce a new combinatorial problem, which we prove NP-complete and show to be a special case of ISAT. Recall that an undirected graph $G = (V, E)$ is called an ***interval graph*** if its vertices can be represented by intervals on the real line such that two vertices are adjacent if and only if their intervals intersect (see [12, 17].) The interval graph sandwich (IGS) problem is the following:

> **INTERVAL GRAPH SANDWICH PROBLEM:**
> INPUT: Two disjoint edge-sets, E^1 and E^2 on the same vertex set V.
> QUESTION: Is there a graph $G = (V, E)$ satisfying $E^1 \subseteq E \subseteq E^1 \cup E^2$ which is an interval graph?

Denote $F = V \times V - \{E^1 \cup E^2\}$. When $E^1 = \emptyset$ or $F = \emptyset$, the answer is trivially yes. When $E^2 = \emptyset$, the problem is polynomial by the algorithm of Booth and Lueker [7]. We show that in the general case, the problem is NP-Complete.

An application in molecular biology: In physical mapping of DNA, information on intersection or non-intersection of pairs of segments originating from a certain DNA chain is known from experiments, without knowledge of the nucleotide sequences of the segments or the chain. The goal is to find out how the segments can be arranged as intervals along a line (the DNA chain), so that their pairwise intersections in that arrangement match the experimental data. (This question, raised by the famous biologist Seymour Benzer [6], was one of the original motivations for the study of interval graphs. In fact, Benzer raised the *decision version* of this question, since at the time the linearity of the DNA was only a hypothesis.) In the graph presentation, vertices correspond to segments and two vertices are connected by an E_1-edge (resp., F-edge) if their segments are known to intersect (resp., not to intersect). E^2-edges correspond the the case where the experimental information on the intersections is inconclusive, or simply unavailable. The decision problem is thus equivalent to the IGS problem.

Because of the intractability of ISAT, MLP, ACSP and ESP attention has been focused on efficient (albeit exponential) backtracking algorithms and on polynomial time approximation algorithms for MLP on $\mathcal{A}_{13}$ (see [1, 31, 32] and the references thereof). On a more positive note, solutions to several restricted cases of ISAT have been known for a long time, and many of these cases correspond to other applications. These will be extended by the new results presented here, and lead us to our second line of specialization, namely, restricted domains. By suitably restricting the input domain of an NP-complete problem, one can often obtain a special class which admits a polynomial time algorithm. In the general case for an interval algebra $\mathcal{A}_i$, each relation set $D(x,y)$ may take any of $2^i - 1$ possible values. We restrict this by designating Δ to denote a particular family of relation sets in $\mathcal{A}_i$ and requiring that each relation set $D(x,y)$ be a member of Δ. We represent each relation set in $\mathcal{A}_3$ by a concatenation of its atomic relations, omitting braces. Hence, $\prec\cap$ represents $\{\prec,\cap\}$, $\prec$ represents $\{\prec\}$, etc. The seven possible relation sets in $\mathcal{A}_3$ in this notation are: $\prec, \succ, \cap$, $\prec\cap, \cap\succ$, $\prec\succ$, $\prec\cap\succ$. Thus, the NP-completeness of the interval graph sandwich problem shows that even when all relation sets are restricted to be from $\Delta_0 = \{\cap, \prec\succ, \prec\cap\succ\}$ (meaning *intersect, disjoint* or *don't care*), ISAT remains NP-complete.

In the temporal reasoning literature, polynomial algorithms have been developed for ISAT and MLP on special restrictions of $\mathcal{A}_{13}$, e.g., by assuming that all events are points instead of intervals [24, 31, 32] or by assuming that the restricted domain satisfy certain convexity conditions [26]. A number of well-known recognition problems in graph theory and partially ordered sets may be viewed as restricted interval satisfiability problems. Five of these, all of which have polynomial time solutions, are given in Table 1 along with their appropriate Δ, see [12, 16, 28].

Table 1. Polynomial interval satisfiability problems in graph theory.

Class	Restricted Domain	Reference
Interval orders	$\{\prec,\succ,\cap\}$	[11]
Interval graphs	$\{\prec\succ,\cap\}$	[15, 13, 7, 22]
Circle (or overlap) graphs	$\{\{\alpha,\alpha^{-1},\equiv\},\{\prec,\succ,\subset,\subset^{-1}\}\}$	[14, 8]
Interval containment graphs	$\{\{\subset,\subset^{-1}\},\{\prec,\succ,\alpha,\alpha^{-1},\equiv\}\}$	[18]
Posets of dimension 2	$\{\{\subset\},\{\subset^{-1}\},\{\prec,\succ,\alpha,\alpha^{-1},\equiv\}\}$	[10, 2, 18]

The results of [3, 5, 4] demonstrate polynomial time solutions for the ESP in $\mathcal{A}_3$ restricted to (i) $\Delta = \{\prec,\succ,\cap\}$ (interval orders) using the so called Π structure and its associated construction algorithms, and (ii) $\Delta = \{\prec\succ,\cap\}$ (interval graphs) using the endpoint-tree structure and its construction algorithms.

We describe here the results of a systematic study on the complexity of the restricted domains in $\mathcal{A}_3$. Since we can assume that two converse relation sets ($\prec$ and $\succ$, or $\prec\cap$ and $\cap\succ$) always appear together in a restricted domain, there are 31 possible restrictions. We classify 27 out of them as either polynomial or NP-complete, leaving open a conjecture that would settle the remaining four. For certain restricted domains special polynomial algorithms are devised. An interesting example is the restricted domain $\mathcal{A}_3 - \prec\!\succ$: By excluding only one out of the seven relation sets, ISAT becomes linearly solvable. For lack of space, we only state here the results for restricted domains without proofs or algorithms, and refer the interested reader to [19].

Another positive result is that the polynomiality of ISAT implies the polynomiality of MLP and the existence of a polynomial representation structure for ACSP. These results apply to each of the algebras $\mathcal{A}_i, i = 3, 6, 7, 13$, and also to any restricted domain in these algebras.

2 NP-Completeness of the Complete Algebras

We need two concepts before we can prove the main result of this section. First, three vertices x, y, z in the graph $G = (V, E)$ are called an *asteriodal triplet* if no two of them are connected by an edge, and for each two of the three, there is a path connecting them which does not pass through any vertex adjacent to the third. Lekkerkerker and Boland observed [25] that an interval graph cannot contain an asteriodal triplet. Second, the Not-All-Equal 3-Satisfiability (NAE-3SAT) problem is a restriction of the 3-Satisfiability problem in which one asks for a truth assignment such that each clause contains at least one true literal and at least one false literal. Schaefer [29] has shown that NAE-3SAT is NP-complete. Note that in this problem we can assume without loss of generality that no clause contains a variable and its negation.

Theorem 1. *The interval graph sandwich problem is NP-Complete.*

Proof. The problem is clearly in NP. We describe a reduction from NAE-3SAT: Let F be a CNF-formula with variables $X_1, \ldots, X_n$ and clauses $C_1, \ldots, C_m$. We construct an instance (V, E^1, E^2) of the IGS problem as follows:

1. Define a vertex p. For each variable $X_i, i = 1, \ldots, n$, define four vertices $x_i, \overline{x}_i, x'_i, \overline{x}'_i$. The vertices $x'_i, \overline{x}'_i$ are called *the private vertices* of variable X_i. The vertices $x_i, \overline{x}_i$ are called *the literal vertices* of X_i. Connect the four vertices to each other and to p as shown in figure 3(I). (Solid arcs are E^1-arcs, dotted arcs are E^2-arcs.)

2. For each clause $C_i = [X_{i1} \bigvee X_{i2} \bigvee X_{i3}]$, $i = 1, \ldots, m$, define three vertices v_i^1, v_i^2, v_i^3, which will be called the *private vertices* of clause C_i. Denote the literal vertices corresponding to the three literals of that clause by x_{i1}, x_{i2} and x_{i3}. Connect these six vertices as shown in figure 3(II).

3. All the arcs which were not required to be in E^1 or outside $E^1 \cup E^2$ by (1) and (2) above are E^2-arcs. Specifically, all the following are E^2-arcs:

3.1 For $i = 1, \ldots, n$, connect each of the vertices $x_i, \overline{x}_i, x'_i, \overline{x}'_i$ to each of $x_j, \overline{x}_j, x'_j, \overline{x}'_j$, $j \neq i$.

3.2. For $i = 1, \ldots, m$, connect each private vertex of clause C_i to each private vertex of clause C_j, $i \neq j$.

3.3. For $i = 1, \ldots, m$, connect each private vertex of clause C_i to p and to each literal vertex except those of the two other literals in clause C_i.

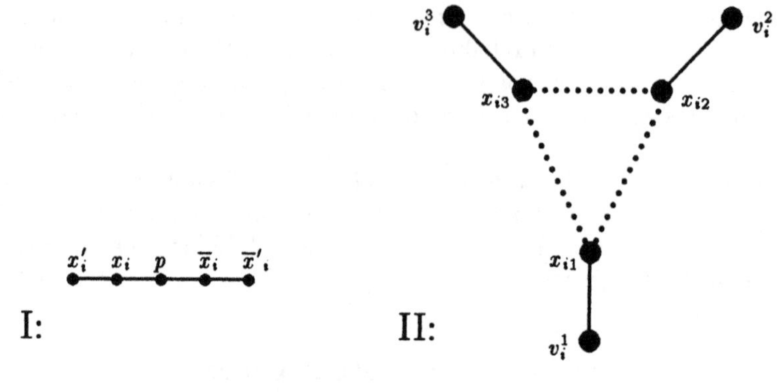

Fig. 3. I: variable subgraph. II: clause subgraph

3.4. For $i = 1, \ldots n$, connect each private vertex of variable X_i to each private vertex of clause $C_j, j = 1, \ldots m$.

Clearly this construction requires polynomial time. Let us now prove its validity: Suppose first that there exists an interval graph sandwich G' for the problem. Fix a realization of G', and denote the interval corresponding to vertex v in the realization by $I(v)$. Denote the endpoints of interval $I(p)$ by p_1 and p_2. By the construction of the variable subgraph (part 1), for each variable X_i, $i = 1, \ldots, n$ the intervals $I(x_i)$ and $I(\overline{x}_i)$ are disjoint, and either $I(x_i)$ meets p_1 and $I(\overline{x}_i)$ meets p_2, or $I(x_i)$ meets p_2 and $I(\overline{x}_i)$ meets p_1. Assign truth values to the variables as follows: $v(X_i) = TRUE$ if and only if $I(x_i)$ meets p_1. By the above argument, this truth assignment is consistent.

Consider now the clause $C_i = [X_{i1} \bigvee X_{i2} \bigvee X_{i3}]$. The intervals $I(x_{i1}), I(x_{i2}), I(x_{i3})$ cannot be pairwise disjoint, since each of them meets one of p_1 and p_2. By the construction of the clause subgraph (part 2), the three intervals cannot have a non-empty intersection, since then in the subgraph corresponding to that clause, v_i^1, v_i^2, v_i^3 will form an asteriodal triplet, which is impossible since the graph is interval. Hence, either one or two of the intervals meet p_1, and so one or two of the literals in each clause are true, as required in NAE-3SAT.

Next, suppose v is a NAE truth assignment which satisfies the formula F. We shall prove that there exists an interval graph sandwich for (E^1, E^2) by creating a sandwich realization for it:

(a) Choose an interval $I(p) = [p_1, p_2]$ arbitrarily, and fix some point p_3 inside it, i.e., $p_1 < p_3 < p_2$. Define intervals $A_1 = [t_1^1, t_1^2]$ and $B_1 = [f_1^1, f_1^2]$ by choosing points $t_1^1, t_1^2, f_1^1, f_1^2$ satisfying

$$t_1^1 < p_1 < t_1^2 < p_3 < f_1^1 < p_2 < f_1^2$$

For $i = 2, \ldots, n$ define inductively intervals A_i, B_i by choosing points $t_i^1, t_i^2, f_i^1, f_i^2$ such that

$$A_i = [t_i^1, t_i^2] \text{ where } t_i^1 < t_{i-1}^1 < p_1 < t_i^2 < t_{i-1}^2$$

$$B_i = [f_i^1, f_i^2] \text{ where } f_{i-1}^1 < f_i^1 < p_2 < f_{i-1}^2 < f_i^2$$

An example of the construction of these intervals is given in figure 4.

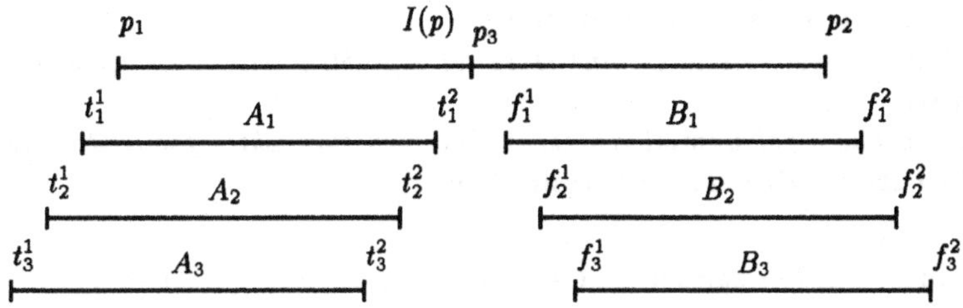

Fig. 4. Construction of the A and B intervals.

(b) If $v(X_i) = TRUE$, then set $I(x_i) = A_i$ and $I(\overline{x}_i) = B_i$. Otherwise, set $I(x_i) = B_i$ and $I(\overline{x}_i) = A_i$. This guarantees that $I(x_i)$ and $I(\overline{x}_i)$ are disjoint, and that one of them meets p_1 and the other meets p_2, as prescribed by (1). The intervals of the private vertices of each variable can now easily be placed so as to satisfy (1).

(c) The arrangement of the literal intervals in part (a) above guarantees that for every two such intervals which have non-empty intersection, no interval is contained in the other. Since v is a not-all-equal truth assignment, for every clause at most two literals are true and at most two are false. Hence, the intervals of the private vertices of each clause can be placed so as to satisfy (2)

The conditions in (3) are automatically satisfied by the above realization, since they pose no additional restrictions. □

Theorem 2. *ISAT is NP-complete for $\mathcal{A}_3$.*

Proof. For a given instance of the IGS problem, construct an instance of ISAT on $\mathcal{A}_3$ as follows: For each edge $(x, y) \in E_1$, E^2 or F, let $D(x, y) = \cap$, $\prec\!\cap\!\succ$ or $\prec\!\diamond\!\succ$, respectively. It is clear that this ISAT problem has a solution if and only if the IGS has one. □

Corollary 3. *ISAT, MLP, ACSP and ESP are NP-hard for $\mathcal{A}_3$, $\mathcal{A}_6$, $\mathcal{A}_7$ and $\mathcal{A}_{13}$.*

Proof. This follows from the observation that the algebra $\mathcal{A}_3$ is contained in each $\mathcal{A}_i$ and that for any $i = 3, 6, 7, 13$, ISAT has a solution if and only if MLP has a non-empty solution if and only if ACSP has a non-empty solution if and only if ESP has a non-empty solution. □

3 Restricted Domain Problems

As stated in the introduction, the proof of Theorem 2.1 shows that ISAT remains NP-complete when restricted to $\Delta_0 = \{\prec\!\diamond\!\succ, \cap, \prec\!\cap\!\succ\}$. The following summarizes our additional results which are detailed in [19].

Theorem 4. *Let Δ_1 be the restricted domain $\mathcal{A}_3 - \prec\!\diamond\!\succ$, that is*

$$\Delta_1 = \{\prec, \succ, \cap, \prec\!\cap, \cap\!\succ, \prec\!\cap\!\succ\}.$$

(1) ISAT(Δ_1) is solvable in linear time.
(2) MLP(Δ_1) is solvable in $O(mn)$ steps for a problem with n events and m explicit relation sets.
(3) There exists a polynomial representation structure which facilitates the solution of ESP on Δ_1 in $O(n)$ steps per realization.

Theorem 5. *ISAT is solvable in $O(n^3)$ time for $\Delta_2 = \{\prec, \succ, \cap, \diamond\}$*

Theorem 6. *ISAT is solvable in linear time for $\Delta_3 = \{\prec, \succ, \prec\cap\succ, \diamond\}$.*

Theorem 7. *ISAT is NP-complete for $\Delta_4 = \{\prec\cap, \cap\succ, \diamond, \prec\cap\succ\}$.*

Since every subset of a restricted domain is polynomial, and every superset of an NP-complete problem is NP-complete, the above results resolve the complexity of 27 out of the 31 possible restricted domains in $\mathcal{A}_3$. We tend to believe that ISAT is NP-complete on $\{\prec\cap, \cap\succ, \diamond\}$. A proof to this conjecture will resolve the remaining four cases.

4 The Relative Complexity of ISAT, MLP and ACSP

Proposition 8. *The minimum labeling problem and the interval satisfiability problem are polynomially equivalent for each of the algebras $\mathcal{A}_i, i = 3, 6, 7, 13$.*

Proof. Omitted in this abstract. □

Proposition 9. *In any of the algebras $\mathcal{A}_i, i = 3, 6, 7, 13$, if the interval satisfiability problem is polynomial, then there exists a polynomial representation structure for the corresponding all consistent solutions problem.*

Proof. (sketch) By Proposition 8, the polynomiality of ISAT implies the polynomiality of MLP. Denote the solution of the MLP by $D = (D^1, D^2, \ldots, D^k)$, where each D^i is a relation set in the minimum labeling solution. The algorithm for ACSP is an exhaustive depth-first search on the solution space defined by the cross product of the sets D^i: In level j of the tree, the sets $D^1, \ldots, D^j$ have been replaced by singletons (atomic relations) and the rest are unchanged. In level i, replace D^i by an atomic relation in D^i and solve ISAT on the resulting problem. If that problem is satisfiable, then move one level down in the enumeration, and replace D^{i+1} by an atomic relation. Otherwise, replace the singleton in level i by a new one, or move one level up if D^i has been exhausted. A consistent realization is determined whenever the algorithm reaches level $k+1$, and the algorithm terminates when level 1 has been exhausted. The consistency check at every level using ISAT oracle allows pruning partially restricted solutions which are already inconsistent, and is the reason for the polynomiality of the algorithm. □

Acknowledgment

Helpful conversations with Fred Roberts and Peter Ladkin are gratefully acknowledged. The initial stage of this work was done while the first author was a visitor at the IBM T.J. Watson Research Center, Yorktown Heights, NY. The work of the second author was done while he visited DIMACS and RUTCOR, Rutgers University, NJ and was supported in part by AFOSR grants 89-0512 and 90-0008, and by NSF grant STC88-09648.

References

1. J. F. Allen. Maintaining knowledge about temporal intervals. *Comm. ACM*, 26:832–843, 1983.
2. K. R. Baker, P. C. Fishburn, and F. S. Roberts. Partial orders of dimension 2. *Networks*, 2:11–28, 1972.
3. A. Belfer and M. C. Golumbic. Counting endpoint sequences for interval orders and interval graphs. to appear in *Discrete Math.*
4. A. Belfer and M. C. Golumbic. The role of combinatorial structures in temporal reasoning. IBM Research Report, (in preparation).
5. A. Belfer and M. C. Golumbic. A combinatorial approach to temporal reasoning. In *Proc. Fifth Jerusalem Conf. on Information Technology*, pages 774–780. IEEE Computer Society Press, 1990.
6. S. Benzer. On the topology of the genetic fine structure. *Proc. Nat. Acad. Sci. USA*, 45:1607–1620, 1959.
7. K. S. Booth and G. S. Lueker. Testing for the consecutive ones property, interval graphs, and planarity using PQ-tree algorithms. *J. Comput. Sys. Sci.*, 13:335–379, 1976.
8. A. Bouchet. Reducing prime graphs and recognizing circle graphs. *Combinatorica*, 7:243–254, 1987.
9. C. H. Coombs and J. E. K. Smith. On the detection of structures in attitudes and developmental processes. *Psych. Rev.*, 80:337–351, 1973.
10. B. Dushnik and E. W. Miller. Partially ordered sets. *Amer. J. Math.*, 63:600–610, 1941.
11. P. Fishburn. Intransitive indifference with unequal indifference intervals. *J. Math. Psych.*, 7:144–149, 1970.
12. P. Fishburn. *Interval Orders and Interval Graphs*. Wiley, New York, 1985.
13. D. R. Fulkerson and O. A. Gross. Incidence matrices and interval graphs. *Pacific J. Math.*, 15:835–855, 1965.
14. C. P. Gabor, K. J. Supowit, and W-L Hsu. Recognizing circle graphs in polynomial time. *J. ACM*, 36:435–473, 1989.
15. P. C. Gilmore and A. J. Hoffman. A characterization of comparability graphs and of interval graphs. *Canad. J. Math.*, 16:539–548, 1964.
16. M. C. Golumbic. *Algorithmic Graph Theory and Perfect Graphs*. Academic Press, New York, 1980.
17. M. C. Golumbic. Interval graphs and related topics. *Discrete Math.*, 55:113–121, 1985.
18. M. C. Golumbic and E. R. Scheinerman. Containment graphs, posets and related classes of graphs. *Ann. N.Y. Acad. Sci.*, 555:192–204, 1989.
19. M. C. Golumbic and R. Shamir. Complexity and algorithms for reasoning about time: A graph-theoretic approach. Technical Report 91-54, DIMACS Center, Rutgers University, NJ, 1991. Submitted.

20. D. G. Kendall. Incidence matrices, interval graphs, and seriation in archaeology. *Pacific J. Math.*, 28:565–570, 1969.
21. D. G. Kendall. Some problems and methods in statistical archaeology. *World Archaeol.*, 1:68–76, 1969.
22. N. Korte and R. H. Möhring. An incremental linear time algorithm for recognizing interval graphs. *SIAM J. Comput.*, 18:68–81, 1989.
23. P. B. Ladkin and R. Maddux. The algebra of constraint satisfaction problems and temporal reasoning. Technical report, Kestrel Institute, Palo Alto, 1988.
24. P. B. Ladkin and R. Maddux. On binary constraint networks. Technical report, Kestrel Institute, Palo Alto, 1988.
25. C. G. Lekkerkerker and J. Ch. Boland. Representation of a finite graph by a set of interval on the real line. *Fundam. Math.*, 51:45–64, 1962.
26. K. Nökel. Convex relations between time intervals. Technical Report SR-88-17, Univ. Kaiserslautern, 1988.
27. C. Papadimitriou and M. Yannakakis. Scheduling interval ordered tasks. *SIAM J. Comput.*, 8:405–409, 1979.
28. F. S. Roberts. *Discrete Mathematical Models, with Applications to Social Biological and Environmental Problems.* Prentice-Hall, Englewood Cliffs, New Jersey, 1976.
29. T. J. Schaefer. The complexity of satisfiability problems. In *Proc. 10th Annual ACM Symp. on Theory of Computing*, pages 216–226, 1978.
30. A. Tarski. On the calculus of relations. *Journal of Symbolic Logic*, 6:73–89, 1941.
31. P. vanBeek. Approximation algorithms for temporal reasoning. In *Proc. Eleventh Int'l. Joint Conf. on Artificial Intelligence (IJCAI-89)*, pages 1291–1296, August 1989.
32. P. vanBeek. Reasoning about qualitative temporal information. In *Proc. Eighth Nat'l. Conf. on Artificial Intelligence (AAAI-90)*, pages 728–734, August 1990.
33. M. Vilian and H. Kautz. Constraint propagation algorithms for temporal reasoning. In *Proc. Fifth Nat'l. Conf. on Artificial Intelligence (AAAI-86)*, pages 337–382, August 1986.

Higher Order Functions in First Order Logics

Andrei Voronkov

ECRC, Arabellastr.17, 8000 Munich 81, Germany (voronkov@ecrc.de)*

Abstract. Most of approaches to extracting programs from (constructive) proofs use type theories. Usually it is argued that first order logic has many drawbacks to be used as a language for programming in logic. In particular, higher order functions are not directly expressible in first order logic. Here we show how to use proof schemes in first order logic for representing higher order functions. We generalize the semantics introduced in [Vor 90] to the proof schemes and show how it is related to extraction of higher order functions from proofs in first order logic.

1 Introduction

Several approaches can be used to derive programs from specifications. One of them is based on extracting programs from constructive proofs. The essential idea of this approach is that under some restrictions a proof of a specification implicitly contains information sufficient to construct a program meeting the specification. Different restrictions give different logics. Most of such logics are *logics of higher types* or *type theories* [Bas 89, Chi 87, Con 86, Coq 88, Hen 92, Nor 84]. Type theories are very helpful in many aspects:

- Rich expressive power. It means that type theories usually can be used for the representation of programming data types as well as for the representation of extracted programs.
- The language of extracted programs is the part of the language of type theories which allows one to use the theories also for manipulations of programs.
- Independently of the language of proofs extracted programs are usually written in a variant of the lambda calculus, i.e. they are essentially pure functional programs. Functional programming greatly benefits from the use of higher order functions. Nevertheless higher order functions which are easily expressible in type theories are not directly representable in first order logic.

Besides it the notion of type theory is sufficiently flexible and allows different modifications which can be used to represent some ideas from programming, e.g. typed vs. untyped programming languages.

The first step in the design of a proof extraction system is to define the logical system in which formal proofs will be written. For writing formal proofs type theories have serious disadvantages. It is much easier to construct proofs in first order theories then in type theories. First order logic has a natural model theoretical semantics, which allows easier understanding of proofs. On the contrary, type theories have much more complicated semantics compared to first order logics. As a consequence, type theories are unnatural for specifying input-output conditions of programs. The

* On leave from the International Laboratory of Intelligent Systems (SINTEL), 630090, Universitetski Prospect 4, Novosibirsk 90, Russia (voronkov@sintel.nsk.su).

specification of a function f, which by any x satisfying $A(x)$ gives y such that $B(x,y)$ is true, in first order logic is written in the form $\forall x(A(x) \supset \exists y B(x,y))$, which is intuitively a natural way to express existence of such a function. In type theories such a specification is usually written in the form $f \in \Pi x : A.\Sigma y : B(x)$. To understand the meaning of this specification one needs to know quite complicated semantics of type theories. Even if such a specification is proved in type theory, it is not trivial to understand that the function of the type $\Pi x : A.\Sigma y : B(x)$ satisfies the specification $\forall x(A(x) \supset B(x, f(x)))$.

The computer implementations of type theories [Chi 87] are also quite complicated and the proofs in this systems are difficult to understand. At the same time there are quite successful implementations of first order constructive logics [Goa 80a, Goa 80b, Hay 88]. In our previous papers we gave a systematic approach to the theory of programming in constructive logic [SV 90, Vor 88, Vor 90, Vor 91b, Vor 91a]. This approach has been used to give a formal definition of constructive logic. The approach is quite general: for example among the results proved in our previous papers are

- The proofs that well-known constructive logics are constructive in the strict sense of our definitions.
- The proofs connecting two notions of constructivism: that of constructive logic and that of the recursion theory.
- The proofs of some relations between the classical model theory and the model theory based on the constructive notion of truth.

The systems described in [Goa 80a, Goa 80b] had already shown the practical importance of first order logics for program extraction. In a forthcoming paper we are planning to show that first order logic can be also used for the purposes claimed to be advantages of type theories, namely the introduction of new types.

In this paper we show how to use *proof schemes* to extract higher order functions from the proofs in first order logic. In Section 2 we give an intuitive example of the use of parameters in proofs to represent higher order functions. In Section 3 we define a constructive notion of truth for parametric formulae. Then in Section 4 we show how to define constructive logics using constructive truth. The notion of constructive logic justifies the use of parameters in the example from Section 2

2 An example

Suppose that we want to specify the function **mapcar** which applies a given function **f** to all elements of a given list **In**. The usual specification of this higher order function can be written in the form of recursive equations:

```
mapcar f nil ⇒ nil
mapcar f (cons x l) ⇒ cons (f x) (mapcar f l)
```

However our approach is to use first order logic without any additional features like recursion. Hayashi [Hay 88] handles recursive equations in his (essentially first order) system, but the logic he uses is quite complicated compared to usual first order logic.

To specify **mapcar** we need to use a language of a constructive theory for proving properties of lists. Such a system can be found e.g. in [Vor 91a]. Here we do not give a full axiomatization of the list theory, but we provide only some essential details instead.

The list theory has three sorts: the sort α of atoms, the sort λ of lists and the sort ν which is the union of α and λ. Some of the special functions and predicates used in the language of the theory are

nil - the constant for empty list;
cons - the list constructor;
$l_1 \sqsubseteq l_2$ - the predicate between lists which is true if l_1 can be obtained from l_2 by deleting several elements from the beginning.

We shall also occasionally use functions **car** giving the first element of a list and **length** giving the length of a list. One of the possible ways to write the specification of **mapcar** in form of a predicate is the following:[2]

```
mapcar(In,Out) ⇔ length(In) = length( Out) ∧
                 (∀X⊑In)¬¬(∃Y⊑Out)(length(X) = length(Y) ∧
                 ¬X=[] ⊃ car(Y) = f(car(X)) )
```

We can in principle use any other specification, because the scheme of the proof given below remains valid for all of them.

Our aim is to prove the following formula specifying the existence of this function:

```
(∀In)(∃Out)mapcar(In,Out).
```

The only rule for lists that will be used in the proof below is *list induction:*

$$\frac{\varphi(\mathrm{nil}) \qquad \begin{array}{c}[\varphi(l)] \\ \vdots \\ \varphi(\mathrm{cons}(u,l))\end{array}}{\forall l \varphi(l)}$$

where u is a variable of the sort ν and l is a variable of the the sort λ. The constructiveness of this rule is easy to prove (see e.g. [Vor 91a]).

Harrop formulae [Har 60] are defined as follows:

1. Any atomic formula is a Harrop formula;
2. If φ, ψ are Harrop formulae, χ an arbitrary formula, then the following formulae are Harrop formulae: $\varphi \wedge \psi$, $\forall x \varphi$, $\neg\chi$, $\chi \supset \varphi$.

We do not provide proofs of Harrop formulae in the example given below, because Harrop formulae have no computational content. It means that the proof of these formulae is necessary for proving correctness of the extracted function, but it does not effect the definition of the function.

A (partial) proof of the above specification in the sequent natural deduction system [Pra 65] is as follows:

```
(1) mapcar(In,Out) ⊢ mapcar([Z|In],[f(Z)|Out])                [Harrop]
(2) (∃Out)mapcar(In,Out) ⊢ (∃Out)mapcar(In,Out)                [axiom]
(3) mapcar(In,Out) ⊢ (∃Out)mapcar([Z|In],Out)                [∃-intro 1]
(4) ⊢ mapcar([],[])                                           [Harrop]
(5) ⊢ (∃Out)(mapcar([],Out))                                 [∃-intro 4]
(6) (∃Out)mapcar(In,Out) ⊢ (∃Out)mapcar([Z|In],Out)         [∃-elim 2,3]
(7) ⊢ (∀In)(∃Out)mapcar(In,Out)                            [ListInd 5,6]
```

[2] The reason to use double negation is that we want **mapcar** to be Harrop formula (see below).

The annotation [Harrop] is used to denote sequents with Harrop formulae in the succedent.

It is easy to see that the proof does not depend on particular properties of the function `f`. Hence we may consider it as a specification of a higher order function which takes `f` and `In` as the input and produces the output `Out = mapcar(f,In)`. This is the main idea of how to synthesize higher order functions from the proofs in first order logic. However to make this idea precise we need to give formal definitions and to prove theorems about correctness of thus extracted functions. We do it in the subsequent sections.

Usually the specifications for program extraction are written in one of the following forms: $(\forall x)(\exists y)Spec(x, y)$ or $(\forall x)(In(x) \supset (\exists y)Out(x, y))$. Suppose that the functional symbol f occurs in this formulae. If there are no occurences of f in the set of axioms of the theory in which proofs are written then the above formulae serve as a specification of an algorithm which takes x and f as the input and gives y as the output.

To give the definition of *truth* of a formula on a model the functions and predicates must be interpreted on this model. After we fixed the model we may construct calculi for proving properties of this model, for instance Peano arithmetic for natural numbers. In the above example we used the symbol `f` which had no interpretation on the intended model. So the above proof can be considered as a scheme in which one can substitute concrete interpreted functions for `f`. To justify the use of uninterpreted functions and such *proof schemes* in a constructive framework we shall change the basic definitions from [Vor 90] in the next sections.

3 Constructive truth for formulae with parameters

This section contains auxiliary definitions concerning the theory of enumerated models and higher type functionals and the definitions of constructive truth for formulae with parameters.

First of all we introduce the definition of *enumerated models* [Ers 80]. Enumerated models and computable functionals of higher types form the basis of our theory of extracting programs from proofs. (More details may be found in [Vor 88, Vor 90]). The motivation to use enumerated models was explained in [Vor 90]. We want to represent programming data types as *models* in the sense of the model theory [Cha 77]. However as we intend to formalize computations over these data types, we need a notion of computability over the models. One of possible ways is to enumerate the elements of the models by natural numbers and to use this enumeration for defining computable functions on the data types. In a way it corresponds to the implementation of data types in programming languages: finally all elements of data types are encoded by sequences of bits in the computer memory. This encoding is invisible to the user of the language, but it is needed to compile programs. In our approach the enumeration of the model is also invisible — all we have is the axioms of some theory describing properties of the data type. However to prove that we can extract programs from proofs (which corresponds to compilation in programming) such encoding is needed.

Definition 1. Let S be a set. An enumeration [Ers 77] of S is any mapping of the set of all natural numbers $\mathfrak{N}$ onto S. An enumerated set is any pair (S, ν) where S is a set and ν is an enumeration of S.

Let $\mathfrak{M} = \langle M, P_0, P_1, \ldots, h_0, h_1, \ldots \rangle$ be a model of a signature σ with predicates $P_0, P_1 \ldots$ and function symbols $h_0, h_1 \ldots$ We shall use $\mathfrak{N}$ to denote the set of all natural numbers.

Definition 2. An enumeration of the model $\mathfrak{M}$ is any enumeration $\nu : \mathfrak{N} \rightarrow M$ of the domain M of $\mathfrak{M}$ such that there exists a binary total recursive function H such that for any $n, y_1, \ldots, y_{m_n} \in \mathfrak{N}$ we have $h_n(\nu y_1, \ldots, \nu y_{m_n}) = \nu H(n, \langle y_1, \ldots, y_{m_n} \rangle)$, where $\langle y_1, \ldots, y_{m_n} \rangle$ is the Gödel number of the tuple $y_1, \ldots, y_{m_n}$. The pair $(\mathfrak{M}, \nu)$ where $\mathfrak{M}$ is a model of the signature σ, and ν is its enumeration is called enumerated model of the signature σ.

We can consider an enumeration of a model $\mathfrak{M}$ as an implementation of the data type corresponding to this model. The restriction on enumerations means that all functions from the signature of the model are computable in this enumeration.

To define the constructive semantics we use the functionals of higher types. For representation of such functionals we choose the Scott's notion of *information systems* [Sco 82]. There is no space to write all the formal definitions concerning the information systems, so here we present only the most essential for us properties.

Information systems allow one to define the functionals of higher types. For any information systems **A**,**B** there exist the information systems $\mathbf{A} \oplus \mathbf{B}$, $\mathbf{A} \otimes \mathbf{B}$ and $\mathbf{A} \rightarrow \mathbf{B}$. We refer reader to [Sco 82] for the complete definitions. The set of all elements of an information system **A** is denoted by $\mid \mathbf{A} \mid$. In any information system **A** there always exists the least element $\perp_{\mathbf{A}}$. The system $\mathbf{A} \rightarrow \mathbf{B}$ is the domain of all *approximable mappings* (or *continuous functions*) from **A** to **B**. The domain $\mathbf{A} \oplus \mathbf{B}$ is essentially the *disjoint union* of the domains **A** and **B**. Its elements are of the form $\mathrm{inl}(a)$ with $a \in \mid \mathbf{A} \mid$, or $\mathrm{inr}(b)$ with $b \in \mid \mathbf{B} \mid$ or $\perp_{\mathbf{A} \oplus \mathbf{B}}$. $\mathbf{A} \otimes \mathbf{B}$ is the *Cartesian product* of **A** and **B**. Elements of $\mathbf{A} \otimes \mathbf{B}$ are pairs of the form $\langle a, b \rangle$ with $a \in \mid \mathbf{A} \mid$ and $b \in \mid \mathbf{B} \mid$.

The information system **N** [Vor 88] is such that the elements of **N** are either $\perp_{\mathbf{N}}$ or natural numbers $0, 1, \ldots$. The information system **1** is defined in such a way that it has only the bottom element $\perp_{\mathbf{1}}$. As it is done in [Vor 88], one can define the notion of a computable element for any information system constructed from **N** and **1** by repeated applications of the constructors $\rightarrow, \otimes, \oplus$.

The notion of *constructive truth* was defined in [Vor 88, Vor 90] for any enumerated model. The definition relies upon the fact that all functions and predicates are interpreted in the enumerated models. However if we are to define constructive truth for the proof schemes containing uninterpreted symbols we have to change the definitions to the case of uninterpreted functions.

As in [Vor 90] we start from the classical truth.

Let $(\mathfrak{M}, \nu)$ be an enumerated model of the signature σ. Let δ is obtained from σ by adding new functional symbols $f_0, \ldots, f_n$. In what follows we call $f_0, \ldots, f_n$ *parameters*. An *interpretation* $\mathfrak{I}$ is any mapping which maps each $f_i, i = 0, \ldots, n$ to a function on $\mathfrak{M}$. Let the signature Δ is obtained from δ by adding constants νi for all natural numbers i with the standard interpretation. We assign to each formula φ of the extended signature Δ an information system $\mathbf{A}_\varphi$ and a relation $a \, \underline{\mathrm{cl}}_{\mathfrak{I}} \, \varphi$ (a classically realizes φ under the interpretation $\mathfrak{I}$) where $a \in \mid \mathbf{A}_\varphi \mid$.

If φ is a formula with free variables $x_0, \ldots, x_n$ then $\forall \varphi$ will denote the formula $\forall x_0, \ldots, x_n \varphi$. If there are no free variables in φ then $\forall \varphi \Leftrightarrow \varphi$.

Definition 3 (The relation $\underline{\mathrm{cl}}_{\mathfrak{I}}$). In (1)-(7) all formulae are closed.

1. $\mathbf{A}_\varphi \Leftrightarrow \mathbf{1}$ for atomic φ and $\perp \underline{\mathrm{cl}}_{\mathfrak{I}} \, \varphi$ iff φ is true in $\mathfrak{M}$ under the interpretation $\mathfrak{I}$.

(Strictly speaking the definition of $\underline{\mathrm{cl}}_{\Im}$ depends of the model $(\mathfrak{M}, \nu)$, so we ought to write $\underline{\mathrm{cl}}_{(\mathfrak{M},\nu),\Im}$ instead of $\underline{\mathrm{cl}}_{\Im}$, but we omit indices where it causes no ambiguities).

2. $\mathbf{A}_{\varphi\wedge\psi} \Leftrightarrow \mathbf{A}_{\varphi} \otimes \mathbf{A}_{\psi}$ and $\langle a, b\rangle \,\underline{\mathrm{cl}}_{\Im}\, \varphi\wedge\psi$ iff $a \,\underline{\mathrm{cl}}_{\Im}\, \varphi$ and $b \,\underline{\mathrm{cl}}_{\Im}\, \psi$.
3. $\mathbf{A}_{\varphi\vee\psi} \Leftrightarrow \mathbf{A}_{\varphi} \oplus \mathbf{A}_{\psi}$ and for $r \in \mid \mathbf{A}_{\varphi\vee\psi} \mid$ we have $r \,\underline{\mathrm{cl}}_{\Im}\, \varphi\vee\psi$ iff one of the following is true:
   (a) for some $a \in \mathbf{A}_{\varphi}$, $r = \mathtt{inl}(a)$ and $a \,\underline{\mathrm{cl}}_{\Im}\, \varphi$;
   (b) for some $b \in \mathbf{A}_{\psi}$, $r = \mathtt{inr}(b)$ and $b \,\underline{\mathrm{cl}}_{\Im}\, \psi$.
   We remind that inl and inr are natural embeddings of $\mid \mathbf{A}_{\varphi} \mid$ and $\mid \mathbf{A}_{\psi} \mid$ into $\mid \mathbf{A}_{\varphi\vee\psi} \mid$.
4. $\mathbf{A}_{\varphi\supset\psi} \Leftrightarrow \mathbf{A}_{\varphi} \rightarrow \mathbf{A}_{\psi}$ and for $f \in \mid \mathbf{A}_{\varphi\supset\psi} \mid$, $f \,\underline{\mathrm{cl}}_{\Im}\, \varphi\supset\psi$ iff for every $a \,\underline{\mathrm{cl}}_{\Im}\, \varphi$ we have $f(a) \,\underline{\mathrm{cl}}_{\Im}\, \psi$.
5. $\mathbf{A}_{\neg\varphi} \Leftrightarrow \mathbf{1}$ and $\bot_{\mathbf{1}} \,\underline{\mathrm{cl}}_{\Im}\, \neg\varphi$ iff for every $a \in \mathbf{A}_{\varphi}$ it is not true that $a \,\underline{\mathrm{cl}}_{\Im}\, \varphi$.
6. $\mathbf{A}_{\exists x\varphi(x)} \Leftrightarrow \mathbf{N} \otimes \mathbf{A}_{\varphi(t)}$, where t is an arbitrary closed term and $\langle n, a\rangle \,\underline{\mathrm{cl}}_{\Im}\, \exists x\varphi(x)$ iff $a \,\underline{\mathrm{cl}}_{\Im}\, \varphi(\nu n)$.
7. $\mathbf{A}_{\forall x\varphi(x)} \Leftrightarrow \mathbf{N} \rightarrow \mathbf{A}_{\varphi(t)}$ and for $f \in \mid \mathbf{A}_{\forall x\varphi(x)} \mid$, $f \,\underline{\mathrm{cl}}_{\Im}\, \forall x\varphi(x)$ iff for every $n \in \mathfrak{N}$ we have $f(n) \,\underline{\mathrm{cl}}_{\Im}\, \varphi(\nu n)$.
8. If there are free variables in φ, then $\mathbf{A}_{\varphi} \Leftrightarrow \mathbf{A}_{\forall\varphi}$, and $a \,\underline{\mathrm{cl}}_{\Im}\, \varphi$ iff $a \,\underline{\mathrm{cl}}_{\Im}\, \forall\varphi$.

A formula φ is classically realizable under the interpretation $\Im$ iff for some $a \in \mid A_{\varphi} \mid$ we have $a \,\underline{\mathrm{cl}}_{\Im}\, \varphi$.

The following theorem proved in [Vor 90] for the language without parameters, explains why this semantics is called "classical realizability":

Theorem 4. *There exists a such that $a \,\underline{\mathrm{cl}}_{(\mathfrak{M},\nu),\Im}\varphi$ iff φ is true in $\mathfrak{M}$ under the interpretation $\Im$.*

This semantics is called classical realizability because the set of all realizable formulae coincides with the set of all classically true formulae. The following definition introduce the set of constructively true formulae as a subset of classically true ones.

Definition 5. Let $a \in \mid A_{\varphi} \mid$. Then $a \,\underline{\mathrm{con}}_{\Im}\, \varphi$ iff $a \,\underline{\mathrm{cl}}_{\Im}\, \varphi$ and a is computable. If $a \,\underline{\mathrm{con}}_{\Im}\, \varphi$ then we will say that a constructively realizes φ. A formula φ is said to be constructively true in the enumerated model $(\mathfrak{M}, \nu)$ under the interpretation $\Im$ (denoted by $(\mathfrak{M}, \nu) \models_{\underline{\mathrm{con}},\Im} \varphi$ iff there is a with $a \,\underline{\mathrm{con}}_{(\mathfrak{M},\nu),\Im}\varphi$.

Up to now this definition differs from that of [Vor 90] only by adding words "under interpretation" when needed. Now we extend it to the parametric case in an obvious way.

Let f_i be n_i-place functions and $\mathbf{F}_i$ be the information systems $\underbrace{\mathbf{N} \otimes \ldots \otimes \mathbf{N}}_{n_i \text{ times}} \rightarrow \mathbf{N}$.

Definition 6 (Relations $\underline{\mathrm{cl}}$ and $\underline{\mathrm{con}}$ for the parametric case). Let $a \in \mathbf{F}_1 \otimes \ldots \otimes \mathbf{F}_n \rightarrow \mathbf{A}_{\varphi}$. Then $a \,\underline{\mathrm{cl}}\, \varphi$ iff for any interpretation $\Im$ we have $a(\langle \Im(f_1), \ldots, \Im(f_n)\rangle)$ $\underline{\mathrm{cl}}_{\Im}\, \varphi$. Similar, $a \,\underline{\mathrm{con}}\, \varphi$ iff for any interpretation $\Im$ we have $a(\langle \Im(f_1), \ldots, \Im(f_n)\rangle) \,\underline{\mathrm{con}}_{\Im}\, \varphi$.

Note. It is easy to modify all our definitions to many-sorted logics, which better correspond to the practice of programming — every programming languages has several different data types and functions/relations working on these data types. However for simplicity we give all the definitions only for the one-sorted case.

The first consequence of this definition is that the classical realizability (the relation $\underline{\mathrm{cl}}$) does not coinside with the classical truth any more (Theorem 8 below). However we can prove soundness: if a formula is realizable, then this formula is true. Soundness is sufficient for using the theory for program extraction: when we extract a program from a proof we need to be sure that the program satisfies the specification given by the end formula of the proof.

Theorem 7. *If there exists a such that $a\,\underline{\mathrm{cl}}_{(\mathfrak{M},\nu)}\varphi$ then φ is true in $\mathfrak{M}$ under any interpretation.*

The following theorem shows that the inverse is not true, unlike the first order case: when one adds function parameters to the language, classical realizability does not coinside with truth in general. In fact we prove even a stronger statement - there exists a formula which is provable in classical first order predicate logic, but which is not realizable.

Theorem 8. *There is an enumerated model $(\mathfrak{M},\nu)$ with a binary predicate P such that the formula $\psi \Leftrightarrow \forall x P(x, f(x)) \vee \neg \forall x P(x, f(x))$ is not classically realizable on $(\mathfrak{M},\nu)$.*

Proof. To give the complete proof one needs to give the complete definitions of how the higher types functionals are represented in information systems, for which we have no space here. So we shall only describe the idea of the proof. Let $\mathfrak{M}$ be the standard model of natural numbers with the identity mapping as the enumeration. Let P be the equality on natural numbers. Assume that the formula ψ is realizable and $a\,\underline{\mathrm{cl}}\,\psi$. Then for every function $g : \mathfrak{N} \to \mathfrak{N}$, $a(g)\,\underline{\mathrm{cl}}\,\forall x P(x, g(x)) \vee \neg \forall x P(x, g(x))$. Let g be the identity mapping, i.e. $g(x) = x$ for all $x \in \mathfrak{N}$. Since $a(g)$ realizes a disjunction, then there is a *finite* piece of information in $a(g)$, which is sufficient to say what part of the disjunction is true. Hence there is a *finite* set S of natural numbers, such that for every function h with $h(x) = x$ on S, $h(x) = x$ for all natural numbers, which is false.

Theorem 8 is not desirable for program synthesis, because systems for extracting programs from proofs often use classical logic in some computationally irrelevant parts of proofs. One can consider for instance the use of Harrop formulae in [Goa 80a, Goa 80b] or the mixed Markov's principle from [Vor 90, Vor 91b]. However below we will show that in both these cases classical logic can be used also in the parametric case. First we shall formulate an interesting property of Harrop formulae.

Theorem 9. *If φ is a Harrop formula, then $\mathbf{A}_\varphi$ has one element $\perp$ which is computable.*

Corollary 10. *Let φ be a Harrop formula. Then the following conditions are equivalent.*

1. *φ is true on $\mathfrak{M}$.*
2. *For every enumeration ν of $\mathfrak{M}$, φ is constructively true on $(\mathfrak{M},\nu)$.*

The same remains true if we change truth to truth under interpretation.

4 Constructive logics with proof schemes

The most important definitions are connected with the notion of *constructive calculus*. Intuitively, the calculus is constructive for some enumerated model iff by any inference rule of this calculus and any tuple of elements realizing its premises one can effectively construct an element realizing its conclusion. Below we give such definitions.

In what follows we will sometimes use informal notions (e.g. saying that a set of formulae is effectively enumerable). But all corresponding formal notions can of course be given.

Definition 11. An inference figure of the signature σ is a finite sequence of formulae $\varphi_1, \ldots, \varphi_n, \varphi$, where $n \geq 0$, of this signature. A calculus $\mathcal{L}$ is any effectively enumerable set of inference figures.

Provability of a formula in a calculus $\mathcal{L}$ is defined as usual: φ is provable iff there is an inference figure of the form $\varphi_1, \ldots, \varphi_n, \varphi$ in $\mathcal{L}$ such that for all $i \in \{1, \ldots, n\}$ φ_i is provable in $\mathcal{L}$.

From now on we assume that an enumerated model $(\mathfrak{M}, \nu)$ of a signature σ is fixed and that δ is the extended signature obtained from σ by adding function symbols $f_0, \ldots, f_n$.

Definition 12. Parametric calculus is any calculus in the signature δ. Parametric proof is a proof in a parametric calculus. Functional symbols $f_0, \ldots, f_n$ are called parameters of such a proof.

Definition 13. A parametric calculus $\mathcal{L}$ is constructive for an enumerated model $(\mathfrak{M}, \nu)$ iff there exists an algorithm α which by any inference figure $\varphi_1, \ldots, \varphi_n, \varphi$ of $\mathcal{L}$ and any $a_1, \ldots, a_n$ such that $a_1 \, \underline{\mathfrak{cl}}_{(\mathfrak{M},\nu)} \varphi_1, \ldots, a_n \, \underline{\mathfrak{cl}}_{(\mathfrak{M},\nu)} \varphi_n$ gives a such that $a \, \underline{\mathfrak{cl}}_{(\mathfrak{M},\nu)} \varphi$.

The definition of constructive calculus is given in such terms that the the notion of constructive calculus is sound w.r.t. constructive truth. Intuitively, the constructive calculi for an enumerated model $(\mathfrak{M}, \nu)$ are exactly the calculi that we can use for program extraction, or for describing computations over the data type represented by $(\mathfrak{M}, \nu)$.

Theorem 14. *Let $\mathcal{L}$ be constructive for $(\mathfrak{M}, \nu)$ and $\vdash_{\mathcal{L}} \varphi$. Then $(\mathfrak{M}, \nu) \models_{\mathrm{con}} \varphi$. Moreover, an element a with $a \, \underline{\mathfrak{con}}_{(\mathfrak{M},\nu)} \varphi$ can be found effectively by a proof of φ in $\mathcal{L}$.*

Proof. Trivial by the length of a proof of φ in $\mathcal{L}$. It is easy to see that we can construct in a computable way some a with $a \, \underline{\mathfrak{cl}}_{(\mathfrak{M},\nu)} \varphi$. Thus this a is computable and $a \, \underline{\mathfrak{con}}_{(\mathfrak{M},\nu)} \varphi$.

Now we shall formulate the main theorem on the use of constructive parametric calculi, which justifies the extraction of higher order functions from proofs:

Theorem 15. *Let $\mathcal{L}$ be a constructive parametric calculus for $(\mathfrak{M}, \nu)$. Then given any proof Π of a closed formula $\forall \bar{x} \exists y \varphi(x, y)$ one can effectively construct a general recursive function g with the following property:*

> *If $\Im$ is an interpretation such that there exist general recursive functions $g_0, \ldots, g_n$ with $\Im(f_i)(\nu m_1, \ldots, \nu m_k) = \nu g_i(m_1, \ldots, m_k)$[3] and $l_1, \ldots, l_n$ are Kleene numbers of $g_1, \ldots, g_n$, then for any tuple $\bar{p}$ of natural numbers the formula $\varphi(\nu \bar{p}, \nu g(l_1, \ldots, l_n, \bar{p}))$ is true on $\mathfrak{M}$ under the interpretation $\Im$.*

[3] This condition means that all parameters f_i are computable in this interpretation.

Proof. Straightforward but tedious. It is sufficient to show how to encode computable elements of the information systems by recursive functions and then to apply Theorem 14.

It is easy to see that this formal statement informally means the following: there exists a (second-order) computable function g meeting the specification

$$(\forall \bar{x})(\forall f_0)\ldots(\forall f_n)\varphi(\bar{x}, g(f_0, \ldots, f_n, \bar{x}))$$

It is also possible to formulate the analogs of Theorem 15 for specifications of partial functions, predicates and partial predicates, as in [Vor 91b].

However the general definition of constructive calculus with the soundness theorem is not sufficient to show the general applicability of the introduced notions. We need to show that the well-known examples of constructive calculi are constructive according to our definitions. We start from the intuitionistic predicate calculus and the intuitionistic (Heyting) arithmetic.

Theorem 16. *The intuitionistic predicate calculus is constructive for every enumerated model* $(\mathfrak{M}, \nu)$.

Proof. Copies the proof of Kleene's realizability of formulae provable in the intuitionistic predicate calculus [Kle 52]. The same functionals that are used in the original proof given by Nelson [Nel 47] can be used in our proof. The representation of the functionals in the form of elements of the information systems is a trivial exercise (the techniques for such a representation may be found in [Sco 82]).

Corollary 17. *Let* $\mathcal{L}$ *be a (non-parametric) calculus in the signature* σ *constructive for* $(\mathfrak{M}, \nu)$ *and* $\mathcal{L}'$ *be obtained from* $\mathcal{L}$ *by adding the rules of the intuitionistic predicate calculus of the signature* δ *to* $\mathcal{L}$*. Then* $\mathcal{L}'$ *is constructive for* $(\mathfrak{M}, \nu)$.

Theorem 18. *The intuitionistic (Heyting) arithmetic is constructive for the standard model of arithmetic* $(\mathfrak{N}, \mathrm{id}_{\mathfrak{N}})$.

Corollary 19. *Let* $\mathcal{L}$ *be a calculus in the signature* σ *constructive for* $(\mathfrak{N}, \mathrm{id}_{\mathfrak{N}})$ *and* $\mathcal{L}'$ *be obtained from* $\mathcal{L}$ *by adding the rules of the intuitionistic predicate calculus plus the induction scheme for parametric formulas to* $\mathcal{L}$*. Then* $\mathcal{L}'$ *is constructive for* $(\mathfrak{N}, \mathrm{id}_{\mathfrak{N}})$.

Theorem 20. *The calculus consisting of all instances of Markov's principle* $\forall x(\varphi \vee \neg\varphi) \supset (\neg\neg\exists x\varphi \supset \exists x\varphi)$ *is constructive for any enumerated model* $(\mathfrak{M}, \nu)$.

Markov's principle is interesting because the intuitionistic arithmetic with Markov's principle is Turing complete: one can extract all computable functions from proofs in this calculus [Vor 91b]. We had already shown that in the parametric case there may be problems with the classical truth. However, we can still use *mixed inference rules* which combine classical and constructive provability, like *mixed Markov's principle* [Vor 90, Vor 91b]:

$$\frac{\vdash_{\mathsf{con}} \forall x(\varphi \vee \neg\varphi) \qquad \vdash_{\mathsf{cl}} \exists x\varphi}{\vdash_{\mathsf{con}} \exists x\varphi}$$

where $\vdash_{\mathsf{cl}}$ and $\vdash_{\mathsf{con}}$ means the classical and the constructive provabilities. We shall not define the semantics of such mixed inference rules here, but we shall prove constructiveness of a stronger form of Markov's principle [Vor 91b]:

Theorem 21. *Let $\mathcal{L}$ be a calculus consisting of any number of formulae of the form $\forall x(\varphi \vee \neg\varphi) \supset \exists x\varphi$, such that the formula $\exists x\varphi$ is true in the model $\mathfrak{M}$. Then $\mathcal{L}$ is constructive for $(\mathfrak{M}, \nu)$, where ν is an arbitrary enumeration of $\mathfrak{M}$.*

In the example from Section 2 we proved the existence of the function `mapcar`. The proof was constructed in the language of list theory [Vor 91a]. In the same way we can easily prove the existence of many other higher order functions. Actually we made such proofs for all built-in higher order functions of the programming language MULISP [MUL 89]. The other higher order functions of MULISP can be defined in MULISP by using higher order function `apply`, which can be defined by the equation `apply` $fx \Leftrightarrow fx$. In our approach it is a trivial exercise to prove the existence of `apply`: the following proof scheme, where f is a parameter, specifies `apply`:

$$\cfrac{\cfrac{f(x) = f(x)}{\exists y(f(x) = y)}}{\forall x \exists y(f(x) = y)}$$

We could also easily prove higher-order functions from the book of Sokolowski [Sok 89] however with several modifications, connected with the type system of S-tandard ML.

Lists comprise a very useful data type in functional programming. The list theory is important for specifying facts about higher order functions, so we shall formulate here a theorem about constructiveness of this theory. This theorem serves as a foundation of using proof schemes in the example from Section 2.

Theorem 22. *The intuitionistic list theory [Vor 91a] is constructive for the model of finite lists.*

Proof. It is sufficient to use functionals defined by recursion in [Vor 91a] as the realizers and to prove that they are computable elements of the information systems.

To stress the generality of our approach to extracting higher order programs from proofs we will formulate the constructiveness of *well-order induction.* Both list induction ListInd, *foundation axiom* for lists from [Vor 91a] and induction on natural numbers Ind can be derived from a very general induction scheme:

$$\frac{(\forall x)((\forall y \prec x)\Phi(y) \supset \Phi(x))}{(\forall x)\Phi(x)}$$

where $\prec$ is any Harrop formula without parameters representing a relation with no infinite descending chains $\ldots \prec a_1 \prec a_0$. A similar induction scheme had been used in [KP 90], as well as in many mathematical books (see e.g. [Bar 75]). This induction scheme can be used to represent many kinds of recursion. It will be the core of the program synthesis system which is currently under development in the Laboratory of Intelligent Systems, Novosibirsk. The following theorem states that the instances of this induction scheme form a constructive calculus.

Theorem 23. *Let $(\mathfrak{M}, \nu)$ be an enumerated model and $\prec$ be a relation on M with the above properties. Then the calculus $\mathcal{L}$ consisting of all instances of the above induction scheme is constructive for $(\mathfrak{M}, \nu)$.*

Proof. For simplicity we consider only the case when φ has no other variables except x. Let a realizes the premise of the rule. We define functionals b, c by the following recursion:

$$b\ x \Leftrightarrow a\ x\ c$$
$$c\ y\ \bot \Leftrightarrow b\ y$$

We prove that b realizes the conclusion of the rule under any interpretation of parameters of φ. To this end we have to prove that for every x, $(b\ x)\,\underline{\mathfrak{cl}}\,\Phi(x)$, or $(a\ x\ c)\,\underline{\mathfrak{cl}}\,\Phi(x)$. Since the relation $\prec$ is well-ordered one can assume that for every $y \prec x$ we have $(b\ y)\,\underline{\mathfrak{cl}}\,\Phi(y)$. Since a realizes the premise of the rule, then $(a\ x)\,\underline{\mathfrak{cl}}\,\forall y \prec x \Phi(y) \supset \Phi(x)$. Thus it is sufficient to prove $c\,\underline{\mathfrak{cl}}\,\forall y \prec x \Phi(y)$, or that for every y, we have $(c\ y)\,\underline{\mathfrak{cl}}\,(y \prec x \supset \Phi(y))$. Consider two cases.

1. $y \prec x$. Then $\bot\,\underline{\mathfrak{cl}}\,y \prec x$ and $(b\ y)\,\underline{\mathfrak{cl}}\,\Phi(y)$. It remains to apply the definition of c.
2. $y \prec x$ is not true. In this case any element realizes $y \prec x \supset \Phi(y)$.

As one can see from the proof, the proof remains valid if the formula expressing the relation $\prec$ contains parameters, but satisfies the well-foundness property for each interpretation of the parameters.

Related work

There are not so many papers related to this paper. In most of the approaches type theories are used. The treatment of higher order functions in type theories is different - as a matter of fact there is no difference between functions and other objects in type theories. A very similar to ours treatment of constructive logics had been used in [Goa 80a, Goa 80b]. However in [Goa 80a, Goa 80b] all functions are interpreted and there is no formal definition of what is constructive logic in general. In [Hay 88] higher order functions can be simulated as follows. The definitions of functions are terms of the logic **PX** from [Hay 88]. There is also a function applying definitions of functions to arguments. In this way it is easy to represent any functions, expressible in pure LISP, including higher order functions. However the resulted logic is complicated compared to usual first order logic.

In the field of mathematical logic there were some similar to ours definition of realizability [NS 82, Pli 78, Pli 86]. However neither of them considered the problem of higher order functions. To this end the most interesting are variants of so called *uniform realizability* intensively studied in e.g. [Pli 78]. Intuitively, a formula containing predicate P is uniformly realizable iff there is a functional which realizes this formula independently of the concrete value of P. Thus the uniform realizability is very similar to the definition that we use. The essential difference is that the uniform realizability had been defined only for natural numbers, which does not allow to use its definition for data types different from natural numbers.

Acknowledgements

I am gratefully acknowledged to Susumu Hayashi and Michel Parigot for interesting discussions. A remark of Alan Bundy about higher order functions in type theories had also stimulated this work.

References

[Bas 89] D.A. Basin. Building theories in Nuprl. In *Logic at Botic'89*, volume 363 of *Lecture Notes in Computer Science*, pages 12–25, 1989.

[Cha 77] C.C.Chang and H.J.Keisler. *Model theory.* North Holland, 1977.

[Chi 87] P. Chisholm. Derivation of a parsing algorithm in Martin-Lőf's theory of types. *Science of Computer Programming*, 8(1):1–42, 1987.

[Con 86] R.L. Constable and e.a. *Implementing Mathematics with the Nuprl Proof Development System.* Prentice Hall, 1986.

[Coq 88] T. Coquand and G Huet. The calculus of constructions. *Information and computation*, 74(213):95–120, 1988.

[Ers 77] Yu.L. Ershov. *The Theory of Enumerations (in Russian)*. Nauka, Moscow, 1977.

[Ers 80] Yu.L. Ershov. *Decidability Problems and Constructive Models (in Russian)*. Nauka, Moscow, 1980.

[Goa 80a] C.A. Goad. Proofs as descriptions of computation. In *5th CADE*, volume 87 of *Lecture Notes in Computer Science*, pages 39–52, 1980.

[Goa 80b] C.A. Goad. Computational uses of the manipulation of formal proofs. Technical Report TR no. STAN-CS-80-819, Stanford Univ. Department of Computer Science, 1980.

[Har 60] R Harrop. Concerning formulas of the types $A \rightarrow B \wedge C$, $A \rightarrow (Ex)B(x)$ in intuitionistic formal system. *J. of Symb. Logic*, 17:27–32, 1960.

[Hay 88] S. Hayashi and H. Nakano. **PX**: *a Computational Logic*. MIT Press, 1988.

[Hen 92] M.C. Henson. Safe positive induction in the programming logic TK. In A.Voronkov, editor, *1st and 2nd Russian Conferences on Logic Programming*, Lecture Notes in Artificial Intelligence, pages 215–231. Springer Verlag, 1992.

[Bar 75] J.Barwise. *Admissible Sets and Structures*. Springer Verlag, 1975.

[Kle 52] S.C. Kleene. *Introduction to Metamathematics*. Van Nostrand P.C., Amsterdam, 1952.

[KP 90] J.-L. Krivine and M. Parigot. Programming with proofs. *J.Inf.Proces. Cybern. EIK*, 26(3):149–167, 1990.

[Nel 47] D. Nelson. Recursive functions and intuitionistic number theory. *Trans. Amer. Math. Soc.*, 61:307–368, 1947.

[NS 82] N.N. Nepeivoda and D.I. Sviridenko. *Towards the Theory for Program Synthesis (in Russian)*, volume 2 of *Trudy Instituta Matematiki*, pages 159–175. Nauka, Novosibirsk, 1982.

[Nor 84] B. Nordström and J.M. Smith. Propositions, types and specifications of programs in Martin-Löf's type theory. *BIT*, 24(3):288–301, 1984.

[Pli 78] V.E. Plisko. Some variants of realizability for predicate formulas. *Izvestiya Akademii Nauk SSSR, Mathematics*, 42(3):636–653, 1978.

[Pli 86] V.E. Plisko. Towards a model theory for languages with constructive semantics (in Russian). In *Soviet Conference on Applications of Mathematical Logic*, pages 154–156, Tallinn, 1986. Institute of Cybernetics.

[Pra 65] D. Prawitz. *Natural deduction*. Almquist and Wicksell, Stockholm, 1965.

[Sco 82] D.S. Scott. Domains for denotational semantics. In *Automata, Languages and Programming*, volume 140 of *Lecture Notes in Computer Science*, pages 577–612, 1982.

[MUL 89] Soft Warehouse Inc. *MULISP Reference Manual*, 1989.

[Sok 89] S. Sokolowski. Applicative high-order programming or standard ML in the battlefield. Technical report, Universität Passau, Fakultät für Mathematik und Informatik, 1989.

[SV 90] S.S. Starchenko and A. Voronkov. On connections between classical and constructive semantics. In *COLOG-88*, volume 417 of *Lecture Notes in Computer Science*, 1990.

[Vor 88] A.A. Voronkov. *Model theory based on a constructive notion of truth, (in Russian)*, volume 8 of *Trudy Instituta Matematiki*, pages 25–42. Nauka, Novosibirsk, 1988. This volume was cover-to-cover translated to English by American Mathematical Society.

[Vor 90] A.A. Voronkov. Towards the theory of programming in constructive logic. In N.Jones, editor, *Proc. of the European Symp. on Programming*, volume 432 of *Lecture Notes in Computer Science*, pages 421–435. Springer Verlag, 1990.

[Vor 91a] A.A. Voronkov. N-realizability: one more constructive semantics. Technical Report 71, Department of Mathematics, Monash University, 1991.

[Vor 91b] A.A. Voronkov. On completeness of program synthesis systems. Technical Report 29, Univ. Paris 7, Equipe de Logique Mathematique, 1991.

Reduction Relations in Strict Applicative Languages

Walter Dosch

Institut für Mathematik, Universität Augsburg
D-8900 Augsburg, Germany

Abstract. We investigate the reduction relations for a strongly typed higher-order applicative language employing function application, conditional, function abstraction and recursion. In particular, we propose a new approach how to correctly implement a strict ("*call-by-value*") semantics in the setting of term rewriting. We study the confluence and termination properties of the reduction system obtained.

1 Introduction

The foundations of functional programming were laid by the λ-calculus (see [3] for a compendium): its reduction rules formalize the evaluation of applicative expressions to some normal form, its models provide a semantic universe for interpreting them. However, at a closer look, the operational and denotational semantics of λ-calculus do not adequately model many applicative programming languages, since there are three major differences:

- In pure λ-calculus, the data structure is coded into the control structure using, for example, Church's numerals. Programming languages, however, are based on the signature of an abstract data type providing sorts, constants, and operators of the underlying data structure. In general, the operators denote partial functions which are undefined for certain arguments.
- Pure λ-calculus is an untyped theory which admits the self-application of functions; in the semantics this leads to limit domains (see [16]). Most functional languages, however, favor a finite type system. Since a finitely typed λ-calculus cannot cope with general recursion (see [15]), there is an explicit fixpoint operation as an independent language concept.
- For the application of functions, the β-reduction of λ-calculus describes a call-by-name semantics, since the argument expression is substituted textually into the body of the abstraction. Most functional languages, however, favor a call-by-value semantics, where the argument expression is evaluated before its value is entered into the body; correspondingly, in the mathematical semantics all denotable functions are strict.

In this paper we investigate the reduction relations for a strongly typed, higher-order functional calculus with a call-by-value semantics based on the data structure of Boolean values and natural numbers. Here applicative expressions are formed from the constants and operators of the data structure using tupling, selection, conditional, function abstraction, function application, and recursion. The reduction rules comprise the data reduction derived from the laws of the underlying abstract data type, the error reduction originating from the application of partial operations to arguments outside their domain, the simplification of the conditional and of the selection, the application of an abstraction to arguments — a restricted form of β-reduction, and the unfolding of (recursive) declarations. Of course, these reduction rules are inspired by the conversion rules of λ-calculus; their study, however, leads among others to the following new results:

- The single reduction relations are strictly resp. strongly confluent.
- The different reduction relations commute strictly resp. strongly with each other.
- The simplification relations including a restricted form of β-reduction, are finitely terminating.
- The normal forms of closed expressions are either values or the symbol for the finite error.

A major difficulty in correctly implementing a strict semantics, arises with the β-reduction $(\lambda x.e_1)(e_2) \rightarrow_\beta e_1[e_2 \textbf{ for } x]$. The straightforward approach to confine the operand e_2 to a normal form, is not correct: If the underlying data structure has partial operations, then there are argument expressions in normal form, which have an undefined meaning. Moreover, if the parameter of the abstraction is of functional type, then the argument can be a recursively defined function which has no (finite) normal form although it denotes a proper function.

To meet a strict semantics, we propose the following solution: We designate a syntactically decidable subset of expressions, called values, that have a defined meaning under all valuations, and restrict the β-reduction to values as arguments.

We assume that the reader is familiar with the foundations of functional programming, in particular term rewriting ([10], [17]), λ-calculus ([3], [7]), and denotational semantics ([11]). The proofs of this summary are contained in [9].

2 Syntax

In this section we shortly introduce the syntax of the expression language together with the syntactic functions. Suitable context conditions are incorporated into the definition such that only context-correct expressions are obtained.

2.1 Basis

Applicative expressions are formed over the signature of an abstract data type.

Definition A *signature* $\Sigma = (\mathcal{S}, \mathcal{K}, \mathcal{F})$ consists of a finite nonempty set $\mathcal{S}$ of *sorts*, a finite pairwise disjoint family $\mathcal{K} = (\mathcal{K}^{\mathbf{s}})_{\mathbf{s} \in \mathcal{S}}$ of *constants*, and a finite pairwise disjoint family of *operators* $\mathcal{F} = (\mathcal{F}^{\mathbf{funct}(\mathbf{s}_1, \ldots, \mathbf{s}_n)\mathbf{s}_{n+1}})_{\mathbf{s}_1, \ldots, \mathbf{s}_{n+1} \in \mathcal{S}\ (n \geq 1)}$.

We base the language on the fixed signature $\Sigma_{NAT} = (\mathcal{S}_{NAT}, \mathcal{K}_{NAT}, \mathcal{F}_{NAT})$ of natural numbers and Boolean values where

$$\mathcal{S}_{NAT} = \{\mathbf{bool}, \mathbf{nat}\}$$
$$\mathcal{K}_{NAT} = \{true, false, 0\}$$
$$\mathcal{F}_{NAT} = \{not,\ and,\ or,\ succ,\ pred,\ add, mult,\ iszero\}$$

with the obvious functionalities. Under mild restrictions, the results of this paper can be generalized to arbitrary partitioned signatures ([9]). Types are constructed from the sorts by forming tuple types and function types.

Definition Given a set $\mathcal{S}$ of sorts, the set $\mathcal{T}$ of *types* over $\mathcal{S}$ is defined inductively:

(1) *Sorts* $\quad \mathcal{S} \subseteq \mathcal{T}$.
(2) *Tuple types* $\quad$ If $\mathbf{t}_1, \ldots, \mathbf{t}_n \in \mathcal{T}$ $(n \geq 1)$, then $\langle \mathbf{t}_1, \ldots, \mathbf{t}_n \rangle \in \mathcal{T}$.
(3) *Function types* $\quad$ If $\mathbf{t}_1, \ldots, \mathbf{t}_{n+1} \in \mathcal{T}$ $(n \geq 1)$, then $\mathbf{funct}(\mathbf{t}_1, \ldots, \mathbf{t}_n)\mathbf{t}_{n+1} \in \mathcal{T}$.

In applicative expressions, parameters are bound by abstractions, and identifiers are introduced by (recursive) declarations.

Definition A *variable family* $\mathcal{V} = \mathcal{P} \,\dot{\cup}\, \mathcal{I}$ is the disjoint union of a family $\mathcal{P} = (\mathcal{P}^{\mathbf{t}})_{\mathbf{t} \in \mathcal{T}}$ of countably infinite, pairwise disjoint sets $\mathcal{P}^{\mathbf{t}}$ of *parameters* and a family $\mathcal{I} = (\mathcal{I}^{\mathbf{t}})_{\mathbf{t} \in \mathcal{T}}$ of countably infinite, pairwise disjoint sets $\mathcal{I}^{\mathbf{t}}$ of *identifiers*. A *basis* $(\Sigma, \mathcal{V})$ of an applicative language consists of a signature Σ and a variable family $\mathcal{V}$ disjoint to Σ.

2.2 Syntax of Applicative Expressions

Definition The family $EXPR = (EXPR^{\mathbf{t}})_{\mathbf{t} \in \mathcal{T}}$ of (*applicative*) *expressions* over a basis $(\Sigma, \mathcal{V})$ with $\Sigma = (\mathcal{S}, \mathcal{K}, \mathcal{F})$ and $\mathcal{V} = \mathcal{P} \,\dot{\cup}\, \mathcal{I}$ is defined inductively:

(1) *Finite error* $\Delta^{\mathbf{t}} \in EXPR^{J}\mathbf{t}$ $(\mathbf{t} \in \mathcal{T})$.
(2) *Variables* $\quad \mathcal{V}^{\mathbf{t}} \subseteq EXPR^{\mathbf{t}}$ $(\mathbf{t} \in \mathcal{T})$.
(3) *Constants* $\quad \mathcal{K}^{\mathbf{s}} \subseteq EXPR^{\mathbf{s}}$ $(\mathbf{s} \in \mathcal{S})$.
(4) *Operators* $\quad \mathcal{F}^{\mathbf{funct}(\mathbf{s}_1, \ldots, \mathbf{s}_n)\mathbf{s}_{n+1}} \subseteq EXPR^{\mathbf{funct}(\mathbf{s}_1, \ldots, \mathbf{s}_n)\mathbf{s}_{n+1}}$.
(5) *Tupling* $\quad$ If $e_i \in EXPR^{\mathbf{t}_i}$ $(i \in [1, n])$, then $\langle e_1, \ldots, e_n \rangle \in EXPR^{\langle \mathbf{t}_1, \ldots, \mathbf{t}_n \rangle}$.
(6) *Selection* $\quad$ If $e \in EXPR^{\langle \mathbf{t}_1, \ldots, \mathbf{t}_n \rangle}$ and $i \in [1, n]$, then $(e[i]) \in EXPR^{\mathbf{t}_i}$.
(7) *Conditional* If $e_1 \in EXPR^{\mathbf{bool}}$ and $e_2, e_3 \in EXPR^{\mathbf{t}}$,
then **if** e_1 **then** e_2 **else** e_3 **fi** $\in EXPR^{\mathbf{t}}$.
(8) *Application* If $e_0 \in EXPR^{\mathbf{funct}(\mathbf{t}_1, \ldots, \mathbf{t}_n)\mathbf{t}_{n+1}}$ and $e_i \in EXPR^{\mathbf{t}_i}$ $(i \in [1, n])$,
then $(e_0(e_1, \ldots, e_n)) \in EXPR^{\mathbf{t}_{n+1}}$.
(9) *Abstraction* If $x_i \in \mathcal{P}^{\mathbf{t}_i}$ pairwise distinct $(i \in [1, n])$ and $e \in EXPR^{\mathbf{t}_{n+1}}$,
then $((\mathbf{t}_1\ x_1, \ldots, \mathbf{t}_n\ x_n)\mathbf{t}_{n+1}\colon e) \in EXPR^{\mathbf{funct}(\mathbf{t}_1, \ldots, \mathbf{t}_n)\mathbf{t}_{n+1}}$.
(10) *Recursion* $\quad$ If $x \in \mathcal{I}^{\mathbf{t}}$ and $e \in EXPR^{\mathbf{t}}$, then $(\mathbf{fix}\ x\colon e) \in EXPR^{\mathbf{t}}$.

The syntactic equality of applicative expressions is denoted by $\hat{=}$.

2.3 Syntactic Characteristics

The expression language employs function application, function abstraction, and recursion; thus it follows the *applicative style* of functional programming (in contrast to [2]). Higher-order functional expressions are built by λ-abstraction over the first-order signature of an abstract data type. The symbols $\Delta^{\mathbf{t}}$ denote the "finite error" that arises from applying partial operations to arguments outside their domain. The expression language constitutes a kernel language in terms of which other language concepts like blocks and declarations can be expressed (see [4]). In writing expressions, brackets may be dropped with the usual conventions.

Example The factorial function $fac \in EXPR^{\mathbf{funct(nat)nat}}$ reads:
$fac \mathrel{\widehat{=}} (\mathbf{fix}\ fc\colon (\mathbf{nat}\ n)\mathbf{nat}\colon \mathbf{if}\ iszero(n)\ \mathbf{then}\ succ(0)\ \mathbf{else}\ mult(n, fc(pred(n)))\ \mathbf{fi}$

2.4 Consistent Renaming and Syntactic Functions

Expressions related by consistently renaming the bound variables are identified at the syntactic level by passing to the quotient algebra.

Definition The family $EXP = (EXP^{\mathbf{t}})_{\mathbf{t} \in T}$ of (*α-congruent*) *expressions* comprises the congruence classes of expressions under the consistent (and clash-free) renaming of bound variables. The equality on EXP is again denoted by $\widehat{=}$.

Free variables are not changed by a consistent renaming. Let $free(e)$ denote the family of free variables of an expression $e \in EXP$. An expression e is called *closed*, if $free(e) = \emptyset$.

Definition The *substitution* $EXP^{\mathbf{t}} \times EXP^{\mathbf{t}_1} \times \cdots \times EXP^{\mathbf{t}_n} \times \mathcal{V}^{\mathbf{t}_1} \times \cdots \times \mathcal{V}^{\mathbf{t}_n} \rightarrow EXP^{\mathbf{t}}$ is defined with the usual care for name clashes: $e[e_1, \ldots, e_n\ \mathbf{for}\ x_1, \ldots, x_n]$ denotes the result of simultaneously replacing in e all free occurrences of x_i by e_i $(i \in [1, n])$.

3 Denotational Semantics

In the denotational semantics we concentrate on the strictness properties of this expression language.

3.1 Semantic Domains

The semantic domains are based on the interpretation of the signature Σ by an appropriate Σ-algebra.

Definition The Σ_{NAT}-algebra $\mathcal{A}$ comprises the *carrier sets* $\mathbf{bool}^{\mathcal{A}} = \{T, F\}$ and $\mathbf{nat}^{\mathcal{A}} = \{0, 1, 2, \ldots\}$, the *constants* $true^{\mathcal{A}} = T$, $false^{\mathcal{A}} = F$ and $0^{\mathcal{A}} = 0$, and the (partial) *operations* $not^{\mathcal{A}}$, $and^{\mathcal{A}}$, $or^{\mathcal{A}}$, $succ^{\mathcal{A}}$, $pred^{\mathcal{A}}$, $add^{\mathcal{A}}$, $mult^{\mathcal{A}}$, and $iszero^{\mathcal{A}}$ with the usual meaning.

Now we associate complete partial orders with the type system.

Definition Given the Σ_{NAT}-algebra $\mathcal{A}$, the *interpretation of the types* associates with every type $\mathbf{t} \in T$ a complete partial order $[\![\mathbf{t}]\!]$ as follows:

(1) Sorts are interpreted by flat partial orders: $[\![\mathbf{s}]\!] = \mathbf{s}^{\mathcal{A}} \cup \{\bot^{\mathbf{s}}\}$ $(\bot^{\mathbf{s}} \notin \mathbf{s}^{\mathcal{A}})$.
(2) Tuple types denote the smash product $[\![(\mathbf{t}_1, \ldots, \mathbf{t}_n)]\!] = [\![\mathbf{t}_1]\!] \otimes \cdots \otimes [\![\mathbf{t}_n]\!]$ of their components.
(3) Function types denote the set of strict continuous functions between their component types extended by the undefined functional object:

$$[\![\mathbf{funct}(\mathbf{t}_1,\ldots,\mathbf{t}_n)\mathbf{t}_{n+1}]\!] = [\,[\![\mathbf{t}_1]\!]\otimes\cdots\otimes[\![\mathbf{t}_n]\!] \rightarrow_{sc} [\![\mathbf{t}_{n+1}]\!]\,]\cup\{\perp^{\mathbf{funct}(\mathbf{t}_1,\ldots,\mathbf{t}_n)\mathbf{t}_{n+1}}\}$$

The major difference to a call-by-name semantics is the use of the smash product and of the domain of strict continuous functions which is enlarged by an undefined functional object. Valuations record the binding of variables to semantic elements.

Definition A *valuation* $\rho = (\rho^{\mathbf{t}}\colon \mathcal{V}^{\mathbf{t}} \rightarrow [\![\mathbf{t}]\!])_{\mathbf{t}\in\mathcal{T}}$ is a family of mappings such that $\perp^{\mathbf{t}} \notin \rho^{\mathbf{t}}(\mathcal{V}^{\mathbf{t}})$ for all $\mathbf{t} \in \mathcal{T}$. ENV denotes the set of all valuations.

3.2 Interpretation of Applicative Expressions

Definition The *interpretation* $[\![\,.\,]\!]\colon EXP^{\mathbf{t}} \rightarrow [ENV \rightarrow [\![\mathbf{t}]\!]]$ *of applicative expressions* of type $\mathbf{t} \in \mathcal{T}$ is defined inductively as follows:

(1) $[\![\Delta^{\mathbf{t}}]\!](\rho) = \perp^{\mathbf{t}}$

(2) $[\![x]\!](\rho) = \rho(x) \quad (x \in \mathcal{V})$

(3) $[\![k]\!](\rho) = k^{\mathcal{A}} \quad (k \in \mathcal{K})$

(4) $[\![f]\!](\rho) = ext(f^{\mathcal{A}})$, where *ext* denotes the (totalization and) strict extension of a (partial) function $(f \in \mathcal{F})$.

(5) $[\![\langle e_1,\ldots,e_n\rangle]\!](\rho) = \begin{cases} (\perp^{\mathbf{t}_1},\ldots,\perp^{\mathbf{t}_n}) & \text{if } [\![e_i]\!](\rho) = \perp^{\mathbf{t}_i} \text{ for some } i \in [1,n] \\ ([\![e_1]\!](\rho),\ldots,[\![e_n]\!](\rho)) & \text{if } [\![e_i]\!](\rho) \neq \perp^{\mathbf{t}_i} \text{ for all } i \in [1,n] \end{cases}$

(6) $[\![(e[i])]\!](\rho) = \pi_i([\![e]\!](\rho))$ where π_i denotes the projection to the i-th component.

(7) $[\![\mathbf{if}\ e_1\ \mathbf{then}\ e_2\ \mathbf{else}\ e_3\ \mathbf{fi}]\!](\rho) = \begin{cases} \perp^{\mathbf{t}} & \text{if } [\![e_1]\!](\rho) = \perp^{\mathbf{bool}} \\ [\![e_2]\!](\rho) & \text{if } [\![e_1]\!](\rho) = T \\ [\![e_3]\!](\rho) & \text{if } [\![e_1]\!](\rho) = F \end{cases}$

(8) $[\![(e_0(e_1,\ldots,e_n))]\!](\rho) = \begin{cases} \perp^{\mathbf{t}_{n+1}} \text{ if } [\![e_i]\!](\rho) = \perp^{\mathbf{t}_i} \text{ for some } i \in [1,n] \\ \qquad \text{or } [\![e_0]\!](\rho) = \perp^{\mathbf{funct}(\mathbf{t}_1,\ldots,\mathbf{t}_n)\mathbf{t}_{n+1}} \\ ([\![e_0]\!](\rho))([\![e_1]\!](\rho),\ldots,[\![e_n]\!](\rho)) \quad \text{otherwise} \end{cases}$

(9) $[\![((\mathbf{t}_1\, x_1,\ldots,\mathbf{t}_n\, x_n)\mathbf{t}_{n+1}\colon e)]\!](\rho) = g$, where $g\colon [\![\mathbf{t}_1]\!]\otimes\cdots\otimes[\![\mathbf{t}_n]\!] \rightarrow [\![\mathbf{t}_{n+1}]\!]$ is given by

$$g(d_1,\ldots,d_n) = \begin{cases} \perp^{\mathbf{t}_{n+1}} & \text{if } d_i = \perp^{\mathbf{t}_i} \text{ for all } i \in [1,n] \\ [\![e]\!](\rho[x_1/d_1]\cdots[x_n/d_n]) & \text{if } d_i \neq \perp^{\mathbf{t}_i} \text{ for all } i \in [1,n]. \end{cases}$$

(10) $[\![(\mathbf{fix}\ x\colon e)]\!](\rho) = \mu(g)$, where $g\colon [\![\mathbf{t}]\!] \rightarrow [\![\mathbf{t}]\!]$ is defined by $g(d) = [\![e]\!](\rho[x/d])$.

Above .[./.] denotes the update operation on environments and μ the least fixpoint operator. Two expressions $e_1, e_2 \in EXP^{\mathbf{t}}$ are called *(semantically) equivalent* (denoted by $e_1 \approx e_2$), if for all $\rho \in ENV$ we have $[\![e_1]\!](\rho) = [\![e_2]\!](\rho)$.

3.3 Strictness Considerations

The functions and functionals described by the expression language are all strict and continuous. Below we illustrate the particular semantic design decisions.

Examples Let $e \in EXP^{\mathbf{nat}}$ denote a closed expression with $[\![e]\!](\rho) = \perp^{\mathbf{nat}}$ for some (and hence for all) $\rho \in ENV$, for example a finite error like *pred*(0) or an infinite error like $(\mathbf{fix}\ x\colon x)$ $(x \in \mathcal{I}^{\mathbf{nat}})$.

a. $[\![\langle 0, e\rangle]\!](\rho) = (\perp^{\mathbf{nat}}, \perp^{\mathbf{nat}})$. The tuple constructor is strict; operationally, the components must be evaluated before the tuple can be constructed.

b. $[\![mult(0,e)]\!](\rho) = \bot^{\mathbf{nat}}$. Basic operations are interpreted as strict functions; operationally, they need the values of all their argument expressions in order to be evaluable.
c. $[\![((\mathbf{nat}\ n)\mathbf{nat}\colon 1)(e)]\!](\rho) = \bot^{\mathbf{nat}}$. An abstraction is interpreted as a strict function of its parameters; operationally, all argument expressions must be evaluated before entering the body of the abstraction.
d. $[\![(\mathbf{nat}\ n)\mathbf{nat}\colon e]\!](\rho) = \Omega^{\mathbf{funct(nat)nat}}$. Here $\Omega^{\mathbf{funct(nat)nat}}$ denotes the *pointwise undefined function* $d \mapsto \bot^{\mathbf{nat}}$ $(d \in [\![\mathbf{nat}]\!])$. Note that abstractions always denote proper functional objects, which, of course, may be undefined for every argument.
e. Let $f \in \mathcal{I}^{\mathbf{funct(nat)nat}}$. Then $[\![(\mathbf{fix}\ f\colon f)]\!](\rho) = \mu(g)$ where $g(d) = [\![f]\!](\rho[f/d]) = d$. Hence g is the identity function and $\mu(g) = \bot^{\mathbf{funct(nat)nat}}$ Thus f denotes the *undefined functional object* $\bot^{\mathbf{funct(nat)nat}}$ modelling nontermination when computing the function.

4 Reduction

Term rewriting represents a general model of evaluating applicative expressions: an expression is successively transformed by replacing in each step a subexpression by an equivalent one. Term rewriting does not narrow the freedom of execution inherent in applicative expressions, since there is no explicit control determining the reduction rule to be applied and the redex for the next reduction step.

Definition A *local R-reduction* on *EXP* is a family $(\rightarrow_{R^{\mathbf{t}}})_{\mathbf{t}\in\mathcal{T}}$ of dyadic relations on $EXP^{\mathbf{t}}$. The *1-step-R-reduction* $\longrightarrow_R$ is the syntax-compatible closure of $\rightarrow_R$; $\longrightarrow_{\hat{\bar{\bar{R}}}}$ denotes its reflexive closure. The *R-reduction* $\Rightarrow_R$ is the reflexive transitive closure of $\longrightarrow_R$. By $\rightarrow_{R_1 \ldots R_n}$ we abbreviate $\rightarrow_{R_1} \cup \cdots \cup \rightarrow_{R_n}$ $(n \geq 1)$; the same convention is used for the closures.

4.1 Values

To meet the strictness constraints of the call-by-value semantics, we introduce a subfamily of expressions, called values (compare [1], [14]), the syntactic form of which will ensure that they have a defined meaning.

Definition For applicative expressions *EXPR* over the basis $(\Sigma_{NAT}, \mathcal{V})$, the family $VAL = (VAL^{\mathbf{t}})_{\mathbf{t}\in\mathcal{T}}$ of *values* is defined inductively:

(1) $\mathcal{P}^{\mathbf{t}} \subseteq VAL^{\mathbf{t}}$ $(\mathbf{t} \in \mathcal{T})$.
(2) $\mathcal{K}^{\mathbf{s}} \subseteq VAL^{\mathbf{s}}$ $(\mathbf{s} \in \mathcal{S})$.
(3) $\mathcal{F}^{\mathbf{funct}(\mathbf{s}_1,\ldots,\mathbf{s}_n)\mathbf{s}_{n+1}} \subseteq VAL^{\mathbf{funct}(\mathbf{s}_1,\ldots,\mathbf{s}_n)\mathbf{s}_{n+1}}$.
(4) If $w \in VAL^{\mathbf{nat}}$, then $(succ(w)) \in VAL^{\mathbf{nat}}$.
(5) If $w_i \in VAL^{\mathbf{t}_i}$ $(i \in [1,n])$, then $\langle w_1, \ldots, w_n \rangle \in VAL^{\langle \mathbf{t}_1,\ldots,\mathbf{t}_n \rangle}$.
(6) If $x_i \in \mathcal{P}^{\mathbf{t}_i}$ are pairwise distinct $(i \in [1,n])$ and $e \in EXPR^{\mathbf{t}_{n+1}}$, then $((\mathbf{t}_1\ x_1, \ldots, \mathbf{t}_n\ x_n)\mathbf{t}_{n+1}\colon e) \in VAL^{\mathbf{funct}(\mathbf{t}_1,\ldots,\mathbf{t}_n)\mathbf{t}_{n+1}}$.

Parameters, constants, basic operators, constructor expressions, tuples of values, and abstractions are values. On the contrary, identifiers, conditionals, function applications, fixpoints, and tuples with non-value components constitute no values, since their meaning may be undefined. The family VAL of values is closed under consistent renaming. Thus we can pass to the quotient $VL = (VL^{\mathbf{t}})_{\mathbf{t} \in T}$ of *(α-congruent) values.*

The family of values is closed under the substitution operation, if parameters are replaced by values only ("substitution convention").

4.2 The Data Reduction

The laws of the abstract data type underlying the expression language lead to data reductions that describe the evaluation of basic operations.

Definition For the Σ_{NAT}-algebra $\mathcal{A}$ the local *data reduction* $\rightarrow_\delta$ on EXP is defined as follows ($y \in VL^{\mathbf{bool}}$, $m, n \in VL^{\mathbf{nat}}$):

$not(true)$	$\rightarrow_\delta false$	$iszero(0)$	$\rightarrow_\delta true$
$not(false)$	$\rightarrow_\delta true$	$iszero(succ(m))$	$\rightarrow_\delta false$
$and(true, y)$	$\rightarrow_\delta y$	$pred(succ(m))$	$\rightarrow_\delta m$
$and(false, y)$	$\rightarrow_\delta false$	$add(0, n)$	$\rightarrow_\delta n$
$or(true, y)$	$\rightarrow_\delta true$	$add(succ(m), n)$	$\rightarrow_\delta succ(add(m, n))$
$or(false, y)$	$\rightarrow_\delta y$	$mult(0, n)$	$\rightarrow_\delta 0$
		$mult(succ(m), n)$	$\rightarrow_\delta add(mult(m, n), n)$

The restriction to values is essential for correctly implementing a strict semantics; for example a rule like $and(false, e) \rightarrow_\delta false$ with an arbitrary expression $e \in EXP^{\mathbf{bool}}$ would model the non-strict sequential or parallel conjunction.

4.3 The Error Reduction

The error reduction originates from the application of partial operations from the underlying abstract data type (compare [18]).

Definition For the Σ_{NAT}-algebra $\mathcal{A}$, the associated local *error reduction* $\rightarrow_\epsilon$ on EXP is defined as follows:

$pred(0)$	$\rightarrow_\epsilon \Delta^{\mathbf{nat}}$	$\langle e_1, \ldots, e_{i-1}, \Delta^{\mathbf{t}_i}, e_{i+1}, \ldots, e_n \rangle$	$\rightarrow_\epsilon \Delta^{\langle \mathbf{t}_1, \ldots, \mathbf{t}_n \rangle}$
$(\Delta^{\langle \mathbf{t}_1, \ldots, \mathbf{t}_n \rangle}[i])$	$\rightarrow_\epsilon \Delta^{\mathbf{t}_i}$	$\mathbf{if}\ \Delta^{\mathbf{bool}}\ \mathbf{then}\ e_2\ \mathbf{else}\ e_3\ \mathbf{fi}$	$\rightarrow_\epsilon \Delta^{\mathbf{t}}$
$(\mathbf{fix}\ x\colon \Delta^{\mathbf{t}})$	$\rightarrow_\epsilon \Delta^{\mathbf{t}}$	$(\Delta^{\mathbf{funct}(\mathbf{t}_1, \ldots, \mathbf{t}_n)\mathbf{t}_{n+1}}(e_1, \ldots, e_n))$	$\rightarrow_\epsilon \Delta^{\mathbf{t}_{n+1}}$
		$(e_0(e_1, \ldots, e_{i-1}, \Delta^{\mathbf{t}_i}, e_{i+1}, \ldots, e_n))$	$\rightarrow_\epsilon \Delta^{\mathbf{t}_{n+1}}$

The clauses describe the origination and the propagation of the finite error through the different language constructs according to their strictness properties.

4.4 Reduction Relations for the Control Structure

Definition The local reduction relations $\rightarrow_\sigma$, $\rightarrow_\gamma$, $\rightarrow_\beta$, and $\rightarrow_u$ on *EXP* are defined as follows ($w_i \in VL^{\mathbf{t}_i}$ for $i \in [1, n]$):

Simplification of the selection	$(\langle w_1, \ldots, w_n \rangle [i]) \rightarrow_\sigma w_i$
Simplification of the conditional	**if** *true* **then** e_2 **else** e_3 **fi** $\rightarrow_\gamma e_2$
	if *false* **then** e_2 **else** e_3 **fi** $\rightarrow_\gamma e_3$
β-reduction	$(((\mathbf{t}_1\ x_1, \ldots, \mathbf{t}_n\ x_n)\mathbf{t}_{n+1}\colon e)(w_1, \ldots, w_n)) \rightarrow_\beta$ $e[w_1, \ldots, w_n$ **for** $x_1, \ldots, x_n]$
Unfold	$(\mathbf{fix}\ x\colon e) \rightarrow_u e[(\mathbf{fix}\ x\colon e)$ **for** $x]$

To meet the strict semantics, in the selection and in the β-reduction the argument expressions are restricted to values.

Definition The *overall reduction* is $\rightarrow_\tau = \rightarrow_{\delta\epsilon\sigma\gamma\beta u}$.

Finally we note that values are closed under τ-reductions.

4.5 Soundness

Definition A relation $\rightarrow_R$ on *EXP* is called *sound* or *meaning preserving*, if for all $e_1, e_2 \in EXP$ with $e_1 \rightarrow_R e_2$ we have $e_1 \approx e_2$.

The soundness of a reduction relation is inherited by its closures. Thus it suffices to show the soundness for the local reduction only. The proof of the following theorem uses the fact that values have a defined interpretation — regardless which meaning is assigned to the free variables occurring.

Theorem The relations $\rightarrow_\delta$, $\rightarrow_\epsilon$, $\rightarrow_\sigma$, $\rightarrow_\gamma$, $\rightarrow_\beta$, $\rightarrow_u$, and $\rightarrow_\tau$ as well as their closures are sound.

5 Confluence

The confluence property of a reduction relation ensures that the final result of a reduction, if there is any, does not depend on the particular reduction path taken.

5.1 Confluence of the Individual Reduction Relations

Definition A local reduction relation $\rightarrow$ on *EXP* is called *confluent*, if for all $e_1, e_2, e_3 \in EXP$ with $e_1 \Rightarrow e_2$ and $e_1 \Rightarrow e_3$ there is an $e_4 \in EXP$ with $e_2 \Rightarrow e_4$ and $e_3 \Rightarrow e_4$. It is called *strictly* resp. *strongly* resp. *locally* (*weakly*) *confluent*, if for all $e_1, e_2, e_3 \in EXP$ with $e_1 \longrightarrow e_2$ and $e_1 \longrightarrow e_3$ there is an $e_4 \in EXP$ with $e_2 \mathrel{\widehat{\longrightarrow}^{=}} e_4$ and $e_3 \mathrel{\widehat{\longrightarrow}^{=}} e_4$ resp. with $e_2 \Rightarrow e_4$ and $e_3 \mathrel{\widehat{\longrightarrow}^{=}} e_4$ resp. with $e_2 \Rightarrow e_4$ and $e_3 \Rightarrow e_4$.

The confluence of the individual reduction relations is summarized in the following table:

Theorem

	strictly confluent	strongly confluent	confluent	locally confluent
$\longrightarrow_\delta$	yes	yes	yes	yes
$\longrightarrow_\epsilon$	yes	yes	yes	yes
$\longrightarrow_\sigma$	yes	yes	yes	yes
$\longrightarrow_\gamma$	yes	yes	yes	yes
$\longrightarrow_\beta$	no	yes	yes	yes
$\longrightarrow_u$	no	yes	yes	yes

Note that the β-reduction is not strictly confluent, since an outer β-contraction may duplicate the β-redexes occurring in the operands. Also unfolding is not strictly confluent, since one u-contraction may create further u-redexes.

In summary, all five reduction relations that do not involve the substitution are strictly confluent; thus two 1-step-reductions meet after at most one further reduction step.

5.2 Commuting of the Reduction Relations

So far the reduction relations have been treated separately. However, for reducing an applicative expression, the different reduction relations have to be combined.

Definition Let $\longrightarrow_R, \longrightarrow_S$ be two local reduction relations on *EXP*. The relation $\longrightarrow_R$ is said *to commute with* $\longrightarrow_S$, if for all $e_1, e_2, e_3 \in EXP$ with $e_1 \Rightarrow_R e_2$ and $e_1 \Rightarrow_S e_3$ there is an $e_4 \in EXP$ with $e_2 \Rightarrow_S e_4$ and $e_3 \Rightarrow_R e_4$. The relation $\longrightarrow_R$ is said *to commute strictly* resp. *strongly* resp. *locally (weakly) with* $\longrightarrow_S$, if for all $e_1, e_2, e_3 \in EXP$ with $e_1 \longrightarrow_R e_2$ and $e_1 \longrightarrow_S e_3$ there is an $e_4 \in EXP$ with $e_2 \widehat{\longrightarrow}^{=}_{S} e_4$ and $e_3 \widehat{\longrightarrow}^{=}_{R} e_4$ resp. with $e_2 \Rightarrow_S e_4$ and $e_3 \widehat{\longrightarrow}^{=}_{R} e_4$ resp. with $e_2 \Rightarrow_S e_4$ and $e_3 \Rightarrow_R e_4$.

Thus a relation on *EXP* is (strictly, strongly, locally) confluent iff it commutes (strictly, strongly, locally) with itself. We summarize the commutation properties of the different reduction relations in the following table:

Theorem

commutes with	$\longrightarrow_\delta$	$\longrightarrow_\epsilon$	$\longrightarrow_\sigma$	$\longrightarrow_\gamma$	$\longrightarrow_\beta$	$\longrightarrow_u$
$\longrightarrow_\delta$	strictly	strictly	strictly	strictly	strongly	strongly
$\longrightarrow_\epsilon$	strictly	strictly	strictly	strictly	strongly	strongly
$\longrightarrow_\sigma$	strictly	strictly	strictly	strictly	strongly	strongly
$\longrightarrow_\gamma$	strictly	strictly	strictly	strictly	strongly	strongly
$\longrightarrow_\beta$	strongly	strongly	strongly	strongly	strongly	commute
$\longrightarrow_u$	strongly	strongly	strongly	strongly	commute	strongly

Note that $\longrightarrow_\delta, \longrightarrow_\epsilon, \longrightarrow_\sigma$, and $\longrightarrow_\gamma$ do not commute strictly with $\longrightarrow_\beta$ or $\longrightarrow_u$, since a β- or an u-contraction may duplicate existing δ-, ϵ-, σ- or γ-redexes.

Since the assumptions of the "lemma of Hindley and Rosen" ([3], Prop. 3.3.5) are fulfilled, we achieve the main result of this section:

Theorem $\rightarrow_\tau$ is confluent on *EXP*.

In summary, all our reduction relations on *EXP* are confluent and therefore Church-Rosser ([6], [12]). For the λI-calculus the Church-Rosser property was first proved in [5], for the λK-calculus in [7], Chapter 4.

5.3 Normal Forms

Normal forms are expressions that are maximally simplified and thus cannot be further reduced.

Definition Let $\rightarrow_R$ be a local R-reduction on *EXP*. An expression *is an (in) R-normal form*, if it does not contain (as subexpression) any R-redex. NF_R denotes the set of R-normal forms. An expression *has an R-normal form*, if there is an R-congruent expression in R-normal form. $NF_R(e)$ denotes the family of R-normal forms of an expression $e \in EXP$.

Expressions in normal form are either values or the symbol for the finite error or they have free variables:

Proposition If $e \in NF_\tau^{\mathbf{t}}$, then $e \in VL^{\mathbf{t}} \cup \{\Delta^{\mathbf{t}}\}$ or $free(e) \neq \emptyset$ $(\mathbf{t} \in \mathcal{T})$.

This leads to a simple characterization of the normal forms of a combinator:

Corollary Let $e \in EXP^{\mathbf{t}}$ be closed $(\mathbf{t} \in \mathcal{T})$. Then $NF_\tau(e) \subseteq VL^{\mathbf{t}} \cup \{\Delta^{\mathbf{t}}\}$.

6 Noetherian Properties

In this section we aim at proving the (non-)termination of reductions on certain subsets of expressions under the various reduction relations.

Definition A local reduction $\rightarrow_R$ on *EXP* is called *Noetherian* (on a subfamily M of expressions), if there is no infinite reduction $e_1 \longrightarrow_R e_2 \longrightarrow_R \ldots$ (starting with some $e_1 \in M$).

6.1 Termination of $\rightarrow_\delta$, $\rightarrow_\epsilon$, $\rightarrow_\sigma$, $\rightarrow_\gamma$, and $\rightarrow_\beta$

The finite termination of the individual reduction relations can be proved by introducing suitable well-founded sets and termination functions (see [8]).

Proposition The relations $\rightarrow_\delta$, $\rightarrow_\epsilon$, $\rightarrow_\sigma$, and $\rightarrow_\gamma$ are Noetherian.

The termination of the β-reduction in this expression language essentially depends on the finite type structure. Observe that in the untyped λ-calculus the β-reduction is not finitely terminating since it allows the simulation of recursion.

Proposition $\rightarrow_\beta$ is Noetherian.

In summary, not only the single reduction relations, but also their union is finitely terminating:

Theorem $\rightarrow_{\delta\epsilon\sigma\gamma\beta}$ is Noetherian.

6.2 (Non-)Termination of $\rightarrow_u$

We aim at a syntactic characterization of those expressions that allow only a finite resp. an infinite number of expansion steps.

Definition An expression $e_1 \in EXP^{\mathbf{t}_1}$ is called *recursive*, if $e_1 \triangleq C[(\mathbf{fix}\, x\colon e_2)]$ with $x \in free(e_2)$ for some $x \in \mathcal{I}^{\mathbf{t}_2}$, $e \in EXP^{\mathbf{t}_2}$ and context C; otherwise it is called *non-recursive*. Let $R = (R^{\mathbf{t}})_{\mathbf{t} \in \mathcal{T}}$ resp. $NR = (NR^{\mathbf{t}})_{\mathbf{t} \in \mathcal{T}}$ denote the family of recursive resp. non-recursive expressions.

The unfolding of recursive expressions again yields recursive expressions. Hence on R unfolding always diverges, whereas on NR it always terminates.

Proposition $\rightarrow_u$ is Noetherian on NR. Every $e \in R$ admits infinite u-reductions.

6.3 (Non-)Termination of $\rightarrow_\tau$

Finally we characterize the (non-)termination of the overall reduction relation.

Proposition $\rightarrow_\tau$ is Noetherian on NR. Every $e \in R$ allows infinite τ-reductions.

Although recursive expressions always allow infinite τ-reductions, they may also possess terminating τ-reductions.

Example Consider again the factorial *fac* from Section 2.3. The expression *fac*(0) has no u-normal form, since the subexpression *fac* is recursive and thus allows an infinite number of unfold steps. However, *fac*(0) has the τ-normal form 1, since upon a γ-contraction all u-redexes are deleted and no further expansion is possible. In operational semantics, *fac* is unfolded by need; that is, a new incarnation is created only if necessary.

7 Conclusion

The confluence, established in Section 5, ensures that the normal form as the final result of a reduction does not depend on the particular reduction path taken. However, it does not ensure that every reduction sequence terminates with the normal form if one exists.

So for operational semantics one selects, out of the set of possible reduction paths, (some of) those reductions that actually reach a normal form whenever there exists one. Such strategies are called safe. Since simplifications always terminate, a safe strategy is essentially determined by the set of recursive declarations to be unfolded in each step. For first order functions the corresponding computation rules and their relationship to denotational semantics have been discussed in detail. The restriction of the β-reduction to values leads to an innermost computation of nested recursive calls. Note that we have disentangled two issues, viz. the unfolding of recursion and the application of an abstraction to arguments, which are usually melted into a single computation step when discussing computation rules.

The aim of this paper was not to study such detailed implementations in terms of abstract machines. Rather we have investigated the basic properties of a reduction semantics. Using Kleene's approximation method, these results provide some kind of basic operational semantics, from which more specific implementations, as described for example in [13], should be derived step by step.

Acknowledgement I gratefully acknowledge valuable comments from my colleague B. Möller on drafts of this paper.

References

1. Asperti, A.: Integrating strict and lazy evaluation: the λ_{sl}-calculus. In: Deransart, P., Małuszynski, J. (eds.): Programming Language Implementation and Logic Programming (PLIP +90). Lecture Notes in Computer Science *456*. Berlin: Springer 1990, 238–254
2. Backus, J.: Can Programming Be Liberated from the von Neuman Style? A Functional Style and its Algebra of Programs. Communications ACM *21*, 613–641 (1978)
3. Barendregt, H.P.: The Lambda Calculus — Its Syntax and Semantics. Revised edition, second printing. Studies in Logic and the Foundations of Mathematics *103*. Amsterdam: North-Holland 1985
4. Bauer, F.L., Berghammer, R., Broy, M., Dosch, W., Geiselbrechtinger, F., Gnatz, R., Hangel, E., Hesse, W., Krieg-Brückner, B., Laut, A., Matzner, T., Möller, B., Nickl, F., Partsch, H., Pepper, P., Samelson K. (†), Wirsing, M., Wössner, H.: The Munich Project CIP. Volume I: The Wide Spectrum Language CIP-L. Lecture Notes in Computer Science *183*. Berlin: Springer 1985
5. Church, A.: The Calculi of Lambda Conversion. Annals of Mathematical Studies *6*. Princeton: Princeton University Press 1941
6. Church, A., Rosser, J.B.: Some Properties of Conversion. Transactions American Mathematical Society *39*, 472–482 (1936)
7. Curry, H.B., Feys, R., Craig, W.: Combinatoric Logic, Volume I. Amsterdam: North-Holland 1958
8. Dershowitz, N.: Termination. In: Jouannaud, J.-P. (ed.): Rewriting Techniques and Applications. Lecture Notes in Computer Science *202*. Berlin: Springer 1985, 180–224
9. Dosch, W.: On a Typed Higher Order Functional Calculus. Ph. D. thesis, Fakultät für Mathematik und Informatik, Technische Universität München, July 1987
10. Huet, G.: Confluent Reductions: Abstract Properties and Applications to Term Rewriting Systems. Journal ACM *27*:4, 797–821 (1980)
11. Loeckx, J., Sieber, K.: The Foundations of Program Verification. Stuttgart: Teubner, Chichester: John Wiley et Sons 1984
12. Newman, M.H.A.: On Theories with a Combinatorial Definition of "Equivalence". Annals of Mathematics *43*:2, 223–243 (1942)
13. Peyton Jones, S.L.: The Implementation of Functional Programming Languages. New York: Prentice Hall 1987
14. Plotkin, G.D.: Call-By-Name, Call-By-Value and the λ-Calculus. Theoretical Computer Science *1*, 125–159 (1975)
15. Schwichtenberg, H.: Definierbare Funktionen im λ-Kalkül mit Typen. Arch. math. Logik u. Grundlagenforschung *17*:3–4, 113–114 (1975/76)
16. Scott, D.: Continuous Lattices. In: Lawere, J.D.: Toposes, Algebraic Geometry and Logic. Lecture Notes in Mathematics *274*. Berlin: Springer 1972, 97–136
17. Staples, J.: Church-Rosser Theorems for Replacement Systems. In: Crossley, J. (ed): Algebra and Logic. Lecture Notes in Mathematics *450*. Berlin: Springer 1975, 281–303
18. Wirsing, M., Pepper, P., Partsch, H., Dosch, W., Broy, M.: On Hierarchies of Abstract Data Types. Acta Informatica *20*, 1–33 (1983)

This article was processed using the LaTeX macro package with LLNCS style

Approximation Algorithms for Minimum Time Broadcast

(Extended abstract)

Guy Kortsarz * David Peleg* †

Abstract

This paper deals with the problem of broadcasting in minimum time. Approximation algorithms are developed for arbitrary graphs, as well as for several restricted graph classes.

1 Introduction

This work concerns efficient algorithms for broadcast in a communication network. The network is modeled by a connected graph $G = (V, E)$ consisting of a set V of vertices, $V = \{v_1, .., v_n\}$ representing the processors, and a set E of edges, $E = \{e_1, ..., e_m\}$ representing the communication lines between the processors. This work assumes the *telephone* communication model (cf. [HHL88]). In this model messages are exchanged during *calls* placed over edges of the network. A round is a series of calls carried out simultaneously. Each round is assumed to require one unit of time, so round t begins at time $t-1$ and ends at time t. A vertex may participate in at most one call during a given round, however there are no limitations on the amount of information that can be exchanged during a given call. At a given round, if a call is placed over an edge e, we say that e is *active* in this round, else it is *idle*. The rule governing the activation of edges at each round is called a *schedule*.

While our communication model is very general, and allows arbitrarily complex communication patterns in the system, it is usually beneficial to define some basic *communication primitives*, which are simple communication procedures from which more involved protocols can be constructed. One important primitive that was studied extensively in the telephone model is *broadcasting* (cf. [HHL88]). A *broadcasting* problem refers to the process where a distinguished vertex originates a message M, that has to become known to all other processors. The efficiency of a broadcast scheme is usually measured by the number of time units it takes to complete the broadcast. Given a scheme S for broadcasting in a graph G, denote the broadcasting

*Department of Applied Mathematics and Computer Science, The Weizmann Institute, Rehovot 76100, Israel.

†Supported in part by an Allon Fellowship, by a Bantrell Fellowship and by a Walter and Elise Haas Career Development Award.

time from v using S by $b(v,G,S)$. Define $b(v,G)$, the ***broadcast time*** of a vertex v in G, as the minimum time for broadcasting a message originated at v in G, i.e., $b(v,G) = \min_S\{b(v,G,S)$. We denote it simply by $b(v)$ when the context is clear. We denote $b(G) = \max_v\{b(v,G)\}$.

For any connected graph G of n vertices and originator u, $b(u) \geq \lceil \log n \rceil$, since in each time unit the number of informed vertices can at most double. Another simple lower bound for $b(v)$ for an arbitrary v is $b(v) \geq Diam(v)$, since a vertex may only send information to a neighboring vertex at each round. An example of a graph for which $b(G) = \lceil \log n \rceil$ is K_n, the complete graph of n vertices.

In any connected graph G, a broadcast from a vertex u determines a spanning tree rooted at u. The parent of a vertex v is the vertex w that transmitted the message to v. Clearly, one may assume that such a vertex is unique. Even when using an arbitrary spanning tree, it is clear that at each step the set of informed vertices grows by at least one. Thus for each network G, $b(G) \leq n - 1$. We can not always improve upon this result. For example, in S_n, the star of n vertices the broadcast time is $b(S_n) = n - 1$.

Given a network $G = (V, E)$ and an originator u, the ***Minimum Broadcast Time*** (MBT) problem is to broadcast the message from u to the rest of the vertices, in $b(u)$ time units. This problem too has received considerable attention in the literature. For example, Slater, Cockayne and Hedetniemi study broadcasting in trees [SCH81], and Farley and Hedetniemi study broadcasting in grid graphs [FH78]. For a comprehensive survey on the subject of gossiping and broadcasting see [HHL88].

Note that the MBT problem in general graphs is NP-complete (cf. [GJ79]) and thus it is unlikely to find an exact solution for it. In this paper we consider approximation schemes for broadcast, namely, algorithms that do not give an exact solution, but rather give a solution that is not "too far" from the optimum. More formally, we call a scheme A for broadcasting on a family of graphs $\mathcal{F}$ a k *– approximation* scheme if for every $G \in \mathcal{F}$ and vertex $v \in V$, $b(v,G,A) \leq k \cdot b(v)$. We say that a scheme S has a (k,k')-approximation ratio if $b(v,G,S) \leq k \cdot b(v) + k'$. A ratio is ***$k$-additive*** if it is an $(O(1),k)$ ratio. We give approximation schemes for broadcast on several networks classes, and analyze their approximation ratio. In particular, we give an approximation algorithm for general graphs with $O(\sqrt{n})$-additive ratio. For ***chordal*** and $O(1)$-separable graphs we have a scheme with ratio $O(\log n)$. We also give an efficient approximation scheme for broadcasting in a special family of graphs called ***trees of cliques***, and some tools for broadcasting in a bounded-face planar graph.

Although we formulate our statements in the telephone model, virtually all our results for broadcast hold also for the message-passing model, assuming that a processor may send at most one fixed size message in each time stamp. Since as far as the broadcast operation is concerned, these two models are equivalent in power.

Several generalizations of the MBT problem appear in the literature. In [Far80], Farley suggests to reconsider the assumption that a vertex may call only neighboring vertices. Farley defines two possible variants of the model using long distance calls, the ***open path*** and the ***open line*** models. In the open path model, communication is carried along vertex disjoint paths. At each round, an informed member v may call a noninformed vertex u on an (arbitrarily long) path, adding u to the set of informed vertices. Two paths corresponding to two different pairs must be vertex disjoint.

We denote the time needed to complete the broadcast from a distinguished vertex v in the graph G in the open path model, by $b_{op}(G,v)$ (or $b_{op}(v)$). We also denote $b_{op}(G) = \max_{v \in V}\{b_{op}(v)\}$. Note that $b_{op}(G) \geq \log n$, however, we can not argue that $b_{op}(G) \geq Diam(G)$. We call the problem of broadcasting from a vertex v in $b_{op}(G)$ time units, OMBT. In this paper we give an approximation algorithm for OMBT with ratio $O(\log n / \log\log n)$. (The open line model is similar, except that the paths used in a communication round need only be *edge* disjoint. The problem of approximating broadcast in this model is essentially solved up to logarithmic factors, since as shown in [Far80] the open line model enables broadcast from an arbitrary vertex in $\lceil \log n \rceil$ time units.)

Returning to the telephone model, another generalization we consider is to assume that the set V_0 of informed vertices at the beginning of the run, need not consist of a single vertex, but can be an arbitrary subset of V. Denote this problem by SMBT, and denote the time needed to broadcast from V_0 by $b(V_0, G)$ or $b(V_0)$. As mentioned in [GJ79], SMBT is NP-complete even for $k = 4$ where k is the bound on the time for completing the broadcast.

In order to approximate the MBT problem, we define in the sequel a problem called *Bipartite Edge Scheduling* (BES) which will be shown to be related to MBT. We give a *pseudo polynomial* solution to BES, and use it in virtually all our approximations for MBT.

2 Preliminaries

We denote the maximal degree of a vertex in a network $G = (V, E)$, by $\Delta(G)$ (or simply Δ, if the context is clear). Throughout the paper we denote the number of vertices of a graph G by n, and the number of edges by m. We denote by Z^+ the set of nonnegative integers. Given a graph $G = (V, E)$ and two vertices $v, w \in V$, we denote the number of edges in a shortest path between v and w by $dist(v, w)$. We denote $Diam(v) = \max_w\{dist(v, w)\}$. The diameter of the graph G is $\max_v\{Diam(v)\}$.

A *cluster* in a graph G is a subset V' of the vertices such that the subgraph induced by V' is *connected*. Two clusters V', V'' are said to be disjoint if $V' \cap V'' = \emptyset$. Two disjoint clusters C_1 and C_2 are said to be independent if there is no edge connecting a vertex of C_1 to a vertex of C_2.

Definition 2.1 *Let $G = (V, E)$ be a graph and let $S = \{v_1, \ldots, v_k\} \subset V$ be a subset of the vertices. A subtree $T = (V_1, E_1)$ of G rooted at a distinguished vertex v is a* shortest path tree leading from v to S *iff $S \subseteq V_1$, each path from v to v_i in T is a shortest path in G, and every leaf of T belongs to S. Denote a SPT leading from a vertex v to a set S by $SPT(v, S)$.*

We now state the definition of a *control graph* of a subset $V' \subseteq v$, in a graph $G = (V, E)$. This definition will be useful in most of our approximation algorithms.

Definition 2.2 *Suppose that the clusters formed when extracting V' from the graph G are $\{C_1, \ldots, C_k\}$. The* control graph *of V' in G is a bipartite graph $D_{V',G} = (V_1, V_2, A)$, where $V_1 = V'$, $V_2 = \{C_1, \ldots, C_k\}$ and A contains an edge (v, C_i) iff there is an edge between v and some vertex of C_i in G.*

3 The Bipartite Edge Scheduling Problem

The *Bipartite Edge Scheduling* (BES) problem is a basic tool we use in our approximation algorithms for MBT. In order to describe the BES problem we need some preliminary definitions. Let $G = (V_1, V_2, A)$ be a bipartite graph, where the vertices of V_1 know a message that has to be broadcasted to the vertices of V_2. I.e., the initial set of informed vertices is V_1. We call each vertex in V_1 a *server* and each vertex in V_2 a *customer*.

The problem imposes an additional requirement. Suppose that each customer $v_2 \in V_2$ has a task t_{v_2} to perform, and the *length* of the task (i.e., the time it takes to complete it) depends upon which vertex of V_1 transmits the message to v_2. I.e., for each edge $e = (v_1, v_2) \in A$ there is a weight $w(e) \in Z^+$, such that if v_1 transmites the message to v_2 then it takes $w(e)$ time units for v_2 to complete the task t_{v_2}, starting from the arrival time of the message (and of course, no vertex of V_2 can start performing its task before it is informed). It is required to minimize the completion time of the entire process, namely, the time by which every vertex in V_2 completes its job.

Thus a solution must determine a function $F : V_2 \longrightarrow V_1$, such that $F(v_2) = v_1$ means that v_2 receives the message from v_1. Clearly, if $F(v_2) = v_1$ then $(v_1, v_2) \in A$ must hold. If $F(v_2) = v_1$ we say that v_1 *controls* (or *dominates*) v_2. Suppose that v controls $u_1, ..., u_k$. Denote $e_i^v = (v, u_i)$ and without loss of generality assume that the vertices are ordered so that $w(e_1^v) \geq w(e_2^v) \geq \ldots \geq w(e_k^v)$. Intuitively, it is logical for v to send the message first to u_1, then to u_2, etc. For a given function F, denote

Definition 3.1 *The* weight *of a function F is* $w(F) = \max_v\{\max_i\{i + w(e_i^v)\}\}$

We are now ready to state the BES problem. Given a bipartite graph $G = (V_1, V_2, A)$ with no isolated vertices, and a weight $w(e) \in Z^+$ for every edge $e \in A$, determine a function $F : V_2 \longrightarrow V_1$ whose weight $w(F)$ is minimal. We call this function F the *minimum control function* for G (or just the minimal function).

It is important to note that in all the applications given in this paper to the *BES* problem, the weights satisfy $\max_e\{w(e)\} \leq n$. Thus in order to use this problem as a basic auxiliary tool for the study of MBT, a *pseudo polynomial* solution will suffice.

A special variant of the *BES* problem arises when for each $v_2 \in V_2$ the weights of the edges entering v_2 are identical. In this case, we might as well associate the weight with v_2 itself. We call this variant of the problem the *Bipartite Vertex Schedule* (BVS) problem. If *all* the weights are identical (thus without loss of generality all the weights are 0), a solution only needs to minimize the maximal number of vertices dominated by a single vertex, i.e., minimize the size of the largest inverse image of F, $\max_v |\{u : F(u) = v\}|$.

We now present a pseudo polynomial solution to the BES problem. Given a positive integer j we check if there exists a corresponding function of weight j. The solution method for this problem involves flow techniques . The original graph is modified as follows. Create a source vertex s and a sink vertex t. For a function of weight j to be feasible, a server v can not dominate a customer u such that $w(v, u) \geq j$. Assume that w_v is the maximal weight that is less than or equal to $j - 1$ of an edge incident to $v \in V_1$. Duplicate v into $w_v + 1$ different copies and arrange the copies in an arbitrary order

$v_1, \ldots, v_{w_v+1}$. For v_1, the first copy of v, create a directed edge (s, v_1), with capacity $j - w_v$, and create a directed edge (v_1, u) with capacity 1, from v_1 to every customer $u \in V_2$ such that $(v_1, u) \in E$. For v_i the i'th copy of v, $i \geq 2$, create a directed edge (s, v_i) with capacity 1, and a directed edge (v_i, u) with capacity 1 to all the customers u such that $(v, u) \in E$ and $w(v, u) \leq w_v - i + 1$. Finally create for each customer $u \in V_2$ a directed edge (u, t) with capacity 1. Call the resulting graph $F_{j,G}$.

Since there are exactly $|V_2|$ edges entering t, and each of them is of capacity 1, the maximal flow can not exceed $|V_2|$. We now claim the following:

Lemma 3.2 *Given a BES problem P on a given graph G and the corresponding construction $F_{j,G}$, the maximal flow is $|V_2|$ iff there exists a function F such that $w(F) \leq j$.*

The minimum weighted function can now be found by using binary search. function (whose weight is j_1). The flow computation is performed for at most a polynomial number of times. Note however that a vertex may be duplicated for a number of times that can equal the maximal number in the input. To summarize, we have established the following.

Theorem 3.3 *There exists a pseudo polynomial algorithm for the BES problem.*

Corollary 3.4 *There exists a pseudo polynomial algorithm for the BVS problem.*

Given a BES instance with a graph $G = (V_1, V_2, E)$, and a weight function w, we give a general pseudo polynomial procedure to solve the scheduling problem.

Algorithm 3.5

1. Compute a minimal function F.
2. Suppose that $v \in V_1$ dominates the vertices $v_1, \ldots, v_k \in V_2$, and without loss of generality assume that $t_{v_i} \geq t_{v_{i+1}}$, for each i.
3. Every vertex v sends the message to the vertices v_i in increasing order of indices.
4. If a vertex $v' \in V_2$ gets the message from v then it finishes its task in $w(v, v')$ time units starting from the arrival time.

Fact 3.6 *The scheduling process terminates in $w(F)$ time units.*

4 Approximating Broadcast in General Graphs

In this section we give an approximation scheme for broadcasting in general graphs, both in the telephone model and in the open path model.

4.1 Approximating MBT

In this section we consider approximation schemes for broadcasting in general graphs, which guarantee a ratio of $(2, O(\sqrt{n}))$. The method used for the approximation is based on dividing the set of vertices into clusters of size $\lceil\sqrt{n}\rceil$, and broadcasting separately on those clusters. This scheme is based upon the following lemma. (The proofs of this and several subsequent lemmas are omitted from this abstract, and are deferred to the full paper.)

Lemma 4.1 *The set of vertices of any graph $G = (V, E)$ can be (polynomialy) decomposed into two sets of clusters $\mathcal{A}$ and $\mathcal{B}$, such that $|\mathcal{A}| \leq \sqrt{n}$, the clusters in $\mathcal{A} \cup \mathcal{B}$ are pairwise disjoint, $(\bigcup\mathcal{A}) \cup (\bigcup\mathcal{B}) = V$, the size of each cluster $C' \in \mathcal{A}$ is $|C'| = \lceil\sqrt{n}\rceil$, the size of each cluster $C' \in \mathcal{B}$ is bounded by $|C'| \leq \sqrt{n}$, and the clusters in $\mathcal{B}$ are pairwise independent.*

Let $G = (V, E)$ be a graph and $V' \subset V$ subset of the vertices. Form the control graph of V', $D_{V',G} = (V_1, V_2, A)$, in G as in Def 2.2. Let the weight of each edge be 0. In this scenario we claim:

Lemma 4.2 *Let F be a minimum control function for $D_{V',G}$. Then $w(F) \leq b(V', G)$.*

In the next lemma we use a shortest paths tree $SPT(v, S)$ rooted at a vertex v and leading to a set S of vertices (see Def. 2.1). Note that it is easy to construct such a tree in time polynomial in $|E|$ using a shortest path tree algorithm; simply construct a shortest path tree T spanning all the graph vertices, and iteratively exclude from it each leaf not belonging to S, until no such leaf exists. Recall that given a tree $T = (V_1, E_1)$ and a vertex $v \in V_1$ it is easy to compute the optimal scheme for broadcasting on T from v (cf. [SCH81]). Let us call the optimal scheme for broadcasting in a tree the *OT scheme*. By Using the OT scheme on $SPT(v, V')$ we can show

Lemma 4.3 *Transmitting a message from a vertex v to a subset $V' \subseteq V, |V'| = l$ of the graph, can be performed in no more than $l - 1 + Diam(v)$ time units.*

We are now ready to approximate broadcast on general graphs.

Algorithm 4.4 *Approximating broadcast in general graphs*
Input: a graph $G = (V, E)$ and a distinguished vertex $v \in V$.

1. Decompose the vertices of V into two sets of clusters $\mathcal{A}$ and $\mathcal{B}$ as in Lemma 4.1.
2. Choose for each cluster C in $\mathcal{A}$ a single representative vertex v_C. Let R denote the set of representatives, $R = \{v_C \,|C \in \mathcal{A}\}$.
3. Transmit the message from v to all the vertices of R by choosing an arbitrary tree $SPT(v, R)$ leading from v to R, and applying the OT scheme to the tree.
4. Choose for each cluster $C \in \mathcal{A}$ an arbitrary spanning tree rooted at its representative v_C, and broadcast (in parallel) in the clusters of $\mathcal{A}$ according to the OT scheme.
5. Construct the bipartite control graph $D_{V',G}$ where $V' = (\bigcup\mathcal{A}) \cup \{v\}$. Compute a minimum control function F. Assume that a vertex v' dominates clusters $C_1, .., C_k \in \mathcal{B}$. Choose for each C_i an arbitrary vertex $v_i \in C_i$ connected to v' and deliver the message from v' to $v_1, .., v_k$ (in arbitrary order). This is done in parallel for all the dominating vertices of V'.

6. Choose for each cluster in $\mathcal{B}$ an arbitrary spanning tree rooted at an informed vertex and transmit the message in parallel to all the vertices in the clusters of $\mathcal{B}$ using the OT scheme in each cluster.

Analyzing the time required by Alg. 4.4, we get the following theorem.

Theorem 4.5 *The broadcast time of* Alg. 4.4 *from a vertex v in a graph G, is bounded by $3 \cdot \sqrt{n} + Diam(v) + b(v)$ time units.* ∎

4.2 Broadcasting in the Open Path Model

Let us turn to the open path communication model. Algorithm 4.4 can be generalized to give a good approximation scheme for the open path broadcasting problem. It is easy to see that Lemma 4.2 holds even in the open path model.

Lemma 4.6 *Let T be a tree rooted at v, with up to k leaves. Then it is possible to broadcast a message from the root v to all the vertices of the tree in the open path model, in no more than $2 \cdot k + \log n$ time units.*

This discussion motivates the following algorithm. Our approach for the approximation for OMBT, is based on the following idea. First we define sets of representatives, $\{R_1, \ldots, R_f\}$, where $R_1 = V$, $|R_f| \leq \log n$ and $f \leq \log n / \log\log n$. To each set R_j and vertex $v \in R_j$ there is a corresponding tree T_j^v, containing exactly $\lceil \log n \rceil$ vertices of R_{j-1}. The trees corresponding to different vertices in R_j are *vertex disjoint*. The main algorithm operates in f stages. First it informs the vertex set R_f. Then it proceeds to inform the sets R_j in reverse order of indices, i.e., at the end of stage i of the main algorithm, the message is known by the set R_{f-i+1}, and the goal of the next stage is for R_{f-i+1} to inform R_{f-i}. We next give Procedure $Choose - Rep$, that chooses the sets R_i of representatives, and the corresponding trees $T_i^v, v \in R_i$. After that, we give the main algorithm that uses $Choose - Rep$ to approximate OMBT.

Throughout the execution of procedure Choose-Rep we extract trees from G. The set of remaining vertices, i.e., the set of vertices not extracted yet from G, will be denoted by V'. The set of clusters in the graph induced by V' will be denoted by $\mathcal{C}$.

Algorithm 4.7 $Choose - Rep$
Input: A graph $G = (V, E)$ and a distinguished vertex $v \in V$.

1. $V' \leftarrow V$, $R_1 \leftarrow V, i \leftarrow 1, \mathcal{C} \leftarrow \{V\}$.
2. **repeat**
   (a) $R_{i+1} \leftarrow \emptyset$.
   (b) **while** $\mathcal{C} \neq \emptyset$ do:
      i. Choose cluster $C \in \mathcal{C}$. Select $\lceil \log n \rceil$ vertices in $C \cap R_i$ arbitrarily, except that if $v \in C$, take v as one of them. Let $v_1, \ldots, v_{\lceil \log n \rceil}$, such that we set $v_1 = v$ if $v \in C$. Select in C a subtree $T_i^{v_1}$ leading from v_1 to $\{v_2, \ldots, v_{\lceil \log n \rceil}\}$.
      ii. Extract $T_i^{v_1}$ from C, and set $V' \leftarrow V' \setminus T_i^{v_1}$.

iii. Set $C \leftarrow C \cup \{B : B$ is a connected component of $C \setminus T^{v_1}, |B \cap R_i| > \lceil \log n \rceil\}$.

end-while

(c) For every tree $T_i^{v_1}$ obtained in stage (b), add its root v_1 to R_{i+1}.

(d) $i \leftarrow i + 1$.

3. **until** $|R_i| \leq \lceil \log n \rceil$.

We now proceed to define the main algorithm. Throughout the algorithm we maintain a set R of informed vertices that equals R_j for some j. The point is that j decreases by one in each iteration, thus at last $R = R_1 = V$.

Algorithm 4.8 *Approximation algorithm for OMBT*

Input: A graph $G = (V, E)$ and a distinguished vertex $v \in V$.

1. Apply procedure $Choose - Rep$ on G and v. Assume that the sets of representatives are $\{R_1, \ldots, R_f\}$.
2. Choose an arbitrary tree leading from v to the other vertices of R_f, and inform all the vertices in R_f using the scheme suggested in the proof of Lemma 4.6.
3. $R \leftarrow R_f, i \leftarrow f$.
4. **repeat**
   (a) Each vertex $u \in R_i$ informs (in parallel) all the vertices in T_i^u using the scheme suggested in the proof of Lemma 4.6.
   (b) Let G_i' denote, $G_i' = G \setminus \bigcup_{u \in R_i} T_i^u$. Let $C_1^i, \ldots, C_s^i$, denote the clusters in the graph induced by G_i'.
   (c) The vertices $\bigcup T_i^u$ inform a vertex v_j in C_j^i, for each $1 \leq j \leq s$, using a minimum control function, as in step 5 of Alg. 4.4.
   (d) Choose for each j, a tree TL_j leading from v_j to the vertices in $R_{i-1} \cap C_j^i$.
   (e) The vertices v_j inform the vertices of TL_j using the scheme of Lemma 4.6.
   (f) $R \leftarrow R_{i-1}, i \leftarrow i - 1$.
5. **until** $i = 1$.

It is clear from the algorithm that when stage 4(e) of Alg. 4.8 is completed, all the vertices of R_{i-1} know the message. It follows that at the end all the vertices are informed.

Theorem 4.9 Algorithm 4.8 *is an* $O(\log n / \log\log n)$ *approximation scheme for OMBT.*

The method of Alg. 4.8 can be used to deal with the MBT problem as well. However, at each stage, broadcasting in a tree T may take $O(\log n + h(T))$ time units, where $h(T)$ is the height of T. Since the diameter of a subcluster of a graph G may largely increase, this may not be a good approximation scheme in the worst case.

However, it is instructive to consider the behavior of Alg. 4.8 on random inputs. Let us consider a random graph $G \in G_{n,p}$. The graph consists of n vertices, where for each pair of vertices $v, w \in V$, the edge $(v, w) \in E$ is drawn with probability p, where p is constant, $0 < p < 1$. For such graphs the scheme of Alg. 4.4 yields only an $O(\frac{\sqrt{n}}{\log n})$ approximation ratio. In contrast, Alg. 4.8 is an $O(\log n / \log\log n)$ approximation scheme for random graphs, with high probability.

5 Separator Based Strategies for Broadcasting

This section examines the idea of using the separability property of a graph in order to achieve fast approximation schemes for broadcasting.

Definition 5.1 *Let $\varphi(n)$ be a nondecreasing function, and let y and ρ be fixed numbers such that* $0 < \rho < 1$.

1. *A graph $G = (V, E)$,* has a *$\langle \rho, y \rangle$ – separator if exists a set $S \subset V$ such that the removal of S leaves no connected component of size greater than $\rho \cdot n$, and $|S| \leq y$.*
2. *A graph $G = (V, E)$ is $\langle \rho, \varphi(n) \rangle$ – separable if every vertex-induced subgraph $G' \subset G$ of n' vertices has a $\langle \rho, \varphi(n') \rangle$ separator.*

Given a $\langle \rho, \varphi(n) \rangle$–separable graph, denote the corresponding separator of every subgraph G' by $sep(G')$.

5.1 Broadcasting Scheme for a Graph with Arbitrary Separator

In order to develop a separator-based broadcasting scheme, we first need to generalize Lemma 4.2. Suppose that a graph G contains a set V' of informed vertices. Denote the clusters created when extracting V' from the graph by $C_1, ..., C_k$. Choose for each C_i an arbitrary nonempty subset $C_i' \subset C_i$. We can use the fact that in broadcasting it is needed to inform the vertices of C_i' to achieve a lower bound on the best possible time for broadcasting. We use the technique developed for solving BES problems. Let us first define a BES instance $B' = BES(V', \{C_1', \ldots, C_k'\})$ as follows.

1. Form the control graph $D_{V',G}$ of V' in G.
2. Put weights on the edges as follows. For an arbitrary vertex $v \in V'$ connected to a vertex in C_i, choose a vertex $v' \in C_i$ connected to v that is closest to the set C_i'. Attach a weight $d^v_{C_i} \equiv dist(v', C_i')$, to the edge (v, C_i).

Lemma 5.2 *If F is a minimal control function for B', then $w(F) \leq b(V', G)$.*

Note, that we can use an algorithm similar to Alg. 3.5 to establish:

Fact 5.3 *In the above scenario, it is possible to inform at least one vertex in C_i', for every i, in no more than $w(F)$ time units.*

It is possible to use Lemma 5.2 in order to construct schemes for broadcasting from a distinguished vertex v in a graph with a "small" separator. Let G be a $\langle \rho, \varphi(n) \rangle$-separable graph. Throughout the run, the set V' will denote the set of already informed vertices.

Algorithm 5.4

1. $V' \leftarrow \{v\}$.

2. Construct a separator $sep(G)$ for G.
3. Build an arbitrary tree $SPT(v, sep(G)) = (V_1, E_1)$ rooted at v and leading to the members of $sep(G)$. Broadcast the message to the vertices of the tree using the OT scheme.
4. $V' \leftarrow V' \cup V_1$.
5. **Repeat**
   (a) Assume the clusters formed when extracting V' from the graph are $C_1, ..., C_k$. Each C_i has a separator $sep(C_i) = C_1^i \cup C_2^i \cup \ldots C_{l_i}^i$, where $C_1^i, C_2^i, \ldots, C_{l_i}^i$ are $sep(C_i)$'s connected components.

   repeat

   i. For each i pick the lowest index $j(i)$ that wasn't chosen yet (for i).
   ii. Build the instance $B' = BES(V', \{C_{j(i)}^i : 1 \leq i \leq k\})$ of the BES problem, as described.
   iii. Send the message to at least one vertex of $C_{j(i)}^i$ for every i and j, using a minimal function F and the scheme suggested in Fact 5.3.

   until the C_j^i's clusters are exhausted for every i and j.

   (b) For every i and j, broadcast the message within C_j^i using the best known scheme for C_j^i. (If no good known scheme exists for the kind of graph C_j^i is, broadcast using an arbitrary tree.)
   (c) $V' \leftarrow V' \cup sep(C_1) \cup \ldots \cup sep(C_k)$.

   Until $V' = V$.

It is easy to see that when Alg. 5.4 terminates, all the vertices in V are informed.

Theorem 5.5 Alg 5.4 *terminates the broadcast process in* $O(\log n) \cdot \varphi(n) \cdot b(v)$ *time units.*

Further, it can be shown that if we can assure that every separator $sep(C)$ is connected and $b(sep(C)) \leq k$ for some integer $k < \varphi(n)$, then the bound is improved to

$$O(\log n) \cdot (b(v) + k). \tag{1}$$

5.2 Applications

In this subsection we give some examples for graph families for which Algorithm 5.4 can be applied. The first example is the one of *chordal graphs.* The following theorem is shown in [GRE84] regarding chordal graphs.

Theorem 5.6 [GRE84] *Any n-vertex chordal graph G contains a (polynomialy computable) maximal clique C such that if the vertices in C are deleted from G, every connected component in the graph induced by any of the remaining vertices is of size at most* $n/2$.

From Theorem 5.6 and Eq. (1) it follows that:

Corollary 5.7 *There exists a polynomial* $2 \cdot \log n + 1$ *approximation scheme for broadcasting on chordal graphs.* ∎

A second example is the family of a c-separable graphs, consisting of graphs for which $\varphi(n) = c$ for some constant c. It follows from Theorem 5.5 that Alg. 5.4 is an $O(\log n)$ approximation scheme for broadcasting in such graphs. Note that *k-outerplanar* graphs are $O(k)$-separable, and that *outerplanar* graphs are $O(1)$-separable. Thus, as a specific cases we haves:

Theorem 5.8 *There exist an* $O(k \cdot \log n)$ *approximation algorithm for broadcasting in a k-outerplanar graph, for a fixed k.*

Corollary 5.9 *There exists a polynomial* $O(\log n)$ *approximation scheme for broadcasting on the family of outerplanar graphs.*

The third example is the well known family of series-parallel graphs. In [FJ90] it is shown that every series-parallel graph is $\langle 2/3, 2 \rangle$-separable and the separator can be found in $O(n)$ time. Thus Alg. 5.4 is a polynomial $O(\log n)$ approximation algorithm for broadcasting on a series parallel graph.

Theorem 5.10 *There exists a polynomial* $O(\log n)$ *approximation algorithm for broadcasting on a series-parallel graph.*

The last example is of the family of *bounded face planar graphs.* The size of a face of a planar graph is the number of vertices in the face, counting multiple visits when traversing the boundary (cf. [Mil86]).

Theorem 5.11 [Mil86] *If G is an embedded planar graph with bounded face size then the graph is* $\langle 2/3, O(\sqrt{n}) \rangle$*-separable, and the separator can be chosen to be a simple cycle, or a single vertex.*

Theorem 5.12 *There exists a polynomial* $O(n^{1/4}/\sqrt{\log n})$ *approximation algorithm for broadcasting in the family of bounded face planar graphs.*

6 Broadcasting in a Tree of Cliques

In this section we switch from general graphs to the other extreme, and give an approximation scheme for a special kind of graph family called *trees of cliques*, generalizing the family of trees.

Definition 6.1 *A graph* $G = (V, E)$ *is a* tree of cliques *(TOC) if*

1. *The vertex set* V *can be decomposed into a disjoint union of sets* $C_1, \ldots, C_k$ *such that each* C_i *induces a clique (i.e., a complete graph) in* G.
2. *The auxiliary graph* $T(G) = (\tilde{V}, \tilde{E})$ *whose vertices are* $\tilde{V} = \{C_1, \ldots, C_k\}$ *and whose edges are* $\tilde{E} = \{(C_i, C_j) \mid$ *there is an edge* $(v_i, v_j) \in E$, *for* $v_i \in C_i, v_j \in C_j\}$ *is a tree.*

To broadcast a message from a vertex v in a TOC, we use the following idea. In order to deliver the message between vertices of different cliques (i.e., from cliques to their clique children), we use the techniques developed for BVS problems. It follows that the total broadcast complexity spent while delivering message between cliques is bounded by $O(b(v))$. Since there is an efficient delivery method for message delivery in a clique, we have.

Theorem 6.2 *There is an* additive $\log n(\log n - \log\log n)$ *approximation algorithm for broadcasting in a* TOC. ∎

We then develop an alternative method for delivering the message inside the cliques. In this method, every vertex participates in the message delivery in its clique only for a small (fixed) number of rounds, and is thus free sooner to help in sending the message down the tree to its clique children. Using this method we establish (in the full paper) some improved bounds in restricted cases.

References

[Far80] A.M. Farley. Minimum time line broadcast network. *Networks*, 10:59–70, 1980.

[FH78] A. Farley and S. Hedetniemi. Broadcasting in grid graphs. *In Proc. Ninth Southeastern Conf. on Combin., Graph Theory and Comput.*, pages 275–288, 1978.

[FJ90] G. Frederickson and R. Janardan. Space-efficient message routing in c-decomposable networks. *SIAM J. on Computing*, 19:164–181, 1990.

[GJ79] M.R. Garey and D.S. Johnson. *Computers and Intractability: A Guide to the Theory of NP-Completeness.* W.H Freeman and Company, 1979.

[GRE84] J.R. Gilbert, D.J. Rose, and A. Edenbrandt. A separator theorem for chordal graphs. *SIAM J. Alg. and Disc. Meth.*, 5:306–313, 1984.

[HHL88] S. Hedetniemi, S. Hedetniemi, and A. Liestman. A survey of gossiping and broadcasting in communication networks. *Networks*, 18:319–349, 1988.

[Mil86] G. Miller. Finding small simple cycle separators for 2-connected planar graphs. *Journal of Computer and System Sciences*, 32:265–279, 1986.

[SCH81] P.J. Slater, E.J. Cockayne, and T. Hedetniemi. Information dissemination in trees. *SIAM J. on Compu.*, 10, 1981.

The Complexity of Reconfiguring Network Models

(Extended abstract)

Y. Ben-Asher * D. Peleg † A. Schuster ‡

Abstract

This paper concerns some of the theoretical complexity aspects of the reconfigurable network model. The computational power of the model is investigated under several variants, depending on the type of switches (or switch operations) assumed by the network nodes. Computational power is evaluated by focusing on the set of problems computable in constant time in each variant. A hierarchy of such problem classes corresponding to different variants is shown to exist and is placed relative to traditional classes of complexity theory.

1 Introduction

In sequential computation there is one widely acceptable model, namely, the *von-Neumann* model. In contrast, there is still no such popular equivalent for parallel computation. In particular, it is not clear which parallel model of computation is the best candidate to bridge the "hardware - software gap," as discussed in [Val90]. The PRAM family is usually considered as the ideal computational environment, for its freedom of restrictions on memory access. At the other extreme, the Fixed Connection Network model (FCN) is viewed to be a "realizable" parallel environment, since each processing element is connected to a constant number of other elements. Recent developments in technology have made several other computational models viable. Such models may be as strong as (or even stronger than) the PRAM model on the one hand, and on the other hand exhibit realizability of the same level as (or even higher than) that of the FCNs.

One of the most promising parallel models of computation is the *Reconfigurable Networks (RN)* model. The basic idea of the RN model is to rely on bus communication, and enable flexible connection patterns, by allowing nodes to connect and

*Department of Mathematics and Computer Science, The Haifa University, Haifa, Israel. E-mail: yosi@mathcs2.haifa.ac.il

†Department of Applied Mathematics and Computer Science, The Weizmann Institute, Rehovot 76100, Israel. E-mail: peleg@wisdom.weizmann.ac.il. Supported in part by an Allon Fellowship, by a Bantrell Fellowship and by a Walter and Elise Haas Career Development Award.

‡Department of Computer Science, Technion, Technion City, Haifa, Israel 32000. E-mail: assafs@cs.technion.ac.il

disconnect their adjacent edges in various patterns. This yields a variety of possible bus topologies for the network, and enables the program to exploit this topological variability in order to speed up the computation.

Informally, a reconfigurable network operates as follows. Essentially, the edges of the network are viewed as building blocks for larger *bus* components. The network dynamically reconfigures itself at each time step, where an allowable configuration is a partition of the network into several connected components, or, a set of edge-disjoint buses. A crucial point is that the reconfiguration process is carried out *locally* at each processor (or *switch*) of the network. That is, at the beginning of each step during the execution of a program on the RN, each switch of the network fixes its *local configuration* by partitioning its collection of edges into some combination of subsets. Adjacent edges that are grouped by a switch into the same subset are viewed as (hardware) connected, so that they form a bus. Any processor connected to an edge participating in the construction of a certain bus, may choose to listen to any incoming or passing message transmitted on that bus.

The basic assumption concerning the behavior of the reconfigurable model (as well as any other bus model) is that in any configuration, the time it takes to transmit along any bus is constant, regardless of the bus length. This assumption is theoretically false, as the speed of signals carrying information is bounded by the speed of light, partially explaining why the RN model and other bus models have not gained wide acceptance initially. Recently, however, implementations were suggested for the RN model, involving a variety of newly developed technologies, including optical communication and optical computing devices. Several dynamically reconfiguring machines involving thousands of switches were actually built [TCS89,GK89,LM89,MKS89,WLH+87], showing that the RN model is *implementable* in massively parallel architectures.

Motivated by the existing implementations, there has been some work on the algorithmic and computational aspects of the RN model. Nakatani [Nak87] considered comparison-based operations like merging, sorting and selection on reconfigurable arrays. Miller, Stout, Reisis and Kumar [MPRS87] and Reisis and Kumar [RP87] considered parallel computations and data movement operations on the reconfigurable mesh. In a recent series of papers, summarized in [Wan91], Wang, Chen and others present many constant time algorithms for RNs. In [BS91,Sch91] the parameter of *bus-usage* is suggested as a measure for the efficiency of RN algorithms. Other papers consider image processing and fault tolerance on RNs.

This expanding volume of algorithms and results calls for a more systematic approach and a theoretical evaluation of the classes of problems solvable using RNs. In particular it is evident that RNs solve large sets of problems in constant time. This power is attributed to the exponential number of global configurations that may be taken by the network at each step. When the problem is solvable by reconfiguring locally according to the input, then the global configuration gives the result instantaneously. Thus, for example, it is shown in [BPRS91] how to sort in constant time using one RN model, and how to solve a $PTIME$-complete problem in constant time using another RN model. Some comparisons and simulations of basic RN models are presented there as well.

In an earlier work, Moshell and Rothstein [MR79] investigated the computational complexity of the *Bus Automata* (BA). The BA model is similar to the RN model. It is composed of a d-dimensional array of finite automata with modifiable channels allowing long-distance communication. Moshell and Rothstein showed that large classes of problems are solvable in constant time on the BA. For example, they showed that the languages recognizable in constant time by a one-dimensional BA are exactly the regular languages.

In this work we extend the ideas from [BPRS91] in order to evaluate the theoretical power of several different RN models. We concentrate on the classes of problems solvable in constant time. Our approach, however, is different from the one given in [MR79] in several aspects. In particular, the underlying topologies assumed for the networks are not necessarily uniform arrays (although we do show equivalence in several cases) and the switches differ in their operation on passing messages. We show that variations in the switching assumptions result in variations in the power of the model. Finally, we present results that relate these models to space-bounded Turing machines and parallel complexity classes.

The rest of this work is organized as follows. Section 2 describes the RN model in more detail. In Section 3, the RN model is compared with the PRAM model, and some connections are established between the corresponding complexity classes. In Section 4 similar comparisons are made with respect to Turing-machine based complexity classes. Section 5 concerns the restriction of the RN model to simple two-dimensional mesh topologies. Section 6 considers the non-monotone RN model. Finally, Section 7 concludes with a discussion and some open problems.

2 Reconfigurable Models of Computation

2.1 The General Model

A reconfigurable network (RN) is a network of switches operating synchronously. The switches residing at the nodes of the network perform the same program, taking local decisions and calculations according to the input and locally stored data. Input and output locations are specified by the problem to be solved, so that initially, each input bit (or item) is available at a single node of the network, and eventually, each output bit (or item) is stored by one.

A single node of the network consists of a computing unit, a buffer and a switch with reconnection capability. The buffer holds either an input or an output item, or something that was previously read from adjacent buses. The power (instruction set) of the computing unit is not central to the discussion, although it varies from section to section. For example, for the simulations of Turing machines by RNs we assume no computation power at all, so that no arithmetic or logic operations are allowed. For the simulations of PRAMs (and by PRAMs) we assume the processor power of the simulating and simulated models to be the same. In many cases, the sole objective of the computing unit is to decide the next state of the switch[1] according to the data stored at the local buffer. In simulating other models by RN's, the size of the buffers

[1]In the sequel, we use the notions of a *switch*, a *processor* and a *network node* interchangeably.

typically remains small. If a *word* (whose length is determined by the bus bandwidth) is moved on the bus in a single step, then the size of the buffer need only be a constant number of words.

A single time step of a RN computation is composed of the following substeps. In substep 1, the network selects a *configuration* H of the buses, and reconfigures itself to H. This is done by local decisions taken at each switch individually, depending on the input, the contents of messages previously read from adjacent buses and local computation results. In substep 2, one or more of the processors connected by a bus transmit a message on the bus. These processors are called the *speakers* of the bus. In substep 3, some of the processors connected by the bus attempt to read the message transmitted on the bus by the speaker(s). These processors are referred to as the *readers* of the bus.

At each time step, a bus may take one of the following three states: *Idle*: no processor transmits, *Speak*: there is a single speaker, and *Error*: there is more than one speaker. An *Error* state, reflecting a collision of several speakers, is detectable by all processors connected by the corresponding bus, but the messages are assumed to be destroyed.

2.2 Variations on Operations

The general RN model, as presented above, does not specify the exact operation of the switches. As already shown in [BPRS91], the specific operation determines the power of the model. We consider four basic variants:

General RN: The switch may partition its collection of edges into any combination of subsets, where all edges in a subset are connected as building blocks for the same bus. Thus the possible configurations are any network partition of edge-disjoint connected subgraphs.

Linear RN (LRN): The switch may partition its collection of edges into any combination of connected pairs and singletons. Hence buses are of the form of a path (or a cycle) and the global configuration is a partition of the network into paths, or a set of edge-disjoint linear buses.

Directed RN (DRN): This model is similar to the Non-Linear RN model, except that edges are directed, so messages travel in one direction only. Consequently, each connected subset of edges is split into *in-edges* and *out-edges*. A message entering the switch for the first time via either one of the in-edges, proceeds via all the out-edges connected to it.

Non-Monotone RN (NMRN): This model is the same as the Directed RN model, but a switch has an additional "inversion" capability. When this operation is activated by the switch, a signal going via the switch is inverted. That is, a "0" ("no signal") turns into a "1" ("signal on") and vice versa.

Note that the notion of a *bus* for DRNs and NMRNs is somewhat different than that of LRNs and RNs. For DRNs and NMRNs suppose some processor z transmits at time step t, and let H_t denote the global configuration that was chosen by the network during step t. Then the message issued by z on some connected set of out-edges reaches the subgraph of H_t consisting of all nodes that may be reached from z by a directed path starting at those out-edges. The notion of ***bus error*** for DRNs and NMRNs changes, too; a node y detects an error during step t if, in the configuration H_t, y is reachable from two different speakers. It may happen that a message issued by some speaker z will be correctly received by a reader, while other readers that are reachable from z detect an error since they are reachable from other speakers too.

2.3 Complexity Classes

Let Σ denote a symbol-set and let $\Sigma^* = \cup_{i\geq 1}\Sigma^i$. A ***problem*** A is a mapping $A : \Sigma^* \longmapsto \Sigma^*$. Using standard reductions, the discussion can be restricted to Boolean problems $A : \Sigma^* \longmapsto \{0,1\}$. An input-instance I for A is said to be ***solved*** by presenting $A(I)$. An ***RN family***, $\mathcal{R} = \{R_N\}_{N\geq 1}$, of reconfiguring networks is a set containing a network construction R_N for each natural N. We say that the family $\mathcal{R}$ ***solves*** a problem A if for every N, R_N solves all size N inputs for A, $\{I : |I| = N\}$.

We consider two measures for computation complexity in the RN model. The ***time*** $T(R)$ is the worst-case number of steps it takes for the computation of the reconfiguring network R to terminate, The ***size*** $S(R)$ is the number of switches in the reconfiguring network R. A reconfiguring network family $\mathcal{R} = \{R_N\}$ has time complexity $f(N)$ if for every $N \geq 1$, a computation of R_N terminates within $T(R_N) = O(f(N))$ steps for all valid input instances of length N. The family $\mathcal{R}$ has size complexity $g(n)$ if for every $N \geq 1$, R_N consists of $S(R_N) = O(g(N))$ switches.

The ***description*** $\mathcal{D}(R)$ of a reconfigurable network R, is a list of $S = S(R)$ triplets of the form $\langle x, \Gamma^x, \texttt{Rules}^x\rangle$, one for each node x of the network. In this description, x is the node's *id*, Γ^x is the list of immediate neighbours of x in the underlying topology R, and $\texttt{Rules}^x$ is a set of configuration and output rules for x (depending on the inputs, the current time step and the data read from adjacent buses in previous time steps). Since we focus on constant-degree networks and constant-time programs, we may assume that a triplet consists of $O(\log S)$ bits. The total network description is thus of size $O(S \log S)$ bits.

The class of reconfigurable networks $\mathcal{RN}(f(N), g(N))$ in the RN model, is the set of families $\mathcal{R}$ with the following properties: (a) $\mathcal{R}$ is of time complexity $f(N)$ and size complexity $g(N)$, and (b) $\mathcal{R}$ is uniformly generated in $SPACE(\log(g(N)))$, i.e., there exists a Turing Machine (TM) M, that given N produces the description of R_N using $O(\log(g(N)))$ cells of its working tape. Other classes are analogously defined for the LRN, DRN and $NMRN$ models. Correspondingly, these are denoted $\mathcal{LRN}(f(N), g(N))$, $\mathcal{DRN}(f(N), g(N))$ and $\mathcal{NMRN}(f(N), g(N))$.

We define the set of problems $RN(f(N), g(N))$ to include any problem A for which there exists a network family $\mathcal{R} \in \mathcal{RN}(f(N), g(N))$ solving A. The problem sets $LRN(f(N), g(N))$, $DRN(f(N), g(N))$ and $NMRN(f(N), g(N))$ are defined analogously.

For example, since a switch in the RN model can simulate a switch in the LRN model, we immediately have that for any two functions $f(N)$ and $g(N)$,

$$LRN(f(N), g(N)) \subseteq RN(f(N), g(N)) .$$

We also need a notion of *uniformity* for the time/size functions. A function $f(N)$ is said to be *constructible* if it is computable by a TM M_f having N as its input and using $O(f(N))$ cells of its working tape.

3 PRAM Algorithms and RN's

In this section we consider the question of how powerful polynomial size RN's are, compared to parallel models of computation with a shared memory unit. In particular we are interested in the common PRAM model (cf. [KR90]). We have (proofs are omitted from this abstract):

Theorem 3.1 *A T-step computation of an N-switch RN with E edges can be simulated by an $O(E)$-processor CRCW PRAM in time $O(T \log N)$.* ▮

The result of Theorem 3.1 complements the following one, derived in [BPRS91].

Theorem 3.2 [BPRS91] *A T-step computation of an N-switch LRN with E edges can be simulated by an $O(E)$-processor EREW PRAM in time $O(T \log N)$.*

Corollary 3.1 [BPRS91] *A problem of input size N that is computable by a $T(N)$-step, polynomial-size LRN (respectively, RN), has an $O(T(N) \log N)$-step EREW (resp., CRCW) PRAM program. In particular, a problem having $O(\log^K N)$-step, polynomial-size LRN's (resp., RN's) with uniformly generated underlying topologies is in (uniform) $EREW^{(K+1)}$ (resp., $CRCW^{(K+1)}$).*

In other words, the corollary implies that problems that are "inherently sequential", i.e., that are "non parallelizable" using traditional parallel models, maintain this property under the RN and the LRN models. Theorem 4.2 implies that this meta-claim holds for the DRN model, too. In Section 6 it is shown that this is not the case for the NMRN model.

As already mentioned, many problems requiring $\Omega(\frac{\log N}{\log \log N})$ steps on a CRCW PRAM (or $\Omega(\log N)$ steps on an EREW PRAM) with polynomial number of processors, can be computed by a constant-time polynomial-size RN. The following theorem shows that this is not the case for the opposite direction.

Theorem 3.3 [BPRS91,WC90b] *A (priority) CRCW PRAM with $P(N)$ processors, $M(N)$ memory cells and $T(N)$ time can be simulated by a $O(T(N))$-step, $P(N) \times M(N)$ mesh operating in the LRN model.*

4 Relations to Turing Machines

In this section we show some basic relations between classes of problems computable in constant time by polynomial-size RN's and classes of problems solvable by space bounded TM's. The reader is referred to [HU79] for an introduction to related terminology that is not explained here.

The main relation between RN's and TM's is expressed in the following lemma. Here, L is the set of problems solvable by a deterministic TM having $O(\log N)$ workspace. The idea behind the proof of the lemma is to construct, for a given Turing machine M in $SPACE(f(N))$, an RN whose switches correspond to the *descriptors* (or "possible states") of M, and whose reconfiguration rules correspond to the rules by which the machine M moves from one configuration to the next. Given such a construction (and once the proper initializations are taken care of), the entire execution of the machine M can be simulated in a single step of the RN, by configuring each switch appropriately and sending a single "signal," starting at the initial configuration and ending at some (accepting or rejecting) configuration. (Again, detailed constructions and proofs are deferred to the full paper.)

Lemma 4.1 *There exists a constant* $c > 0$ *such that for every constructible* $f(N)$, $SPACE(f(N)) \subseteq RN(O(1), c^{\max(f(N), \log N)})$. ∎

Corollary 4.1 $L \subseteq RN(O(1), poly(N))$. ∎

In particular, all logspace reductions are carried in constant time in the RN model using a polynomial number of switches. This will be useful later when we consider the class $PTIME$ and its relation to the NMRN model. We can further generalize Lemma 4.1 and drop the constructibility restriction for TM's with high space requirements.

Lemma 4.2 *There exists a constant* $c > 0$ *such that for every* $f(N) = \Omega(N)$, $SPACE(f(N)) \subseteq RN(O(1), c^{f(N)})$. ∎

Lemma 4.2 implies a universality result for the RN model. The same result was previously shown for the Bus Automata model [Rot76].

Corollary 4.2 *For every decidable problem A there exists a family of RN's solving it in constant time.* ∎

Note that circuits are also a universal model, hence the results from [BPRS91] that are reviewed at Section 5 imply a stronger version of Corollary 4.2, namely a universality result for the LRN model.

Corollary 4.3 *For every decidable problem A there exists a family of LRN's solving it in constant time.* ∎

Let us next relate linear RN's to space bounded TM's.

Theorem 4.1 $LRN(O(1), poly(N)) \subseteq L$. ∎

In summary, Theorems 3.1, 4.1 and 4.1 give

$$LRN(O(1), poly(N)) \subseteq L \subseteq RN(O(1), poly(N)) \subseteq CRCW^1 .$$

Finally, we relate the power of non-deterministic TM's and DRN's. The next-move mapping δ of a non-deterministic TM may have several choices for the next machine configuration, given a certain descriptor. The non-deterministic TM accepts its input if there exists any sequence of choices of moves that leads to an accepting state. In particular, NL is the set of problems solvable by a non-deterministic TM having $O(\log N)$ workspace. Our last result in this section is that $NL = DRN(O(1), poly(N))$.

Lemma 4.3 *There exists a constant* $c > 0$ *such that for every constructible* $f(N)$, $NSPACE(f(N)) \subseteq DRN(O(1), c^{\max(f(N), \log N)})$. ▮

Corollary 4.4 $NL \subseteq DRN(O(1), poly(N))$. ▮

It is instructive to understand why Lemma 4.3 fails when the undirected RN model is used. Intuitively, this is because when simulating a nondeterministic machine M, the buses configured in order to represent the flow of computation are no longer in the shape of a simple path. Consequently, the signal transmitted by the switch $s(d_0)$ of the simulating RN (corresponding to the initial configuration d_0 of the simulated M) may take in-edges in the "opposite" direction and hence reach switches corresponding to descriptors that may not be reached by M in a valid sequence of moves. This is actually an inherent problem of the RN model; when taking some configuration, the switch can not control the exits that an incoming signal may take. This observation may lead to upper bounds on the computational power of the RN model in order to "separate" it from the DRN model.

Theorem 4.2 $DRN(O(1), poly(N)) \subseteq NL$. ▮

Finally we note that, although no direct simulation is shown, the equivalence of $DRN(O(1), poly(N))$ and NL implies $DRN(O(1), poly(N)) \subseteq CRCW^1$ (cf. [KR90]).

5 Universality of the Mesh

In this section we show that the two-dimensional mesh is computation universal and achieves high speedup. A problem A is in the class $Mesh\_LRN(t(N), r(N), c(N))$ if for each N, the $r(N) \times c(N)$ mesh solves all size N inputs to A in $t(N)$ steps. Similar definitions apply for the RN, DRN and NMRN models. Let us first review several results for the LRN model.

We follow [KR90] for the definitions of *circuits* and their *depth*. Given a family of (bounded fan-in) circuits $C = \{C_i\}$, $i \geq 1$, we say that C is in $CKT(D(N))$ if the depth of C_N is $O(D(N))$ for each N. The size of a circuit is its number of edges. A circuit C of size $|C|$ is *uniform* if its description can be generated by a TM using $O(\log |C|)$ workspace. A problem A is in $CKT(D(N))$ if there is a family of uniform circuits $\{C_N\}_{N \geq 1}$ in $CKT(D(N))$, that solves A.

Lemma 5.1 [BPRS91] *For every* $\epsilon > 0$, $CKT(d) \subseteq LRN(O(1), 2^{(1+\epsilon)d})$, *and hence* $NC^1 \subseteq LRN(O(1), poly(N))$ *and* $NC^2 \subseteq LRN(O(1), O(N^{\log N}))$.

In fact, the result is stronger: there exist uniform "universal" constructions computing all functions of the same circuit complexity.

Lemma 5.2 [BPRS91] *For every fixed $\epsilon, c > 0$ there exists a constructible (universal) LRN network of size $O(N^{c(1+\epsilon)})$ computing in constant time all functions that are computable by circuits of depth $c \log N$.*

The above results can be used to prove the universality of the mesh. In principle, the construction of the rectangle is similar to the universal LRN construction of [BPRS91] (also cf. [Sch91]), with some modifications. The K to K permutation networks that are used therein are replaced by $K \times K$ meshes. Combined with an appropriate initialization network, the total width of the resulting construction is N, and its length is $KN^{(1+\epsilon)c}$ (we use $K \leq N$). The number of switches involved is minimized by using the relation given in [BPRS91, Theorem 4.3], and yields $K = N$ and $\epsilon = 2/(\log N - 2)$ as the optimal choices. Detailed description is omitted.

Theorem 5.1 $NC^1 \subseteq Mesh\_LRN(O(1), N, poly(N))$. ∎

Suppose that we would like to compute some function having a circuit of depth $O(c \log N)$ on a given LRN mesh M whose dimensions are fixed (and are not a function of N). Let $L_1 \times L_2$ be the dimensions of M. The specific $N \times KN^{(1+\epsilon)c}$ rectangle used in the proof of Theorem 5.1 may be embedded on M, e.g., in a snake-like form. If the rectangle fits into M as a whole, then we are done. As N gets larger, however, computation can not be completed in a single sweep. Rather, it is executed in *supersteps.* Detailed description is omitted again.

Corollary 5.1 *If $L_1 \geq N$ and $L_2 > 2N$, then a problem having a $O(c \log N)$ depth circuit is computable by the $L_1 \times L_2$ LRN mesh in $O(N^{(1+2/(\log N-2))c+1}/(L_1(L_2-2N)))$ steps.* ∎

The requirements $L_2 > 2N$ and $L_1 \geq N$ may be eased considerably, by choosing $K \ll N$. Then, we need $L_2 > 2K$ and $L_1 \geq K$. The price for this modification is in the original rectangle construction becoming longer, so that the computation takes more steps.

Corollary 5.2 *For all $K \geq 16$, if $L_1 \geq K$, $L_2 > 2K$ and $L_1^2/K^2 \leq N$, then a problem that is computable by a circuit of depth $O(c \log N)$ can be computed by the $L_1 \times L_2$ LRN mesh in $O(N/L_1 + KN^{(1+2/(\log K-2))c}/(L_1(L_2-2K)))$ steps.* ∎

Using the construction of Cai and Lipton [CL89], this bound can be improved further for the case $K \geq 5$. The computation takes $O(N/L_1 + N^{1.81c}/(L_1(L_2-2K)))$ steps on the $L_1 \times L_2$ LRN mesh.

We now turn to showing that in the RN model, any general network R can be simulated by a mesh M whose size is approximately the square of that of R's size.

Lemma 5.3 $RN(O(1), S(N)) = Mesh\_RN(O(1), O(S(N)), O(S(N)))$. ∎

6 Non-Monotonic Reconfiguring Networks

This section investigates the power of the NMRN model. It is instructive to note that although this model is the most popular for implementations (e.g. [GK89]), it is also more powerful than the commonly accepted parallel models (assuming $PTIME \neq NC$), even those equipped with a shared memory unit. The main result of this section is the following theorem.

Theorem 6.1 $PTIME = NMRN(O(1), poly(N))$.

The $\subseteq$ direction of the theorem is implied by the following lemma.

Lemma 6.1 [BPRS91] *Any circuit of depth d and constant fan-in can be simulated by a non-monotonic RN in constant time and maximum bus length d.* ∎

As a more illustrative example to the power of non monotonic RN, let us consider the well studied problem of computing the *Lexicographically-First Maximal Independent Set (Lex-MIS)* in a given graph. This problem is often used as a canonical example for a $PTIME$-complete problem just as is the CVP. In [BPRS91] it is shown that $Lex - MIS$ can be solved in constant time by a $\sqrt{N} \times \sqrt{N}$ mesh in the $NMRN$ model.

Lemma 6.2 [BPRS91] $Lex - MIS \in Mesh\_NMRN(O(1), \sqrt{N}, \sqrt{N})$.

From Lemma 5.3 and Theorem 4.1 we have

$$L \subseteq Mesh\_RN(O(1), poly(N), poly(N)) \subseteq Mesh\_NMRN(O(1), poly(N), poly(N)),$$

enabling us to conclude that $PTIME \subseteq Mesh\_NMRN(O(1), poly(N), poly(N))$.

The remaining direction in the proof of Theorem 6.1 involves a simple emulation of the networks.

7 Discussion

Our results for the relations between reconfigurable complexity classes and parallel and traditional complexity classes are summarized in Figure 1. Established connections are drawn by arrows. Downward vertical arrows hold trivially and are omitted.

The importance of these relations is in indicating how hard a problem may turn to be. For example, consider the *Transitive Closure (TC)* problem. Wang and Chen [WC90a] showed that

$$TC \in RN(O(1), N^3)\ ; \qquad TC \in Mesh\_RN(O(1), N^2, N^2)\ .$$

The TC problem is related to the $s-t$ connectivity problem: "given two nodes s, t in a graph G, is there a path starting at s and leading to t?". The solution of the TC for a graph G gives the answer for this problem for all pairs of nodes s and t in G. The $s-t$ connectivity problem is known to be in RL. Showing $TC \in LRN(O(1), poly(N))$ would put TC in L, resolving a long-standing problem. Thus, although the constant time RN algorithm for TC is not very complicated, we expect a solution for TC in the (constant-time polynomial-size) LRN model to be either very difficult or impossible.

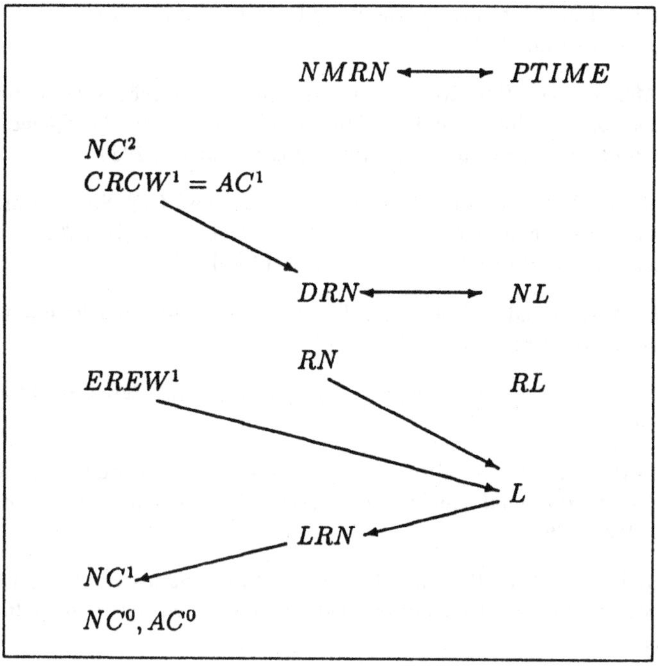

Figure 1: Reconfigurable complexity classes (classes are constant-time and polynomial-size).

References

[BPRS91] Y. Ben-Asher, D. Peleg, R. Ramaswami, and A. Schuster. The power of reconfiguration. *Journal of Parallel and Distributed Computing*, pages 139–153, 1991. Special issue on Massively Parallel Computation.

[BS91] Y. Ben-Asher and A. Schuster. Data gathering on reconfigurable networks. Technical Report Technical Report #696, Technion, October 1991.

[CL89] J. Cai and R.J. Lipton. Subquadratic simulations of circuits by branching programs. In *Proceedings of the 30th Symposium on Foundation of Computer Science*, pages 568–573. IEEE, 1989.

[GK89] J.P. Gray and T.A. Kean. Configurable hardware: A new paradigm for computation. In C.L. Seitz, editor, *Proceedings of the 10th Caltech conference on VLSI*, pages 279–295, Cambridge, MA, March 1989. MIT Press.

[HU79] J.E. Hopcroft and J.D. Ullman. *Introduction to Automata Theory, Languages and Computation.* Addison-Wesley Publishing Company, 1979.

[KR90] R.M. Karp and V. Ramachandran. A survey of parallel algorithms for shared-memory machines. In J. van Leeuwen, editor, *Handbook of Theoretical Computer Science.* North Holland, Amsterdam, 1990.

[LM89] H. Li and M. Maresca. Polymorphic-torus network. *IEEE Trans. on Computers*, 38(9):1345–1351, 1989.

[MKS89] O. Menzilcioglu, H.T. Kung, and S.W. Song. Comprehensive evaluation of a two-dimensional configurable array. In *Proceedings of the 19th Symposium on Fault-Tolerant Computing*, pages 93–100, Chicago, Illinois, 1989.

[MPRS87] R. Miller, V.K. Prasanna-Kumar, D.I. Reisis, and Q.F. Stout. Parallel computations on reconfigurable meshes. Technical Report TR IRIS#229, Dept. of Computer Science, University of Southern California, 1987.

[MR79] J.M. Moshell and J. Rothstein. Bus automata and immediate languages. *Information and Control*, 40:88–121, 1979.

[Nak87] T. Nakatani. *Interconnections by Superposed Parallel Buses.* PhD thesis, Princeton University, 1987.

[Rot76] J. Rothstein. On the ultimate limitations of parallel processing. In *Proceedings of the International Conference on Parallel Processing (best paper award)*, pages 206–212, 1976.

[RP87] D. Reisis and V.K. Prasanna-Kumar. VLSI arrays with reconfigurable busses. In *Proceedings of the 1st International Conference on SuperComputing*, pages 732–742, 1987.

[Sch91] A. Schuster. *Dynamic Reconfiguring Networks for Parallel Computers: Algorithms and Complexity Bounds.* PhD thesis, Hebrew University, Jerusalem, ISRAEL, August 1991.

[TCS89] X. Thibault, D. Comte, and P. Siron. A reconfigurable optical interconnection network for highly parallel architecture. In *Proceedings of the 2nd Symposium on the Frontiers of Massively Parallel Computation*, 1989.

[Val90] L.G. Valiant. General purpose parallel architectures. In J. van Leeuwen, editor, *Handbook of Theoretical Computer Science.* North Holland, Amsterdam, 1990.

[Wan91] B.F. Wang. *Configurational computation: a new algorithm design strategy on processor arrays with reconfigurable bus systems.* PhD thesis, National Taiwan University, June 1991.

[WC90a] B. Wang and G. Chen. Constant time algorithms for the transitive closure and some related graph problems on processor arrays with reconfigurable bus systems. *IEEE Transactions on Parallel and Distributed Systems*, 1(4), 1990.

[WC90b] B.F. Wang and G.H. Chen. Two dimensional processor array with a reconfigurable bus system is at least as powerful as CRCW model. *Information Processing Letters*, 36(1):31–36, 1990.

[WLH+87] C.C. Weems, S.P. Levitan, A.R. Hanson, E.M. Riseman, J.G. Nash, and D.B. Shu. The image understanding architecture. Technical Report COINS TR 87-76, University of Massachusetts at Amherst, 1987.

Optimal Mapping in Direct Mapped Cache Environments

(Extended Abstract)

S. Gal[1] and Y. Hollander[2] and A. Itai[2] *

[1] IBM Israel Science and Technology
Technion City, Haifa, Israel
[2] Computer Science Dept.
Technion City, Haifa, Israel

Abstract. In this paper we study positioning strategies for improving the performance of a memory system with a direct mapped cache. A positioning technique determines for every program item, (instruction or data), its address in main memory.
Assuming the Independent Reference Model, we break the general positioning problem into two: the collision minimization, and the grouping problems; and show optimal algorithms for both problems. Using these algorithms we derive an optimal algorithm for the general positioning problem. Also, we show that the quality of a class of natural assignments that distribute the items almost arbitrarily is good as long as the optimal hit ratio is sufficiently large. For the case of more restricted positionings, we find an optimal assignment for the special case of the pair assignment.
In addition we look at the expected performance gain of two frequently suggested cache features. The cache bypass feature supports the access of items in memory without loading the item into the cache. We show an assignment with best possible hit ratio which is almost always better then the optimal hit ratio. Also, it is shown that a random cache which alters the assignment of an item randomly cannot improve the expected hit ratio.
These optimal positioning algorithms can be easily integrated into an optimizing compiler. The access probabilities can be estimated statically by sophisticated compilation techniques or dynamically from traces. For programs that implement accesses to a data structure where the current step is independent of previous steps it seems that optimal hit ratio can be achieved.

1 Introduction

Typical storage systems consist of a hierarchy of several levels: The topmost level is small, fast, and expensive; each successive level is larger, slower and cheaper. This structure has been promoted since it offers expected access time close to that of the fastest level while keeping the average cost per memory cell near the cost of the cheapest level. In this paper we concentrate on the top two levels of the hierarchy, i.e., the relatively small processor cache and below it the much larger main memory.

* Visiting AT&T Bell Laboratories, 600 Mountain Avenue, Murray Hill, New Jersey

Both main memory and cache are organized as an array of lines with identical line size. To access an item the processor first checks whether the line holding the item is in the cache. If it is not there, a *cache miss* occurs and the the entire line is loaded from main memory into the cache. Due to the huge difference in the access times between cache and main memory, the performance penalty caused by a main memory access is significant. Therefore, memory system performance is measured by the *hit ratio*, H/A, where H is the number of *cache hits* (accesses that are not cache misses) and A is the total number of memory accesses. Cache organizations that exhibit best hit ratios are typically large and require complex management.

Since processor speeds have increased much faster than memory speeds, performance has become increasingly dependent on another factor – the cache access time. The best access time is achieved by small caches with simple management schemes. To this end, mappings are required to be *static* – each memory line is mapped to a single predetermined cache line, and *direct* – the cache line is determined only by the memory line. However, such caches have lower hit ratios. Extensive comparisons [6] have shown that in this tradeoff between high hit ratio and minimal access time, direct mapped caches are the preferred solution. Therefore, current research in the field has focused on improving the hit ratio of direct mapped caches by considering different positioning (mappings) of the program items to memory lines.

The number of cache misses is minimized in two steps: Grouping the program items into groups, and minimizing the inter-group collisions. Let i and i' be two program items residing in main memory lines m, m', which are mapped to the same cache line c. Whenever i' is referenced after i a cache miss occurs. These misses, called *collisions*, could be avoided by mapping m' to a cache line $c' \neq c$.

This collision minimization problem can be defined formally: Given the access sequence of the program, find an assignment of the program items to memory lines such that the expected number of misses is minimal. In [7] it is shown that finding an optimal mapping for a given access sequence is NP-Complete.

On the other hand, grouping techniques exploit the fact that whenever a main memory line is loaded into the cache, additional items (those sharing the same line) are also loaded, and if the next access is to one of these items, there is no cache miss. In particular, if all items mapped to the same main memory line are accessed consecutively, then only the first reference of each line is a miss. Therefore, it is desirable to group items in the same main memory line if they are typically accessed one after the other.

The grouping problem can be easily transformed to a graph theoretical problem: Each vertex in the graph represents a memory item. An edge (v_1, v_2) exists if v_2 is accessed shortly after v_1 or vice versa. In [7] we showed that for a cache with a single line that can hold at most two items this problem is equivalent to matching, and hence solvable in polynomial time. For larger lines the problem is NP-complete.

As a first approximation, we use the Independent Reference Model (IRM) to model the program's access pattern. In this model we assume that the probability to access an item is known and is independent of previous references. For this model we find optimal algorithms for both the collision minimization and the grouping problems. Then, using these algorithms we derive an optimal algorithm for the general positioning problem. Furthermore, we look at another natural heuristic, which distributes the items almost arbitrarily between the different lines. We show that if the hit ratio of the optimal positioning is sufficiently large then this heuristic compares favorably with the optimum.

Another interesting class of positionings is when the items are distributed evenly between the lines. We show an optimal algorithm for the special case of the pair assignment. The pair assignment is the case when the number of cache lines is exactly half the number of the program items, and the mapping assigns each cache line with equal number of program items.

In addition, we examine a frequently suggested feature for improving the cache hit ratio: The cache bypass mechanism enables accessing an item in main memory without loading it into the cache. This feature improves the hit rate since when rarely accessed items are never loaded into the cache, more frequently accessed items can stay in cache for longer periods. For a cache with the bypass feature, we show a positioning with the best possible (the upper bound) cache hit ratio.

Finally, we show that a random cache where the assignment of an item is determined by a coin tossing with a given probability does not improve the expected hit ratio

In this extended abstract we only present our results. The more technical proofs will appear in the full paper. The rest of the paper is organized as follows: In Section 2 we discuss previous work done in the area of program items positioning. Next we define exactly the cache model and the program access pattern representation. In Sections 4,5 and 6 we give the optimal algorithms for the collision minimization, the grouping and the general positioning problems. In Section 7 we consider positioning that have some restrictions on their structure. Next we consider the possibility of bypassing the cache (Section 8) and the random cache (Section 9). Section 10 completes the paper with conclusions.

2 Related Work

Most previous work showed that intelligent positioning of program items improves the memory system performance by reducing the number of cache misses. The different works assumed different cache and program models. However, no comparison regarding the relative power of the different program models, e.g., full trace, call graph etc, was done. Furthermore, for a given model it was not clear, whether the problems can be solved efficiently and if so, were the suggested algorithms optimal?

Early work concentrated on virtual memory environments. Since pages can be put anywhere in memory the focus was given mostly to the grouping problem. Hartfield and Gerald [4] used a graph clustering algorithm to group routines that executed one after the other onto the same page. Hartly [5] employed duplication of code modules and inline expansion to extend locality.

On the cache memory level more attention was given to techniques that minimize the number of collisions. Agarwal et al. [1] suggested to sort procedures on the basis of the frequency of call, and assigning the frequently called ones to different cache blocks. Hwu and Chang [9] looked at direct mapped instruction caches. They used profile data to guide in the positioning of basic blocks. McFarling [8], looking at direct mapped instruction caches, used profile data for excluding instructions from being loaded into the cache and therefore, avoid replacing more frequently used instructions that are already loaded. He, also suggested a mapping technique that reduces the expected number of collisions. Gupta and Chi [3] worked on instruction caches and suggested code duplication and code propagation to reduce cache pollution (instructions that are fetched into the cache and never used).

3 The Model

We first define both the program access pattern representation and the cache model.

3.1 The Program Model

Programs reference both instructions and data elements, which we collectively call *program items* and number them $1, 2, \ldots, n$. We shall assume that all program items have the same size.

The program runtime behavior can be represented in several ways, the most detailed of which is its trace. The trace is an ordered list of all memory references made by the program for a specific input. Since usually traces are huge, considering the full trace is often impractical. One alternative is to use a sample of the trace and hope that it accurately represents the entire trace.

As a first approximation, we assume the Independent Reference Model (IRM). According to this approach the program trace is modeled as a sequence of independent, identically distributed random variables Y_t with:

$$Pr(Y_t = j) = p_j \quad \text{for all } t \text{ and } 1 \leq j \leq n.$$

Thus, the runtime behavior of a program with n items is represented by ***appearance probabilities*** $p_1, \ldots, p_n$. This model was previously assumed for probabilistic analysis of demand paging algorithms in environments with full associative caches (see, [2]).

3.2 The Cache Model

According to our model, memory is not homogeneous but consists of a *cache* of L *lines* of fast memory, and a slower memory consisting of L *blocks*. The ith block is mapped to the ith cache line, i.e., when a referenced program item is not in the cache, a *cache miss* occurs, the item is loaded from the slow memory into the cache; if the item resides in the ith block, it is loaded into the ith cache line, replacing the item occupying that line. Such a mapping is called *direct mapping*: Each item is mapped to a single line and this assignment is unchanged during the entire execution.

4 The Collision Minimization Problem

Our goal is to minimize the expected number of the collisions by mapping competing items into different cache lines. Let S be partition of the program items $1..n$ into L disjoint sets $S = S_1, S_2, \ldots, S_L$. Let E_i be the event that item i was referenced. Using Bayes' formula we obtain:

$$Pr_S(hit) = \sum_{k=1}^{n} Pr(hit \mid E_k) * p_k = \sum_{i=1}^{L} \sum_{k \in S_i} Pr(hit\ in\ S_i \mid E_k) * p_k$$

Since we have assumed independence between the present and the previous reference, $Pr(hit\ in\ S_i \mid E_k)$ is equal to the probability that the previous reference to line i was made by item k, which is equal to $p_k / \sum_{j \in S_i} p_j$. Thus, the probability of a cache hit becomes:

$$Pr_S(hit) = \sum_{i=1}^{L} \frac{\sum_{k \in S_i} {p_k}^2}{\sum_{k \in S_i} p_k}. \tag{1}$$

We are looking for is an assignment of the program items that maximizes (1). Consider first the case that $L = 2$. Also, assume that the appearance probabilities are nonincreasing, i.e.,

$$p_1 \geq p_2 \geq \ldots \geq p_n.$$

We shall show that it is always optimal to assign item 1 to the first cache line and all other items to the second one. This rule, which we call "Separate the largest", leads to an assignment which is somewhat counterintuitive. For example, if we have 101 items, the first with probability 1% and the others with equal probability of 0.99% then this rule puts 1% of the probability weight into the first line and 99% into the second line. This may seem strange, yet it is optimal as the theorem following the next lemma shows.

Lemma 1. *Let A and B be any disjoint mutually exclusive sets of the items $2..n$. Then*

$$p_1 + \frac{\sum_2^n p_i^2}{\sum_2^n p_i} \geq \frac{p_1^2 + \sum_A p_i^2}{p_1 + \sum_A p_i} + \frac{\sum_B p_i^2}{\sum_B p_i}. \tag{2}$$

If $p_1 > p_n$ then inequality (2) is strict.

The proof is technical and will appear in the full paper. It is easy to generalize (2) for the case of L lines:

Theorem 2. *The optimal cache assignment of L lines is to assign each of the items $1, 2, \ldots, L-1$ to different lines and all remaining items $L, L+1, \ldots, n$ to line L.*

Proof sketch: By induction on the number of cache lines. We use the generalization of Lemma 1 for the induction step. □

5 The Grouping Problem

In previous sections we assumed that a cache line can hold only a single program item. However, often each cache line can hold more than that. In this section we study the effect that this increase of line capacity has on the expected hit probability. The model we assume here is of a cache that has a single line ($L = 1$) and the line capacity (denoted by C) is greater than 1. In such a cache, the only way to reduce the number of misses is to take advantage of the fact that on a cache miss, not only the referenced item is loaded into the cache, and accessing any of these additional items will not cause a cache miss.

A grouping $G = G_1, \ldots, G_K$ is a partition of the program items into K disjoint subsets such that $|G_j| \leq C$ for $1 \leq j \leq K$.

Let E_i be the event that item i is referenced. Then, the hit probability is the sum of the hit probabilities for the different items which is:

$$Pr_G(hit) = \sum_{i=1}^{n} Pr(hit \mid E_i) * p_i = \sum_{j=1}^{K} \sum_{i \in G_j} Pr(hit\, in\, G_j \mid E_i) * p_i.$$

Since we have assumed independence between the present and the previous reference $Pr(hit\, in\, G_j \mid E_i)$ is equal to the probability that the previous reference was to one of the elements in G_j which is equal to $\sum_{l \in G_j} p_l$. Thus, the probability of a cache hit becomes:

$$\begin{aligned} Pr_G(hit) &= \sum_{j=1}^{K} \sum_{i \in G_j} p_i \sum_{l \in Gj} p_l \\ &= \sum_{j=1}^{K} \Big(\sum_{i \in G_j} p_i\Big)^2. \end{aligned} \tag{3}$$

We are looking for a grouping that maximizes (3). In the next theorem we show that ordering the items by decreasing probability, taking the first C items as G_1, the next C items as G_2 and so on is optimal.

Theorem 3. *Let* $1..n$ *be the set of the program items with appearance probabilities* $p_1 \geq p_2 \geq \ldots \geq p_n$. *Let* $G = G_1, \ldots, G_K$ *be a grouping of the program items such that for each* $1 \leq j < K$, $G_j = (j-1)*C+1, \ldots, j*C$ *and* $G_K = (K-1)*C+1, \ldots, n$. *Then, for every grouping* A:

$$Pr_A(hit) \leq Pr_G(hit). \tag{4}$$

Proof. Every grouping G defines a set C_G of K super variables such that $C_j = \{\sum_{i \in S_j} p_i : 1 \leq j \leq K\}$. Maximizing equation (3) can also be seen as finding the maximum of the function f of K variables:

$$f(C_1, \ldots, C_K) = \sum_{j=1}^{K} C_j^2.$$

under the constraint that $C_i \geq 0$ and $\sum C_j = 1$.

Consider a pair C_i, C_j such that $C_i \geq C_j$ and fix all the other variables. Thus $C_i + C_j = X$ is a constant, and f becomes a function of a single variable C_i.

$$f(C_i) = C_i^2 + (X - C_i)^2 + \sum_{l \neq i,j} C_l^2.$$

Differentiating f with respect to C_i yields

$$\begin{aligned} \frac{\partial f}{\partial C_i} &= 4C_i - 2X \\ &= 2(C_i - C_j) \geq 0. \end{aligned}$$

Thus, f is a nondecreasing function of C_i. Therefore, putting maximum probability in C_i maximizes f. Since we used the fact that the total sum of the probabilities equals 1, only to show that $C_i + C_j$ is a constant, the same proof is valid also when $\sum C_k$ = constant < 1, and the same argument can be applied on the remaining probabilities until all of them are grouped. □

6 The Positioning Problem

After considering separately the two subproblems of the positioning problem, we are ready to look for an optimal mapping in the general case. We assume that the cache has several lines, each of which can hold several program items, i.e., $L \geq 1$ and $C \geq 1$.

A *mapping* S is a partitioning of the program items into L disjoint sets $\{S_j \mid 1 \leq j \leq L\}$. All items within S_j are mapped to the same cache line (j). The items within each S_j are further divided into disjoint groups $G_{j,l}$ with each $|G_{j,l}| \leq C$. Suppose item i belongs to $G_{j,l}$. If a cache miss occurs when referencing item i, the entire group $G_{j,l}$ is loaded into the cache.

In the full paper we use the results of the previous sections to find an optimal mapping:

Theorem 4. *Let* $1, 2, \ldots, n$ *be the set of the program items with appearance probabilities* $p_1 \geq p_2 \geq \ldots \geq p_n$. *The optimal mapping* S *to a cache with* $L \geq 1$ *lines and line capacity* $C \geq 1$ *is as follows: The first* $L-1$ *blocks hold the first* $(L-1)C$ *items in order of decreasing probabilities, and the last block holds all the remaining items, i.e.,* $S_1 = \{1, \ldots, C\}$, $\ldots$, $S_{L-1} = \{(L-2)*C+1, \ldots, (L-1)*C\}$, *and* $S_L = \{\{(L-1)*C+1, \ldots, L*C\}, \{L*C+1, \ldots, (L+1)*C\}, \ldots, \{\lfloor \frac{n}{C} \rfloor * C+1, \ldots, n\}\}$

Proof sketch: Group according to Theorem 3 and then consider the items of each group as one super-variable, and apply Theorem 2. □

7 Restricted Mappings

Our previous results concerning the optimal positioning are somehow surprising. We did not assume any restrictions on the partitioning and indeed, the optimal assignment to lines distributes the items unevenly between the different lines: a single line is assigned most of the items while the rest of the lines are assigned with C items each. This kind of partitioning might be impractical for some architectures since it would require that one block be large enough to hold all but $(L-1)C$ items.

In the next subsection we look at partitions that obey some restrictions on their structure. First, we consider partitions where each of the L most probable items, $p_1, \ldots, p_L$, are assigned to a different line and the remaining items are distributed arbitrarily among the lines. This family of partitions seems reasonable, items with high probability do not interfere with each other and hopefully the penalty caused by items with low appearance probability is small.

In subsection 7.2 we consider partitions into groups of equal size and show an optimal solution for a special case, the pair assignment case.

7.1 Almost Arbitrary Partitions

Here we consider only the family of partitions ARB that distribute all but the L most probable items arbitrarily. For simplicity, we assume that the cache line can hold only a single item at a time. In the following theorem we bound the difference between the hit probability of the optimal partitioning and the expected hit probability of a partition $S \in ARB$

Theorem 5. *Let $1, 2, \ldots, n$ be the set of the program items with appearance probabilities $p_1 \geq p_2 \geq \ldots \geq p_n$. Let $S = \{S_1 = \{1, \ldots\}, S_2 = \{2, \ldots\}, \ldots, S_L = \{L, \ldots\}\} \in ARB$ be a partitioning of the program items, then*

$$Pr_{OPT}(hit) - Pr_S(hit) \leq \frac{1}{4}. \tag{5}$$

Proof. We will prove the theorem only for $L = 2$. For the general case the proof is identical. Let us denote by $d_i = (\sum_{j \in S_i} p_j) - p_i$. We will show that

$$p_1 + \frac{p_2^2 + \ldots + p_n^2}{p_2 + \ldots + p_n} - \left(\frac{\sum_{i \in S_1} p_i^2}{p_1 + d_1} + \frac{\sum_{i \in S_2} p_i^2}{p_2 + d_2} \right) \leq \frac{1}{4}.$$

Note that

$$\begin{aligned} Pr_S(hit) &= \frac{\sum_{i \in S_1} p_i^2}{p_1 + d_1} + \frac{\sum_{i \in S_2} p_i^2}{p_2 + d_2} \geq \frac{p_1^2}{p_1 + d_1} + \frac{p_2^2}{p_2 + d_2} \qquad (6) \\ &= \frac{p_1^2 + p_1 d_1 - p_1 d_1}{p_1 + d_1} + \frac{p_2^2 + p_2 d_2 - p_2 d_2}{p_2 + d_2} \\ &= p_1 + p_2 - \frac{p_1 d_1}{p_1 + d_1} - \frac{p_2 d_2}{p_2 + d_2} \qquad (7) \end{aligned}$$

from (7) and the fact that $p_2 \geq \frac{p_2^2 + \ldots + p_n^2}{p_2 + \ldots + p_n}$ we conclude that:

$$Pr_{opt}(hit) - Pr_s(hit) \leq \frac{p_1 d_1}{p_1 + d_1} + \frac{p_2 d_2}{p_2 + d_2}. \tag{8}$$

The expression on the right hand side of (8) is an n variable function. The hit probabilities difference can be bounded by finding the maximum of this function, subject to the constraint

$$p_1 + p_2 + d_1 + d_2 = 1.$$

Using Lagrange multipliers we can show $p_i = d_j = \frac{1}{4}$. Substituting p_i and d_j in f the maximum is found to be $\frac{1}{4}$. □

We now show a lower bound on the performance of ARB. Again, let $S \in ARB$ and for convenience let $R = \sum_{i=1}^{L} p_i$. Since $Pr_{OPT}(hit) \leq R$ it remains to find a lower bound on $Pr_S(hit)$.

Theorem 6. *Let $1, 2, \ldots, n$ be the set of the program items with appearance probabilities $p_1 \geq p_2 \geq \ldots \geq p_n$. Let $S = \{S_1 = \{1, \ldots\}, S_2 = \{2, \ldots\}, \ldots, S_L = \{L, \ldots\}\} \in ARB$ be a partitioning of the program items, then*

$$P_S(hit) \geq R^2$$

Proof.

$$Pr_S(hit) \geq \sum_{j=1}^{L} \frac{p_j^2}{p_j + d_j} \tag{9}$$

since an inequality similar to (6) holds also for a cache with L lines. The expression on the right hand side of (9) is a function of the variables $d_1, \ldots, d_L$. Thus, the hit probability can be bounded by finding the minimum of this function. Using Lagrange multipliers we can show the requested result. □

From the above theorem it is obvious that:

$$\frac{Pr_S(hit)}{Pr_{OPT}(hit)} \geq R.$$

These two bounds are tight. Let $p_1 \geq p_2 \geq \ldots \geq p_{L-1} > p_L = p_{L+1} = \ldots = p_n = \epsilon$ be the access probabilities. For the above probabilities it is always possible to choose a partition S such that $d_j + p_j = p_j/R$ for every $1 \leq j \leq L$. For such S the expected hit probability is:

$$\sum_{j=1}^{L} \frac{p_j^2}{p_j/R} = R^2 + o(\epsilon)$$

Therefore, for the above case the heuristic's quality is $o(R) + \epsilon$ and if $R = 0.5$ then $Pr_{OPT}(hit) - Pr_S(hit) \approx R - R^2 = \frac{1}{4}$.

Thus, ARB is a poor heuristic for small R, but in that case, even OPT does not perform well. When $Pr_{OPT}(hit)$ is large, since $R - p_L \leq Pr_{OPT}(hit) \leq R$ then R is also large and therefore, $Pr_{S \in ARB}(hit) \geq R^2$ is also relatively large.

7.2 Pair Assignment

The pair assignment is the case when the number of cache lines is exactly half the number of the program items, i.e., $L = n/2$. In this case we look for an optimal solution that assigns exactly two items to each line. The model assumed here is of a cache with L lines and line capacity 1.

Let $S = (S_1, \ldots, S_L)$ be a pair assignment of the program items $1, \ldots, 2L$ such that $S_j = \{i_{j_1}, i_{j_2}\}$ for $1 \leq j \leq L$. The expected hit probability of S is:

$$\sum_{j=1}^{L} \frac{p_{i_{j_1}}^2 + p_{i_{j_2}}^2}{p_{i_{j_1}} + p_{i_{j_2}}}. \tag{10}$$

In the following theorem we show how to maximize (10).

Theorem 7. *Let $1, 2, \ldots, 2L$ be the set of the program items with appearance probabilities $p_1 \geq p_2 \geq \ldots \geq p_{2L}$. Let $OPT = \{\{1, 2L\}, \{2, 2L-1\}, \ldots, \{L, L+1\}\}$ be a pair assignment. Then, for every pair assignment S*

$$Pr_{OPT}(hit) \geq Pr_S(hit).$$

Proof. Let $S = \{\{1,k\},\{j,2L\},\ldots\}$ such that $p_k > p_{2L}$, and $p_1 > p_j$. Let $S' = \{\{1,2L\},\{j,k\},\ldots\}$ the pair assignment generated by exchanging items k and $2L$ in S. We will show that S is not optimal since $Pr_{S'}(hit) > Pr_S(hit)$.

It is sufficient to show that:

$$\frac{p_j^2+p_k^2}{p_j+p_k}+\frac{p_1^2+p_{2L}^2}{p_1+p_{2L}} > \frac{p_1^2+p_k^2}{p_1+p_k}+\frac{p_{2L}^2+p_j^2}{p_j+p_{2L}}.$$

The proof is technical and will appear in the full paper.

Thus, we proved that it is always best to pair p_1 and p_{2L}. Now we can use the same argument for the remaining items and pair items 2 and $2L-1$ and so on. □

8 Cache Bypass

Cache bypassing, i.e., the ability to avoid loading into the cache a referenced item seems to be attractive. Obviously, an optimal offline algorithm will not load into the cache an item that is referenced only once before being replaced. The decision whether to load a given item into the cache when referenced can be done each time the item is referenced or alternatively it can be done only once prior to execution (statically).

Since we do not know the reference pattern, we only consider the static approach. From examining the optimal assignment's hit probability it is obvious that the upper bound on the expected hit probability for a cache with L lines is:

$$\sum_{j=1}^{L} p_j \tag{11}$$

since $\frac{\sum_{j=L}^{n} p_j^2}{\sum_{j=L}^{n} p_j} \le p_L$. But (11) is also the expected hit probability if only items $1,\ldots,L$ are loaded into the cache and all references to other items bypass cache. Thus, we can estimate the gain attainable by employing a cache bypassing feature. Similarly, the same argument holds for a cache with line capacity larger then 1.

9 Can Randomization Help?

A natural question from the theoretical point of view is whether adding randomization to the direct mapped cache mechanism improves performance. In a random cache, each memory line can be mapped to one of k predetermined cache lines. When a cache miss occurs, the specific memory line is determined by a coin tossing with a given probability. More practically, the random cache can be used as a model for the ***k-set associative*** cache memory where each memory line is mapped to one of k cache lines and the specific line is determined by a replacement algorithm such as LRU.

Our cache model is of a random cache with 2 lines and line capacity 1. Let $S = \{S_1, S_2\}$ be a partition of the program items with an arbitrary program item $i \in S_1$. Also, for convenience let us use the following notations: $c_1 = \sum_{j\in S_1} p_j - p_i$ and

$c_2 = \sum_{j \in S_2} p_j$ for the probability sums for the different lines and $t_1 = \sum_{j \in S_1} p_j^2 - p_i^2$ and $t_2 = \sum_{j \in S_2} p_j^2$ for sum of probability squares for the different lines.

The function

$$g(x) = \frac{t_1 + x^2 p_i^2}{c_1 + xp} + \frac{t_2 + (1-x)^2 p_i^2}{c_2 + (1-x)p_i} \tag{12}$$

represents the expected hit probability when item i is assigned to the first line a proportion x of the time and to the second line with proportion $1-x$ of the time. In the following theorem we look for the proportion that maximizes the hit probability.

Theorem 8. *Let $S = \{S_1, S_2\}$ be a partitioning of the program items. Then for all* $0 < x < 1$

$$g(x) < \max\{\frac{t_2 + p_i^2}{c_2 + p_i} + \frac{t_1}{c_1}, \frac{t_1 + p_i^2}{c_1 + p_i} + \frac{t_2}{c_2}\}. \tag{13}$$

Proof sketch: We show that $g(x)$ is convex for this interval and therefore obtains its maximal value either in $x = 0$ or in $x = 1$ which corresponds to the right hand side of (12). □

It follows from theorem 8 that it is always better to assign each item to one of the lines instead of randomly switching it between the two lines. This theorem can be easily extended for a cache with $k \geq 2$ lines.

10 Conclusions

In this paper we studied positioning strategies for improving the performance of a memory system with a direct mapped cache. Since the two basic problems, the collision minimization and the grouping problems, are NP-Complete for the full trace program model we assumed as a first approximation the Independent Reference Model as our program model. We presented optimal algorithms for both the collision minimization and the grouping problems. Then, combining both results we have shown an optimal assignment for the general positioning problem.

Since the optimal assignments distributed the items in an uneven way we have considered an assignment with more restricted structure. We looked at a natural heuristic, which distributes the items almost arbitrarily between the different lines. For positionings generated by this heuristic we showed that if the hit ratio of the optimal positioning is sufficiently large then the quality of the heuristic when compared to the optimal is good. Also, we have shown an optimal assignment for the pair assignment case.

The cache bypassing feature is a well known option for improving cache performance. We showed that an assignment with best possible hit ratio which is almost always better then the optimal assignment is possible. Finally, we considered the question of a random cache. We have shown that a random cache which alters the assignment of an item randomly can not improve the expected hit ratio.

These optimal assignments can be easily integrated into an optimizing compiler. The access probabilities can be estimated statically by sophisticated compilation techniques or dynamically from traces. For programs that implement accesses to a data structure it seems that best possible hit ratio can be achieved.

References

1. A. Agarwal, P. Chow, M. Horowitz, J. Acken, A. Saltz, and J. Hennessy. On chip caches for high performance processors. In *Proc. of Conf. on Advanced Research in VLSI*, pages 1–24, Stanford Univ.,Univ. of California, Berkeley, March 87. edited by P. Losleben.
2. P. A. Franaszek and T.J. Wagner. Some distribution free aspects of paging algorithm performance. *JACM*, 21(1):31–39, January 74.
3. Rajiv Gupta and Chi-Hung Chi. Improving instruction cache behavior by reducing cache pollution. In *Proceedings Supercomputing 90*, pages 82–91, November 1990.
4. D. J. Hartfield and J. Gerald. Program restructuring for virtual memory. *IBM Systems Journal*, 10(3):168–192, 1971.
5. S. J. Hartly. Compile-time program restructuring in multiprogrammed virtual memory systems. *IEEE Trans. on SW Eng.*, 14(11):1640–1644, November 1988.
6. M. D. Hill. *Aspects of Cache Memory and Instruction Buffer Performance*. PhD thesis, Univ. of California, Berkeley, 1987.
7. Yona Hollander and Alon Itai. The offline mapping problem for direct mapped caches is NP-complete. In preparation, 91.
8. Scott McFarling. Program optimization for instruction caches. In *Third International Conf. on Architectural Support for Programming Languages and Operating Systems*, pages 183–191, April 89.
9. Wen mei W. Hwu and Pohua P. Chang. Achieving high instruction cache performance with an optimizing compiler. In *Proc. 16th. Sym. on Computer Architecture*, pages 242–250, Jerusalem, Israel, May 89.

This article was processed using the LaTeX macro package with LLNCS style

New Algorithms for Generalized Network Flows

Edith Cohen[1] * and Nimrod Megiddo[2] **

[1] AT&T Bell Laboratories, Murray Hill, NJ 07974.
[2] IBM Research, Almaden Research Center, San Jose, CA 95120, and School of Mathematical Sciences, Tel Aviv University, Tel Aviv, Israel.

Abstract. This paper is concerned with generalized network flow problems. In a generalized network, each edge $e = (u, v)$ has a positive "flow multiplier" a_e associated with it. The interpretation is that if a flow of x_e enters the edge at node u, then a flow of $a_e x_e$ exits the edge at v.
The uncapacitated generalized transshipment problem (UGT) is defined on a generalized network where demands and supplies (real numbers) are associated with the vertices and costs (real numbers) are associated with the edges. The goal is to find a flow such that the excess or deficit at each vertex equals the desired value of the supply or demand, and the sum over the edges of the product of the cost and the flow is minimized. Adler and Cosares [1] reduced the restricted uncapacitated generalized transshipment problem, where only demand nodes are present, to solving a system of linear inequalities with two variables per inequality. The algorithms presented in [2, 3, 4] result in a faster algorithm for restricted UGT.
Generalized circulation is defined on a generalized network with demands at the nodes and capacity constraints on the edges (i.e., upper bounds on the amount of flow). The goal is to find a flow such that the flow excesses at the nodes are proportional to the demands and maximized. We present a new algorithm that solves the capacitated generalized flow problem by iteratively solving instances of UGT. The algorithm can be used to find an optimal flow or an approximation. When used to find a constant factor approximation, the algorithm yields a bound which is not only more efficient than previous algorithms but also strongly polynomial. It is believed to be the first strongly polynomial approximation algorithm for generalized circulation. The existence of such an approximation algorithm is interesting since it is not known whether the exact problem has a strongly polynomial algorithm.

* Research was done while the first author was attending Stanford University and IBM Almaden Research Center. Research partially supported by ONR grant ONR-N00014-91-C-0026 and by NSF PYI Grant CCR-8858097, matching funds from AT&T and DEC.
** Research partially supported by ONR-N00014-91-C-0026

1 Introduction

A *generalized network* is a digraph $G = (V, E)$ given together with positive *flow multipliers* a_e $(e \in E)$ associated with the edges. The multiplier a_e $(e \in E)$ is interpreted as a gain factor (when $a_e > 1$) or a loss factor (when $a_e < 1$) of flow along the edge e; if x_e units of flow enter the edge e, then $a_e x_e$ units exit. Generalized network flows are also known in the literature as *flows with losses and gains.* They can be used to model many situations that arise in financial analysis [7, 8, 11].

The uncapacitated generalized transshipment problem (UGT) is defined on a generalized network, where costs are given for the edges and supplies or demands are given for the nodes. The goal is to find a flow of minimum cost, which satisfies the supply and demand requirements. Adler and Cosares [1] gave an algorithm for solving restricted instances of UGT where there are many sources and no sinks. Their algorithm is based on solving the dual linear programming problem. In this case the constraints of the dual problem comprise a TVPI[3] system with a special property, which we call *monotonicity*, namely, in each inequality there is at most one positive and at most one negative coefficient. Hence, the results of [2, 3, 4] imply better time bounds for restricted UGT.

In the generalized circulation problem (GC) we consider a generalized network where (nonnegative) demands are associated with the nodes and capacities are associated with the edges. The goal is to find a feasible flow which maximizes the fraction of the satisfied demand. Goldberg, Plotkin, and Tardos [8] presented an algorithm for the more general capacitated generalized transshipment problem without costs. Their algorithm is based on solving an instance of GC with a single supply node, the *source*, and performs additional computation of $O(mn)$ time. We present a scheme for solving generalized circulation problems by iteratively relaxing the capacity constraints. An iteration features (i) solving an instance of UGT on the same network with costs chosen with respect to the capacities, (ii) scaling the flow to a feasible one, and (iii) replacing the capacities by the residual capacities calculated relative to the latter flow.

Our scheme introduces a general method of approximating a solution to linear programming problems of the following form:

$$(P) \qquad \begin{aligned} \text{Maximize } & t \\ \text{subject to } & \boldsymbol{Ax} = t\boldsymbol{b} \\ & \boldsymbol{Ux} \le \boldsymbol{d} \\ & \boldsymbol{x} \ge \boldsymbol{0}\,, \end{aligned}$$

where $\boldsymbol{A} \in R^{n\times m}$, $\boldsymbol{O} \le \boldsymbol{U} \in R^{\ell\times m}$, $\boldsymbol{b} \in R^n$, and $\boldsymbol{0} \le \boldsymbol{d} \in R^\ell$. The system $\boldsymbol{Ux} \le \boldsymbol{d}$ may be viewed as a set of generalized capacity constraints. Denote by t^* the maximum of (P). Suppose that for $\boldsymbol{c} \ge \boldsymbol{0}$ the following problem is relatively easy:

$$(E) \qquad \begin{aligned} \text{Minimize } & \boldsymbol{c}^T\boldsymbol{x} \\ \text{subject to } & \boldsymbol{Ax} = \boldsymbol{b} \\ & \boldsymbol{x} \ge \boldsymbol{0}\,. \end{aligned}$$

[3] Two Variables per Inequality

We will show that by solving a single instance of (E) (with a suitable $\boldsymbol{c}$) a feasible solution $(\boldsymbol{x}', t') \in R^{n+1} \times R$ of (P) can be found such that $t' \geq t^*/\ell$.

Consider the generalized circulation problem with the relaxed goal of computing a flow which satisfies a fraction of the demand which approximates within a constant factor the best attainable fraction. For the relaxed problem, the scheme described above yields a strongly polynomial time algorithm, which we also believe is the fastest known algorithm in a certain range of the input parameters. This scheme also yields an algorithm for obtaining an optimal solution, which is the fastest known for a certain range of the input parameters.

In Section 2 we define the UGT problem and review the algorithm of Adler and Cosares [1]. In Section 3 we introduce the approximation algorithm and apply it to the generalized circulation problem. In Section 4 we introduce bidirected generalized networks and discuss the UGT and generalized circulation problems on these networks. Section 5 contains concluding remarks.

Note that for instances of the problems mentioned above we need to consider cases where $m = \Omega(n^2)$. The algorithms presented here handle multiple edges within the stated time bounds.

2 The Generalized Transshipment Problem

Given a graph $G = (V, E)$, for every $i \in V$ we denote by $\text{in}(i)$ and $\text{out}(i)$ the sets of edges that go into and out of i, respectively.

Problem 2.1 [Uncapacitated Generalized Transshipment (UGT)]
Given is a generalized network, consisting of a graph $G = (V, E)$ with flow multipliers a_e and edge-costs c_e $(e \in E)$, and supplies (or demands) b_i $(i \in V)$. Find a flow function $\boldsymbol{x} = (x_e)_{e \in E}$ to solve the following:

$$\begin{aligned} \text{Minimize } & \sum_{e \in E} c_e x_e \\ \text{subject to } & \sum_{e \in \text{in}(i)} a_e x_e - \sum_{e \in \text{out}(i)} x_e = b_i \quad (i \in V) \\ & x_e \geq 0 \quad (e \in E) . \end{aligned}$$

When $b_i < 0$ (resp., $b_i > 0$), we call i a *sink* (resp., *source*). The dual linear programming problem can be stated as follows. Find $\pi_1, \ldots, \pi_n$ to solve the following:

$$\begin{aligned} \text{Maximize } & \sum_{i=1}^{n} b_i \pi_i \\ \text{subject to } & \pi_i - a_e \pi_j \leq c_e \quad (e = (i,j) \in E) . \end{aligned}$$

Note that the set of constraints of the dual problem is monotone in the sense defined above.

In this section we consider restricted instances of UGT where either there are only sinks ($\boldsymbol{b} \geq \boldsymbol{0}$) or there are only sources ($\boldsymbol{b} \leq \boldsymbol{0}$). Adler and Cosares [1] proposed a scheme for solving a subclass of linear programming problems in standard form[4] where each variable appears in at most two equations. In particular,

[4] In the standard form the constraints are in the form $Ax = b$, $x \geq \boldsymbol{0}$.

that scheme is applicable to restricted UGT instances. They showed that these instances can be solved by using one application of Megiddo's algorithm for TVPI systems [12]. An application of the faster algorithms for TVPI systems presented in [2, 3, 4] can be used instead. Hence, restricted UGT instances can be solved in $O\left(mn^2(\log m + \log^2 n)\right)$ time, deterministically, and when using randomization, in $O\left(n^3 \log n + mn(\log m \log^3 n + \log^5 n)\right)$ expected time.

We now characterize the problems to which the scheme of [1] applies. Consider a linear programming problem in standard form

$$(SF) \qquad \begin{aligned} \text{Minimize } & \boldsymbol{c}^T \boldsymbol{x} \\ \text{subject to } & \boldsymbol{A}\boldsymbol{x} = \boldsymbol{b} \\ & \boldsymbol{x} \geq \boldsymbol{0} \end{aligned}$$

where each column of $\boldsymbol{A} \in R^{n \times m}$ contains at most two non-zeros. Denote by $\boldsymbol{x}^* \in R^m$ an optimal solution of (SF). Note that the dual of (SF) amounts to maximizing an arbitrary objective function subject to a TVPI system. Consider the problems

$$(SF_i) \qquad \begin{aligned} \text{Minimize } & \boldsymbol{c}^T \boldsymbol{x} \\ \text{subject to } & \boldsymbol{A}\boldsymbol{x} = b_i \boldsymbol{e}^i \\ & \boldsymbol{x} \geq \boldsymbol{0} \end{aligned}$$

$(i = 1, \ldots, n)$[5] suppose $\boldsymbol{x}^{(i)}$ is an optimal solution of (SF_i), $i = 1, \ldots, n$. The scheme of [1] applies to (SF) if $\boldsymbol{x}^* = \sum_{i:b_i \neq 0} \boldsymbol{x}^{(i)}$.

We now sketch the ideas used in the scheme of [1]. Let $\pi_i^{\min}$ (resp., $\pi_i^{\max}$) denote the minimum (resp., maximum) value of π_i subject to the TVPI system of constraints $\boldsymbol{A}^T \boldsymbol{\pi} \leq \boldsymbol{c}$. If $\pi_i^{\max} = \infty$ (resp., $\pi_i^{\min} = -\infty$), then (SF) is feasible only if $b_i \leq 0$ (resp., $b_i \geq 0$). If $b_i \neq 0$, a vector $\boldsymbol{x}^{(i)}$ as defined above can be constructed from a minimal subset of the dual constraints which implies (i) $\pi_i \leq \pi_i^{\max}$ if $b_i > 0$, or (ii) $\pi_i \geq \pi_i^{\min}$ if $b_i < 0$. The edges which correspond to such a minimal system comprise a generalized augmenting path [9] of flow into node i (i.e., a flow generating cycle and a path from a node on the cycle to node i). The vector $\boldsymbol{x}^{(i)}$ is obtained by adjusting the flow values on the edges while pushing flow along this augmenting path.

It is easy to see that the scheme of [1] applies to restricted UGT instances. Consider a UGT instances where $\boldsymbol{b} \geq \boldsymbol{0}$ (the arguments are similar for the case of $\boldsymbol{b} \leq \boldsymbol{0}$). The system of dual constraints is monotone, so by a single application of the algorithm of [2, 3, 4] we determine $\pi_i^{\max}$ for $i = 1, \ldots, n$ (see the sections on monotone systems in [2, 3, 4]). If $\pi_i^{\max} < \infty$, the algorithm also computes a minimal subset of dual constraints which implies that $\pi_i \leq \pi_i^{\max}$. The vector $\boldsymbol{x}^{(i)}$ can be constructed using this information. If $\pi_i^{\max} = \infty$ and $b_i > 0$, the UGT system is not feasible. Otherwise, $\boldsymbol{x}^* = \sum_{i:b_i > 0} \boldsymbol{x}^{(i)}$ is a solution.

[5] e^i is such that $e^i_j = 0$, $i \neq j$ and $e^i_i = 1$.

3 Generalized Circulation

Vaidya, 89 [16]	$O(n^2m^{1.5}\log(n\gamma))$
Kapoor and Vaidya, 88 [10]	$O(n^{2.5}m^{1.5}\log(n\gamma))$
Goldberg, Plotkin and Tardos, 88 [8]	$O(n^2m^2\log n\log^2\gamma)$

Table 1. Some previous results on generalized circulation

Definition 3.1 Consider a generalized network $G = (V, E)$, where demands $b_i \geq 0$ $(i = 1, \ldots, n)$ are associated with the nodes and capacities $c_{ij} \geq 0$ (possibly $c_{ij} = \infty$) are associated with the edges.

1. A *generalized flow* is a nonnegative flow function $\boldsymbol{x} = (x_e)_{e\in E}$ for which there exists a scalar $\hat{t} = \hat{t}(\boldsymbol{x})$ such that

$$\sum_{e\in\mathrm{in}(i)} a_e x_e - \sum_{e\in\mathrm{out}(i)} x_e = \hat{t}b_i \quad (i = 1, \ldots, n)$$

   i.e., the flow $\boldsymbol{x}$ satisfies a fraction $\hat{t}$ of the demand.
2. A generalized flow is said to be *feasible* if

$$x_e \leq c_e \quad (e \in E) .$$

Problem 3.2 [Generalized Circulation]
Given is a generalized network with demands and capacities as above. Find a feasible generalized flow $\boldsymbol{x}^*$ such that $\hat{t}(\boldsymbol{x}^*)$ is maximized. Denote $t^* \equiv \hat{t}(\boldsymbol{x}^*)$.

We refer to t^* as the *optimal* value. A feasible generalized flow $\boldsymbol{x}$ is said to be *optimal* if $\hat{t}(\boldsymbol{x}) = t^*$, and ϵ*-optimal* if $\hat{t}(\boldsymbol{x}) \geq (1-\epsilon)t^*$.

Vaidya [16] gave an $O(n^2m^{1.5}\log(n\gamma))$ time algorithm for the problem, where γ is an upper bound for all the numerators and denominators of the capacities, multipliers, and costs. Vaidya's bound is based on a specialization of his currently fastest known general purpose linear programming algorithm and relies on the theoretically fast matrix multiplication algorithms. The previously fastest known algorithm, due to Kapoor and Vaidya [10], does not rely on fast matrix multiplication, and has a bound worse by a factor of $\sqrt{n}$. A new result by Murray [13] is based on a different specialization of Vaidya's linear programming algorithm to generalized flow. Murray's generalized circulation algorithm matches the bound of [16] and does not rely on fast matrix multiplication. The algorithms of [10, 13, 16] are applicable to the more general min-cost generalized flow problem. A different algorithm, of a somewhat more combinatorial nature, was given by Goldberg, Plotkin and Tardos [8]. These results are summarized in Table 1.

3.1 A Generalized Circulation Algorithm

The algorithms discussed above are designed to find an optimal flow. We introduce an algorithm for Problem 3.2 which is based on iteratively obtaining a $(1 - 1/m)$-optimal flow and then considering the problem on the residual network. Hence, an ϵ-optimal flow can be computed in $O(m \log \epsilon^{-1})$ iterations. Note that $O(m)$ iterations suffice for any constant ϵ. The optimal value can be found within $O(m|t^*|)$ iterations, where $|t^*|$ is the number of bits of accuracy required. Note that $|t^*| \leq m \log(n\gamma)$, where γ is the maximum value of any numerator or denominator of a capacity or a multiplier in the network.

We discuss the complexity of each iteration. In Subsection 3.2 we introduce an approximation method that allows us to find a $(1 - 1/m)$-optimal feasible generalized flow by solving a single UGT instance on the same generalized network, where the capacity constraints are relaxed and costs are introduced. It follows that each iteration of our algorithm amounts to solving an instance of the restricted UGT problem.

The resulting deterministic and randomized bounds for computing an ϵ-optimal generalized circulation are summarized in Table 2. We believe our algorithm is more practical than [16]. When the algorithm is used to find an approximate solution, we achieve strongly polynomial time bounds which are also strictly better than those of [8, 10], and better than those of [16] in a certain range of the parameters (e.g., when the size of the binary encoding of capacities and multipliers is large). The algorithm also yields improved time bounds for obtaining an optimal solution in a certain range of the parameters, e.g., when we know the number of bits in the binary encoding of t^* is small.

Computing an ϵ-optimal flow:	
expected time	$O\left(m \log \epsilon^{-1}\left(n^3 \log n + mn(\log m \log^3 n + \log^5 n)\right)\right)$
deterministic	$O\left(m^2 n^2 \log \epsilon^{-1}(\log m + \log^2 n)\right)$
Computing the optimal solution:	
expected time	$\tilde{O}\left(\lvert t^*\rvert(mn^3 + m^2 n)\right)$
deterministic	$\tilde{O}(\lvert t^*\rvert m^2 n^2)$

Table 2. Bounds for generalized circulation

Note that when $\epsilon = 1/q(m,n)$, for some polynomial q, an ϵ-optimal flow can be found in strongly polynomial time. It is still not known whether a strongly polynomial time algorithm exists for finding an optimal solution. This question is of a particular interest because generalized circulation is one of the simplest classes of linear programming problems for which no strongly polynomial algorithm is yet known [8, 15].

3.2 Obtaining an Approximation

Consider linear programming problems of the following form:

$$\begin{aligned} \text{Maximize } & t \\ \text{subject to } & \boldsymbol{Ax} = t\boldsymbol{b} \\ & \boldsymbol{Ux} \leq \boldsymbol{d} \\ & \boldsymbol{x} \geq \boldsymbol{0} \end{aligned}$$

where $\boldsymbol{A} \in R^{n \times m}$, $\boldsymbol{O} \leq \boldsymbol{U} \in R^{\ell \times m}$, $\boldsymbol{b} \in R^n$, and $\boldsymbol{0} \leq \boldsymbol{d} \in R^\ell$. We refer to the constraints $\boldsymbol{Ux} \leq \boldsymbol{d}$ as *generalized capacity constraints.* A vector $\boldsymbol{x} \geq \boldsymbol{0}$, such that $\boldsymbol{Ax} \propto \boldsymbol{b}$ ($\boldsymbol{Ax}$ is proportional to $\boldsymbol{b}$) and $\boldsymbol{Ux} \leq \boldsymbol{d}$ is called *feasible.* For a feasible vector $\boldsymbol{x}$, denote by $\hat{t}(\boldsymbol{x})$ the scalar $\hat{t}$ such that $\boldsymbol{Ax} = \hat{t}\boldsymbol{b}$. Denote by $(\boldsymbol{x}^*, t^*)$ an optimal solution (so that $t^* = \hat{t}(\boldsymbol{x}^*)$). A feasible vector $\boldsymbol{x}$ is *ϵ-optimal* if $\hat{t}(\boldsymbol{x}) \geq (1-\epsilon)t^*$.

Suppose that for $\boldsymbol{0} \leq \boldsymbol{c} \in R^m$ it is relatively easy to compute a vector $\boldsymbol{x} \geq \boldsymbol{0}$ which minimizes $\boldsymbol{c}^T\boldsymbol{x}$ subject to $\boldsymbol{Ax} = \boldsymbol{b}$. We refer to problems of this form as *uncapacitated* instances, whereas an instance of the original problem is referred to as a *capacitated* one. Note that when the capacitated problem is an instance of generalized circulation, $\boldsymbol{U}$ is a diagonal matrix with at most $m = |E|$ rows. The corresponding uncapacitated problem is an instance of UGT on the same network, where only demand nodes are present.

We present an algorithm for constructing a $(1 - 1/\ell)$-optimal vector $\boldsymbol{y}$. The algorithm amounts to solving a single instance of the uncapacitated problem. Let $\boldsymbol{D} = \text{diag}(\boldsymbol{d})$, i.e., $\boldsymbol{D}$ is a diagonal matrix with the coordinates of $\boldsymbol{d}$ in its diagonal. Let $\boldsymbol{p}^T = \boldsymbol{e}^T\boldsymbol{D}^{-1}\boldsymbol{U}$, where $\boldsymbol{e}$ is a vector of 1's, and cosider the linear cost function $\boldsymbol{p}^T\boldsymbol{x}$. Note that $\boldsymbol{p}^T = \sum_{i=1}^{\ell} \boldsymbol{U}_{i\bullet}/d_i$. It is easy to verify that the following properties hold:

1. If $\boldsymbol{x}$ is feasible then $\boldsymbol{p}^T\boldsymbol{x} \leq \ell$.
2. If $\boldsymbol{Ax} \propto \boldsymbol{b}$, $\boldsymbol{x} \geq 0$, and $\boldsymbol{p}^T\boldsymbol{x} \leq 1$, then $\boldsymbol{x}$ is feasible.
3. If $\boldsymbol{p}^T\boldsymbol{x}^* > 0$, then $\boldsymbol{p}^T\boldsymbol{x}^* \geq 1$ (since for some i, $\boldsymbol{U}_{i\bullet}\boldsymbol{x}^* = d_i$).

Consider a vector $\boldsymbol{y} \geq 0$ such that $\boldsymbol{Ay} \propto \boldsymbol{b}$ and $\boldsymbol{p}^T\boldsymbol{y} = 1$ which maximizes $\hat{t}(\boldsymbol{y})$. Note that the vector $\ell\boldsymbol{y}$ maximizes $\hat{t}(\boldsymbol{x})$ among all vectors $\boldsymbol{x} \geq 0$ such that $\boldsymbol{Ax} \propto \boldsymbol{b}$ and $\boldsymbol{p}^T\boldsymbol{x} \leq \ell$. In particular, $\hat{t}(\ell\boldsymbol{y}) \geq t^*$, and hence, $\hat{t}(\boldsymbol{y}) \geq t^*/\ell$. Such a vector $\boldsymbol{y}$ can be obtained by normalizing a vector $\boldsymbol{x} \geq 0$ which minimizes $\boldsymbol{p}^T\boldsymbol{x}$ subject to $\boldsymbol{Ax} = \boldsymbol{b}$. Also, $\boldsymbol{y}$ is feasible and therefore provides the desired approximation. A formal description of the algorithm follows.

Algorithm 3.3 [Compute a $(1 - 1/\ell)$-optimal vector]

1. Solve the following instance of the uncapacitated problem:

$$\begin{aligned} \text{Minimize } & \boldsymbol{p}^T\boldsymbol{x} \\ \text{subject to } & \boldsymbol{Ax} = \boldsymbol{b} \\ & \boldsymbol{x} \geq \boldsymbol{0}\,. \end{aligned}$$

   If it is infeasible, then conclude that $\boldsymbol{x} = \boldsymbol{0}$ is the only feasible vector of the capacitated instance. Otherwise, let $\boldsymbol{x}$ be the solution.

2. If $\boldsymbol{p}^T\boldsymbol{x} = 0$ then for every $r \geq 0$, the vector $r\boldsymbol{x}$ is feasible, and hence the capacitated problem is unbounded.
3. Otherwise, when $\boldsymbol{p}^T\boldsymbol{x} \neq 0$, compute the largest number r (which must exist in this case) such that $r\boldsymbol{U}\boldsymbol{x} \leq \boldsymbol{d}$. Conclude that $r\boldsymbol{x}$ is $(1 - 1/\ell)$-optimal.

Correctness Consider the vector $\boldsymbol{x}$ computed in step 1 of the algorithm. Note that $\hat{t}(\boldsymbol{x}) = 1$. Hence, $\hat{t}(r\boldsymbol{x}) = r\hat{t}(\boldsymbol{x}) = r$.

Proposition 3.4 $\boldsymbol{p}^T\boldsymbol{x} = 0$ *if and only if the capacitated problem is unbounded.*

Proof. Suppose first that $\boldsymbol{p}^T\boldsymbol{x} = 0$. Note that for all $r \geq 0$, $r\boldsymbol{p}^T\boldsymbol{x} = 0$, and hence, $r\boldsymbol{x}$ is feasible. Also, for all $r \geq 0$, $\hat{t}(r\boldsymbol{x}) = r$. Hence, the problem is unbounded. Second, suppose the problem is unbounded. There exists a vector $\boldsymbol{x}$ such that $r\boldsymbol{x}$ is feasible for all $r \geq 0$. It follows that $\boldsymbol{p}^T(r\boldsymbol{x}) = r\boldsymbol{p}^T\boldsymbol{x} \leq \ell$ for all $r \geq 0$. Hence, $\boldsymbol{p}^T\boldsymbol{x} = 0$.

The following proposition concludes the correctness proof.

Proposition 3.5 *If t^* is finite, then $r \geq t^*/\ell$.*

Proof. For $k \geq 0$, denote

$$R(k) = \max\{\hat{t}(\boldsymbol{y}) \mid \boldsymbol{p}^T\boldsymbol{y} \leq k, \boldsymbol{A}\boldsymbol{y} \propto \boldsymbol{b}, \boldsymbol{y} \geq 0\} \text{ , and}$$
$$R^*(k) = \max\{\hat{t}(\boldsymbol{y}) \mid \boldsymbol{p}^T\boldsymbol{y} \leq k, \boldsymbol{y} \text{ is feasible}\} \text{ .}$$

Obviously, (i) R and R^* are increasing functions, (ii) $R \geq R^*$, (iii) for every $a > 0$, $R(ak) = aR(k)$, and (iv) $t^* \leq R^*(\ell)$.

For the vector $\boldsymbol{x}$ (computed in step 1), $R(\boldsymbol{p}^T\boldsymbol{x}) = 1$, and hence $R(r\boldsymbol{p}^T\boldsymbol{x}) = r$. Since $\boldsymbol{p}^T\boldsymbol{x} > 0$, it follows that $r\boldsymbol{U}_{i\bullet}\boldsymbol{x} = d_i$ for some $1 \leq i \leq \ell$. Hence, $r\boldsymbol{p}^T\boldsymbol{x} \geq 1$. It follows that

$$t^* \leq R^*(\ell) \leq R(\ell) \leq R(\ell r\boldsymbol{p}^T\boldsymbol{x}) = \ell r R(\boldsymbol{p}^T\boldsymbol{x}) = \ell r \text{ .}$$

4 Bidirected Generalized Networks

In the previous sections we discussed generalized networks where the flow multipliers are positive numbers. We refer to the edges in these networks as head-tail edges. A head-tail edge produces a nonnegative amount of flow at the tail end of the edge and a proportional nonpositive amount at the head end. In bidirected generalized networks we allow two additional types of edges: head-head and tail-tail. The properties of edges of these types are shown in Figure 1. Note that a tail-tail edge can be viewed as a head-tail edge with a negative multiplier. Bidirected generalized networks are more general than bidirected networks (see [11]). In biderected networks the multipliers associated with the edges are always unity. Bidirected networks were first considered by Edmonds [6] who related them to non-bipartite matching theory. In this section we apply the methods discussed in previous sections to flow problems on bidirected generalized networks.

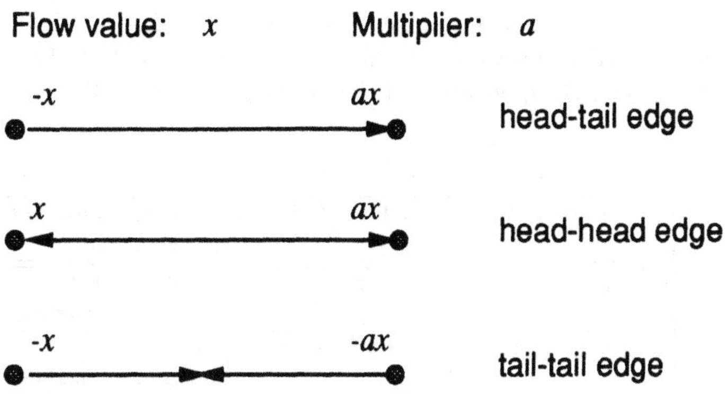

Fig. 1. Edge types of a bidirected generalized network

4.1 UGT on Bidirected Networks

We discuss the application of the scheme of Adler and Cosares for solving the UGT problem on bidirected networks. A bidirected UGT problem has the form:

$$\begin{aligned} \text{Minimize} \quad & \boldsymbol{c}^T \boldsymbol{x} \\ \text{subject to} \quad & \boldsymbol{A}\boldsymbol{x} = \boldsymbol{b} \\ & \boldsymbol{x} \geq 0 \,, \end{aligned}$$

where $\boldsymbol{b} \in R^n$, $\boldsymbol{c} \in R^m$, and the matrix $\boldsymbol{A} \in R^{n \times m}$ has at most two non-zero entries in each column. Note that head-tail edges correspond to columns where the two entries have opposite signs, head-head edges correspond to columns with two positive entries, and tail-tail edges correspond to columns with two negative entries. The dual of this problem is:

$$\begin{aligned} \text{Maximize} \quad & \boldsymbol{b}^T \boldsymbol{y} \\ \text{subject to} \quad & \boldsymbol{A}^T \boldsymbol{y} \leq \boldsymbol{c} \,, \end{aligned}$$

where the constraints have the TVPI property. Recall that when only head-tail edges are present, the dual has monotone constraints. When both head-tail and tail-tail edges are allowed, $\boldsymbol{A}^T$ is called a *pre-Leontief* matrix (see [5]), and it is known that in this case there exists a vector which maximizes all variables simultaneously. The scheme of Adler and Cosares applies when $\boldsymbol{b} \geq \boldsymbol{0}$. Similarly, when both head-tail and head-head edges are present, $-\boldsymbol{A}^T$ is a pre-Leontief matrix, and hence, there exists a vector which minimizes all variables simultaneously. The scheme of Adler and Cosares applies here when $\boldsymbol{b} \leq \boldsymbol{0}$. When all three types of edges are present, the dual constitutes a general TVPI system. The algorithm of [2, 3, 4] can be used to find a vector which maximizes or minimizes a single variable. The scheme of Adler and Cosares applies here to cases where $\boldsymbol{b} = \pm \boldsymbol{e}^i$. The UGT instances for which the scheme of Adler and Cosares applies are listed in Table 3. These instances can be solved by a single application of the algorithms of [2, 3, 4].

Allowed edge types	*structure of the dual* $A^T y \leq c$	– *supply/demand vectors* – *TVPI needed*
head-tail	monotone TVPI	$b \leq 0$ or $b \geq 0$ monotone (maximize $\pm e^T y$)
head-tail, tail-tail	A^T is pre-Leontief	$b \geq 0$ monotone (maximize $e^T y$)
head-tail, head-head	$-A^T$ is pre-Leontief	$b \leq 0$ monotone (minimize $e^T y$)
all types	general TVPI	$b_j = \pm 1$, $b_i = 0$ $(i \neq j)$ general (maximize/minimize y_j)

Table 3. Solving UGT on bidirected generalized networks

4.2 Generalized Circulation on Bidirected Networks

We consider applying the approximation algorithm of Section 3 to generalized circulation problem where the underlying network is bidirected. Recall that the approximation algorithm iteratively computes a feasible flow and in the following iteration considers the residual graph. Since tail-tail edges give rise to head-head edges in the residual graph (and vice versa), we only consider networks where all three edge types are present. Note that when all three edge types are present the Adler-Cosares scheme applies to UGT instances where there is a single source or a single sink (that is, $\boldsymbol{b} = \boldsymbol{e}_i$ or $\boldsymbol{b} = -\boldsymbol{e}_i$ for some i $(1 \leq i \leq n)$.

It follows that the approximation scheme presented in Section 3 can be used to solve bidirected generalized circulation instances where $\boldsymbol{b} = \pm \boldsymbol{e}_i$ for some i $(1 \leq i \leq n)$.

5 Concluding Remarks

In this paper we presented algorithms for the uncapacitated generalized transshipment (UGT) problem and the generalized circulation (GC) problem. We also considered the UGT and GC problems on bidirected generalized networks. To solve UGT, we combined a scheme by Adler and Cosares [1], which reduces the restricted UGT problem where either only demand nodes or only supply nodes are present to solving the dual linear programming problem, with the algorithms given in [2, 3, 4]. The combination yielded better time bounds for restricted UGT instances.

In order to utilize the UGT algorithms for solving the capacitated GC problem, we introduced an iterative approximation algorithm. In each iteration, we consider a UGT instance, with costs which "capture" the relaxed capacities. The solution of this UGT instance yields an approximate solution for the GC instance. The next iteration considers the residual graph.

We now comment on the parallel running times of the algorithms mentioned above. We denote $f(n) = \tilde{O}(g(n))$ if there is a k such that $f(n) = O(g(n)(\log n)^k)$. The parallel complexity of the algorithms of [2, 3, 4] is $\tilde{O}(n)$ either deterministically with $O(mn)$ processors, or with randomization with $O(m + n^2)$ ones. The algorithms for the restricted UGT instances have the same complexity. The approximation algorithm for GC runs in $\tilde{O}(mn \log \epsilon^{-1})$ time using $O(mn)$ processors for the deterministic bound and $O(m + n^2)$ processors for the randomized one.

The existence of a strongly polynomial algorithm for the unrestricted UGT problem (where many sources and sinks are allowed) remains an open question. The dual of the UGT problem calls for optimizing a general objective function subject to monotone system. The following reduction (similar to [14]) demonstrates the difficulty of the problem. An instance of capacitated generalized transshipment can be reduced in linear time to an instance of UGT with $3m$ edges and $n + 2m$ nodes. The reduction is as follows. Consider an instance of generalized circulation on a network $G = (V, E)$ where $d_v \in R$ is the supply or demand at v $(v \in V)$, and a_e, u_e, and c_e are the multiplier, capacity, and cost, respectively, associated with the edge e $(e \in E)$. The corresponding instance of the UGT problem $G' = (V \cup W \cup W', E')$ preserves the supplies and demands at the nodes in V. Each edge $e \in E$ has two corresponding nodes $w_e \in W$ and $w'_e \in W'$, and three edges in E' which form an undirected path. The node w_e has a demand u_e and the node w'_e has a supply $-u_e$. Suppose $e = (v_1, v_2)$ is an edge in G. The corresponding edges in G' are (i) (v_1, w) with multiplier 1 and cost c_e, (ii) (w', w) with multiplier 1 and cost 0, and (iii) (w', v_2) with multiplier a_e and cost 0.

References

1. I. Adler and S. Cosares. Strongly polynomial algorithms for linear programming problems with special structure. *Oper. Res.*, 1991. To appear.
2. E. Cohen. *Combinatorial Algorithms for Optimization Problems.* PhD thesis, Department of Computer Science, Stanford University, Stanford, Ca., 1991.
3. E. Cohen and N. Megiddo. Improved algorithms for linear inequalities with two variables per inequality. In *Proc. 23rd Annual ACM Symposium on Theory of Computing,* pages 145–155. ACM, 1991.
4. E. Cohen and N. Megiddo. Improved algorithms for linear inequalities with two variables per inequality. Technical Report RJ 8187 (75146), IBM Almaden Research Center, San Jose, CA 95120-6099, June 1991.
5. R. W. Cottle and A. F. Veinott Jr. Polyhedral sets having a least element. *Math. Prog.*, 3:238–249, 1972.
6. J. Edmonds. An introduction to matchings. In *Engineering Summer Conference.* The Univ. of Michigan, Ann Arbor, 1967. Mimeographed notes.
7. F. Glover, J. Hultz, D. Klingman, and J. Stunz. Generalized networks: a fundamental computer-based planning tool. *Management Science*, 24(12), August 1978.
8. A. V. Goldberg, S. K. Plotkin, and É. Tardos. Combinatorial algorithms for the generalized circulation problem. In *Proc. 29th IEEE Annual Symposium on Foundations of Computer Science*, pages 432–443. IEEE, 1988.

9. M. Gondran and M. Minoux. *Graphs and Algorithms.* John Wiley & Sons, New York, 1984.
10. K. Kapoor and P. M. Vaidya. Speeding up Karmarkar's algorithm for multicommodity flows. *Math. Prog.*, 1991. To appear.
11. E. L. Lawler. *Combinatorial optimization: networks and matroids.* Holt, Reinhart, and Winston, New York, 1976.
12. N. Megiddo. Towards a genuinely polynomial algorithm for linear programming. *SIAM J. Comput.*, 12:347–353, 1983.
13. S. Murray. An interior point conjugate gradient approach to the generalized flow problem with costs and the multicommodity flow problem dual. Manuscript, 1991.
14. J. B. Orlin. A faster strongly polynomial minimum cost flow algorithm. In *Proc. 20th Annual ACM Symposium on Theory of Computing*, pages 377–387. ACM, 1988.
15. É. Tardos. A strongly polynomial algorithm to solve combinatorial linear programs. *Oper. Res.*, 34:250–256, 1986.
16. P. M. Vaidya. Speeding-up linear programming using fast matrix multiplication. In *Proc. 30th IEEE Annual Symposium on Foundations of Computer Science*, pages 332–337. IEEE, 1989.

This article was processed using the LaTeX macro package with LLNCS style

Factoring Polynomials via Relation-Finding

Victor S. Miller

IBM, Thomas J. Watson Research Center
Mathematical Sciences Department
Yorktown Heights, NY 10598

Abstract. In this paper we describe a new algorithm for fully factoring polynomials defined over the rationals or over number-fields. This algorithm uses as an essential subroutine, any fast relation finding algorithm for vectors of real numbers. Unlike previous algorithms which work on one factor at a time, the new algorithm finds all factors at once.
Let P be a polynomial of degree n, height $H(P)$ (= sum of the absolute values of P's coefficients), logarthmic height $h(P) = \log H(P)$. If we use the HJLS relation-finding algorithm of Hastad, Just, Lagarias and Schnorr, our algorithm has running time $O(n^{5+\epsilon}h(P))$ if fast multiplication is used, and $O(n^{6+\epsilon}h(P))$ if ordinary multiplication is used. This is an improvement by a factor of n over the algorithm of Schönhage, the previously best known.

1 Introduction

In the seminal paper [LLL82], Lenstra, Lenstra and Lovasz gave the first known algorithm for factorization of a polynomial $P(x) \in \mathbb{Q}[x]$, whose running time is polynomial in n (= $\deg P$), and in $h(P)$ (the logarithmic height of P). This algorithm proceeds by finding the smallest degree rational factor divisible by a particular local factor (over a p-adic field or over the real field), by means of a process of lattice basis reduction in a succession of lattices. To find the entire factorization, the polynomial must be reduced by the factor just found, and the whole process iterated with the deflated polynomial.

In this paper, we give a new simpler algorithm which uses as an essential subroutine any algorithm for finding integer relations among a collection of real vectors. This algorithm has the virtue of only requiring $\log n$ application of the integer-relation algorithm, as opposed to $\log n$ applications of lattice-basis reduction for each factor. It also finds the complete factorization in one step. The running time is $O(n^{5+\epsilon}h(P))$ if fast multiplication is used, and $O(n^{6+\epsilon}h(P))$ if ordinary multiplication is used. This saves a factor of n over the best known algorithm due to Schönhage [Sch84] (which also may be recast in terms of relation–finding). Last, the fact that the relation–finding actually produces all factors is much easier to understand than the rather subtle fact that a Lovasz-reduced lattice of the multiples of a particular local polynomial factor yields a rational factor.

2 Idempotents and Factors

In [GMT89] Gianni, Miller and Trager describe how the process of of Hensel-lifting factors modulo p^n can be more efficiently realized as refining the approximation of idempotents.

In the following, let K be either a number field (a finite extension of $\mathbb{Q}$), or a function field (a finite extension of $k(x)$, where k is a finite field). In the number field case, let Z denote the ring $\mathbb{Z}$ of ordinary integers. In the function field case, let Z denote the ring $k[x]$.

Definition 1. A factor $f(x)|P(x)$ is called an *exact factor* if $\gcd(f(x), P(x)/f(x)) = 1$.

Let $\pi : K[x] \to A$ denote the canonical projection.

Proposition 2. *Let $P(x) \in K[x]$ be a polynomial of degree n. There is a one-to-one correspondence between idempotents $e \in A$, where A is the algebra $K[x]/(P(x))$, and the exact factors $f(x)|P(x)$, $f(x) \in K[x]$. This correspondence may be calculated by one application of the extended Euclidean algorithm whose input is two polynomials of degree $\leq n$.*

Proof. If $e \in A$ is an idempotent, then $\pi^{-1}(eA)$ is an ideal in $K[x]$. Thus, there is a unique monic polynomial $f(x) \in K[x]$ generating this ideal. This polynomial is the polynomial corresponding to e. Now, since $\pi{-}1(eA)$ contains $\pi^{-1}(\{0\})$, we must have $f(x)|P(x)$. Now let $g(x)$ be the unique polynomial of degree $< n$ in $\pi^{-1}(\{e\})$, $g(x) = h(x)f(x)$ for some $h(x) \in K[x]$. Because $\pi(g)$ is an idempotent, we have $h(x)f(x)^2 = f(x) \bmod P(x)$, or $h(x)f(x) + j(x)(P(x)/f(x)) = 1$ for some polynomial $j(x) \in K[x]$. That is, $f(x)$ is an exact factor of P. Conversely, an exact factor $f(x)$ yields $h(x)f(x) + j(x)(P(x)/f(x)) = 1$ for some h and j. □

Proposition 3. *If α is a root of the polynomial $P(x)$, then*

$$e_\alpha = \pi(\frac{1}{P'(\alpha)}\frac{P(x)}{x-\alpha})$$

, is a primitive idempotent of dimension 1, in the algebra $A = K[x]/(P(x))$. This idempotent corresponds to α, in the sense that, if $g(x)$ is any polynomial, then $\pi(g(x))e_\alpha = g(\alpha)e_\alpha$.

Let $|\ |$ be an absolute value of K (which can be archimedean in the number field case). Let $\hat{K}$ denote the completion of K with respect to this absolute value. Now $A = K[x]/(P(x))$ is a finite dimensional vector space over K. By $|\ |$ on elements of A we will mean a vector space norm on A compatible with the absolute value on K. Finally, by $||\ ||$ we will mean the operator norm induced by $|\ |$. That is $||a|| := \sup_{x,|x|=1} |\rho(a)x|$, where $\rho : A \to M_n(K)$ is the left regular representation of A, with respect to some basis. With this norm, A becomes a normed algebra: $||ab|| \leq ||a||||b||$ for all $a, b \in A$, in addition to the usual properties of a norm.

Now, to find good upper bounds for things of the form $||a||$, we can use, for example, the expression for this norm when the underlying vector space norm is the L^2 norm: $||a||$ is the square root of the largest eigenvalue of $\rho(a)^t\rho(a)$. A particularly convenient basis for this calculation, is the basis consisting of the e_α where α ranges over the roots of $P(x)$. This yields: $||f|| = \sup_\alpha |f(\alpha)|$, where α ranges over the roots of P. To estimate the sup we can use the simple bound $|\alpha| \leq \max(1, |a_1|+\cdots+|a_n|)$.

3 Refining Approximate Idempotents

The fundamental construction is the refining of approximate idempotents. We recall that an idempotent of an algebra A is an element $e \in A$ such that $e^2 = e$. If A is a unital (has an element 1) Noetherian ring, it has only a finite number of idempotents. There is a natural partial order on idempotents: We have $e \leq f$ if $ef = e$. An idempotent is *primitive* if it is non-zero and minimal with respect to the just defined partial order. Finally, if A is a finite-dimensional algebra then define $\dim e := dim_K eA$. It is clear, that $e \leq f$ implies $\dim e \leq \dim f$. Thus $\dim e = 1$ implies that e is primitive.

The following is taken from [GMT89]. An *approximate idempotent*, in a finite dimensional algebra A will be an element $\bar{e} \in A$ such that $||\bar{e}^2 - \bar{e}|| < 1/4$. An approximate idempotent can be uniquely refined to a unique idempotent. We define

$$\bar{e}' = 3\bar{e}^2 - 2\bar{e}^3 \tag{1}$$

It is straightforward to calculate that

$$\bar{e}'^2 - \bar{e}' = (\bar{e}^2 - \bar{e})^2(-3 + 4(\bar{e}^2 - \bar{e})) \tag{2}$$

Thus, if $||\bar{e}^2 - \bar{e}|| \leq \varepsilon < 1/4$, then $||\bar{e}'^2 - \bar{e}'|| \leq \varepsilon^2(3+4\varepsilon) \leq 4\varepsilon^2$. This yields quadratic convergence.

4 Relations among idempotents

The essential idea of this algorithm is that one may find the set of primitive idempotents in $B := A \otimes_K \hat{K}$ by means of analysis (the refining of approximate idempotents). The factors that we seek correspond to the primitive idempotents in A. If M denotes the additive subgroup in B generated by the set of primitive idempotents, then $M \cap A$ is the additive subgroup generated by the primitive idempotents in A (here we identify A with its image under the canonical embedding $A \to B$) see Proposition 4. This intersection may be calculated by finding the generators of the set of integer relations among the idempotents in B expressed as vectors in "A-coordinates". This process works because we can give a good bound for the maximum possible coefficient of such a relation, and because the real numbers involved are known to be algebraic numbers in a particular number field. Thus we can give a good lower bound for the smallest non-zero real-number that can possible arise in the relation-finding algorithm.

Finally, once we have a basis for the module of integer relations, we can use that to obtain the idempotents by means of a partition refinement algorithm.

Proposition 4. *Let A be a finite dimensional algebra over a field K, and L be an extension field of K. Let E be the additive subgroup generated by the idempotents of $A \otimes L$. Then $E \cap A$ is the additive subgroup of idempotents in A (here we identify A with its image under the canonical embedding of A into $A \otimes L$).*

Proof. First, we may assume that L is algebraically closed, because the canonical map from A to $A \otimes L$ is injective. Next, the galois group G, of L/K acts on $A \otimes L$ via the second factor. If $\sigma \in G$, and $e \in A \otimes L$ is a primitive idempotent, then so is e^σ. Thus G permutes the primitive idempotents. For each primitive idempotent e define $\psi(e)$ = sum of conjugates of e. It is now clear, that if a sum of idempotents is in A it is fixed under G, and so is a sum of elements of the form $\psi(e)$. However, each $\psi(e)$ is an idempotent in A. □

5 Outline of the Algorithm

The first part of the algorithm involves finding good starting points for the idempotent refinement process. This is furnished by the Proposition 3

To use this proposition we find approximations to the roots of $P(x)$, and then find the corresponding approximate idempotent. We may find sufficiently good approximations to all the complex roots of P by using the splitting–circle method of Schönhage [Sch82, Sch87] in time $O(n^3 B^{1+\epsilon})$, where B is the number of bits of precision necessary. We shall see below that B may be taken as $\log \operatorname{disc}(P)$, which, by a theorem of Mahler [Mah64] is $O(n \log nh(P))$. Thus, all roots needed below may be calculated in time $O(n^{4+\epsilon} h(P))$.

Second, we need to find a basis of A, so that the Z-module generated by that basis contains all idempotents. This is furnished by the following:

Proposition 5. *Let $D = \det(\operatorname{Tr}(z_i z_j))$ the discriminant of the basis z_i of A. Then the module generated by $\frac{1}{D} z_i$ contains all idempotents.*

Third, Let z_i and w_i, $i = 1, \ldots, n$, are linearly independent sets of elements of a vector space V over $\mathbb{Q}$, and M and N are respectively the additive subgroups generated by them. Let L be the module of relations $\{a_i \in \mathbb{Z} : a_1 z_1 + \cdots + a_n z_n + a_{n+1} w_1 + \cdots + a_{2n} w_n = 0\}$. Then $\{a_1 z_1 + \cdots + a_n z_n, a \in L\}$ is the intersection $M \cap N$.

We now use Proposition 4 to actually construct the additive subgroup generated by the rational idempotents.

Next, we use the relation finding algorithm of Hastad, Just, Lagarias and Schnorr [HJLS89] to calculate the above intersection. In order to do this we need to find upper bounds on the integers necessary to find the basis of all relations. Note, that one one side, a set of generators of the module of relations is contained in the relations among all idempotents with the basis z_i of A. So, a bound of 1 may be taken for the coefficients of the idempotents.

In order to bound the z_i we proceed as follows: Every idempotent in A must be a sum of a set of idempotents of the form e_α. We first note the trivial bound, that for any root α of p that $\alpha \le \max(1, nH(p))$, where $H(p) = \max_i |a_i|$, and from the formula given for e_α that every coefficient of e_α is $O(nH(p)^n)$. Since we are going to use the basis (x^k/D) where D is the discriminant, an upper bound on the size of the coefficients is thus $O(n(\log n + h(p)))$, by using the bound $\log \operatorname{disc} A = O(n(\log nh(p))$ (see Mahler [Mah64]).

We then use the Simultaneous Relations Algorithm of [HJLS89, p. 875], to calculate the intersection:

Algorithm 6. *On input the real vectors $x_1, \ldots, x_l \in \mathbb{R}^n$ and $k, r \in \mathbb{N}$ this algorithm either finds r independent simultaneous integer relations $c_1, \ldots, c_n$ for $x_1, \ldots, x_n$ or it proves that $\lambda_r(x_1, \ldots, x_n) \geq 2^k$.*

Here $\lambda_r(x_1, \ldots, x_n)$ means the r-th succesive minimum of the lattice generated by $x_1, \ldots, x_n$

This algorithm halts in time $O(n^3(k+n))$ arithmetic operations on real numbers.

To apply this algorithm, we may take $k = \lg U(A)$.

Let K_j denote the field $\mathbb{Q}(\alpha_j)$ When one looks at the coefficients of of the vectors involved in the algorithm, one finds that they will be algebraic integers in a particular complex embedding of $\mathbb{Q}[x]/(P(x))$ (namely, the field K_j in the j-th coordinate).

Because we are working with real numbers which are algebraic integers, we can establish a bound:

Proposition 7. *Let $\alpha_1, \ldots, \alpha_n$ be elements in a number field K of degree n, with $|\ |$ an archimedean absolute value on K. Let $M = \sup_{\sigma,i} |\alpha_i^\sigma|$ where σ ranges over all complex embeddings of K. Let $a_0, a_1, \ldots, a_n \in \mathbb{Z}$ and $H \geq |a_i|$. Let $L = a_0 + a_1\alpha_1 + \cdots + a_n\alpha_n$. Then, either $L = 0$ or $L \geq 1/((n+1)HM)^{n-1}$.*

This proposition allows us to determine the accuracy necessary to insure that the relation finding algorithm indeed finds all relations. In our case we may take H to be any upper bound on all the roots of P

Taking logarithms, we find that the number of bits necessary is $O(n((\log n)^2 + h(p)))$.

Fix notation by supposing that w_i is the n-dimensional vector with 1 in the i-th position and 0 elsewhere, and that e_i is the approximation to the idempotent e_{α_i} written with respect to the basis x^i/D of A. Now, the output of the relation finding algorithm will be n basis vectors of the form $a_{ij} \in \mathbb{Z}$, with $i = 1, \ldots, n$ and $j = 1, \ldots, 2n$, so that $a_{i1}e_1 + \cdots + a_{in}e_n + a_{i(n+1)}w_1 + \cdots + a_{i(2n)}w_n = 0$. Because, the e_i are linearly independent over $\mathbb{Q}$, it is easy to see that $a_{i1}e_1 + \cdots + a_{in}e_n$ are a basis for the intersection that we are seeking. The task remains to find the idempotents, primitive in A that generate this module. We can do this by means of a partition refinement algorithm:

Proposition 8. *Define a relation on the set of e_i by $e_i \mathcal{R} e_j$ if for all $k \leq n$ we have $a_{ik} = a_{jk}$. This is clearly an equivalence relation. Then the elements $\sum e_i$ where the sum is taken over an equivalence class in $\mathcal{R}$ form the set of primitive idempotents in A.*

Proof. Note that since each idempotent in A is a sum over a set of primitive idempotents in $A \otimes \mathbb{C}$, that $a_{ik} = a_{jk}$ occurs whenever e_i and e_j are conjugate under the action of galois. Furthermore, if they aren't conjugate, then there is a k such that $a_{ik} \neq a_{jk}$. The latter happens because the e_i form a complete set of primitive idempotents. □

The relation $\mathcal{R}$ may be calculated by a trivial algorithm in time $O(n^2)$, and by a slightly more sophisticated partition-refinement algorithm in time $O(n \log n)$.

Putting everything together yields:

Theorem 9. *There is an algorithm to fully factor a polynomial $P(x) \in \mathbb{Q}[x]$ which has running time* $O(n^4(\log n + h(p)^2))$ *arithmetic operations. Each of these operations is performed on numbers of* $O(n(\log n)^2 + h(p))$ *bits.*

By contrast the LLL algorithm [LLL82] takes $O(n^6 h(p)^2)$ operations on numbers of size $O(n^3 h(p))$ bits. The improved Schönhage factorization algorithm [Sch84] takes $O(n^{6+\epsilon} + n^4(\log|f|)^2 + \varepsilon)$ bit operations.

Note that that the bound on the sizes of the numbers involved appears to be unduly pessimistic, as it is based on very crude estimates from a generalization of Liouville's theorem on irrationality measures. Also note, that all calculations may be made with n-dimensional real vectors, as opposed to n-dimensional complex vectors. Namely, we need only to start with idempotents defined over $\mathbb{R}$. Whenever we have a complex root α we consder the real idempotent $e_\alpha + e_{\bar{\alpha}}$ instead of the two idempotents e_α and $e_{\bar{\alpha}}$. These, in fact, constitute the set of primitive real idempotents, as α ranges over all roots of P.

6 Conclusion

We have described an algorithm for polynomial factorization with running time polynomial in the degree and the logarithmic height of the polynomial. This algorithm uses relation-finding instead of lattice basis reduction (though, clearly the two are closely connected). The essential step uses relation finding to find the intersection of two modules, which is much more straitforward than the modules of the L^3 algorithm. In addition, this algorithm may use other relation-finding methods, such as the new PSLQ method of Feguson and Bailey [FB91], or the older PSOS method of the same authors [BF89].

References

[BF89] David H. Bailey and Helaman R. P. Ferguson. Numerical results on relations between fundamental constants using a new algorithm. *Math. Comp.*, 53:649–656, 1989.

[FB91] Helaman R. P. Ferguson and David H. Bailey. A polynomial time, numerically stable integer relation algorithm. Technical report, Supercomputing Research Center, 17100 Science Drive, Bowie, MD 20715, December 1991.

[GMT89] Patrizia Gianni, Victor Miller, and Barry Trager. Decomposition of algebras. In *ISAAC '88*, Lecture Notes in Computer Science. Springer–Verlag, 1989.

[HJLS89] Johann Hastad, B. Just, Jeffrey C. Lagarias, and Claus P. Schnorr. Polynomial time algorithms for finding integer relations among real numbers. *Siam J. Comput.*, 18:859–881, 1989.

[KM86] Ravi Kannan and Lyle A. McGeoch. Basis reduction and evidence for transcendence of certain numbers. In *Foundations of software technology and theoretical computer science (New Delhi, 1986)*, volume 241 of *Lecture Notes in Comput. Sci.*, pages 263–269. Springer, Berlin-New York, 1986.

[LLL82] Arjen K. Lenstra, Hendrik W. Lenstra, Jr., and Laszlo Lovasz. Factoring polynomials with rational coefficients. *Mathematische Annalen*, 261:515–534, 1982.

[Mah64] Kurt Mahler. An inequality for the discriminant of a polynomial. *Michigan Math. J.*, 11:257–262, 1964.

[Sch82] Arnold Schönhage. The fundamental theorem of algebra in terms of computational complexity. Technical report, Math. Inst. Univ. Tübingen, 1982.

[Sch84] Arnold Schönhage. Factorization of univariate integer polynomials by diophantine approximation and an improved basis reduction algorithm. In *Automata, languages and programming (Antwerp, 1984)*, volume 172 of *Lecture Notes in Computer Science*, pages 436–447, Berlin-New York, 1984. Springer–Verlag.

[Sch87] Arnold Schönhage. Equation solving in terms of computational complexity. In *Proceedings of the International Congress of Mathematicians, 1986*, volume 1, pages 131–153. American Mathematical Society, 1987.

This article was processed using the LaTeX macro package with LLNCS style

New Resultant Inequalities and Complex Polynomial Factorization

Victor Pan

Lehman College, CUNY, Bronx, NY 10468.
Supported by NSF Grant CCR 9020690 and PSC-CUNY Award 662478

Abstract. We deduce some new probabilistic estimates on the distances between the zeros of a polynomial $p(x)$ by using some properties of the discriminant of $p(x)$ and apply these estimates to improve the fastest deterministic algorithm for approximating polynomial factorization over the complex field. Namely, given a natural n, positive ϵ, such that $\log(1/\epsilon) = O(n \log n)$, and the complex coefficients of a polynomial $p(x) = \sum_{i=0}^{n} p_i x^i$, such that $p_n \neq 0$, $\sum_i |p_i| \leq 1$, we compute (within the error norm ϵ) a factorization of $p(x)$ as a product of factors of degrees at most $n/2$, by using $O(\log^2 n)$ time and n^3 processors under the PRAM arithmetic model of parallel computing or by using $O(n^2 \log^2 n)$ arithmetic operations. The algorithm is randomized, of Las Vegas type, allowing a failure with a probability at most δ, for any positive $\delta < 1$ such that $\log(1/\delta) = O(\log n)$. Except for a narrow class of polynomials $p(x)$, these results can be also obtained for ϵ such that $\log(1/\epsilon) = O(n^2 \log n)$.

1 Introduction

Randomization is already a classical tool for designing effective numerical and algebraic algorithms over finite fields (see, for instance, [16]), but over infinite fields, randomization is usually limited to verification of polynomial identities and to avoiding singularities (see [12], [18]). We are going to demonstrate the power of randomization in a new area, for approximate factorization (over the complex field) of a monic univariate polynomial of degree n,

$$p(x) = \sum_{i=0}^{n} p_i x^i = p_n \prod_{j=1}^{n} (x - x_j) \, , \qquad \|p(x)\| = \sum_i |p_i| \, , \tag{1}$$

that is, given a set of complex coefficients $p_0, p_1, \ldots, p_n$ and a positive ϵ, we seek approximations $x_1^*, \ldots, x_n^*$ to the zeros $x_1, \ldots, x_n$ of $p(x)$ such that

$$\|p(x) - p_n \prod_{j=1}^{n} (x - x_j^*)\| \leq \epsilon \, , \tag{2}$$

assuming the polynomial norm

$$\|\sum_i u_i x^i\| = \sum_i |u_i| \, .$$

The requirement (2) is motivated by the observation that in practice of computation, the coefficients of $p(x)$ are most frequently available only within certain truncation errors. For the worst case input polynomial $p(x)$, where $|x_j| \leq 1$, for all j (this assumption is no loss of generality, since we may scale x), (2) implies the more classical requirement that

$$|x_j - x_j^*| < \tilde{\epsilon}\,, \qquad \text{for all } j\,, \tag{3}$$

as long as $\tilde{\epsilon} \geq 4.4|p_n|(2\epsilon)^{1/n}$, $2|p_n|\epsilon < 40^{-n}$ (see appendix in [15]). Moreover, for many polynomials $p(x)$, the bound (2) implies (3) already for $\tilde{\epsilon} = O(\epsilon/\max_j |p'(x_j)|)$.

For polynomials $p(x)$ with multiple or clustered zeros, (2) implies (3), with $\tilde{\epsilon}$ tending to be larger than ϵ as $\epsilon \to 0$.

Example 1. $p(x) = x^n$ has the only zero $x_1 = x_2 = \ldots = x_n = 0$, whose multiplicity is n. $p(x) + \epsilon = x^n + \epsilon$ has the zeros $x_j = \epsilon^{1/n}\omega^j$, $j = 1, \ldots, n$; $\omega = \exp(2\pi\sqrt{-1}/n)$, so that $\tilde{\epsilon} = \epsilon^{1/n}$.

Example 1 suggests that, for polynomials with multiple or clustered zeros, computing the factorization under (2) is numerically better conditioned than the zero finding problem under (3).

More important for us, the same example also suggests that after a small random perturbation of the coefficients of $p(x)$, the zeros of the resulting polynomial $p(x) + \Delta(x)$, with $\|\Delta(x)\| = \epsilon$, tend to stay apart from each other at the distance at least of the order of $(1/n)\epsilon^{1/n}$ [even if they correspond to the multiple or clustered zeros of $p(x)$], so that such a perturbation promises to eliminate a major obstacle to a rapid convergence of many known algorithms for polynomial factorization, namely, those which converge slowly on the input polynomials whose zeros form clusters.

Substantiation of this intuitive argument is not straightforward, however.

In this paper we achieve some progress towards such a substantiation, by exploiting some properties of the resultant of $p(x)$ and of its derivative [or of the discriminant of $p(x)$]. Based on these properties, we estimate the *m-th diameter* $d_m = d_m(x_1, \ldots, x_n)$ of the set $\{x_1, \ldots, x_n\}$,

$$d_m = \min_{|T|=m} \max_{i,j \in T} |x_i - x_j|\,, \qquad m = 2, 3, \ldots, n\,, \tag{4}$$

where the minimum is over all the cardinality m subsets of the set $\{1, 2, \ldots, n\}$ [that is, d_m denotes the minimum diameter of a subset of m elements of the set $\{x_1, \ldots, x_n\}$, so that, in particular, $d_n = \max_{1 \leq i,j \leq n} |x_i - x_j|$]. More precisely, we estimated the m-th diameter of the set of the zeros of the polynomials

$$p(x) + x^h \Delta\,, \qquad \text{for} \qquad h = 0, 1, \ldots, n\,,$$

for a random complex Δ uniformly distributed on the circle $|\Delta| = \rho$, and for a fixed small positive ρ. We have set $m = n/2$ (assuming n even) and proved that, with a probability at least $1/(2n+1)$, the reciprocal of the m-th diameter of the set of the zeros of $p(x) + x^h\Delta$ is bounded by$O(1/\rho^{4/(n-2)})$ (as $\rho \to 0$) if $h = 0$, and moreover, for a large class of the input polynomials $p(x)$ [not including $p(x) = x^n$], the maximum of such a reciprocal over all integers h, $0 \leq h \leq n$, is bounded by $O(1/\rho^{4/(n-2)n})$ [see (18), (53) and Proposition 4 below, for more specific estimates].

We also examined the resulting effect of the perturbation of $p(x)$ on the computation of the factorization of $p(x)$ by means of the effective factorization algorithm of [17] and of its further improvement based on some techniques of [13]. The resulting hybrid algorithm recursively computes the *complete numerical factorization* (2) of $p(x)$ and supports the record running time bounds for this computation, both in terms of arithmetic and Boolean (bit) operations involved. The intermediate steps compute *incomplete numerical factorizations* of $p(x)$. If the degrees of the output factors are less than, say, $1/2$ of the input degree in every recursive step, then in at most $\lfloor \log_2 n \rfloor$ recursive steps, complete numerical factorization (2) is computed, and the worst case bounds on the sequential and parallel running times of the entire algorithm decrease roughly by the factors of n and $n/\lfloor \log_2 n \rfloor$, respectively. This is because, in the worst case, for each i, recursive step i splits its input polynomial of degree $n+1-i$ into two factors of degrees 1 and $n-i$, respectively, so that $n-1$ recursive steps are required to compute a complete recursive factorization (2).

By using the cited lower bounds on the distances among the zeros of the slightly perturbed polynomial, $p(x)+x^h \Delta$, we prove that, with a probability bounded away from 0, for a random choice of Δ, practically the *same algorithm* splits such a perturbed polynomial into factors of degrees less than $n/2$. Thus, the randomization alone *strictly improves* the performance of the original algorithms.

The same randomization techniques can be recursively applied to split the computed factors of $p(x)$. In each new recursive step, however, the randomization gives us less and less advantages (see section 8 on the details), and we may end up with shifting to the original deterministic factorization algorithm at some recursive step at which using randomization gives us no advantage anymore.

Below, we will formally state our main results in the form of Theorem 1, which presents our estimates for the error and for the parallel and sequential computational complexity of a single step of splitting $p(x)+\Delta$ (for a random Δ, $|\Delta|=\rho$) into factors of degrees less than $n/2$. We note that our randomization is of Las Vegas type, where no undetected errors may occur (the algorithm may output FAILURE but with a low and controlled probability).

For simplicity, we will use the arithmetic (rather than Boolean) complexity estimates, which is adequate since our deviation from the original algorithms of [17] and [13] does not actually affect the required precision of the computation. We will assume the customary RAM and PRAM models of sequential and parallel arithmetic computations, respectively (see [1], [9]), and will adopt the customary notation $O_A(t,p)$, which means that $O(t)$ parallel arithmetic steps and p processors suffice in the parallel implementation of the solution algorithm. (Here and hereafter, we use the "O" notation assuming that $n \to \infty$ and $\epsilon, \rho \to 0$.) $O_A(t,p)$ also implies $O_A(ts, p/s)$, for any integer $p/s > 0$, which gives us the sequential time bound $O_A(tp,1)$, for $s=p$ (Brent's principle [7]).

We will assume hereafter that

$$\|p(x)\| = 1\ , \tag{5}$$

$$1/4 \le r(C,p(x)) = \max_j |x_j - C| \le 1\ , C = (1/n)\sum_j x_j = -p_{n-1}/(np_n)\ . \tag{6}$$

We may closely approximate $r(C,p(x))$ at the cost $O_A(\log n, n)$ (see Proposition 5 below), and if $r(C,p(x)) > 1$ or if $r(C,p(x)) < 1/4$, we may shift to a polynomial

$$q(y) = ap(by+c) = q_n \prod_{j=1}^{n} (y - y_j)\ ,$$

for fixed complex a, b and c such that $ab \neq 0$,

$$\|q(y)\| = 1 , \qquad 1/4 < r(\widetilde{C}, q(y)) = \max_j |y_j| \leq 1 , b\widetilde{C} = \sum_j (x_j - c) .$$

The cost of shifting from $p(x)$ to $q(y)$ is also $O_A(\log n, n)$ (see [2]).

Here is our main result, which we will prove in sections 6 and 7.

Theorem 1. *Suppose that we are given complex coefficients $p_0, \ldots, p_n$ of the polynomial $p(x)$ of (1), satisfying (5), (6), and four positive α, β, δ and ϵ such that*

$$\alpha \geq 1 > \delta > 0 , \quad \beta \geq 1 , \quad n|p_n|20^{-n} > \epsilon , \quad \log(1/\epsilon) = O(n^\alpha (\log n)^\beta) . \tag{7}$$

Then there exists a randomized algorithm (of Las Vegas type) that either reports a failure with a probability at most δ or, otherwise, computes an incomplete numerical factorization of $p(x)$ (within error norm ϵ) into a product of polynomials, each of degree less than $n/2$. The algorithm supports the following parallel and sequential complexity estimates for this computation:

$$c_A = O_A(n^{\alpha-1}(\log n)^{\beta+1} \ , \ n^3 \log(1/\delta)/(\log n)^\beta) , \tag{8}$$

$$(sc)_A = O_A(n^{\alpha+1}(\log n)^{\beta+1} + n(\log n)^2 \log(1/\delta), 1) . \tag{9}$$

Remark 1. If

$$\log(1/\delta) = O(\log n) , \tag{10}$$

then the estimates (8) and (9) are simplified as follows:

$$c_A = O_A(n^{\alpha-1}((\log n)^{\beta+1} \ , \ n^3(\log n)^{1-\beta}) , \tag{11}$$

$$(sc)_A = O_A(n^{1+\alpha}(\log n)^{\beta+1}, 1) . \tag{12}$$

[In the summary, we cited (11) and (12) for $\alpha = \beta = 1$.]

Remark 2. We also show (in section 9) how the complexity bounds (8) and (9) can be ensured, for a large class of input polynomials $p(x)$, even provided that the upper bound of (7) on $\log(1/\epsilon)$ is increased by the factor of n, to

$$\log(1/\epsilon) = O(n^{\alpha+1}(\log n)^\beta) .$$

We organize the remaining part of the paper as follows: In section 2 we estimate some correlations between the absolute value of the discriminant of $p(x)$ [or of the resultant $R(p, p')$ of $p(x)$ and $p'(x)$] and the m-th diameter of the set of zeros of $p(x)$. In section 3 we estimate $|R(p + \Delta, p')|$ as a function in Δ. In section 4 we show our hybrid deterministic algorithm. In section 5 we combine the results of sections 2–4 into our basis lemma (Proposition 9). In section 6 we summarize our study in the form of a parallel algorithm. In section 7 we modify this algorithm for the sequential computation and will deduce the complexity estimates of Theorem 1. In section 8 we comment on the recursive application of our algorithms. In section 9 we improve our estimated error bounds over a large class of the input polynomials $p(x)$.

Hereafter, all logarithms are to the base 2, and each polynomial zero of multiplicity μ is counted as μ zeros.

Acknowledgements. I wish to thank Joseph Lewittes and John Reif, for helpful comments and stimulating discussions, and also C. Engle for her assistance with typing the manuscript.

2 The Magnitude of the Resultant and the Distances between Polynomial Zeros

In this section we will relate the distances between some zeros of a polynomial $p(x)$ of (1) to the absolute value of R, the resultant of this polynomial and its derivative $p(x)$. We will make use of the two following expressions for R:

$$R = R(p_0, \ldots, p_n) = (-1)^{n(n-1)/2} p_n^{2n-1} \prod_{1 \le i < j \le n} (x_i - x_j)^2 \; ; \tag{13}$$

R equals the determinant of the $(2n-1) \times (2n-1)$ Sylvester (resultant) matrix,

$$R = \det S \; , \quad S = \begin{bmatrix} p_n & & O & (np_n) & & O \\ \vdots & \ddots & & \vdots & \ddots & \\ p_2 & \cdots & p_n & (2p_2) & & \\ p_1 & \cdots & p_{n-1} & p_1 & \cdots & (np_n) \\ p_0 & \cdots & p_{n-2} & & & \\ & \ddots & \vdots & & \ddots & \vdots \\ O & & p_0 & O & & p_1 \end{bmatrix} . \tag{14}$$

(14) implies, in particular,

Proposition 2. *The resultant R is a polynomial in $p_1, p_2, \ldots, p_n$ with integer coefficients, having the total degree $2n-1$.*

We will recall (4), ignore the case of multiple zeros, assuming for a moment that $R \neq 0$, and will immediately deduce from (13) the following

Proposition 3. *For any integer m, $1 \le m \le n$, let us denote that*

$$D = D(p_0, \ldots, p_n) = |R(p_0, \ldots, p_n)/p_n^{2n-1}| \; . \tag{15}$$

Then

$$D \le d_n^{n(n-1)} (d_m/d_n)^{m(m-1)} \; , \qquad m = 1, 2, \ldots, n \; . \tag{16}$$

We deduce from (16) that

$$D \le d_n^{n(n-1)} (d_m/d_n)^{m(m-1)} \; . \tag{17}$$

Hereafter, we will assume that n is even, $n = 2m$, so that $m(m-1) = n(n-2)/4$. Then we will deduce from (17) that

$$D/d_n^{n(3n-2)/4} \le d_m^{n(n-2)/4} \; , \quad D^{4/n(n-2)}/d_n^{(3n-2)/(n-2)} \le d_m \; . \tag{18}$$

3 Probabilistic Lower bound on the Magnitude of the Resultant

Let Δ denote a random complex parameter under the uniform probability distribution on the circle

$$|\Delta| = \rho \tag{19}$$

where the value ρ will be fixed later on. We are going to deduce some probabilistic lower bound on $|R_h(\Delta)| = |R(p_0, \ldots, p_{h-1}, p_h + \Delta, p_{h+1}, \ldots, p_n)|$, $\quad 0 \le h \le n$ [compare (13)]. Recall Proposition 2 and rewrite $R_h(\Delta)$ as a polynomial in Δ,

$$R_h(\Delta) = \sum_{i=0}^{n} r_{h,i}\Delta^i = r_{h,k}\prod_{j=1}^{k}(x - x_{j,h}(\Delta)) , \qquad k = k(h) \le n , \tag{20}$$

where $r_{h,i}$ are polynomials in $p_0, \ldots, p_n$ with integer coefficients and have total degrees at most $2n - 1 - i$, $i = 0, 1, \ldots, n$. Furthermore,

$$r_{h,1} = \partial R / \partial p_h , \qquad h = 0, 1, \ldots, n , \tag{21}$$

$$r_{0,n} = 0 , \quad r_{0,n-1} = (-1)^{n(n-1)/2}(np_n)^n . \tag{22}$$

The next simple result is the basis for our algorithms.

Proposition 4. *For a random Δ, under the uniform probability distribution on the circle (19), for any pair of nonnegative integers $h \le n$, $u \le n$, and for any fixed positive ρ, we have:*

$$|R_h(\Delta)| > 0.5|r_{h,u}|\rho^u \tag{23}$$

with a probability at least $1/(2k(h)+1) \ge 1/(2n+1)$, where $k(h)$ is defined by (20).

Proof. Let j be an integer such that

$$|r_{h,u}|\rho^u \le |r_{h,j}|\rho^j = \max_{0 \le i \le n}(|r_{h,i}|\rho^i) , \qquad 0 \le j \le n-1 . \tag{24}$$

It is well-known from analytic function theory that

$$\int_{|\Delta|=\rho} (R_h(\Delta)/\Delta^{j+1})\, d\Delta = 2\pi\sqrt{-1}\, r_{h,j} .$$

Representing Δ as $\rho\exp(2\pi\sqrt{-1}\,\phi)$, we obtain that

$$(1/\rho^j)\int_0^{2\pi} |R_h(\Delta)|\, d\phi = \int_0^{2\pi} |R_h(\Delta)/\Delta^{j+1}|\,\rho\, d\phi \ge 2\pi|r_{h,j}| ,$$

$$\frac{1}{2\pi}\int_0^{2\pi} |R_h(\Delta)|\, d\phi \ge |r_{h,j}|\,\rho^j ,$$

so that $|r_{h,j}|\rho^j$ is a lower bound on the average value of $|R_h(\Delta)|$ on the circle (19). To complete the proof, we compare this bound with the following upper bound: $|R_h(\Delta)| \le \sum_{i=0}^{k(h)} |r_{h,i}|\rho^i \le (k(h)+1)|r_{h,j}|\rho^j$, and recall (24).

Hereafter, denote that

$$\tilde{p}_{h,n} = p_n + \Delta \text{ if } h = n; \quad \tilde{p}_{h,n} = p_{h,n} \text{ otherwise.}$$

Assume that $\tilde{p}_{h,n} \neq 0$ for all h. Recall (20) and, similarly to the definitions (15) and (4), denote that

$$D_h(\Delta) = |R_h(\Delta)/\tilde{p}_{h,n}^{2n-1}| \, ,$$

$$d_{h,k}(\Delta) = \min_{|J|=k} \max_{i,j \in J} |x_{h,i}(\Delta) - x_{h,j}(\Delta)| \, , \qquad k = 2, 3, \ldots, n \, , \quad h = 0, 1, \ldots, n \, ,$$

and rewrite (18) as

$$(D_h(\Delta))^{4/n(n-2)} / (d_{h,n}(\Delta))^{(3n-2)/(n-2)} \leq d_{h,m}(\Delta) \, , \quad m = n/2 \, . \tag{25}$$

Rewrite $(3n-2)/(n-2)$ as $3 + 4/(n-2)$, combine (23) and (25), and obtain that

$$d_{h,m}(\Delta) > (0.5 \, | \, r_{h,u} \tilde{p}_{h,n}^{1-2n} | \rho^u)^{4/n(n-2)} / (d_{h,n}(\Delta))^{3+4/(n-2)} \, , \tag{26}$$

$u, h = 0, 1, \ldots, n$, with a probability at least $1/(2n+1)$.

In particular, substitute (22) into (26), for $h = 0$, $u = n - 1$, and arrive at the inequality

$$d_{0,m}(\Delta) > (0.5 n^n)^{4/n(n-2)} |\rho/p_n|^{4(n-1)/n(n-2)} / d_{0,n}(\Delta)^{3+4/(n-2)} \, , \tag{27}$$

where $\lim_{n \to \infty} (0.5 n^n)^{4/n(n-2)} = 1$.

Also, substitute (21) into (26), for $u = 1$ and $h = 0, 1, \ldots, n$, to obtain that

$$d_{h,m}(\Delta) > (0.5 | \tilde{p}_{h,n}^{1-2n} \frac{\partial R}{\partial p_h} | \rho)^{4/n(n-2)} / (d_{h,n}(\Delta))^{3+4/(n-2)} \, . \tag{28}$$

4 A Deterministic Algorithm for Polynomial Factorization

Hereafter, $S(C, r)$ will denote the square on the complex plane, with the center C and with the sides parallel to the real and imaginary axes and having length $2r$. $D(C, r)$ will denote the disc on the complex plane, with the center C and radius r. We assume that $S(C, r)$ and $D(C, r)$ denote closed complex domains.

$\tilde{R}/r$ is called the *isolation ratio* of the square $S(C, r)$ or of the disc $D(C, r)$ if $\tilde{R}$ is the minimum value such that the domains $S(C, \tilde{R}) - S(C, r)$ or, respectively, $D(C, \tilde{R}) - D(C, r)$ contain a zero of $p(x)$.

We next recall some known results.

Proposition 5. *Given the coefficients $p_0, \ldots, p_n$, a complex C and a constant θ, $0 < \theta < 1$, it is possible, at the cost $O_A(\log n, n)$, to evaluate r such that*

$$\theta r \leq r(C, p(x)) = \max_{1 \leq j \leq n} |C - x_j| \leq r \, . \tag{29}$$

Remark 3. $d_n \leq 2r(C, p(x)) \leq 2r$, under the notation of (29).

Proposition 5 relies on an old algorithm of Turan (see [19], [20]) complemented with more recent estimates for the complexity of its blocks.

Proposition 6. *([13]). Let a complex C and a positive r be two given values that satisfy (6) and (29). Then there exists a natural $H = H(n,r) = O(\log n)$ such that, for every $K > H$, it is possible, at the cost $O_A(K \log n, n^2)$, to compute complex C_i, real r_i, and natural $g \geq 2$ and $k_i \geq 1$, $i = 1, \ldots, g$, such that for all i,*

$$r_i \leq rn/2^K \ , \tag{30}$$

and $S(C_i, r_i)$ has an isolation ratio at least 3 and contains exactly k_i zeros of $p(x)$; furthermore, $\sum_{i=1}^{g} k_i = n$, and $S(C_j, r_j) \cap S(C_h, r_h)$ is empty if $1 \leq j < h \leq g$.

Proposition 7. *Let $S(C_i, r_i)$, the squares defined in Proposition 6, for $i = 1, \ldots, g$, be given to us, together with the associated integers k_i and with a positive ϵ^*. Let us denote*

$$b = b(\epsilon^*) = (1/n)\log(1/\epsilon^*) \ . \tag{31}$$

Then, at the cost $O_A(\log n \log(bn), gn \log b/\log(bn))$, the coefficients of $g \leq n$ monic polynomials $p_1(x), \ldots, p_g(x)$ can be computed such that the polynomial $p_i(x)$ has exactly k_i zeros, all lying in $S(C_i, r_i)$, $i = 1, \ldots, g$, and

$$\|p(x) - p_1(x) \ldots p_g(x)\| \leq \epsilon^* \ . \tag{32}$$

Proposition 7 follows from the results of [17] (Corollary 4.3 and section 12) applied to the discs $D(C_i, r_i\sqrt{2})$, $i = 1, \ldots, g$; such a disc $D(C_i, r_i\sqrt{2})$ contains exactly k_i zeros of $p(x)$ [lying in the square $S(C_i, r_i)$] and has an isolation ratio at least $3/\sqrt{2} > 2$ (compare Remark 4 below).

Combining Propositions 5–7, we devise

Algorithm 1. Input: the complex coefficients $p_0, \ldots, p_{n-1}$ of a polynomial $p(x)$ of (1) and a positive ϵ^*.

Output: positive integers $g > 1$, $k_1, \ldots, k_g$ (such that $k_1 + \cdots + k_g = n$) and the coefficients of monic polynomials $p_i(x)$ of degrees k_i, $i = 1, \ldots, g$, satisfying (32).

Stage 1. Compute C and r satisfying (6) and (29).

Stage 2. Compute the squares $S(C_i, r_i)$ defined in Proposition 6.

Stage 3. Compute a factorization (32), by following Proposition 7.

We immediately deduce the bounds

$$C_A^* = O_A((K + \log(bn))\log n, n^2) \tag{33}$$

on the parallel cost of the computation by algorithm 1, where b has been defined in Proposition 7 and where we may choose any K exceeding $H = O(\log n)$. (Later on, we will see some advantages of choosing a larger value of K.)

We may recursively apply algorithm 1 in whose input set we replace $p(x)$ by the polynomials $p_1(x), \ldots, p_g(x)$, as long as they have degrees exceeding 1 (these g applications can be performed concurrently, and similarly in the further recursive steps). The maximum degree of the output polynomials of algorithm 1 is $n - g + 1$ or less, so that in at most $n - 1$ its applications and at the overall cost bounded by $O_A((K+\log(bn))n \log n, n^2)$, we will arrive at the factorization (2) of $p(x)$ into linear factors. Here, we impose the same error bound ϵ^* for the numerical factorization of all the auxiliary polynomials that we factorize in this recursive process. We choose this bound ϵ^* sufficiently small, so as to ensure the error bound ϵ for the complete numerical factorization (2). Specifically, we are guided by the next proposition from section 5 of [17], which relates ϵ^* to ϵ:

Proposition 8. *Let*

$$\|p(x) - p_1(x) \cdots p_h(x)\| \le \epsilon h/n\ , \quad \|p_1(x) - f(x)g(x)\| \le \epsilon^*\ ,$$

$$\epsilon^* = \frac{\epsilon \|p_1(x)\|}{n 2^n \|p(x)\|}\ .$$

Then

$$\|p(x) - f(x)g(x)p_2(x) \cdots p_h(x)\| \le (h+1)\epsilon/n\ .$$

Due to Proposition 8, it is sufficient to choose

$$\epsilon^* = \frac{\epsilon \|w(x)\|}{n 2^n \|p(x)\|} \ge \frac{\epsilon}{n 2^n \|p(x)\|} \tag{34}$$

whenever algorithm 1 is applied to a monic polynomial $w(x)$ in the recursive process described above.

Next suppose that, by modifying the first step of this recursive process, we may ensure a more rapid decrease of the degrees of the factors, such that

$$\max_{1 \le i \le g}\ \deg\, p_i(x) < 0.5\ \deg\, p(x) = n/2\ ,$$

and similarly at all the next recursive steps. Then it would have sufficed to use $\lfloor \log_2 n \rfloor$ (rather than $n-1$) concurrent recursive steps of application of algorithm 1 [as before, we ensure the desired output error bound ϵ by imposing the error bound ϵ^* of (34) at all the recursive steps].

We easily estimate that in this case the complexity of recursive step i is $O_A((K + \log(bn)) \log n, n^2/2^i)$, for $i = 1, 2, \ldots, \lfloor \log n \rfloor$, which implies that the overall complexity of the complete numerical factorization of $p(x)$ into linear factors is $O_A((K + \log(bn)) \log^2 n, n^2/\log n)$. (To arrive at this bound, we apply Brent's principle of [7] by slowing down those recursive steps that otherwise would have used more than $n^2/\log n$ processors.)

These estimates show that algorithm 1 performs more effectively in the cases where the factors computed at its recursive steps have smaller degrees. In the next sections we will apply a randomization technique to split $p(x)$ into factors of degrees less than $n/2$.

Remark 4. Algorithm 1 is a simplification (based on the results of [13]) of the algorithm of [17]. The recursive step of [17] splits $p(x)$ into two factors, whose zeros lie inside and, respectively, outside a fixed disc that has an isolation ratio of the order of $1 + 1/n$. Since we deal with the squares $S(C_i, r_i)$ of Propositions 6, 7, having isolation ratios at least 3, the computation of the splitting by using algorithm 1 is substantially simpler than the similar computation in [17].

5 How to Ensure a Balanced Partition of the Set of Zeros

In the next result, we use D and r defined by (15) and (29).

Proposition 9. *Let the integer K of Proposition 6 be chosen such that*

$$2^{K-0.5} > n(2r)^{4(n-1)/(n-2)} / D^{4/(n(n-2))} . \tag{35}$$

Then $2\sqrt{2}r_i < d_m$, for $i = 1, \ldots, g$, that is, every square $S(C_i, r_i)$, $i = 1, \ldots, g$, of Proposition 6 contains less than $m = n/2$ zeros of $p(x)$.

Proof. Proposition 9 immediately follows from the comparison of the upper bound (30) on r_i with the lower bound (18) on d_m. [Compare also Remark 3 and observe that the diameter of the square $S(C_i, r_i)$ equals $2\sqrt{2}\,r_i$.]

Remark 5. As an exercise, the reader may extend (18) and Proposition 9, as well as our subsequent study, by choosing a smaller m, say, $m = \sqrt{n}$.

Proposition 9 can be immediately extended to the case where $p(x)$ is replaced by $p(x) + \Delta$, for Δ of (19), D by $D_0(\Delta)$ (see section 3) and similarly r of (29) by $r_0(\Delta)$; in particular, we may rewrite the assumption (35) as follows:

$$D_0(\Delta) > (2r_0(\Delta))^{(n-1)n}\, n^{(n-2)n/4}\, 2^{-(K-0.5)(n-2)n/4} . \tag{36}$$

Now let d, K and ρ be such that $d \geq 2r_0(\Delta)$,

$$0.5|r_{0,n-1}\,p_n^{1-2n}|\rho^{n-1} \geq d^{(n-1)n}\, n^{n(n-2)/4} / 2^{(K-0.5)n(n-2)/4} . \tag{37}$$

Apply Proposition 4 for $h = 0$, $u = n - 1$ and deduce that [with a probability at least $1/(2n+1)$] we have:

$$\begin{aligned} D_0(\Delta) = |R_0(\Delta) / p_n^{2n-1}| &> 0.5|r_{0,n-1} / p_n^{2n-1}|\rho^{n-1} \\ &\geq d^{(n-1)n}\, n^{n(n-2)/4}\, 2^{-(K-0.5)n(n-2)/4} . \end{aligned}$$

Since $d \geq 2r_0(\Delta)$, the latter inequality implies (36), and, consequently, implies the extension of Proposition 9 to the case where the polynomial $p(x) + \Delta$ replaces $p(x)$.

6 The Factorization Algorithm

Now we are ready to summarize our previous study, by devising the following randomized (of Las Vegas type) algorithm:

Algorithm 2. Input: the complex coefficients $p_0, \ldots, p_{n-1}$ of a polynomial $p(x)$ of (1), a positive ρ such that

$$r(C, p(x)) \leq 2r(C, p(x) + \Delta) \leq 3r(C, p(x)) \quad \text{if} \quad |\Delta| = \rho\,, \quad C = -p_{n-1}/(np_n) \tag{38}$$

(compare Remark 6 below), and a tolerance δ to the probability of a failure, $0 < \delta < 1$ [compare (7)].

Output: FAILURE with a probability at most δ or, otherwise, an integer g, $g > 2$, a complex value Δ, $|\Delta| = \rho$, and the coefficients of g polynomials $p_i^*(x, \Delta)$ having degrees less than $n/2$ and satisfying the inequality (40) below.

Stage 1. Successively compute the values

$$\nu = \lceil (2n+1) \log(1/\delta) / \log 3 \rceil \,, \tag{39}$$

then C and r satisfying (6) and (29), for $\Theta = 0.99$ (compare Remark 6 below), then $d = 3.1\,r$, and finally, the minimum positive integer K exceeding H of Proposition 6 and satisfying (37). Choose ν independent random values Δ on the circle $|\Delta| = \rho$, under the uniform probability distribution.

Stage 2. For all such values Δ and for $\Delta = 0$, concurrently compute $D_0(\Delta)$. If (36) has been satisfied for none of the values Δ, end this computation and output FAILURE. Otherwise, fix some Δ for which (36) holds, apply algorithm 1 to the polynomial $p(x) + \Delta$ in order to compute and to output a natural $g > 2$ and the coefficients of the polynomials $p_i^*(x, \Delta)$ that approximate g distinct nonconstant factors $p_i(x, \Delta)$ of $p(x) + \Delta$, for $i = 1, \ldots, g$, such that

$$p(x) + \Delta = \prod_{i=1}^{g} p_i(x, \Delta) \; ; \quad \|p(x) + \Delta - \prod_{i=1}^{g} p_i^*(x, \Delta)\| \leq \rho \; ;$$

$$\|p(x) - \prod_{i=1}^{g} p_i^*(x, \Delta)\| \leq 2\rho \; , \tag{40}$$

and end the computations. [Note that 2ρ plays the role of ϵ^* of (32), (34) and algorithm 1.]

Let us next show the correctness of the algorithm. First observe that $d = 3.1\,r \geq 3.1\,r\big(C, p(x)\big)$ [due to (29)]. Recall (38) and obtain that $d \geq 2.05\,r(C, p(x) + \Delta)$. Extend (29) by replacing $p(x)$ by $p(x) + \Delta$ and r by $r_0(\Delta)$, and obtain that $d \geq 2.05\,\Theta\, r_0(\Delta)$. Substitute $\Theta = 0.99$ and obtain that

$$d > 2r_0(\Delta) \; . \tag{41}$$

Now apply Proposition 4, for $h = 0$, $u = n-1$, and deduce that, with a probability at least $1/(2n+1)$,

$$|R_0(\Delta)| > 0.5 r_{0,n-1} \rho^{n-1} \; ,$$

which implies that

$$D_0(\Delta) = |R_0(\Delta) \,/\, p_n^{2n-1}| > 0.5\, r_{0,n-1} |p_n^{1-2n}| \rho^{n-1} \; .$$

The latter inequality implies (36) since we have chosen the value of K satisfying (37). Therefore, we may apply Proposition 9 extended to the case of the input polynomial $p(x) + \Delta$. Then, application of algorithm 1 at stage 2 of algorithm 2 gives us a numerical factorization of $p(x) + \Delta$ satisfying (40), and we observe that the probability of a failure in an application of stage 2 to $p(x) + \Delta$ for all the ν values $\Delta \neq 0$ is at most $(1 - 1/(2n+1))^{\nu} < 1/3^{\log(1/\delta)/\log 3} = \delta$ [see (39)].

Remark 6. The assumption (38) surely holds for any sufficiently small positive ν. In particular, we may deduce from Appendix A of [15] that it is sufficient if

$$2\rho < 40^{-n} |p_n| \; . \tag{42}$$

Of course, the reader may replace the "magic" numbers 2 and 3 in (38) and the value $\Theta = 0.99$ by various other candidate values, so as to preserve the correctness of algorithm 2, respectively modifying (42).

7 Computational Complexity Estimates

Next, we will assume that $p(x)$ and x have been scaled so that

$$d \leq 1 \tag{43}$$

and will estimate the parallel complexity c_A of performing algorithm 2. Clearly, c_A is dominated by the complexity of computing $D_0(\Delta)$ for all the ν values Δ [bounded by $O_A(\log^2 n, \nu n^2 / \log n)$, due to [14]] and of applying algorithm 1 [see (33)], so

$$c_A = O_A\left[(K + \log(bn)) \log n, n^2(1 + \nu/(K + \log(bn)))\right] \tag{44}$$

where K denotes the minimum integer exceeding H (defined in Proposition 6) and satisfying (37), $bn = -1 + \log(1/\rho)$ [compare (31)] and ν is defined by (39).

Now observe that (40) implies (32), for any $\rho \leq \epsilon^*/2$ and for $p_i(x) = p_i^*(x, \Delta)$, $i = 1, \ldots, g$. Suppose that α, β, δ and ϵ are given as in Theorem 1, such that (7) holds. Then (38) holds for $\rho = \epsilon^*/2$ [see (34) and Remark 6]. Set $\rho = \epsilon^*/2$ and apply algorithm 2. By the definition of K given at stage 1 of this algorithm,

$$K = \max\{H + 1, \lceil K^* \rceil\} \tag{45}$$

$H = O(\log n)$, and setting $K = K^*$ turns (37) into an equation, that is,

$$2^{(K^*-0.5)n(n-2)/4} = 2d^{(n-1)n}\, n^{(n-2)n/4}\, |p_n^{2n-1} / r_{0,n-1}\rho^{n-1}| \,.$$

Substitute (22), take logarithms on both sides, divide the resulting equation by $n(n-2)/4$ and obtain that

$$K^* = 0.5 + 4/(n-2)n + (1 - 4/(n-2)) \log n + ((4n-4) / (n-2)n) \log |p_n d^n / \rho| \,. \tag{46}$$

Replace ρ by $\epsilon^*/2$, recall (5), (43) and Proposition 9, and deduce that

$$K = O(\log n + (1/n) \log(1/\epsilon)) = O(\log(n/\epsilon^{1/n}) \,. \tag{47}$$

We also have that

$$bn = O(\log(1/\epsilon^*)) \,, \tag{48}$$

$$\nu = O(n \log(1/\delta)) \tag{49}$$

[compare (31), (39)]. Combining (44)–(49), we obtain that $K + \log(bn) = \phi(n, \epsilon) = (\log(\log(1/\epsilon) + (n/\epsilon^{1/n})))$, and furthermore that

$$c_A = O_A(\phi(n, \epsilon) \log n, n^3 \log(1/\delta) / \phi(n, \epsilon)) \,. \tag{50}$$

In particular, if

$$\log(1/\epsilon) = O(n^\alpha (\log n)^\beta \,, \quad \text{for a fixed} \quad \beta \geq 1 \,,$$

then $\log\log(1/\epsilon) = O(\log n)$; $\log(1/\epsilon^{1/n}) = O(n^{\alpha-1}(\log n)^\beta)$, and we arrive at (8).

To deduce the bound (9), we modify stage 2 of algorithm 2 as follows:

a) compute $R_0(\Delta)$ for n values Δ equal to all the n-th roots of 1; for each value of Δ, such an evaluation amounts to computing the determinant of a Sylvester matrix, for the sequential cost $O_A(n(\log n)^2, 1)$ ([4], [5], [11]); this means $O_A((n \log n)^2, 1)$ for all the values Δ;

b) compute the coefficients of $R_0(\Delta)$ as a polynomial in Δ [see (14) and (20)] by means of the inverse FFT, for the cost $O_A(\log n, n)$ or $O_A(n \log n, 1)$ ([1]);
c) define ν by (39) and compute $D_0(\Delta)$, for ν random and independent values Δ on the circle $|\Delta| = \rho$, for the overall cost $O_A((\nu + n)\log^2 n, 1)$ ([1], [4], [6]);
d) among these ν values, choose the value Δ that maximizes $|D_0(\Delta)|$ and output FAILURE if (36) does not hold, for this value of Δ;
e) otherwise, if (36) holds, apply algorithm 1 to the polynomial $p(x)+\Delta$, at the cost $(C)^*_A = O_A((K + \log(bn))\log n, n^2)$, bounded according to (33), (45)–(48); by Brent's principle of [7], this implies the parallel cost bound $(sC)^*_A = O_A(n^2(K + \log(bn))\log n, 1)$.

We will refer to the resulting algorithm as to *algorithm 3*.

Summarizing all these estimates for the complexity of performing algorithm 3 and assuming (7), (38), (39), we arrive at the bound (9) on the sequential complexity of computing the approximate factorization (2), thus proving Theorem 1.

8 Extension to Recursive Factorization

Unless FAILURE has been output, stages 1 and 2 of algorithms 2 or 3 can be repeated with each of the polynomials $p_i(x, \Delta)$ of degree $k_i > 1$ replacing $p(x)$, with k_i replacing n in (37), and with

$$\nu_i = \lceil (2k_i - 1)\log(1/\delta) \,/\, \log 3 \rceil$$

replacing ν of (39). Then the failure probability is at most δ at this factorization stage for all the $p_i^*(x, \Delta)$. The difficulty with this extension of algorithms 2 and 3 is that in order to compute the factorization of $p_i^*(x, \Delta)$, we need to replace n by k_i in both (37) and (46), so that at this step, our estimate gives us $K = O((1/k_i)\log(1/\rho))$, rather than $K = O((1/n)\log(1/\rho))$. At the subsequent recursive steps, we need to replace k_i, in this expression for K, by smaller and smaller values. This means that we need to choose larger and larger values of K to ensure the desired bound on the approximation error of the factorization. This way we increase the running time of the algorithm. Thus, at some recursive step, the estimated time of our randomized computation may exceed the estimated time bound for the recursive step of the deterministic algorithm (based on algorithm 1), to which we shall shift at this point. It is desired, of course, to decrease the error of the factorization, so as to take advantage of the randomization as long as possible, reaching the factors of $p(x)$ that have smaller degrees. To achieve this, we will next slightly modify our randomization approach.

9 Decreasing Upper Bounds on the Factorization Error

Algorithms 2 and 3 and their analysis in section 7 relied on (22) and (27). For a large class of input polynomials $p(x)$, we may reach the same asymptotic complexity bounds (8) and (9) assuming that, roughly,

$$\log(1/\epsilon) = O(n^{1+\alpha}(\log n)^{\beta}) \,, \tag{51}$$

that is, for a large class of inputs, we may arrive at a superior approximation to the factorization of $p(x)$ by using roughly the same amount of computational resources. [We refer to (55), (56) below, for a more precise statement of the assumption (51).] The improvement is important in the recursive application of the factorization algorithms (see the previous section).

Let us supply some details. Denote

$$w_h = 0.5|\tilde{p}_{h,n}^{1-2n}\,\partial R/\partial p_h|\ , \quad h = 0, 1, \ldots, n\ , \tag{52}$$

substitute this expression on the right side of (28), also replacing $d_{h,n}(\Delta)$ by d of (41), $d \geq d_{h,n}(\Delta)$, and obtain that

$$d_{h,m}(\Delta) > (w_h\rho)^{4/n(n-2)}\,/\,d^{3+4/(n-2)}\ . \tag{53}$$

We need to choose K such that $dn\sqrt{2}/2^K < d_{h,m}(\Delta)$, due to Proposition 6. Assume that $w_h \neq 0$ and extend Proposition 9 replacing (45), (46) by the following expression:

$$K = \max\{H+1, \lceil 0.5 - \frac{4}{n(n-2)}\log(w_h\rho) + \log n + \frac{4n-4}{n-2}\log d\rceil\}\ . \tag{54}$$

Assume that $\rho = \epsilon/2$ and $d \leq 1$ [compare (43)], and deduce that

$$K = O(\log n + (1/n^2)\log(1/(w_h\epsilon))) = O(\log n\,/\,(w_h\epsilon)^{1/n^2})\ ,\ \text{unless } w_h = 0\ .$$

This is a considerable improvement of (47) unless w_h is small. Clearly, w_h does not decrease as $\epsilon \to 0$, and (52) and Proposition 2 imply that

$$w_h \geq 0.5\,z\,|z\tilde{p}_{h,n}|^{1-2n}$$

if $z \neq 0$, zp_i are integers for all i and $\partial R/\partial p_h \neq 0$. Furthermore, we may evaluate $\partial R/\partial p_h$, for $h = 0, 1, \ldots, n$, at the same asymptotic computational cost [bounded by $O_A(\log^2 n, n^2/\log n)$ or alternatively by $O_A(n\log^2 n, 1)$] that we need for the evaluation of R. We achieve this just by applying to R the parallel algorithm of [8], which extends the sequential algorithm of [3], [10]. [The algorithm of [8] computes all the first order partial derivatives of any polynomial $p(y_1, \ldots, y_s)$ at the cost $O_A(t, p)$, provided that an algorithm is available that computes $p(y_1, \ldots, y_s)$ at the cost $O_A(t, p)$, by using only arithmetic operations, with no branchings.]

Thus, initially, we may compute $\partial R/\partial p_h$ and $w_h\rho$, for $h = 0, 1, \ldots, n$, then choose h for which w_h is maximum, and finally compare $w_h\rho$ with $0.5\,n^n\,|\rho\,/\,p_n|^{n-1}$ [see (22), (23)]. If the latter value is greater, we shall go to algorithms 2 or 3 with no changes. Otherwise, we shall apply one of these algorithms, replacing $D_0(\Delta)$ by $D_h(\Delta)$ and K of (45), (46) by K of (54).

In the latter case, we shall replace $\phi(n, \epsilon)$ in (50) by $\log(\log(1/\epsilon) + n/(\epsilon w_h)^{1/n^2})$, and thus shall arrive at the overall complexity estimates (8) and (9) assuming that

$$\log\log(1/\epsilon) = O((\log n)^\beta)\ , \tag{55}$$

$$\log(1/(\epsilon w_h)) = O(n^{\alpha+1}(\log n)^\beta)\ , \quad \text{for fixed} \quad \alpha \geq 1\ ,\ \beta \geq 1\ . \tag{56}$$

[(55) and (56) turn into (51) if, say, $1/w_h = O(1)$.]

References

1. Aho, A. V., Hopcroft, J. E., Ullman, J. D.: The Design and Analysis of Computer Algorithms, Addison-Wesley, 1976.
2. Aho, A. V., Steiglitz, K., Ullman, J. D.: Evaluating polynomials at fixed set of points, SIAM J. Comput. **4** (1975) 533–539.
3. Baur, W., Strassen, V.: On the complexity of partial derivatives, Theoretical Comp. Sci. **22** (1983) 317–330.
4. Bini, D., Pan, V.: Numerical and Algebraic Computations with Matrices and Polynomials, **1**, **2**, Birkhäuser, Boston, 1992.
5. Bitmead, R. R., Anderson, B. D. O.: Asymptotically fast solution of Toeplitz and related systems of linear equations, Linear Algebra and Its Applic. **34** (1980) 103–116.
6. Borodin, A., Munro, I.: The Computational Complexity of Algebraic and Numeric Problems, American Elsevier, New York, 1975.
7. Brent, R. P.: The parallel evaluation of general arithmetic expressions, J. ACM **21**(2) (1974) 201–206.
8. Kaltofen, E., Singer, M.: Size efficient parallel algebraic circuits for partial derivatives, Tech. Report 90-32, Comp. Sci. Dept., RPI, Troy, NY, 1990.
9. Karp, R. M., Ramachandran, V.: A survey of parallel algorithms for shared memory machines, in Handbook Theor. Computer Science, North-Holland, Amsterdam, 1990.
10. Linnainmaa, S.: Taylor expansion of the accumulated rounding errors, BIT **16** (1976) 146–160.
11. Musicus, B. R.: Levinson and fast Choleski algorithms for Toeplitz and almost Toeplitz matrices, Internal Report, Lab. of Electronics, MIT, 1981.
12. Pan, V.: Complexity of parallel matrix computations, Theoretical Comp. Sci. **54** (1987) 65–85.
13. Pan, V.: Sequential and parallel complexity of approximate evaluation of polynomial zeros, Computers and Math. (with Applic.) **14**(8) (1987) 591–622.
14. Pan, V.: Parametrization of Newton's iteration for computations with structured matrices and applications, Computers and Math. (with Applics.), (1992).
15. Pan, V.: Randomized incomplete numerical factorization of a polynomial over the complex field, Tech. Rep. TR 031.91, Int. Comp. Sci. Inst., Berkeley, CA, 1991.
16. Rabin, M.: Probabilistic algorithms in finite fields, SIAM J. Comp. **9**(2) (1980) 273–280.
17. Schönhage, A.: The fundamental theorem of algebra in terms of computational complexity, ms, Dept. of Math., U. of Tübingen, Tübingen, Germany, 1982.
18. Schwartz, J. T.: Fast probabilistic algorithms for verification of polynomial identities, J. of ACM **27**(4) (1980) 701–717.
19. Turan, P.: Power sum method and approximative solution of algebraic equations, Math. of Comp. **29**(129) (1975) 311–318.
20. Turan, P.: On a New Method of Analysis and Its Applications, Wiley & Sons, New Jersey, 1984.

This article was processed using the LaTeX macro package with LLNCS style

Can Symmetric Toeplitz Solvers be Strongly Stable?

Elliot Linzer

IBM Research, P.O. Box 218, Yorktown Heights, NY 10598, USA

Abstract. We describe symmetric positive definite Toeplitz systems for which the floating point vector that is closest to the actual solution is not the solution of a nearby symmetric Toeplitz system. With these systems we are able to show that a large class of Toeplitz solvers are not strongly stable for solving symmetric (or symmetric positive definite) Toeplitz systems; i.e., the computed solution is not necessarily the solution of a nearby symmetric Toeplitz system. This class of algorithms includes Gaussian elimination and seems to include all known fast and superfast Toeplitz solvers; certainly, it includes the better known ones. These results strongly suggest that all symmetric Toeplitz solvers are not strongly stable.

1 Introduction

An $n \times n$ set of symmetric Toeplitz equations is a set of equations of the form

$$\mathbf{Tx} = \mathbf{y}, \tag{1}$$

where

$$\mathbf{x} = \begin{pmatrix} x_1 \\ x_2 \\ \vdots \\ x_n \end{pmatrix}, \qquad \mathbf{y} = \begin{pmatrix} y_1 \\ y_2 \\ \vdots \\ y_n \end{pmatrix},$$

and

$$\mathbf{T} = \left(\rho_{|j-k|}\right)_{j,k=1}^{n}$$

is a symmetric Toeplitz matrix. Toeplitz matrices arise in a large variety of physical applications [Bun85]. The need for efficient algorithms to solve large systems of Toeplitz equations has led many researchers to study Toeplitz solvers.

So called *fast Toeplitz solvers* solve $n \times n$ Toeplitz systems using only $O(n^2)$ arithmetic operations [Lev47, Tre64, Kai86, Bla86]. More recently, several *superfast* algorithms have been discovered that use only $O(n \log^2 n)$ operations [BGY80, AG86].

The study of the numerical properties of Toeplitz solvers began with G. Cybenko, who showed that, when certain fast Toeplitz solvers are used to solve well-conditioned symmetric positive definite (hereafter, s.p.d.) Toeplitz systems, the computed solution is close to the actual solution [Cyb78, Cyb80]. We say that those fast Toeplitz solvers are *weakly stable* for solving s.p.d. Toeplitz systems. Although attempts have been made to improve the numerical performance of fast Toeplitz solvers for indefinite Toeplitz systems [Swe86], a weakly stable fast algorithm for general Toeplitz matrices has not been found.

An algorithm for solving symmetric Toeplitz systems is said to be *strongly stable* if the solution that it computes is the solution of a nearby symmetric Toeplitz system. In the next section, these types of stability are discussed in more detail. Because the definitions that appear in the literature for the different types of stability are somewhat vague, we also give a precise definition of what we will mean by strong stability.

Before a physical problem is reduced the the mathematical problem of solving a set of structured linear equations, errors may have already been introduced due to measurement noise, quantization, etc. If an algorithm is strongly stable, then computational errors that occur during the solution of the linear system are not qualitatively worse than those incurred prior to representing the problem as the solution of a linear system.

In Section 3, we describe s.p.d. Toeplitz systems for which the floating point vector that is closest to the actual solution is not the solution of a nearby symmetric Toeplitz system. We then use these systems to show that a large set of symmetric Toeplitz solvers are not strongly stable. In Section 4, we present a set of numerical experiments designed to demonstrate that Levinson's algorithm is not strongly stable. In Section 5, we show that if we use a slightly tighter definition of strong stability than the definition given in Section 2, then we can prove that all algorithms for solving 2×2 or 3×3 symmetric Toeplitz systems are not strongly stable.

2 Conditioning and stability

Consider the solution of a set of linear equations of the form

$$\mathbf{M}\mathbf{x} = \mathbf{y}. \tag{2}$$

The condition number of $\mathbf{M}$, defined as $\kappa(\mathbf{M}) = ||\mathbf{M}||\;||\mathbf{M}^{-1}||$, determines the sensitivity of the solution to small changes in $\mathbf{M}$ and $\mathbf{y}$. In particular, if $\hat{\mathbf{x}}$ is the solution of

$$(\mathbf{M} + \sigma\mathbf{G})\hat{\mathbf{x}} = \mathbf{b} + \sigma\mathbf{g},$$

then for consistant matrix and vector norms [GL83]

$$\frac{||\hat{\mathbf{x}} - \mathbf{x}||}{||\mathbf{x}||} \le \kappa(\mathbf{M})\left(\frac{||\sigma\mathbf{G}||}{||\mathbf{M}||} + \frac{||\sigma\mathbf{g}||}{||\mathbf{b}||}\right) + O(\sigma^2). \tag{3}$$

If $\kappa(\mathbf{M})$ is large then $\mathbf{M}$ is said to be *ill-conditioned*; small changes in the inputs ($\mathbf{M}$ and $\mathbf{b}$) can lead to large changes in the the solution.

We will now summarize definitions of various types of stability from [Bun85]. An algorithm for solving $\mathbf{M}\mathbf{x} = \mathbf{y}$ is said to be stable for a class of matrices $\mathcal{A}$ if the solution that it computes in finite precision arithmetic, $\hat{\mathbf{x}}$, is the solution of a nearby system; i.e., if $(\mathbf{M} + \mathbf{G})\hat{\mathbf{x}} = \mathbf{y} + \mathbf{g}$, for some $||\mathbf{G}|| \ll ||\mathbf{M}||$ and $||\mathbf{g}|| \ll ||\mathbf{y}||$ whenever $\mathbf{M} \in \mathcal{A}$. This is the classical approach to the analysis of the numerical properties of matrix inversion [GL83, Bun87, Wil65]. In this paper, we consider $\mathcal{A} = \{n \times n$ nonsingular symmetric Toeplitz matrices$\}$ and $\mathcal{A} = \{n \times n$ s.p.d. Toeplitz matrices$\}$. If there exists such a $\mathbf{G}$ that also satisfies $(\mathbf{M} + \mathbf{G}) \in \mathcal{A}$ then the algorithm is said to be *strongly stable*. If $\mathbf{M}$ is well-conditioned and $\mathbf{x}$ is computed with a stable algorithm, then from (3) it can be seen that $||\hat{\mathbf{x}} - \mathbf{x}|| \ll ||\mathbf{x}||$. An algorithm is weakly stable over a class of matrices $\mathcal{A}$ if $||\hat{\mathbf{x}} - \mathbf{x}|| \ll ||\mathbf{x}||$ whenever $\mathbf{M} \in \mathcal{A}$ and $\mathbf{M}$ is well conditioned.

The definitions from [Bun87] are a bit vague, and for our purpose (disproving strong stability), it is necessary to make the definitions more precise. In particular, we must say exactly what we mean by the symbol "$\ll$", and we must define a model for roundoff errors.

Let a and b be real numbers, let $op = + \; - \; *$ or $/$, let $c = a\;(op)\;b$, and let $\hat{c}$ be the computed value of c. Following [Atk89, GL83], we will assume that

$$|\hat{c} - c| \leq |c|\,\delta. \tag{4}$$

We will use (4) as the model for floating point computations. Thus, to prove weak stability, stability, or strong stability we can only rely on (4) and not on information that might give a more precise idea about what kind of roundoff can be expected. Similarly, to prove that an algorithm is not strongly stable we need to show that if we choose the outcome of each elementary operation in a manner which is consistent with (4), then for a particular $\mathbf{M}$ and $\mathbf{y}$ the computed solution is not the solution of a nearby linear system of the same type (or is not the solution of a nearby linear system for stability; or is not close to the true solution for a well-conditioned matrix for weak stability). A more precise model (e.g., one which exactly defines the mapping $a\;(op)\;b \rightarrow \hat{c}$) would make stability easier to prove and the lack of stability harder to prove.

Let us now implicitly define the "$\ll$" symbol that we have used in the description of strong stability by giving a precise definition to strong stability.

Definition 1. An algorithm for solving solving $\mathbf{Mx} = \mathbf{y}$ is said to be strongly stable for a class of matrices $\mathcal{A}$ if $\exists K > 0$ for which (4) can be used to show that the computed solution, $\hat{\mathbf{x}}$, has the property that

$$\lim_{\delta \to 0} \; \mathrm{MAX}_{\mathbf{y},\mathbf{M}} \; \mathrm{MIN}_{\mathbf{g},\mathbf{G}} \left(\frac{||\mathbf{G}||}{||\mathbf{M}||} + \frac{||\mathbf{g}||}{||\mathbf{y}||} \right) = 0,$$

where the maximum is taken over $\mathbf{M} \in \mathcal{A}$, $\kappa(\mathbf{M}) \leq K/\delta$ and all non-zero $\mathbf{y}$, and the minimum is take over $\mathbf{M} + \mathbf{G} \in \mathcal{A}$ and $(\mathbf{M} + \mathbf{G})\hat{\mathbf{x}} = \mathbf{y} + \mathbf{g}$.

This definition is given for a particular problem size n, and therefore error growth as n increases will not prevent an algorithm from being called strongly stable. Because all norms over finite dimensional spaces are equivalent [GL83, page 12], the particular norm used to calculate the limit in the above definition will have no affect on whether or not an algorithm is strongly stable. A stricter interpretation of "$\ll$" (e.g., that $\frac{||\mathbf{G}||}{||\mathbf{M}||} + \frac{||\mathbf{g}||}{||\mathbf{y}||} = O(\delta)$) would make strong stability harder to prove and the lack of strong stability easier to prove. Similar definitions can be formulated for stability and weak stability.

It can be seen from (2) that the computed solution, $\hat{\mathbf{x}}$, will always satisfy

$$\mathbf{M}\hat{\mathbf{x}} = \mathbf{y} + \mathbf{g},$$

where

$$\|\mathbf{g}\| \leq \kappa(\mathbf{M}) \frac{\|\hat{\mathbf{x}} - \mathbf{x}\|}{\|\mathbf{x}\|} \|\mathbf{y}\|. \tag{5}$$

If $\mathbf{M}$ is well conditioned (that is, if $\kappa(\mathbf{M})$ is small) and a weakly stable algorithm was used to compute $\hat{\mathbf{x}}$, then (5) implies that $\|\mathbf{g}\| \ll \|\mathbf{y}\|$. It follows that the differences between the various types of stability only become apparent when ill-conditioned matrices are used. Indeed, if the set of matrices $\mathcal{A}$ has the property that there exits a number K that satisfies $\kappa(\mathbf{M}) < K$ whenever $\mathbf{M} \in \mathcal{A}$, then if an algorithm for solving (2) is weakly stable it is also strongly stable.

By taking the maximum over $\kappa(\mathbf{M}) \leq K/\delta$, we allow an algorithm to be strongly stable even if the computed solution does not solve a nearby system of the same type if the matrix involved is so ill-conditioned, relative to the machine precision, that the computed solution can anyway be expected to be essentially meaningless. (This assumption is always explicit or implicit when backwards error analysis is used, as in [GL83, page 67], where without assumptions on the condition number the so called *growth factor* that appears in the error analysis of Gaussian elimination, and depends on the elements of the *compute* reduced matrix, cannot be bounded as a function of n even when full or partial pivoting is used.) We thus keep the definition of strong stability loose enough to allow algorithms described as strongly stable in [Bun87] to still be called strongly stable but do not make it so loose – say by only considering matrices for which $\kappa(\mathbf{M}) \leq K$ – so that the distinction between the different types of stability would disappear.

3 The main results

In this section, we will show that a large class of $n \times n$ symmetric Toeplitz solvers are not strongly stable. In the terminology of Definition 1, we will take the maximum over $\mathbf{M} \in \{n \times n \text{ s.p.d. Toeplitz matrices}\}$ and the minimum over $(\mathbf{M} + \mathbf{G}) \in \{n \times n \text{ symmetric Toeplitz matrices}\}$, and show that the limit is not equal to 0. We will thus disprove strong stability for symmetric Toeplitz solvers as well as s.p.d. Toeplitz solvers.

For $n \geq 2$ and $1 > \epsilon > 0$, denote by $\mathbf{R}$ the $n \times n$ s.p.d. Toeplitz matrices given by

$$\mathbf{R} = \begin{pmatrix} 1 & 0 & \cdots & 0 & \epsilon - 1 \\ 0 & \ddots & \ddots & & 0 \\ \vdots & \ddots & \ddots & \ddots & \vdots \\ 0 & & \ddots & \ddots & 0 \\ \epsilon - 1 & 0 & \cdots & 0 & 1 \end{pmatrix}.$$

The two-norm condition number of $\mathbf{R}$ is $\kappa_2(\mathbf{R}) = (2-\epsilon)/\epsilon$; thus, for small ϵ the matrix $\mathbf{R}$ is ill-conditioned. Denote by $\mathbf{y}_1$ the n point vector given by

$$\mathbf{y}_1 = \begin{pmatrix} 1 + \delta/(2\epsilon) \\ 0 \\ \vdots \\ 0 \\ 1 + (\epsilon - 1)\delta/(2\epsilon) \end{pmatrix}.$$

The linear system

$$\mathbf{R}\mathbf{x} = \mathbf{y}_1 \tag{6}$$

has the exact solution

$$\mathbf{x} = \begin{pmatrix} 1/\epsilon + \delta/(2\epsilon) \\ 0 \\ \vdots \\ 0 \\ 1/\epsilon \end{pmatrix}.$$

Denote the computed solution by $\hat{\mathbf{x}} = (\,\hat{x}_1 \quad \cdots \quad \hat{x}_n\,)^t$. Let $\hat{\mathbf{x}}$ satisfy

$$(\mathbf{R} + \mathbf{A})\,\hat{\mathbf{x}} = \mathbf{y}_1 + \mathbf{b} \tag{7}$$

where $\mathbf{b} = (\,b_1 \quad \cdots \quad b_n\,)^t$ and $\mathbf{A} = (a_{|j-k|})_{j,k=1}^n$ is a symmetric Toeplitz matrix. Let $a = a_0 - a_{n-1}$, and let $b = b_1 - b_n$. Left multiplying each side of (7) by the the n-point row vector $1/(2-\epsilon)\ (\,1 \quad 0 \quad \cdots \quad 0 \quad -1\,)$, we obtain

$$\frac{1}{2-\epsilon}\sum_{j=2}^{n-1}(a_j - a_{n-j+1})\,\hat{x}_j + \left(1 - \frac{a}{2-\epsilon}\right)(\hat{x}_1 - \hat{x}_n) = \delta/(2\epsilon) + \frac{b}{2-\epsilon}. \tag{8}$$

Consider the class of algorithms used to solve symmetric Toeplitz systems that do not use the first element of the solution computed solution vector, $\hat{x}_1$, to compute the other elements of the solution vector. This class of algorithms seems to include all known fast and superfast Toeplitz solvers; certainly, it includes Levinson's algorithm [Lev47], Schur's algorithm [Kai86] and any algorithm based on the Gohberg-Semencul formula [GF74] or similar inversion formulae.

For such an algorithm the following scenario is possible (that is, it cannot be disproved by using (4)). The last $n-1$ elements of the solution vector are all computed exactly, but roundoff error does occurs during the last elementary operation used to compute x_1. In particular, since

$$|\, x_1 - 1/\epsilon \,| < \delta \,|\, x_1 \,|,$$

it can occur that $\hat{x}_1 = 1/\epsilon$, $\hat{x}_n = x_n = 1/\epsilon$ and $\hat{x}_2 = x_2 = \hat{x}_3 = x_3 = \cdots \hat{x}_{n-1} = x_{n-1} = 0$. Indeed, it is possible that $1/\epsilon$ will be the closest floating point number to x_1, as when ϵ is a negative power of two. In this scenario, the left hand side of (8) is zero, so we can infer that

$$b = (\epsilon - 2)\delta/(2\epsilon). \tag{9}$$

If $1 > \epsilon = O(\delta)$, then $\|\mathbf{y}_1\| = O(1)$ and $|\, b \,| = O(1)$, which imply that $|\, b \,| \,/\|\mathbf{y}_1\| = O(1)$, whence

$$\frac{\|\mathbf{b}\|}{\|\mathbf{y}_1\|} \geq O(1). \tag{10}$$

Equation (10) shows that for any δ we can choose an s.p.d. Toeplitz system (i.e., (6) with a small enough ϵ) for which the solution computed with an algorithm from the above described class will not be the solution of any nearby symmetric Toeplitz systems; that is, $\|\mathbf{b}\|/\|\mathbf{y}_1\| \geq O(1)$. By choosing ϵ as a negative power of 2, this computed solution is in fact the closest floating point vector to the actual solution.

To show the lack of strong stability in the formal sense of Definition 1, note that if $\epsilon = 2\delta/K$ then $\kappa_2(\mathbf{R}) < K/\delta$ but $\|\mathbf{b}\|/\|\mathbf{y}_1\| \geq O(K)$. Thus, all Toeplitz solvers from the above described class are not strongly stable for the solution of symmetric or s.p.d. Toeplitz systems.

With (6), we showed that symmetric Toeplitz solvers that do not use the computed value of x_1 to compute the remaining elements of $\mathbf{x}$ vector are not strongly stable. With

$$\mathbf{R}\mathbf{x} = \mathbf{y}_2 = \begin{pmatrix} 1 + (\epsilon - 1)\delta/(2\epsilon) \\ 0 \\ \vdots \\ 0 \\ 1 + \delta/(2\epsilon) \end{pmatrix}, \tag{11}$$

the same arguments, *mutatis mutandis*, can be made to show that all algorithms that do not use the computed value of x_n to compute the other elements of the solution vector are not strongly stable for the solution of symmetric or s.p.d. Toeplitz systems. This second class of algorithms includes Gaussian elimination without pivoting or with partial pivoting (because the pivots will always lie on the main diagonal).

4 Numerical experience

In Section 3, the reliance on (4) simplified the analysis of the numerical accuracy of algorithms; the model is quite simple and allows us to calculate limits as $\delta \to 0$. Nonetheless, it is somewhat artificial; worst case actual machine computations may be more or less accurate than a worse case analysis of (4) would suggest. (They may be more accurate because the machine might not "choose" the outcome of computations as cleverly as we did, and they may be less accurate because (4) does not account for the possibility of overflows.) We have therefore performed a set of numerical experiments to test the strong stability of Levinson's algorithm.

The experiments were performed in IEEE standard single precision arithmetic ($\delta \approx 2^{-24}$). The version of Levinson's algorithm given in [Cyb78] was used to solve the 10×10 system

$$\mathbf{R}\mathbf{x} = \mathbf{z}, \tag{12}$$

where $\mathbf{R}$ is defined in the last section and

$$\mathbf{z} = \begin{pmatrix} 1 + 2^{-25}/\epsilon \\ 0 \\ \vdots \\ 0 \\ 1 + (\epsilon - 1)2^{-25}/\epsilon \end{pmatrix},$$

for $\epsilon = 2^{-1}, 2^{-2}, \ldots 2^{-25}$. We then computed $\hat{x}_1 - \hat{x}_{10}$ in double precision arithmetic.

Let $\hat{\mathbf{x}}$ satisfy

$$(\mathbf{R} + \mathbf{C})\hat{\mathbf{x}} = \mathbf{z} + \mathbf{d}, \tag{13}$$

where $\mathbf{C} = (c_{|j-k|})_{j,k=1}^{n}$ and $\mathbf{d} = (\, d_1 \quad \cdots \quad d_n \,)^t$.

For $\epsilon = 2^{-1}, 2^{-2}, \ldots 2^{-23}$ the results of the expeiments were $\hat{x}_1 - \hat{x}_{10} = 0$ and $\hat{x}_2 = \hat{x}_3 \cdots = \hat{x}_9 = 0$. Left multiplying each side of (13) by $1/(2-\epsilon)\,(\,1 \quad 0 \quad \cdots \quad 0 \quad -1\,)$, we see that, for Levinson's algorithm computed in single precision arithmetic,

$$d_1 - d_n = (\epsilon - 2)\delta/(2\epsilon) \qquad \epsilon = 2^{-1}, 2^{-2}, \ldots 2^{-23}.$$

For that $\epsilon \geq 2^{-25}$, $||\mathbf{z}||_1 = 2 + 2^{-25}$. Because $||\mathbf{d}||_1 \geq |\, d_1 - d_n \,|$, we can obtain

$$\frac{||\mathbf{d}||_1}{||\mathbf{z}||_1} \geq \frac{(2-\epsilon)2^{-25}}{\epsilon(2+2^{-25})} > 0.1874\frac{2^{-23}}{\epsilon} \qquad \epsilon = 2^{-1}, 2^{-2}, \ldots 2^{-23},$$

showing that as ϵ decrease to 2^{-23} the symmetric Toeplitz system that is closest to (12) and has $\hat{\mathbf{x}}$ as a solution moves steadily away from (12).

For $\epsilon = 2^{-24}$, the results were $\hat{x}_1 - \hat{x}_{10} = 1$ and $\hat{x}_2 = \hat{x}_3 \cdots = \hat{x}_9 = 0$. For this computed solution vector, left multiplying each side of (13) by $1/(2 - 2^{-24})\,(\,1 \quad 0 \quad \cdots \quad 0 \quad -1\,)$ shows that $c_0 - c_{n-1} + d_1 - d_n = 1 - 2^{-25}$. Because $||\mathbf{R}||_1 = 2 - 2^{-24}$ and $||\mathbf{C}||_1 \geq c_0 - c_{n-1}$, we can deduce that

$$\frac{||\mathbf{C}||_1}{||\mathbf{R}||_1} + \frac{||\mathbf{d}||_1}{||\mathbf{z}||_1} \geq \frac{1 - 2^{-25}}{2 + 2^{-25}} > 0.499.$$

For $\epsilon = 2^{-25}$ overflows occurred when Levinson's algorithm was used to solve (6) (because $\mathbf{R}$ is then numerically singular).

5 Changing the definition

It is, of course, tautological that whether or not an algorithm is strongly stable depends on the definition of strong stability. In this section, we show that by slightly tightening the definition of strong stability we can deduce that all algorithms are not strongly stable for the solution of 2×2 and 3×3 symmetric or s.p.d. Toeplitz systems.

Instead of simply requiring that the limit in Definition 1 be equal to 0, we require that $||\mathbf{G}||/||\mathbf{M}|| + ||\mathbf{g}||/||\mathbf{y}|| = O(\delta)$. Thus for an algorithm to be strongly stable for the solution of symmetric (or s.p.d.) Toeplitz systems, we now require that $\exists\, C < \infty$ such that (4) can be used to show that when the algorithm is used to solve (1) (and, for s.p.d. Toeplitz solvers, whenever $\mathbf{T}$ is also positive definite) the computed solution, $\hat{\mathbf{x}}$, satisfies $(\mathbf{T} + \mathbf{A})\hat{\mathbf{x}} = \mathbf{y} + \mathbf{b}$, where $\mathbf{A}$ is Toeplitz and $||\mathbf{A}||/||\mathbf{T}|| + ||\mathbf{b}||/||\mathbf{y}|| \leq \delta C + O(\delta^2)$,

With this tighter definition of strong stability, we will see that there are 2×2 and 3×3 s.p.d. Toeplitz systems for which there are no floating point vectors that solve a nearby symmetric Toeplitz system. By contrast, when we used the looser definition of Section 3 we were only able to show the existence of s.p.d. Toeplitz systems for which the floating point vector closest to the actual solution did not solve any nearby symmetric Toeplitz systems.

Consider *any* algorithm used to solve (6). If $n = 2$ or $n = 3$, (8) reduces to

$$\left(1 - \frac{a}{2-\epsilon}\right)(\hat{x}_1 - \hat{x}_n) = \delta/(2\epsilon) + \frac{b}{2-\epsilon}. \tag{14}$$

The above equation implies that one of the following three conditions must hold:

1. $|\hat{x}_1 - \hat{x}_n| < (4/3) * \delta/(2\epsilon) = 2\delta/(3\epsilon)$,
2. $a = O(1)$ or
3. $b = O(\delta/\epsilon)$.

Assume that the algorithm used to compute $\hat{\mathbf{x}}$ is strongly stable. Thus the second condition cannot hold. From here until the end of the section, we will consider values of ϵ for which $\epsilon = O(\sqrt{\delta})$. Thus the third condition cannot hold. Hence we will assume that the first condition holds; i.e., that

$$|\hat{x}_1 - \hat{x}_n| < 2\delta/(3\epsilon). \tag{15}$$

Equation (4) cannot guarantee that there are floating point numbers that are greater than $3/(4\epsilon)$ and yet differ by less than $2\delta/(3\epsilon)$. This point is best illustrated by considering a floating point system that uses L bit mantissas; i.e., a system that represents only those positive numbers of the form $2^E * M$, where E is an integer (the exponent) and M is an integer in the interval $[2^{L-1}, 2^L - 1]$. This floating point system is consistent with (4) if the computed value of $a(op)b$ is the nearest floating point number to $a(op)b$ and $\delta = 2^{-L}$. If $\epsilon = (3/4)2^{-P}$ for a positive integer P, then floating point numbers greater than $3/(4\epsilon)$ differ by at least $2^{P-L} = 3\delta/(4\epsilon) > 2\delta/3\epsilon$. If either $\hat{x}_1 \leq 3/(4\epsilon)$ or $\hat{x}_n \leq 3/(4\epsilon)$, then $||\hat{\mathbf{x}} - \mathbf{x}|| / ||\mathbf{x}|| = O(1)$. We choose ϵ so that $\epsilon = (3/4)2^{-P} = O(\sqrt{\delta})$ for some integer P. Thus we can infer from (15) that

$$||\hat{\mathbf{x}} - \mathbf{x}|| / ||\mathbf{x}|| = O(1). \tag{16}$$

Because $\kappa(\mathbf{R}) = O(1/\epsilon) = O(\sqrt{1/\delta})$, we can use (3) and (16) to obtain $||\mathbf{A}||/||\mathbf{R}|| + ||\mathbf{b}||/||\mathbf{y}|| \geq O(\sqrt{\delta})$. It follows that with this tighter definition of strong stability all algorithms for solving 2×2 or 3×3 symmetric (or s.p.d.) Toeplitz systems are not strongly stable. Because for $n = 2$ or $n = 3$ there are no floating point vectors that are solutions of systems close to (6) when floating point computations are modeled by using numbers with binary mantissas, the results of this section hold even if a more realistic model than (4) is used for floating point computation.

6 Discussion

When Bunch defined weak stability, stability and strong stability in [Bun87], he gave examples of algorithms for which weak stability had been proved but stability had not been proved, and algorithms for which stability had been proved but strong stability had not been proved. Nonetheless, he did not show that any weakly stable algorithm is in fact not stable, or that any stable algorithm is in fact not strongly stable. In [Lin90], the author showed that transform based circular deconvolution is weakly stable but not strongly stable. In this paper, we have more examples of algorithms which are weakly stable but not strongly stable; fast Toeplitz solvers that are weakly stable for solving s.p.d. Toeplitz systems are not strongly stable. Moreover, because Gaussian elimination with partial pivoting is stable for solving nonsingular systems, it is also stable for solving symmetric Toeplitz systems. We have shown in Section 3 that Gaussian elimination with partial pivoting is not strongly stable for the solution of symmetric Toeplitz systems. Thus we now have an example of an algorithm which is stable but not strongly stable. Finding an example of an algorithm which is weakly stable but not stable remains an open problem.

The key fact that has allowed us to prove that a large class of symmetric Toeplitz solvers are not strongly stable, and that for a tight definition of strong stability allowed us to show that no 2×2 or 3×3 Toeplitz solvers are strongly stable, was that there are Toeplitz systems for which a solution vector that is slightly perturbed elementwise does not solve any nearby symmetric Toeplitz systems. A similar situation prevails with circulant matrices, and it seems likely that strong stability can be disproved for similar classes of algorithms that invert circulant systems (although only a single algorithm is dealt with in [Lin90]).

The title of this paper asks whether any symmetric Toeplitz solver can be strongly stable. It is certainly possible to invent algorithms for which the techniques of Section 3 cannot be used to formally disprove strong stability. However, because there are symmetric Toeplitz systems for which an approximate solution, with only a small relative perturbation in a single element, does not solve a nearby symmetric Toeplitz system, it seems highly unlikely that any algorithm is strongly stable for the solution of symmetric Toeplitz systems.

Moreover, this property of slightly perturbed solutions not solving nearby systems of the same type is a property of Toeplitz *systems* rather then Toeplitz *solvers*. Thus, it seems rather misleading to talk about an *algorithm* not being strongly stable for the solution of a certain type of problem if there may not be any strongly stable algorithms for solving that problem. These problems are inherently difficult to solve in a strongly stable way using floating point arithmetic. Because it seems unlikely that any strongly stable algorithms exist for a type of linear system where slightly perturbed solutions are not solutions of nearby systems of the same type, it seems natural to ask whether we are dealing with such systems before we ask whether a particular algorithm is strongly stable.

References

[AG86] G. S. Ammar and W. B. Gragg. The generalized Schur algorithm for the superfast solution of Toeplitz systems. In M. Pindor J. Gilewicz and W. Siemaszko, editors, *Rational Approximation and its Application in Mathematics and Physics*. Springer, 1986.

[Atk89] K. E. Atkinson. *An Introduction to Numerical Analysis*. Wiley, New York, NY, 1989.

[BGY80] R. P. Brent, F. G. Gustavson, and D. Y. Y. Yun. Fast solution of Toeplitz systems equations and computation of Padé approximations. *J. Algorithms*, 1:259–295, 1980.

[Bla86] R. E. Blahut. *Fast Algorithms for Digital Signal Processing*. Addison-Wesley, Reading, MA, 1986.

[Bun85] J. R. Bunch. Stability of methods for solving Toeplitz systems of equations. *SIAM J. Sci. Stat. Comput.*, 6:349–364, 1985.

[Bun87] J. R. Bunch. The weak and strong stability of algorithms in numerical linear algebra. *Linear Algebera Appl.*, 88/89:49–66, 1987.

[Cyb78] G. Cybenko. *Error Analysis of Some Signal Processing Algorithms*. PhD thesis, Princeton University, Princeton, NJ, 1978.

[Cyb80] G. Cybenko. The numerical stability of the Levinson-Durbin algorithm for Toeplitz systems of equations. *SIAM J. Sci. Stat. Comput.*, 1:303–309, 1980.

[GF74] I. C. Gohberg and I. A. Fel'dman. *Convolution Equations and Projection Methods for their Solution*. American Mathematical Society, Providence, RI, 1974.

[GL83] G. H. Golub and C. F. Van Loan. *Matrix Computations*. Johns Hopkins, Baltimore, MD, 1983.

[Kai86] T. Kailath. A theorem of I. Schur and its impact on modern signal processing. In I.C. Gohberg, editor, *I. Schur Methods in Operator Theory and Signal Processing*. Birkhauser-Verlag, 1986.

[Lev47] N. Levinson. The Wiener rms error criterion in filter design and prediction. *J. Math. Phys.*, 25:261–278, 1947.

[Lin90] E. Linzer. On the stability of transform-based circular deconvolution. Techinical Report RC-16337, IBM Research, Yorktown Heights, NY, 1990. To appear in *SIAM J. Numer. Anal.*

[Swe86] D. R. Sweet. The use of pivoting to improve the numerical performance of Toeplitz solvers. In J. M. Speiser, editor, *Advanced Algorithms and Architectures for Signal Processing*. SPIE, 1986.

[Tre64] W. F. Trench. An algorithm for the inversion of finite Toeplitz matrices. *J. SIAM*, 12:512–522, 1964.

[Wil65] J. Wilkinson. *The Algebraic Eigenvalue Problem*. Clarendon Press, Oxford, England, 1965.

This article was processed using the LaTeX macro package with LLNCS style

Bounds On Parallel Computation of Multivariate Polynomials

Ilan Sade* Amir Averbuch

Deptartment of Computer Science
School of Mathematical Sciences, Tel Aviv University
Tel Aviv 69978, Israel
E-mail: sade@math.tau.ac.il

Abstract. We consider the problem of fast parallel evaluation of multivariate polynomials over a field **F**. We define "maximal-degree" ($max_{\deg}$) of a multivariate polynomial f as $\max_i deg_{x_i}(f(x_1,\ldots,x_n))$ $i=1,\ldots,n$.
The first lower bound result states that if a circut **G** evaluates a multivariate polynomial f, where its nodes are capable of performing $(+,*)$, then the depth(**G**) is not less than $\log_2\lceil max_{\deg}(f)\rceil$. This result is a generalization of Kung's[K] results for a univariate polynomial which is $\log_2\lceil deg\, f\rceil$.
In the second part, we consider the circuit **G** which evaluates an arbitrary polynomial f in n variables with $max_{\deg}(f) \triangleq d_p > 1$.
We present two algorithms that achieve better performance than the classical results of Hyafil[H] and Valiant et al. [VSBR] for most classes of multivariate polynomials. For the class of " dense " polynomials the results are closed to the theorethical bound $\log C$, where C is the sequential complexity.
The algorithms generalize Munro-Paterson[MP] method for the univariate case. It should be noticed that the bound obtained by Hyafil[H] and Valiant, Skyum, Berkowitz and Rackoff[VSBR] is not sufficiently tight for the worst-sequential case (dense multivariate polynomials) and their bound can be reduced by the factor of $\log d$ while the number of required processors is only $O(C)$. The best improvement is achieved in a case of a "dense" multivariate polynomial. A polynomial is dense if the computation necessitates $\Omega(d_p^n)$ sequential steps.
The simple algorithm requires only $n\log d_p + O(n\sqrt{\log d_p})$ parallel steps .The second algorithm has parallel complexity , measured by the depth of the circuit , $depth(\mathbf{G}) \le n(\log\, d_p+\beta)+\log\, n+\sqrt{\log\, d_p}$ where $\beta \le \sqrt{\log d_p}$. If $C=\Omega(d_p^n)$ then it is less than $\log C+\sqrt{n\cdot\log C}$ where C is the number of sequential steps, and it requires only $O(C)$ processors.
The second algorithm is slightly better than the " simple" one. The improvement is achieved when β is small. The improvement of both algorithms in the parallel complexity and the number of processors with respect to Valiant is significant for most classes of multivariate polynomials.
Key words :Complexity of parallel computation, Multivariate polynomials, Design and analysis of parallel algorithms , Maximal-degree, Dense polynomial.

* This author was supported by Eshkol Fellowship No. 0375 administered by the Israeli Ministry of Science.

1 Introduction

Hyafil[H] proved that any multivariate polynomial $f(x_1,\ldots,x_n)$ of degree d that can be computed with C sequential steps, can be computed in parallel in $O(\log d)(\log C + \log d)$ steps. His method requires, in general, $C^{\log d}$ processors. Therefore, even if C and d are both polynomially bounded in terms of n (the number of indeterminates) the number of processors required is not polynomially bounded.

Valiant et. al.[VSBR] improved Hyafil's result by reducing the number of required processors to $O(Cd)^\beta$ processors for an appropriate β.

In the first part of the paper we prove a lower bound for the parallel time and at the second part of the paper we consider the worst sequential case, which we define as "dense" polynomial. For this case, we prove that the parallel time is only $O(\log C)$ and the number of required processors is only $O(C)$ which are both better than the previous mentioned general results. It stressed the necessity of parallelization for the computation of "dense" multivariate polynomials.

Definition 1. Let $\mathbf{F}$ be a field and let $\mathbf{F}[x_1,\ldots,x_n]$ be the ring of polynomials over indeterminates $x_1,\ldots,x_n$ with coefficients from $\mathbf{F}$.

A program f over $\mathbf{F}$ is a sequence of instructions:

$$v_i \longleftarrow v_i' \circ v_i'' \quad i = 1,\ldots,C$$

where for each value i :

I. $v_i', v_i'' \in \mathbf{F} \cup \{x_1,\ldots,x_n\} \cup \{v_1,\ldots,v_{i-1}\}$
II. $\circ$ is one of the ring operations $\{+,*\}$.

Subtraction can be simulated by using $(-1) \in \mathbf{F}$. The formal polynomial evaluation at v_i can be defined as $f(v_i)$. The degree of $f(v_i)$ is denoted by $d(v_i)$.

The computational model is a circuit with nodes capable of performing "add" and "multiply" operations.

We assign to each node v_i a vector of n elements $\mathbf{deg}(v_i) = \{deg_1(v_i,\ldots,deg_n(v_i)\}$ where for $l = 1,\ldots,n$, we define $deg_l(v_i) = deg_{x_l} f(v_i)$ and

$$d(v_i) \triangleq \sum_{l=1}^{n} deg_l(v_i) \quad max_{\mathbf{deg}}(v_i) \triangleq \max_l deg_l(v_i)$$

The degree of a scalar in the field is 0, the degree of an indetereminate x_l is the unit vector $\mathbf{e_l}$ $\;l = 1,\ldots,n$. In case of a multiplication node v_i then $deg_l(v_i) = deg_l(v_i') + deg_l(v_i'')$ $\;l = 1,\ldots,n$, and in case of an addition node then $deg_l(v_i) = \max(deg_l(v_i'), deg_l(v_i''))$ $\;l = 1,\ldots,n$.

2 Lower Bound

Kung[K] derived a lower bound for the parallel processing time of rational expressions in the case of a univariate function ($n = 1$) [Th. 6.1.3 in [BM]].

We generalize the result to a multivariate polynomial case.

Theorem 1 *The lower bound on the paraellel computation time of any multivariate polynomia* $f(x_1,\ldots,x_n)$ *is* $\lceil \log_2(max_{\deg} f(x_1,\ldots,x_n)) \rceil$.

This theorem can be stated using the arithmetic circuit model as:

Theorem 2 *If a circuit* **G** *evaluates* f *then* $depth(\mathbf{G})$ *is not less than* $\log_2(max_{\deg} f(x_1,\ldots,x_n))$.

Proof: The proof is similar to Kung[K], where the degree of the univariate polynomial should be replaced by the $max_{\deg}$ of a multivariate polynomial. □

Corollary 1 *The same theorem can be generalized to any multivariate rational function by defining* $max_{\deg}$ *of a function* $\frac{p(x_1,\ldots,x_n)}{q(x_1,\ldots,x_n)}$ *as* $\max\{max_{\deg}(p), max_{\deg}(q)\}$.

3 The complexity of the problem

Hyafil[H] showed that any polynomial P of degree d that can be computed with $C(P)$ $\{+,-,*\}$ operations serially, can be computed in parallel in time proportional to $\log d(\log C + \log d)$. Unfortunately, his method, in general, requires $C^{\log d}$ processors.

Valiant-Skyum-Berkowitz-Rackoff[VSBR] showed that any multivariate polynomial of degree d that can be computed serially in C steps can be computed in parallel in $O(\log d)(\log C + \log d))$ steps using $(Cd)^{O(1)}$ processors.

We define a "dense polynomial" as a polynomial of n indeterminates that has $max_{\deg} = d_p$, where its evaluation requires $\Omega(d_p^n)$ serial steps. We present an algorithm, that in a case where the multivariate polynomial is "dense", then its parallel time is almost $\log C$ and the number of processors is $O(C)$.

Dense polynomials are actually representing the worst-case analysis for serial evaluation and the aim of this paper is to show that its parallelization will speed-up the computation.

Our main result indicates that Valiant et. al.[VSBR] bound is not sufficiently tight in the case of dense multivariate polynomials. Their result for the parallel complexity is quite good for sparse systems where $C = O(nd)$. But for denser systems, their bound can be improved. Our result for the parallel complexity is quite closed to $\log C$, which is the theoretical but not achievable optimum for any PRAM parallel system.

Definition 2 *Let* $T(d_p, n)$ *be the time that parallel computation of polynomials in* n *varaibles and* $max_{\deg} = d_p$ *necessiated on array of sufficient number of processors.*

We, first, consider the simple algorithm, which eventually improves Valiant et. al. bound for dense multivariate polynomials.

The simple algorithm. Let f be an arbitrary polynomial in n variables with $max_{\deg}(f) = d_p$.

$$f(x_1 \ldots x_n) = \sum_{i=0}^{d_p} c_i(x_2 \ldots x_n) x_1^i. \tag{1}$$

By definition, we have:

$$T(d_p, n) = T(d_p, n-1) + T(d_p, 1) \tag{2}$$

Since the best bound for the single-variable polynomial is [MP]:

$$T(d_p, 1) = \log d_p + O(\sqrt{\log d_p}) \tag{3}$$

Hence,

$$T(d_p, n) = n \cdot \log d_p + n \cdot O(\sqrt{\log d_p}) \tag{4}$$

This result is $O(\log C)$. If the polynomial is "dense" , the result is $\log C + O(\sqrt{n \log C})$.

We shall try to decrease the bound closer to the theoretical limit which is $\log C$. Although the simple algorithm is quite closed to the limit.

Definition 3 *Let $D(r) = \frac{1}{2}r(r+1)+1$ where r is a natural number. Hence, $D(r) = D(r-1) + r$.*

Assumptions: Let f be an arbitrary polynomial in n variables with $max_{\text{deg}} = d_p$ where $2^{D(r-2)} \leq d_p < 2^{D(r-1)}$.

The exact location of d_p in $[2^{D(r-2)},\ 2^{D(r-1)})$ is determined by β, $\beta = D(r-1) - \log d_p$. Hence, $0 < \beta \leq r - 1$.

Let $Q(r, n)$ be $\max(T(d_p(r), n))$ where the maximum is taken over all the relevant polynomials.

Lemma 1 $Q(r, n) \geq D(r) + \log n$.

Proof: The proof is done by induction on n.

$Q(r, 1) = D(r)$ See [MP].

$Q(r, n+1) \geq Q(r, n) + 1$ since at least one more operation is needed to evaluate a polynomial in $n+1$ variables.

Substitutting the induction hypothesis into $Q(r, n+1)$ and using the fact that $1 + \log n \geq \log(n+1)$ and we have:

$$Q(r, n+1) \geq Q(r, n) + 1 \geq D(r) + \log n + 1 \geq D(r) + \log(n+1) \tag{5}$$

The hypothesis holds for $n+1$. □

Lemma 2 *Let f be an arbitrary polynomial in n variables with $max_{\text{deg}}(f) = d_p$, $2^{D(r-2)} \leq d_p < 2^{D(r-1)}$, then there exists a circuit which evalu f with depth $= T(d_p, n) \leq nD(r-1) + \log n + r$.*

Proof: The proof is done by introducing an algorithm based on Munro-Paterson[MP] splitting technique.

The proof is proceed by induction on r. The induction hypothesis is done on the depth: $T(d_p, n) \leq Q(r, n) = nD(r-1) + \log n + r$. We assume that there exists a circuit which evaluates any arbitrary multivariate polynomial in $depth = Q(r, n)$. To verify for $r = 1$:

$$P_1(x_1, \ldots, x_n) = \sum_{i_1=0}^{1} \cdots \sum_{i_n=0}^{1} a_{i_1 \ldots i_n} x_1^{i_1} \ldots x_n^{i_n} \tag{6}$$

Obviously, there are at most 2^n possible operands in the summation due to all possible combinations. Therefore, at most n parallel additions after $\log n$ parallel time for multiplications in each monomial and one multiplication by the coefficient. In total: $n + \log n + 1 = nD(0) + \log n + 1$. (Munro and Paterson proved the lemma for a single variable case).

So for $n = 1$ we have that $Q(r, 1) = D(r)$.

To prove the lemma we construct the difference equation:

$$T(d_p(r+1), n) \leq Q(r+1, n) = rn + 1 + \max(Q(r, n), D(r-1) + r + \log n)$$
$$= rn + 1 + \max(Q(r, n), D(r) + \log n) \quad (7)$$

This equation emerged from the nature of the circuit which is typical to the splitting method.

Any arbitrary polynomial f with high parallel degree can be composed from lower parallel degree polynomials.

Assume that $max_{\text{deg}}(f) = d_p = 2^{D(r)} - 1$ then f can be decomposed as:

$$f(x_1, \ldots, x_n) = \sum_{i_1=0}^{2^r-1} \cdots \sum_{i_n=0}^{2^r-1} q_{i_1 \ldots i_n}(x_1 \ldots x_n) x_1^{i_1 2^{D(r-1)}} \cdots x_n^{i_n 2^{D(r-1)}} \quad (8)$$

Each of the polynomials $q_{i_1 \ldots i_n}(x_1 \ldots x_n)$ has max_{deg} less than $2^{D(r-1)}$.

According to the induction hypothesis each $q_{i_1 \ldots i_n}(x_1 \ldots x_n)$ takes at most $Q(r, n)$ time units.

In parallel each monomial $x_1^{i_1 2^{D(r-1)}} \ldots x_n^{i_n 2^{D(r-1)}}$ can be computed in at most $D(r-1) + r + \log n$ time units.

Then the stage of the summation and multiplication takes at most $nr + 1$ parallel steps.

Now we use the result of Lemma 1 and have $Q(r+1, n) = rn + 1 + Q(r, n)$ and w know that $Q(1, n) = n + \log n + 1$. By the summation:

$$Q(r+1, n) = Q(1, n) + n \sum_{j=1}^{r} j + r = n + \log n + r + 1 + n\frac{r(r+1)}{2}$$

$$= n[1 + \frac{r(r+1)}{2}] + \log n + r + 1 = nD(r) + \log n + r + 1 \quad (9)$$

Hence $Q(r+1, n) = nD(r) + \log n + r + 1$ or $Q(r, n) = nD(r-1) + \log n + r$. □

Lemma 3 *The depth of the circuit of f is bounded by: $n(\log d_p + \beta) + \log n + O(\sqrt{\log d_p})$ for $d_p > 1$. β is determined by the location of d_p on the strip $2^{D(r-2)} \leq d_p < 2^{D(r-1)}$. $0 < \beta < \sqrt{\log d_p}$.*

proof: Since $\log d_p = D(r-1) - \beta$ and $r \approx \sqrt{\log d_p}$ then

$$depth = T(d_p, n) \leq n(\log d_p + \beta) + \log n + \sqrt{\log d_p} \quad \square$$

Theorem 3 *An arbitrary dense polynomial in n variables can be computed in parallel in less than $\log C + \sqrt{n \cdot \log C}$ steps using only $O(C)$ processors. In fact, the bound is quite closed to the theoretical time limit which is $\log C$.*

Proof: By defintion, C the serial complexity of the computation of a dense polynomial, is $\Omega(d_p{}^n)$. By applying the circuit described in Lemma 2 and Lemma 3, we have the required circuit. The number of processors required for the fast parallel evaluation is computed as follows:

Let $N(n,r)$ denote the maximum number of processors required at the r-th stage in evaluating an arbitrary polynomial in n variables. According to the architecture of the circuit, we have:

$$N(n,r+1) = 2^{rn}N(n,r) + \{generators \quad of \quad all \quad high \quad powers\} +$$

$$\{monomials \quad generators \quad , multipliers \quad and \quad summation\} \tag{10}$$

where we know that $N(n,1) < 3 \cdot 2^n$.

In Eq. (10) the first term $2^{nr} \cdot N(n,r)$ dominates the others. Generation of all high powers requires $O(n \cdot 2^{D(r)})$ processors. The multiplications and the summation require $O(2^{nr})$ processors. Thus, we can say:

$$N(n,r+1) = 2^{rn}N(n,r) + O(n \cdot 2^{D(r)}) + O(2^{nr}) \tag{11a}$$

$$N(n,r+1) = 2^{rn}N(n,r) + \alpha_1 n 2^{D(r)} + \alpha_2 2^{nr} \tag{11b}$$

$$N(n,1) < 3 \cdot 2^n \tag{12}$$

The leading term is $2^{rn} \cdot N(n,r)$. Therefore, after $r-1$ iteratio we can have that

$$N(n,r) = O(2^{n(\frac{r(r-1)}{2}+1)} = O(2^{nD(r-1)}) = O(2^{n \log d_p}) \tag{13}$$

The final result is $O(2^{n \log d_p}) = O(d_p^n)$ which is $O(C)$ in the case of dense multivariate polynomial. □

The results are better than Hayfil[H] and Valiant et. al.[VSBR] for this case. Generally speaking, we may say that when the system becomes denser, the bound is $O(\log C)$, which is a better bound than Hyafil and Valiant et. al. bound.

4 Conclusions

1. The obtained circuit is almost optimal in time, since $\log C$ is the theoretical optimum for any PRAM parallelization.
2. The circuit can be implemented in a "modular" VLSI-architecture using only $O(C)$ processors. The structure is dictated either by the simple algorithm or by the later one.
3. The criterion for parallel complexity of multivariate polynomials evaluation in n varaiables should be expressed by n and the "maximal-degree" ($max_{\deg}$).

References

[BM] Borodin, A., Munro, I.: The Computational Complexity of Algebraic and Numeric problems, American Elsevier Publishing Company, 1975.

[K] Kung, H.: New Algorithm and Lower Bounds for the Parallel Evaluation of Certain Rational Expressions and Recurrences, J. ACM, vol. **23**, no. 2 (1976) 252-261.

[H] Hyafil, K.: On the Parallel Evaluation of Multivariate Polynomials, Proc., 10th ACM Symposium on Theory of Computing, (1978) pp. 193-195.

[VSBR] Valiant, L.G., Skyum, S., Berkowitz, S., Rackoff, C.: Fast Parallel Computation of Polynomials using Few Processors, SIAM J. Comput., **12**, No. 4, (1983) 641-644.

[MP] Munro, I., Paterson, M.: Optimal Algorithms for Parallel Polynomial Evaluation, J. of Computer and System Science **7**(1973) 189-198.

This article was processed using the LaTeX macro package with LLNCS style

Time-Lapse Snapshots

Cynthia Dwork
IBM Almaden Research Center

Maurice Herlihy
DEC Cambridge Research Lab.

*Serge A. Plotkin**
Stanford University

*Orli Waarts***
Stanford University

Abstract. A snapshot scan algorithm takes an "instantaneous" picture of a region of shared memory that may be updated by concurrent processes. Many complex shared memory algorithms can be greatly simplified by structuring them around the snapshot scan abstraction. Unfortunately, the substantial decrease in conceptual complexity is quite often counterbalanced by an increase in computational complexity.
In this paper, we introduce the notion of a *weak snapshot scan*, a slightly weaker primitive that has a more efficient implementation. We propose the following methodology for using this abstraction: first, design and verify an algorithm using the more powerful snapshot scan, and second, replace the more powerful but less efficient snapshot with the weaker but more efficient snapshot, and show that the weaker abstraction nevertheless suffices to ensure the correctness of the enclosing algorithm.
We give two examples of algorithms whose performance can be enhanced while retaining a simple modular structure: bounded concurrent timestamping, and bounded randomized consensus. The resulting timestamping protocol is the fastest known bounded concurrent timestamping protocol. The resulting randomized consensus protocol matches the computational complexity of the best known protocol that uses only bounded values.

1 Introduction

Synchronization algorithms for shared-memory multiprocessors are notoriously difficult to understand and to prove correct. Recently, however, researchers have identified several powerful abstractions that greatly simplify the conceptual complexity of many shared-memory algorithms. One of the most powerful of these is *atomic snapshot scan* (in this paper we sometimes omit the word "scan"). Informally, this is a procedure that makes an "instantaneous" copy of memory that is being updated by concurrent processes. More precisely, the

* Research supported by NSF Research Initiation Award CCR-900-8226, by U.S. Army Research Office Grant DAAL-03-91-G-0102, by ONR Contract N00014-88-K-0166, and by a grant from Mitsubishi Electric Laboratories.

** Research supported by NSF grant CCR-8814921, U.S. Army Research Office Grant DAAL-03-91-G-0102, ONR contract N00014-88-K-0166, and IBM fellowship.

problem is defined as follows. A set of n asynchronous processes share an n-element array A, where P is the only process that writes $A[P]$[3]. An atomic snapshot is a read of all the elements in the array that appears to occur instantaneously. Formally, scans and updates are required to be *linearizable* [20], *i.e.* each operation appears to take effect instantaneously at some point between the operation's invocation and response.

Atomic snapshot scan algorithms have been constructed by Anderson [3] (bounded registers and exponential running time), Aspnes and Herlihy [6] (unbounded registers and $O(n^2)$ running time), and by Afek, Attiya, Dolev, Gafni, Merritt, and Shavit [2] (bounded registers and $O(n^2)$ running time). Chandy and Lamport [13] considered a closely related problem in the message-passing model.

Unfortunately, the substantial decrease in conceptual complexity provided by atomic snapshot scan is often counterbalanced by an increase in computational complexity. In this paper, we introduce the notion of a *weak snapshot scan*, a slightly weaker abstraction than the atomic snapshot scan. The advantage of using weak snapshot is that it can be implemented in $O(n)$ time. Thus, the cost of our weak snapshot scan is asymptotically the same as the cost of a simple "collect" of the n values. Our primitive, however, is much more powerful. Moreover, the best known atomic snapshot requires atomic registers of size $O(nv)$, where v is the maximum number of bits in any element in the array A. In contrast, our weak snapshot requires registers of size $O(n+v)$ only.

Our results indicate that weak snapshot scan can sometimes alleviate the trade-off between conceptual and computational complexity. We focus on two well-studied problems: bounded concurrent timestamping and randomized consensus. In particular, we consider algorithms for these problems based on an atomic snapshot. In both cases, we show that one can simply replace the atomic snapshot scan with a weak snapshot scan, thus retaining the algorithms' structure while improving their performance.

The weak snapshot algorithm presented here was influenced by work of Kirousis, Spirakis, and Tsigas [23], who designed a linear-time atomic snapshot algorithm for a *single* scanner. In this special case our algorithm solves the original atomic snapshot problem as well.

One important application of snapshots is to bounded *concurrent timestamping*, in which processes repeatedly choose labels, or timestamps, reflecting the real-time order of events. More specifically, in a concurrent timestamping system processes can repeatedly perform two types of operations. The first is a *Label* operation in which a process assigns itself a new label; the second is a *Scan* operation, in which a process obtains a set of current labels, one per process, and determines a total order on these labels that is consistent with the real time order of their corresponding *Label* operations.[4]

Israeli and Li [21] were the first to investigate bounded *sequential* timestamp systems, and Dolev and Shavit [17] were the first to explore the *concurrent* version of the problem. The Dolev-Shavit construction requires $O(n)$-sized registers and labels, $O(n)$ time for a label operation, and $O(n^2 \log n)$ time for a scan. In their algorithm each processor is assigned a single multi-reader single-writer register of $O(n)$ bits. Extending the Dolev-Shavit solution in a non-trivial way, Israeli and Pinhasov [22] obtained a bounded concurrent timestamp system that is linear in time and label size, but uses registers of size $O(n^2)$. An alternative

[3] One can also define multi-writer algorithms in which any process can write to any location.

[4] Observe that the scan required by the timestamping is not necessarily identical to the atomic snapshot scan. Unfortunately, the two operations have the same name in the literature.

implementation of their algorithm uses *single*-reader-single-writer registers[5] of size $O(n)$, but requires $O(n^2)$ time to perform a *Scan*. Later, Dwork and Waarts [18] independently obtained a completely different linear-time solution, not based on any of the previous solutions, with a simpler proof of correctness. The drawback of their construction is that it requires registers and labels of size $O(n \log n)$.

Dolev and Shavit observed that the *conceptual* complexity of their concurrent timestamping algorithm can be reduced by using atomic snapshot scan. We show that, in addition, the algorithm's *computational* complexity can be reduced by simply replacing the snapshot scan with the weak snapshot, making no other changes to the original algorithm. The resulting bounded concurrent timestamping algorithm is linear in both time and the size of registers and labels, and is conceptually simpler than the Dolev-Shavit and Israeli-Pinhasov solutions.

Another important application of atomic snapshots is *randomized consensus*: each of n asynchronous processes starts with an input value taken from a two-element set, and runs until it chooses a *decision value* and halts. The protocol must be *consistent:* no two processes choose different decision values; *valid:* the decision value is some process' preference; and randomized *wait-free:* each process decides after a finite expected number of steps. The consensus problem lies at the heart of the more general problem of constructing highly concurrent data structures [19]. Consensus has no deterministic solution in asynchronous shared-memory [16]. Nevertheless, it can be solved by *randomized* protocols in which each process is guaranteed to decide after a finite *expected* number of steps. Randomized consensus protocols that use unbounded registers have been proposed by Chor, Israeli, and Li [14] (against a "weak" adversary), by Abrahamson [1] (exponential running time), by Aspnes and Herlihy [7] (the first polynomial algorithm), by Saks, Shavit, and Woll [27] (optimized for the case where processes run in lock step), and by Bracha and Rachman [11] (running time $O(n^2 \log n)$).

Protocols that use bounded registers have been proposed by Attiya, Dolev, and Shavit [8] (running time $O(n^3)$), by Aspnes [5] (running time $O(n^2(p^2+n))$, where p is the number of active processors), and by Bracha and Rachman [10] (running time $O(n(p^2+n))$). The bottleneck in Aspnes' algorithm is atomic snapshot. Replacing this atomic snapshot with our more efficient weak snapshot improves the running time by $\Omega(n)$ (from $O(n^2(p^2+n))$ to $O(n(p^2+n))$), and yields a protocol that matches the fastest known randomized consensus algorithm that uses only bounded registers, due to Bracha and Rachman [10]. Both our consensus algorithm and the one in [10] are based on Aspnes' algorithm. The main difference is that the solution of Bracha and Rachman is specific to consensus, whereas our algorithm is an immediate application of the primitive developed in this paper.

The remainder of this paper is organized as follows. Section 2 gives our model of computation and defines the weak snapshot primitive. Some properties of weak snapshots appear in Section 3. The remaining sections describe the weak snapshot algorithm and its applications.

2 Model and Definitions

A *concurrent system* consists of a collection of n asynchronous *processes* that communicate through an initialized shared memory. Each memory location, called a *register*, can be written by one "owner" process and read by any process. Reads and writes to shared registers are assumed to be *atomic*, that is, they can be viewed as occurring at a single instant of time. In order to be consistent with the literature on the discussed problems, our time and space

[5] All other results mentioned are in terms of multi-reader-single-writer registers.

complexity measures are expressed in terms of read and write operations on single-writer multi-reader registers of size $O(n)$. Polynomial-time algorithms for implementing large single-writer/multi-reader atomic registers from small, weaker, registers are well known [12, 24, 25, 26].

An algorithm is *wait-free* if there is an *a priori* upper bound on the number of steps a process might take when running the algorithm, regardless of how its steps are interleaved with those of other processes. All algorithms discussed in this paper are wait-free.

An *atomic snapshot memory* supports two kinds of abstract operations: *Update* modifies a location in the shared array, and *Scan* instantaneously reads (makes a copy of) the entire array. Let U_i^k (S_i^k) denote the *k*th *Update* (*Scan*) of process i, and v_i^k the value written by i during U_i^k. The superscripts are omitted where it can not cause confusion. An operation A *precedes* operation B, written as "$A \longrightarrow B$", if B starts after A finishes. Operations unrelated by precedence are *concurrent*. Processes are *sequential*: each process starts a new operation only when its previous operation has finished, hence its operations are totally ordered by precedence.

Correctness of an atomic snapshot memory is defined as follows. There exists a total order "$\Longrightarrow$" on operations such that:

- If $A \longrightarrow B$ then $A \Longrightarrow B$.
- If *Scan* S_p returns $\bar{v} = \langle v_1, \ldots, v_n \rangle$, then v_q is the value written by the latest *Update* U_q ordered before S_p by $\Longrightarrow$.

The order "$\Longrightarrow$" is called the *linearization* order [20]. Intuitively, the first condition says that the linearization order respects the "real-time" precedence order, and the second says that each correct concurrent computation is equivalent to some sequential computation where the scan returns the last value written by each process.

We define a *weak snapshot* as follows: we impose the same two conditions, but we allow "$\Longrightarrow$" to be a *partial order*[6] rather than a total order. We call this order a *partial linearization order*. If $A \Longrightarrow B$ we say that B *observes* A.

This weaker notion of correctness allows two scans S and S' to disagree on the order of two *Updates* U and U', but only if all four operations are concurrent with one another. Scanning processes must agree about *Updates* that happened "in the past" but may disagree about concurrent updates. Thus, in a system with only one scanner, atomic snapshots and weak snapshots are equivalent. Similarly, the two types of snapshots are equivalent if no two updates occur concurrently.

3 Properties of Weak Snapshots

The reader can easily verify that weak snapshots satisfy the following axioms:

- **Regularity**: For any value v_a^i returned by S_b^j, U_a^i begins before S_b^j terminates, and there is no U_a^k such that $U_a^i \longrightarrow U_a^k \longrightarrow S_b^j$.
- **Monotonicity of *Scans***: If S_a^i and S_b^j are two scans satisfying $S_a^i \longrightarrow S_b^j$, ($a$ and b could be the same process), and if S_a^i observes update U_c^k (formally, $U_c^k \Longrightarrow S_a^i$), then S_b^j observes U_c^k.

[6] In this paper, all partial orders are irreflexive.

- **Monotonicity of *Updates***: If U_a^i and U_b^j are two *Update* operations (possibly by the same process), such that $U_a^i \longrightarrow U_b^j$, and if S_c^k is a *Scan* operation, possibly concurrent with both U_a^i and U_b^j, such that S_c^k observes U_b^j ($U_b^j \Longrightarrow S_c^k$), then S_c^k observes U_a^i.

Roughly speaking, weak snapshots satisfy all the properties of atomic snapshots except for the consistency property which states: If *Scans* S_a^i, S_b^j return $\bar{v} = \langle v_1, \ldots v_n \rangle$ and $\bar{v}' = \langle v_1' \ldots v_n' \rangle$, respectively, then either $U_k \not\longrightarrow U_k'$ for every $k = 1, \ldots, n$, or vice versa.

Define the *span* of a value v_p^i to be the interval from the start of U_p^i to the end of U_p^{i+1}. Clearly, values written by successive *Updates* have overlapping spans. The following lemma formalizes the intuition that a weak snapshot scan returns a possibly existing state of the system.

Lemma 1. *If a weak snapshot scan returns a set of values $\bar{v}$, then their spans have a non-empty intersection.*

Proof: Let v_p^i and v_q^j be in $\bar{v}$ such that the span of v_p^i is the latest to start and the span of v_q^j is the first to end. Then, it is enough to show that the spans of v_p^i and v_q^j intersect. Suppose not. Then $U_q^j \longrightarrow U_p^i$. By the definition of span, $U_q^{j+1} \longrightarrow U_p^i$, and hence $U_q^{j+1} \Longrightarrow U_p^i$, which violates the requirement that each *Scan* return the latest value written by the latest *Update* ordered before it by $\Longrightarrow$. ■

Let a *Scan* S of a weak snapshot start at time t_s, end at time t_e, and return a set of values $\bar{v}$. Lemma 1 implies that there is a point t in which the spans of all these values intersect. There may be more than one such point; however, the Regularity property of weak snapshots and Lemma 1 imply that there is at least one such point t such that $t_s \leq t \leq t_e$. This is because the first clause in the definition of regularity implies that the span of v_a^i begins before t_e, while the second clause implies that the span of v_a^i ends after t_s. We will refer to the latest such point t by t_{scan} of S.

4 Weak Snapshot

Intuitively, in order to be able to impose partial order on the scans and updates, we need to ensure that a scan that did not return value v_a^j of processor a because v_a^j is too new, will not return a value v_b^i that was written by processor b *after* b saw v_a^j. By the properties of weak snapshot, if the scan returns v_b^i, then it must be ordered after b's update in the partial order. Since this update has to be ordered after a's update, we have that a's update has to be ordered before the scan. This contradicts the assumption that the scan saw neither v_a^j nor any later update by a.

If each value returned by the *Scan* is the value written by the latest update that terminated before a specific point in the *Scan*, the above situation does not occur. This observation, due to Kirousis, Spirakis, and Tsigas [23], motivates our solution. Roughly speaking, in our solution, at the start of a scan, the scanner produces a new number, called *color*, for each other process. When a process wants to perform an update, it reads the colors produced for it (one color by each scanner) and tags its new value with these colors. This enables the scanner to distinguish older values from newer ones.

The next subsection describes a solution that uses an unbounded number of colors. Later we will show how to simulate this solution using only a bounded number of colors. The simulation uses a simplification of the *Traceable Use* abstraction defined by Dwork and Waarts in [18].

4.1 Unbounded Weak Snapshot

We follow the convention that shared registers appear in upper-case and private variables in lower-case. In order to simplify the presentation, we assume that all the private variables are persistent. If a variable is subscripted, the first subscript indicates the unique process that writes it, and the second, if present, indicates the process that uses it. Each process b has variables VALUE_b, which stores b's current value, PCOLOR_b, QCOLOR_b, each of which stores an n-element array of colors, and VASIDE_{bc}, for each $c \neq b$. We frequently refer to $\text{PCOLOR}_b[c]$ as PCOLOR_{bc} (analogously for $\text{QCOLOR}_b[c]$). In this section, we assume that all these variables are stored in a single register. Section 4.4 describes how to eliminate this assumption. The code for the *Update* and *Scan* operations appears in Figures 1 and 2, respectively; the code for the *Produce* operation, called by *Scan*, appears in Figure 3. At the start of a scan, the scanner b produces a new color for each updater c and stores it in PCOLOR_{bc}. It then reads VALUE_c, VASIDE_{cb}, and QCOLOR_{cb} atomically. If QCOLOR_{cb} is equal to the color produced by b for c (and stored in PCOLOR_{bc}), b takes VASIDE_{cb} as the value for c, otherwise b takes VALUE_c.

The updater b first reads PCOLOR_{cb} and then writes its new VALUE_b atomically with $\text{QCOLOR}_{bc} := \text{PCOLOR}_{cb}$ for all c. At the same time it updates VASIDE_{bc} for all c that the updater detects have started to execute a concurrent *Scan*.

The intuition behind the use of the VASIDE variable can be best described if we will consider an example where we have a "fast" updater b and a "slow" scanner c, where c executes a single *Scan* while b executes many *Updates*. In this case, the updater will update VALUE_b each time, but will update VASIDE_{bc} only once, when it will detect that c is scanning concurrently. Intuitively, VASIDE_{bc} allows the scanner c to return a value for process b that was written by b during an update started no later than the end of the color producing step of the current scan. Therefore, such value can depend only on values that are not more recent than the values returned by the *Scan*.

1. For all $c \neq b$, read $qcolor_b[c] := \text{PCOLOR}_{cb}$
2. For all $c \neq b$, if $qcolor_b[c] \neq \text{QCOLOR}_{bc}$
   then $vaside_b[c] := \text{VALUE}_b$
3. Atomically write:
   $\text{VALUE}_b :=$ new value
   For all $c \neq b$, $\text{VASIDE}_{bc} := vaside_b[c]$
   For all $c \neq b$, $\text{QCOLOR}_{bc} := qcolor_b[c]$

Fig. 1. *Update* Operation for Process b.

We superscript the values of variables to indicate the execution of *Update* or *Scan* in which they are written. For example PCOLOR^l_{bc} is the value of PCOLOR_{bc} written during *Scan* S^l_b. Next, we construct an explicit partial linearization order $\Longrightarrow$ as follows. Define $U^j_q \Rightarrow S^i_p$ to hold if S^i_p takes the value originally written by U^j_q. (Note that S^i_p may read this value from

1. Call *Produce*
2. For all $c \neq b$ atomically read:
   $value_b[c] :=$ VALUE$_c$
   $qcolor_b[c] :=$ QCOLOR$_{cb}$
   $vaside_b[c] :=$ VASIDE$_{cb}$
3. For all $c \neq b$
   If $qcolor_b[c] \neq pcolor_b[c]$
   then $data_b[c] := value_b[c]$
   else $data_b[c] := vaside_b[c]$
4. Return $(data_b[1], \ldots, \text{VALUE}_b, \ldots, data_b[n])$

Fig. 2. *Scan* Operation for Process b.

1. For all $c \neq b$ $pcolor_b[c] :=$ PCOLOR$_{bc} + 1$
2. Atomically write for all $c \neq b$ PCOLOR$_{bc} := pcolor_b[c]$

Fig. 3. *Produce* Operation for Process b.

VASIDE$^k_{qp}$, where $k > j$). Define $\Longrightarrow$ to be the transitive closure of $\longrightarrow \cup \Rightarrow$. It follows from the following two lemmas that the *Scan* and *Update* procedures yield a weak snapshot memory.

Lemma 2. *The relation $\Longrightarrow$ is a partial order.*

Lemma 3. *For each process, our weak scan returns the value written by the latest update ordered before that scan by $\Longrightarrow$.*

Recall that v^k_q denotes the value originally written by U^k_q. Let U^j_q be the last update by process q to be ordered before S^i_p by $\Longrightarrow$. The proof of the lemma relies on the following claim.

Claim 4. *U^j_q terminates before S^i_p reads* VALUE$_q$. *Moreover, U^j_q does not read* PCOLOR$^i_{pq}$.

4.2 Review of the *Traceable Use* Abstraction

We use a simplified version of the *Traceable Use* Abstraction of Dwork and Waarts [18] in order to convert the unbounded weak snapshot described in the previous section into a bounded one. We start by reviewing the abstraction. Recall that in the unbounded solution, when process b produces a new color for process c, this new color was never produced by b for c beforehand. This feature implies that when b sees VALUE$_c$ tagged by this new color it knows that this VALUE$_c$ is too recent (was written after the scan began), and will not return it as the result of its scan. However, the same property will follow also if when b produces a new color for c, it will simply choose a color that is guaranteed not to tag c's value unless b

produces it for c again. To do this b must be able to detect which of the colors it produced for c may still tag c's values. This requirement can be easily satisfied by incorporating a simplified version of the *Traceable Use* abstraction.

In general, the goal of the *Traceable Use* abstraction is to enable the colors to be *traceable*, in that at any time it should be possible for a processor to determine which of its colors might tag any current or future values, where by "future value" we mean a value that has been prepared but not yet written. Although we allow a color that is marked as "in use" not to be used at all, we require that the number of such colors will be bounded.

The simplified version of the *Traceable Use* abstraction has three types of wait-free operations: *Consume*, *Reveal* and *Garbage Collection*.

- *Consume*: Allows the calling processor to obtain the current color produced for it by another processor. It takes two parameters: the name c of the processor from which the color is being consumed, and the name of the color (that is, the shared variable holding the color). It returns the value of the consumed color.
- *Reveal*: Allows a processor to update a vector containing its colors. It takes two parameters: the name of the vector and a new value for the vector.
- *Garbage Collection*: Allows a processor to detect all of its colors that are currently "in use". It takes a list of shared variables in which the garbage collector's colors reside. It returns a list of colors that may currently be in use.

It is important to distinguish between shared variables of an algorithm that uses the *Traceable Use* abstraction and auxiliary shared variables needed for the implementation of the abstraction. We call the first type of variables *principal* shared variables, and the second type *auxiliary*. Only principal shared variables are passed to the *Garbage Collection* procedure. For example, in the weak snapshot system the only principal shared variables are PCOLOR_{pq} and QCOLOR_{pq} for any p and q.

For $1 \leq i \leq n$, let R_i^k (C_i^k) denote the kth *Reveal* (*Consume*) operation performed by processor i. X_i^k denotes the vector written by i during R_i^k. Let b consume a color X_c from c. Then X_c is said to be *in use* from the end of the *Consume* operation until the beginning of b's next *Consume* from c. In addition, all colors revealed by i appearing in any principal shared variables are also said to be in use. We require the following properties:

- **Regularity:** For any color X_p^a consumed by C_i^k, R_p^a begins before C_i^k terminates, and there is no R_p^b such that $R_p^a \longrightarrow R_p^b \longrightarrow C_i^k$.
- **Monotonicity:** Let $C_i^k, C_j^{k'}$ (where i and j may be equal) be a pair of *Consume* operations returning the colors X_p^a, X_p^b. If $C_i^k \longrightarrow C_j^{k'}$ then $a \leq b$.
- **Detectability:** If a color v revealed by processor b was not seen by b during *Garbage Collection*, then v will not be in use unless b reveals it again.
- **Boundedness:** The ratio between the maximum number of colors detected by b during *Garbage Collection* as possibly being in use and the maximum number of colors that can actually be in use concurrently is bounded by a constant factor.

The regularity and monotonicity properties of the *Traceable Use* guarantee the regularity and monotonicity properties of the bounded weak snapshot system. Detectability guarantees that a processor will be able to safely recycle its colors. Boundedness guarantees that by taking the local pools to be sufficiently large, the producer will always find colors to recycle.

The implementation of the *Traceable Use* abstraction described in [18] assumes following restrictions:

- **Conservation:** If a color v_c consumed by C_i^k from c is still used by i when it performs a new *Consume* from c, $C_i^{k'}, k' > k$, then at the start of $C_i^{k'}$ this color is in one of i's principal shared variables.
- **Limited Mobility:** A color consumed by b and stored in a principal shared variable X_b cannot be moved to a different principal shared variable Y_b (*i.e.*, removed from X_b and placed in Y_b).

We show that the simplified *Traceable Use* under these restrictions suffices for our weak snapshot algorithm.

4.3 Bounded Weak Snapshots

For simplicity of exposition, we first present an algorithm that uses registers of size $O(nv)$, where v is the maximum number of bits in any process' value. In Subsection 4.4 we show how to modify this algorithm so that registers of size $O(n+v)$ will suffice. In order to convert the unbounded solution to a bounded one, we replace the *Produce* operation shown in Figure 3 by the *Produce* operation shown in Figure 4. The meaning of the notation in Step 1.3 of the new *Produce* operation is that all n colors $pcolor_b[i]$, $1 \leq i \leq n$, are written atomically to PCOLOR_{bi}.

1.a. For all $1 \leq i \leq n$ $X[i] :=$ *Garbage Collection*($\text{PCOLOR}_{bi}, \text{QCOLOR}_{ib}$)
1.b. For all $c \neq b$, choose $pcolor_b[c] \notin X[c]$
1.c. *Reveal* ($\text{PCOLOR}_b, pcolor_b$)

Fig. 4. *Produce* Operation for Process b.

Also, Line 1 of the *Update* operation shown in Figure 1 is replaced by the following:

1. For all $c \neq b$, $qcolor_b[c] := Consume(c, \text{PCOLOR}_c b)$.

The complexity of *Traceable Use* given in [18] is $O(n)$ per each *Consume* or *Reveal*, and $O(n^2)$ per each *Garbage Collection*. However, in our particular case a trivial modification of the implementation in [18] reduces the cost of *Garbage Collection* to $O(k)$, where k is the number of variables passed as parameters to the *Garbage Collection* procedure. Also, it is easy to see that we can get by with a constant number of colors for each pair of processes.

4.4 Reducing the Register Size

The weak snapshot described above uses registers of size $O(nv)$ where v is the maximum number of bits in any value VALUE_b. This is due to the fact that an updater b may set aside a different value for each scanner c in a variable VASIDE_{bc}, and all these values are kept in a single register. To reduce the size of the registers, each updater b, will store VASIDE_{bc} in a separate register for each c. Only after this has been accomplished, b atomically updates VALUE_b and, for all $c \neq b$, VCOLOR_{bc}.

The modifications to the code are straightforward. Lines 2 and 3 of the code for the *Scan* (Figure 2) are replaced by Lines 2' and 3' below.

2'. For all $c \neq b$ atomically read:
    $value_b[c] := \text{VALUE}_c$
    $qcolor_b[c] := \text{QCOLOR}_{cb}$
3'. For all $c \neq b$
    If $qcolor_b[c] \neq pcolor_b[c]$
        then $data_b[c] := value_b[c]$
        else read $data_b[c] := \text{VASIDE}_{cb}$

Lines 2 and 3 of the code for the *Update* operation (Figure 1) are replaced by the following Lines $2'$ and $3'$.

2'. For all $c \neq b$, if $qcolor_b[c] \neq \text{QCOLOR}_{bc}$ then $vaside_b[c] := \text{VALUE}_b$
    $\text{VASIDE}_{bc} := vaside_b[c]$
3'. Atomically write:
    $\text{VALUE}_b :=$ new value
    For all $c \neq b$, $\text{QCOLOR}_{bc} := qcolor_b[c]$

Observe that the only difference between the modified and the original algorithm is that the shared variables VASIDE_{qp} and VALUE_q are not read atomically together by *Scan* and not written atomically together by the *Update*.

The only way we can get an execution of the modified algorithm that does not correspond to an execution of the original algorithm is when the *Scan* reads VALUE_q^k and $\text{VASIDE}_{qp}^{k'}$ and returns the latter, where $\text{VASIDE}_{qp}^{k} \neq \text{VASIDE}_{qp}^{k'}$. We now show that this can not happen.

Since VASIDE_{qp} is written before VALUE_q, we have that $k' > k$. Since the scan S_p^i returns the value it read from VASIDE_{qp}, we have $\text{PCOLOR}_{pq}^i = \text{QCOLOR}_{qp}^k$. By the Detectability property, U_q^k consumes color PCOLOR_{pq}^i. By Monotonicity, for all $k \leq k_1 \leq k'$, $U_q^{k_1}$ consumes same color. Hence none of $U_q^{k_1}$ changed the value in VASIDE_{qp}, i.e. $\text{VASIDE}_{qp}^k = \text{VASIDE}_{qp}^{k'}$.

5 Applications

In this section, we explore two applications of the weak snapshot: bounded concurrent timestamping and randomized consensus. First we take the bounded concurrent timestamping protocol of Dolev and Shavit [17], and show that the labels can be stored in an abstract weak snapshot object, where each access to the labels is through either the weak snapshot *Update* or the weak snapshot *Scan* operation. The resulting protocol has running time, label size, and register size all $O(n)$.

We then take the elegant randomized consensus protocol of Aspnes [5], and show that replacing atomic snapshot with weak snapshot leads to an algorithm with $O(n(p^2+n))$ expected number of operations. This is an improvement of $\Omega(n)$ over the original algorithm.

5.1 Efficient Bounded Concurrent Timestamping

In a *concurrent timestamping system*, processes repeatedly choose *labels*, or timestamps, reflecting the real-time order of events. More precisely, there are two kinds of operations: *Label* generates a new timestamp for the calling process, and *Scan* returns an indexed set of labels $\bar{\ell} = \langle \ell_1, \ldots, \ell_n \rangle$ and an irreflexive total order $\prec$ on the labels.

For $1 \leq i \leq n$, let L_i^k (S_i^k) denote the kth *Label* (*Scan*) operation performed by processor i (processor i need not keep track of k, this is simply a notational device allowing us to describe long-lived runs of the timestamping system). Analogously, ℓ_i^k denotes the label obtained by i during L_i^k. Correctness is defined by the following axioms:

- **Ordering:** There exists an irreflexive total order $\Longrightarrow$ on the set of all *Label* operations, such that:
  - **Precedence:** For any pair of *Label* operations L_p^a and L_q^b (where p and q may be equal), if $L_p^a \longrightarrow L_q^b$, then $L_p^a \Longrightarrow L_q^b$.
  - **Consistency:** For any *Scan* operation S_i^k returning $(\bar{\ell}, \prec)$, $\ell_p^a \prec \ell_q^b$ if and only if $L_p^a \Longrightarrow L_q^b$.
- **Regularity:** For any label ℓ_p^a in $\bar{\ell}$ returned by S_i^k, L_p^a begins before S_i^k terminates, and there is no L_p^b such that $L_p^a \longrightarrow L_p^b \longrightarrow S_i^k$.
- **Monotonicity:** Let $S_i^k, S_j^{k'}$ (where i and j may be equal) be a pair of *Scan* operations returning the vectors $\bar{\ell}, \bar{\ell}'$ respectively which contain labels ℓ_p^a, ℓ_p^b respectively. If $S_i^k \longrightarrow S_j^{k'}$ then $a \leq b$.

Dolev and Shavit describe a *bounded* concurrent timestamping system that uses atomic multi-reader registers of size $O(n)$ and whose *Scan*[7] and *Label* operations take time $O(n^2 \log n)$ and $O(n)$ respectively. They also mention that the labels can be stored in an abstract atomic snapshot object, where each access to the labels is through either atomic snapshot *Update* or *Scan* operation. More specifically, they would replace the *Collect* performed during the *Label* operation by an atomic snapshot *Scan*, would replace the simple writing of the new label with an atomic snapshot *Update*, and would replace their entire original *Scan* with an atomic snapshot *Scan*.

However, as they note, this transformation has drawbacks. The size of the atomic registers in all known implementations of atomic snapshot memory is $O(nv)$, where v is the size of the local value of each processor, and hence the size of the atomic registers in the resulting timestamping system is $O(n^2)$ (because here v is a label, and their label is of size n). Second, since both *Update* and *Scan* operations of the snapshot take $O(n^2)$ steps, then while the running time of the *Scan* operation in the resulting timestamping system improves, the running time of the *Label* operation increases to $O(n^2)$.

We show that one can replace the atomic snapshot abstract object in the Dolev-Shavit timestamping system by the weak snapshot object. Note that this leads to a solution without the above-mentioned drawbacks. More precisely, we get a timestamping system with linear running time, register size and label size.

Next we prove that the resulting system is indeed a bounded concurrent timestamping system.

[7] Note that this *Scan* is different from our weak snapshot *Scan*.

Theorem 5. *Our modification of the Dolev-Shavit algorithm yields a bounded concurrent timestamping system.*

Proof: Regularity and Monotonicity follow directly from the analogous properties of the weak snapshot (more specifically, they follow from the Regularity and the Monotonicity of Scans properties of weak snapshot). To complete the proof we need to show the Ordering property.

Consider an execution of our algorithm and focus on the sequence of labelling operations. In our algorithm, when a process performs a *Label* operation it collects the labels of the other processes using a weak snapshot *Scan*, while in the original algorithm of Dolev and Shavit these labels are obtained using a simple *Collect*. However, for every execution of our algorithm, there exists an execution of the Dolev-Shavit algorithm that produces the same sequence of the labelling operations. This is due to the fact that the set of labels read by a weak snapshot scan can be also read by a collect executed in the same time interval, and because the result of a labelling operation in the Dolev-Shavit algorithm depends only on the set of labels collected during this operation. This implies that there exists an irreflexive total order on the labelling operations in the execution of our algorithm that is consistent with the precedence relation on the labelling operations. (The ordering is the one guaranteed by the proof of the Dolev-Shavit algorithm on the corresponding execution of their algorithm.)

Given an execution, the total order on the labelling operations defined by Dolev and Shavit is as follows: if one labelling operation reads the label produced by another labelling operation, then the first operation is ordered after the second. To get the total order, take the transitive closure of this partial order and extend it to a total order by considering the values of the labels.

The next step is to show that the order produced by a *Scan* operation of our algorithm is consistent with this total order. A *Scan* operation of our algorithm is just a weak snapshot *Scan*. Consider a weak snapshot *Scan* that returns a set of labels $\bar{\ell}$. To compute the order between these labels, our algorithm makes direct use of the appropriate procedure in the Dolev-Shavit algorithm. Therefore, it remains to show that the order on these labels produced by this procedure is consistent with the total order defined above.

Define a modified execution of our algorithm where we stop each process after it completes the labelling operation that generates its label in $\bar{\ell}$. Observe that the Monotonicity of Scans property of weak snapshots implies that none of the labelling operations in the original execution that generated labels in $\bar{\ell}$ can observe labels that were not written in the modified execution. Consider a *Scan* of the original Dolev-Shavit algorithm that is executed at the end of this modified execution. The *Scan* of Dolev-Shavit reads the same labels as in $\bar{\ell}$. The ordering of the labels computed by this *Scan* is consistent with the ordering on the labelling operations in the modified execution, and hence the ordering of the labels produced by our algorithm is also consistent with the total order on the labels defined by the modified execution.

We claim that the total order on *Label* operations obtained for the original execution (from which we obtained the modified one) is consistent with the total order obtained by the modified execution. In other words, we have the original (infinite) execution and a modified (truncated) execution. Consider labelling operations that appear only in both executions and the two total orders defined on these operations. Note that the only way these two total orders could be inconsistent is if there exists a labelling operation in the original execution that generated a label in $\bar{\ell}$ and that read a label (during its weak snapshot *Scan*) that was not written in the modified execution. However, since the labels in $\bar{\ell}$ are read by a weak snapshot *Scan*, the "Monotonicity of Scans" property of weak snapshots implies that this is impossible. ■

5.2 Efficient Randomized Consensus

In a *randomized consensus protocol*, each of n asynchronous processes starts with a *preference* taken from a two-element set (typically $\{0, 1\}$), and runs until it chooses a *decision value* and halts. The protocol is correct if it is *consistent:* no two processes choose different decision values; *valid:* the decision value is some process's preference; and *randomized wait-free:* each process decides after a finite expected number of steps. When computing a protocol's expected number of steps, we assume that scheduling decisions are made by an *adversary* with unlimited resources and complete knowledge of the processes' protocols, their internal states, and the state of the shared memory. The adversary cannot, however, predict future coin flips.

Our technical arguments require some familiarity with the randomized consensus protocol of Aspnes [5]. This protocol makes two uses of atomic snapshot, both of which can be replaced by our weak snapshot. The protocol is centered around a *robust weak shared coin* protocol, which is a kind of collective coin flip: all participating processes agree on the outcome of the coin flip, and an adversary scheduler has only a slight influence on the outcome. The n processes collectively undertake a one-dimensional random walk centered at the origin with absorbing barriers at $\pm(K + n)$, for some $K > 0$. The shared coin is implemented by a shared counter. Each process alternates between reading the counter's position and updating it. Eventually the counter reaches one of the absorbing barriers, determining the decision value. While the counter is near the middle of the region, each process flips an unbiased local coin to determine the direction in which to move the counter. If a process observes that the counter is within n of one of the barriers, however, the process moves the counter deterministically toward that barrier. The code for the robust shared coin appears in Figure 5.

```
FUNCTION SharedCoin
repeat
c := read(counter)
if c ≤ (K + n) then decide 0
elseif c ≥ (K + n) then decide 1
elseif c ≤ −K then decrement(counter)
elseif c ≥ K then increment(counter)
else
        if LocalCoin=0 then decrement(counter)
        else increment(counter)
```

Fig. 5. Robust Weak Shared Coin Protocol (Aspnes[5])

Aspnes implements the shared counter as an n-element array of atomic single-writer multi-reader registers, one per process. To increment or decrement the counter, a process updates its own field. To read the counter, it atomically scans all the fields. Careful use of modular arithmetic ensures that all values remain bounded. The expected running time of this protocol, expressed in primitive reads and writes, is $O(n^2(p^2 + n))$, where p is the number of processes that actually participate in the protocol.

The shared counter at the heart of this protocol is *linearizable* [20]: There exists a total order "$\Longrightarrow$" on operations such that:

- If $A \longrightarrow B$ then $A \Longrightarrow B$.
- Each *Read* operation returns the sum of all increments and decrements ordered before it by $\Longrightarrow$.

We replace the linearizable counter with a different data abstraction: by analogy with the definition of weak snapshot, a *weak counter* imposes the same two restrictions, but allows $\Longrightarrow$ to be a partial order instead of a total order. Informally, concurrent *Read* operations may disagree about concurrent increment and decrement operations, but no others. We can construct a weak counter implementation from Aspnes's linearizable counter implementation simply by replacing the atomic snapshot scan with a weak snapshot scan. We now argue that the consensus protocol remains correct if we replace the linearizable counter with a more efficient weak counter.

The proof of the modified consensus protocol depends on the following lemma which is analogous to a similar lemma in [5]. Recall from Section 3 that for each *Scan* operation returning a vector $\bar{v}$ of values, there is an associated time t_{scan}, the latest time between the start and end times of the *Scan* at which the spans of the values in $\bar{v}$ intersect.

Let R_p^i (I_q^j, D_q^j) denote p's (q's) i^{th} (j^{th}) read (increment, decrement) operation.

Lemma 6. *If R_p^i returns value $v \geq K + n$, then all reads whose t_{scan} is not smaller than the t_{scan} of R_p^i will return values $\geq K + 1$. (The symmetric claim holds when $v \leq -(K + n)$.)*

The protocol also uses an atomic snapshot to make the protocol's running time depend on p, the number of active processes. For this purpose, in addition to the shared counter used for the random walk, the protocol also keeps two additional counters, called *active* counters (implemented in the same way as the "random walk" counter), to keep track of the number of active processes that start with initial values 0 and 1. Each process increments one active counter before it modifies the random walk counter for the first time. (More specifically, if the processor starts with initial value 0, it increments the first active counter, and otherwise it increments the second.) All three counters (that is, the shared coin counter and the two active counters) are read in a single atomic snapshot scan.

The proof of the expected running time of the protocol hinges on the following lemma, which holds even if we replace the atomic snapshot scan by a weak snapshot scan. Define the *true position* of the random walk at any instant to be the value the random walk counter would assume if all operations in progress were run to completion without starting any new operations.

Lemma 7. *Let τ be the true position of the random walk at t_{scan} of R_p. If R_p returns values c, a_0, and a_1 for the random walk counter and the two active counters, then $c - (a_0 + a_1 - 1) \leq \tau \leq c + (a_0 + a_1 - 1)$.*

6 Conclusions

We have defined the weak snapshot scan primitive and constructed an efficient implementation of it. We have given two examples of algorithms designed using the strong primitive of atomic snapshot scan for which it was possible to simply replace the expensive atomic snapshot with the much less expensive weak snapshot scan. Indeed, it seems that in many cases atomic snapshot scan can be simply replaced by weak snapshot scan. Our construction relied on the *Traceable Use* abstraction of Dwork and Waarts [18]. Alternatively, we could have used the weaker primitives of Tromp [28] or of Kirousis, Spirakis, and Tsigas [23].

In a similar spirit to the weak snapshot, one can define a weak concurrent timestamping system, which, roughly speaking, satisfies the properties of the standard timestamping system except that the ordering $\Longrightarrow$ on *Label* operations and the $\prec$ orders on labels are *partial* rather than total. Such a timestamping system is interesting for two reasons: it is conceptually simple and it can replace standard timestamping in at least one situation: Abrahamson's randomized consensus algorithm [1].

In conclusion, we can generalize our approach as follows. Consider a concurrent object with the following sequential specification. [8]

- **Mutator** operations modify the object's state, but do not return any values. Mutator operations executed by different processes commute: applying them in either order leaves the object in the same state.
- **Observer** operations return some function of the object's state, but do not modify the object.

A concurrent implementation of such an object is *linearizable* if the precedence order on operations can be extended to a total order $\Longrightarrow$ such that the value returned by each observer is the result of applying all the mutator operations ordered before it by $\Longrightarrow$. This kind of object has a straightforward wait-free linearizable implementation using atomic snapshot scan ([6]). A *weakly linearizable* implementation is one that permits $\Longrightarrow$ to be a partial order instead of a total order. This paper's contribution is to observe (1) that weakly linearizable objects can be implemented more efficiently than any algorithm known for their fully linearizable counterparts, and (2) there are certain important applications where one can replace linearizable objects with weakly linearizable objects, preserving the application's modular structure while enhancing performance.

Acknowledgement

We would like to thank Jim Aspnes, Hagit Attiya, and Nir Shavit for helpful discussions.

References

1. K. Abrahamson, On Achieving Consensus Using a Shared Memory, *Proc. 7 ACM Symposium on Principles of Distributed Computing*, pp.291-302, 1988, .
2. Y. Afek, H. Attiya, D. Dolev, E. Gafni, M. Merritt, and N. Shavit, Atomic Snapshots of Shared Memory, *Proc. 9 ACM Symposium on Principles of Distributed Computing*, pp. 1-13, 1990.
3. J. Anderson, Composite Registers, *Proc. 9 ACM Symposium on Principles of Distributed Computing*, pp. 15-30, August 1990.

[8] This definition is similar to Anderson's notion of a *pseudo read-modify-write* (PMRW) operation [4]. Anderson, however, requires that all mutators commute, not just those applied by different processes.

4. J. Anderson, and B. Groselj, Beyond Atomic Registers: Bounded Wait-free Implementations of Non-trivial Objects, *Proc. 5th International Workshop on Distributed Algorithms*, Delphi, Greece, October 1991.
5. J. Aspnes, Time- and Space-Efficient Randomized Consensus, to appear in the *Journal of Algorithms*. An earlier version appears in *Proc. 9 ACM Symposium on Principles of Distributed Computing*, pp. 325-331, 1990.
6. J. Aspnes and M.P. Herlihy Wait-Free Data Structures in the Asynchronous PRAM Model, *Proc. 2nd Annual Symposium on Parallel Algorithms and Architectures*, July 1990, pages 340–349, Crete, Greece.
7. J. Aspnes and M.P. Herlihy, Fast Randomized Consensus using Shared Memory, *Journal of Algorithms*, 11(3):441-461, 1990.
8. H. Attiya, D. Dolev, and N. Shavit, Bounded Polynomial Randomized Consensus, *Proc. 8 ACM Symposium on Principles of Distributed Computing*, pp. 281-294, 1989.
9. H. Attiya, N. Lynch, and N. Shavit, Are Wait-Free Algorithms Fast?, *Proc. 9 IEEE Symposium on Foundations of Computer Science*, pp. 363-375, 1990. Expanded version: Technical Memo MIT/LCS/TM-423, Laboratory for Computer Science, MIT, February 1990.
10. G. Bracha and O. Rachman, Approximated Counters and Randomized Consensus, Technical Report Technion 662, 1990.
11. G. Bracha and O. Rachman, Randomized Consensus in Expected $O(n^2 \log n)$, *Proc. 5th International Workshop on Distributed Algorithms*, Greece, 1991.
12. J.E. Burns and G.L. Peterson, Constructing Multi-reader Atomic Values from Non-atomic Values, *Proceedings of the Sixth ACM Symposium on Principles of Distributed Computing*, pages 222–231, 1987.
13. K. M. Chandy and L. Lamport, Distributed Snapshots: Determining Global States of Distributed Systems, *Acm Trans. on Computer Systems 3:1,1985*, pp. 63–75.
14. B. Chor, A. Israeli, and M. Li, On processor coordination using asynchronous hardware, *Proc. 6th ACM Symposium on Principles of Distributed Computing*, pages 86–97, 1987.
15. E. W. Dijkstra, Solution of a problem in concurrent programming control, *Communications of the ACM 8:165*, 1965.
16. D. Dolev, C. Dwork, and L Stockmeyer. On the minimal synchronism needed for distributed consensus, *Journal of the ACM 34:1*, pp. 77–97, January, 1987.
17. D. Dolev and N. Shavit, Bounded Concurrent Time-Stamp Systems are Constructible!, *Proc. 21 ACM Symposium on Theory of Computing*, pp. 454-465, 1989.
18. C. Dwork and O. Waarts, Simple and Efficient Bounded Concurrent Timestamping or Bounded Concurrent Timestamp Systems are Comprehensible!, IBM Research Report RJ 8425, October 1991. Also, to appear in *Proc. 24 ACM Symposium on Theory of Computing*, 1992.
19. M.P. Herlihy. Wait-free Synchronization, *ACM Transactions on Programming Languages and Systems*, 13(1):124–149, January 1991.
20. M.P. Herlihy and J.M. Wing, Linearizability: A Correctness Condition for Concurrent Objects, *ACM Transactions on Programming Languages and Systems*, 12(3):463–492, July 1990.
21. A. Israeli and M. Li, Bounded Time Stamps, *Proc. 28 IEEE Symposium on Foundations of Computer Science*, 1987.
22. A. Israeli and M. Pinhasov, A Concurrent Time-Stamp Scheme which is Linear in Time and Space, *manuscript*, 1991.
23. L. M. Kirousis, P. Spirakis and P. Tsigas, Reading Many Variables in One Atomic Operation Solutions With Linear or Sublinear Complexity, *Proc. 5th International Workshop on Distributed Algorithms*, 1991.
24. L. Lamport, Concurrent reading and writing. *Communications of the ACM*, 20(11):806–811, November 1977.
25. L. Lamport, The Mutual Exclusion Problem, Part I: A Theory of Interprocess Communication, *J. ACM 33(2)*, pp. 313-326, 1986.

26. G. Peterson, Concurrent Reading While Writing, *ACM Transactions on Programming Languages and Systems* 5(1), pp. 46-55, 1983.
27. M. Saks, N. Shavit, and H. Woll, Optimal Time Randomized Consensus - Making Resilient Algorithms Fast in Practice, Symposium on Discrete Algorithms, pp. 351-362, 1990.
28. J. Tromp, How to Construct an Atomic Variable, *Proc. 3rd International Workshop on Distributed Algorithms, LNCS 392*, 1989.

This article was processed using the LaTeX macro package with LLNCS style

Concurrent Timestamping Made Simple

Rainer Gawlick, Nancy Lynch, and Nir Shavit

Massachusettes Institute of Technology, Laboratory of Computer Science
545 Technology Square, Cambridge MA 02139, USA

Abstract. Concurrent Timestamp Systems (CTSS) allow processes to temporally order concurrent events in an asynchronous shared memory system. Bounded memory constructions of a CTSS are extremely powerful tools for concurrency control, and are the basis for solutions to many coordination problems including mutual exclusion, randomized consensus, and multiwriter atomic registers. Unfortunately, known bounded CTSS constructions seem to be complex from the algorithmic point of view. Due to the importance of bounded CTSS, the rather involved original construction by Dolev and Shavit was followed by a series of papers that tried to provide more easily verifiable CTSS constructions.

In this paper, we present what we believe is the simplest, most modular, and most easily proven bounded CTSS algorithm known to date. The algorithm is constructed and its correctness proven using several tools. Our algorithm combines the labeling method of the Dolev-Shavit CTSS with the atomic snapshot algorithm proposed in Afek et al. in a way that limits the amount of interleavings that can occur. We prove the correctness of our algorithm by showing that it implements a simple, unbounded, real-number based CTSS specification. Our proof methodology is based on forward simulation techniques of the I/O Automata model.

1 Introduction

The paradigm of concurrent timestamping is at the heart of solutions to some of the most fundamental problems in multiprocessor concurrency control. Examples of such problems include *fcfs*-mutual-exclusion [9], construction of a multi-reader-multi-writer atomic register [16], and randomized consensus [3]. A simple bounded construction of a CTSS would imply simple solutions to most of these extensively researched problems.

A timestamp system is somewhat like a ticket machine at an ice cream parlor. People's requests to buy the cream are time-stamped based on a numbered ticket (label) taken from the machine. Any person, in order to know in what order the requests will be served, can scan through all the labels and establish the total order among them. A *concurrent* timestamp system (CTSS) is a timestamp system in which each one of the processes can either take a new ticket or scan the other's tickets concurrently and without having to wait for any other processes. Since the CTSS algorithm is wait-free, it is highly suited for fault-tolerant and real-time applications (see [6]).

Israeli and Li, in [7], were the first to isolate the notion of bounded timestamping (timestamping using bounded size memory) as an independent concept, developing an elegant theory of bounded *sequential* timestamp systems, that is, timestamp systems in a world where no two operations are ever concurrent. Dolev and Shavit [4] were the first to define and construct a bounded *concurrent* time stamp system. However, to quote [5]: "their algorithm is ingenious but its proof is long and involved." (To be exact, it is 43 pages long.)

Because of the importance of the concurrent timestamping problem, the original solution by Dolev and Shavit has been followed by a series of papers directed at providing a simpler bounded CTSS algorithm. Israeli and Pinchasov [8] have simplified the [4] algorithm and its proof by modifying the labeling scheme of [4], introducing a new label scanning method, and strengthening the ordering-of-events based formal proof by reasoning about global states. (However, it still takes over 40 pages...) Dwork and Waarts [5] have taken a totally different approach, by having their bounded construction simulate a new and simpler type of unbounded CTSS construction in which processes choose from "local pools" of label values instead of a "global pool" as in [4, 8]. However, in order to bound the number of possible label values in the local pools, they are forced to introduce a form of amortized garbage collection. This greatly complicates their algorithm. (Their algorithm only has an informal operational proof.)

In this paper, we present a novel bounded algorithm that we believe is the simplest, most modular, and most easily proven CTSS algorithm known to date (our complete *formal* proof takes 15 pages.) Our basic approach is to decompose the problem into several distinct pieces.

- We base our algorithm on the atomic snapshot primitive introduced by Afek et. al [1] (we use it as a black box). This primitive allows a process to collect an "instantaneous" view of an array of shared registers, without waiting during the operation. [1] gives an implementation of this primitive from atomic single writer multireader registers. By using a snapshot primitive, we limit the amount of interleavings that can occur in the proof.
- The operation of choosing a new label given a set of older ones was a point of difficulty in all former algorithms. Based on the snapshot operation, we introduce a much simplified version of labeling algorithm of [4].
- Proving that the bounded algorithm is a correct CTSS has in the past led to long and involved inductive arguments. We overcome this problem by introducing a CTSS specification that uses label values taken from the unbounded range of positive reals. It is easy to show that the unbounded real-number based specification implements the CTSS axioms given in [4]. Our proof follows by showing that our bounded algorithm implements the real-number based specification. The proof methodology will be based on the forward simulation techniques of the I/O Automata model. (Forward simulations (see [14] for discussion and references) are a powerful technique that has been studied in the semantics community, and is given here a "practical" application).

The most efficient bounded CTSS implementations [5, 8] require $O(n)$ time per operation. Though one might think that a high price in complexity must be paid for our algorithm's modularity and ease of proof, this is not the case. The size of the labels is only $O(n)$, and the time complexity of our algorithm is that of the underlying atomic snapshot algorithm. Given that the complexity of snapshot implementations is constantly improving, currently requiring no more than $O(n\sqrt{n})$ reads and writes per operation [2], there is hope that the complexity of our simple, bounded timestamp system will continue to improve.

2 I/O Automata Model

We present our algorithm in the context of the I/O Automata model. This model, introduced by Lynch and Tuttle [13], represents algorithms as *I/O Automata* which are characterized by ***states***, ***initial states***, ***actions***, and state transitions called ***steps***. A step that results from an action is denoted by (s, π, s') where s is the original state, π is the action, and s' is the new state. Actions are classified into *external actions*, those visible to the user of the algorithm, and *internal actions*, which are not visible to the user. An *execution* of an I/O Automaton is an alternating sequence of states and actions that can be produced if the algorithm is executed starting from an initial state. The *behavior* of an execution is the projection of the execution on the external actions of the I/O Automaton. The set of all possible behaviors of an I/O Automaton A is called *behaviors*(A).

The I/O Automata model represents problems as a set of allowable behaviors. An I/O Automaton A is said to *solve* a problem if *behaviors*(A) is a subset of the behaviors that define the problem[1]. We say that an I/O Automaton A *implements* another I/O Automaton B if *behaviors*(A) $\subseteq$ *behaviors*(B). Our correctness proof uses the following theorem [13] on simulation proofs.

Theorem 1. *Let A and B be I/O Automata and* R *a relation over the states of A and B. Suppose:*

1. *If a is an initial state of A, then there exists an initial state b of B such that $(a, b) \in$ R.*
2. *Suppose a is a reachable state of A and and b is a reachable state of B such that $(a, b) \in$ R. If (a, π, a') is a step of A then there exists a state b' of B such that (b, π, b') is a step of B and $(a', b') \in$ R.*

Then behaviors(A) $\subseteq$ behaviors(B).

3 An Unbounded Concurrent Timestamp System

This section introduces a simple unbounded real-number based specification of a concurrent timestamp system, UCTSS. It is easy to show that this specification meets the CTSS axioms of [4].

The code for the operations of UCTSS is given in Figure 1. The system has n processes indexed by $\{1 \dots n\}$. Each process p_i in UCTSS can perform two operations, SCAN_i and LABEL_i. The operation LABEL_i allows process p_i to associate a label (timestamp) with a given value. The operation SCAN_i allows process p_i to determine the order among values based on their associated labels. ORDER_i and MAKELABEL_i,

[1] Actually, the concept of *solving* a problem is defined by *fair behavior* inclusion rather that *behavior* inclusion. Addressing this point is straightforward.

which are used by SCAN$_i$ and LABEL$_i$ respectively, are defined in Figure 2. SNAP$_i$, which is defined by Afek et al. in [1], atomically reads an array of single writer multireader registers. UPDATE$_i$, also defined by [1], writes a value to a single register in the array of single writer multireader registers read by SNAP$_i$. Since SNAP$_i$ and UPDATE$_i$ are atomic operations, each line of SCAN$_i$ and LABEL$_i$ represents an atomic operation. Furthermore, SNAP$_i$ and UPDATE$_i$ are wait-free, therefore their use does not compromise the wait-free properties of our timestamp algorithm. In terms of the I/O Automata model BeginScan$_i$, EndScan$_i(\bar{o_i}, \bar{v_i})$, BeginLabel$_i(nv_i)$, and EndLabel$_i$ are the external actions; ORDER$_i$, MAKELABEL$_i$, and UPDATE$_i$ are the internal actions.

```
SCAN_i
        BeginScan_i
        ORDER_i(SNAP_i((t_1, v_1)...(t_n, v_n)))
        EndScan_i(ō_i, v̄_i)

LABEL_i
        BeginLabel_i(nv_i)
        MAKELABEL_i(SNAP_i(t_1 ... t_n))
        UPDATE_i((t_i, v_i), (nt_i, nv_i))
        EndLabel_i
```

Fig. 1. Code for UCTSS and BCTSS

ORDER$_i((t_1, v_1) \ldots (t_n, v_n))$
  $\bar{v_i} := (v_1 \ldots v_n)$
  $\bar{o_i} :=$ the sequence of indexes where j appears before k in o_i iff $(t_j, j) \ll (t_k, k)$

MAKELABEL$_i(t_1 \ldots t_n)$
  if $i \neq i_{max}$
    then $nt_i := t_{max} + X$ where X is nondeterministically selected from $\Re^{>0}$

Fig. 2. Code for MAKELABEL$_i$ of UCTSS and ORDER$_i$ of UCTSS and BCTSS

UCTSS uses labels that are non-negative real numbers. The ordering between labels is based on the usual $<$ order of $\Re^{\geq 0}$. The ordering used in the ORDER$_i$ function is represented by the symbol $\ll$, and is a lexicographical order between label and process index pairs. Specifically:

$(\ell_i, i) \ll (\ell_j, j)$ iff either $\ell_i < \ell_j$ or $\ell_i = \ell_j$ and $i < j$.

The state of UCTSS is defined by the shared state and the local state of each of the n processes. The set of variable pairs (t_i, v_i) where t_i contains the current label (timestamp) of process p_i, and v_i represents the value associated with label t_i, constitute the shared state. The shared state is accessed only by using the SNAP$_i$ and UPDATE$_i$ primitives. SNAP$_i$ atomically reads from the shared state. The code for the atomic actions ORDER$_i$ and MAKELABEL$_i$ makes multiple references to t_i and v_i. The references are to local copies of the shared variables which are read by the SNAP$_i$ primitive. UPDATE$_i(A, B)$ copies the local value B to the shared register A.

The local state of each process consists of the variables nt_i, $\bar{o_i}$, $\bar{v_i}$, nv_i, and pc_i. nt_i contains the new label determined by MAKELABEL$_i$, $\bar{o_i}$ is an array of process indexes containing the ordering of the processes returned by EndScan$_i(\bar{o_i}, \bar{v_i})$, $\bar{v_i}$ is an array of values containing the values associated with the labels used to determine $\bar{o_i}$, nv_i contains the new value passed by BeginLabel$_i(nv_i)$, and pc_i contains the actions enabled for p_i in the current state. Finally, the state of UCTSS has derived variables t_{max} and i_{max}. $t_{max} = \text{MAX}(t_1 \ldots t_n)$ and i_{max} be the largest process index i such that $t_i = t_{max}$. The initial values of the state variables are: $t_i = nt_i = 0$, $\bar{o_i} = (1 \ldots n)$, $\bar{v_i} = (0 \ldots 0)$, $v_i = nv_i = 0$, and $pc_i = \{\text{BeginScan}_i, \text{BeginLabel}_i(nv_i)\}$.

Informally, in order for LABEL$_i$ to function correctly, MAKELABEL$_i$ must set nt_i to a value that is greater than or equal to t_{max}. When $i \neq i_{max}$ we can see immediately that $nt_i > t_{max}$. When $i = i_{max}$, nt_i retains it current value. Since MAKELABEL$_i$ is the only action that modifies nt_i, nt_i must still have the value that was assigned during the previous execution MAKELABEL$_i$. Hence, $nt_i = t_i$. When $i = i_{max}$, $t_i = t_{max}$, thus $nt_i = t_{max}$.

4 A Bounded Concurrent Timestamp System

In this section we present our bounded implementation of a concurrent timestamp system, BCTSS. BCTSS differs from UCTSS in three ways: the structure of the labels, the order between labels, and the manner in which MAKELABEL$_i$ determines new labels. In all other aspects BCTSS and UCTSS are identical. Recall that a label in UCTSS is an element of $\Re^{\geq 0}$. In BCTSS, labels are taken from a different domain. In order to construct the new domain we introduce the set $\mathcal{A} = \{1 \ldots 5\}$. We define the order $\prec_{\mathcal{A}}$ and the function NEXT on the elements of $\mathcal{A}$.

$$1 \prec_{\mathcal{A}} 2,3,4,5; \quad 2 \prec_{\mathcal{A}} 3,4,5; \quad 3 \prec_{\mathcal{A}} 4; \quad 4 \prec_{\mathcal{A}} 5; \quad 5 \prec_{\mathcal{A}} 3.$$

The graph in Figure 3 represents $\prec_{\mathcal{A}}$, where $a \prec_{\mathcal{A}} b$ iff there is a directed edge from b to a.

$$\text{NEXT}(k) = \begin{cases} k+1 \text{ if } k \in \{1,2,3,4\} \\ 3 \quad\quad \text{if } k = 5 \end{cases}$$

A BCTSS label is an element of $\mathcal{A}^{n-1}$, where n is the number of processes in the system. We refer to elements of $\mathcal{A}^{n-1}$ using array notation. Specifically, the hth digit of label ℓ will be denoted by $\ell[h]$. Since we have redefined the label type, we must specify the order that is to be used between elements of $\mathcal{A}^{n-1}$ for the $\ll$ order in the ORDER$_i$ action. The order between elements of $\mathcal{A}^{n-1}$ is represented by the symbol $\prec$ and will be a lexicographical order based on $\prec_{\mathcal{A}}$. Specifically:

> $\ell_i \prec \ell_j$ iff there exists $h \in \{1 \ldots n-1\}$ such that $\ell_i[h'] = \ell_j[h']$ for all $h' < h$ and $\ell_i[h] \prec_{\mathcal{A}} \ell_j[h]$.

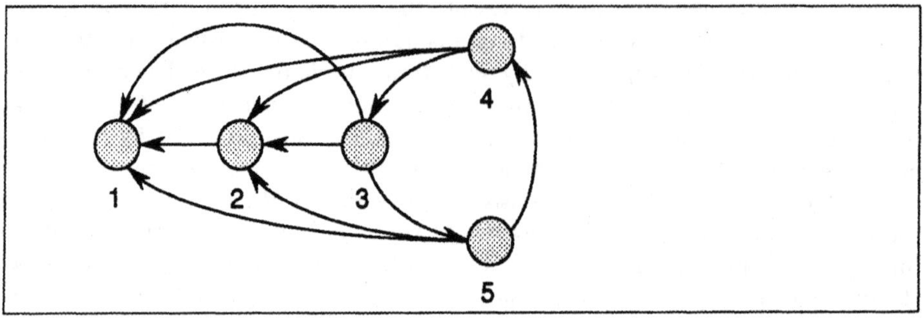

Fig. 3. A graphical illustration of the $\prec_{\mathcal{A}}$ order between the elements of $\mathcal{A} = \{1 \ldots 5\}$

Example 1. $4 \ldots 4.5.2 \prec 4 \ldots 4.3.1$.

Lemma 2. *If ℓ_1 and ℓ_2 are elements of $\mathcal{A}^{n-1}$ then exactly one of the following is true: $\ell_1 \prec \ell_2$, $\ell_2 \prec \ell_1$, or $\ell_1 = \ell_2$.*

We define the following notation and functions for BCTSS labels:

Definition 3. For any $h \in \{0 \ldots n-1\}$, $\ell_1 \stackrel{h}{=} \ell_2$ iff $\ell_1[h'] = \ell_2[h']$ for all $h' \leq h$. Note that $\ell_1 \stackrel{n-1}{=} \ell_2$ implies that $\ell_1 = \ell_2$.

Definition 4. For any $h \in \{1 \ldots n-1\}$, $\ell' = \text{NEXTLABEL}(\ell, h)$ iff $\ell' \stackrel{h-1}{=} \ell$, $\ell'[h] = \text{NEXT}(\ell[h])$ and $\ell'[h'] = 1$ for all $h' \in \{h+1 \ldots n-1\}$.

Definition 5. For any $h \in \{1 \ldots n-1\}$, $\ell' \in \text{CYCLE}(\ell, h)$ iff $\ell' \stackrel{h-1}{=} \ell$ and $\ell'[h] \in \{3, 4, 5\}$.

Lemma 6. *A set $\mathcal{L}$ of labels is not totally ordered by $\prec$ iff there exist $\ell_1, \ell_2, \ell_3 \in \mathcal{L}$ and $h \in \{1 \ldots n-1\}$ such that $\ell_1 \stackrel{h-1}{=} \ell_2 \stackrel{h-1}{=} \ell_3$ and $\{\ell_1[h], \ell_2[h], \ell_3[h]\} = \{3, 4, 5\}$.*

Proof. $\Rightarrow$ The $\prec$ ordering on $\mathcal{L}$ is irreflexive by definition and is antisymmetric by Lemma 2. Therefore, it must be that transitivity does not hold. Specifically there exist $\ell_1, \ell_2, \ell_3 \in \mathcal{L}$ such that $\ell_1 \prec \ell_2 \prec \ell_3$, and $\ell_1 \not\prec \ell_3$. By Lemma 2 it cannot be that $\ell_1 = \ell_3$, therefore $\ell_3 \prec \ell_1$. Since $\prec$ is a lexicographical order, there must exist $h \in \{1 \ldots n-1\}$ such that $\ell_1 \stackrel{h-1}{=} \ell_2 \stackrel{h-1}{=} \ell_3$ and $\ell_1[h] \prec_{\mathcal{A}} \ell_2[h] \prec_{\mathcal{A}} \ell_3[h]$ and $\ell_1[h] \not\prec_{\mathcal{A}} \ell_3[h]$. Now by definition of $\mathcal{A}$, $\{\ell_1[h], \ell_2[h], \ell_3[h]\} = \{3, 4, 5\}$.
$\Leftarrow$ This direction is straightforward.

We now define some functions on the states of BCTSS. In order to reason about the states of the system we introduce the notation $b.x$ to refer to the variable x in state b. For a state b and any label ℓ in state b:

Definition 7. For any $h \in \{0 \ldots n-1\}$, $\text{AGREE}(b.\ell, h) = \{j \mid b.t_j \stackrel{h}{=} b.\ell\}$.

Definition 8. For any $h \in \{0 \ldots n-1\}$, $\text{NUM}(b.\ell, h) = |\text{AGREE}(b.\ell, h)|$.

Definition 9. For any $h \in \{0 \ldots n-1\}$, $\text{NUM}_i(b.\ell, h) = |\text{AGREE}(b.\ell, h) - \{i\}|$.

Definition 10. A *choice vector* for state b is any vector $(b.\ell_1 \ldots b.\ell_n)$ such that $b.\ell_i \in \{b.t_i, b.nt_i\}$ for each i.

Definition 11. $\text{TOT}(b) = \mathit{true}$ iff the set of values in every choice vector is totally ordered by $\prec$; otherwise $\text{TOT}(b) = \mathit{false}$.

Recall that the second difference between UCTSS and BCTSS is the $\ll$ ordering that is used in ORDER_i. We define $\ll$ for BCTSS lexicographically, i.e.:

$(\ell_i, i) \ll (\ell_j, j)$ iff either $\ell_i \prec \ell_j$ or $\ell_i = \ell_j$ and $i < j$.

In any state b in which $\text{TOT}(b) = \mathit{true}$, $\ll$ defines a total order.

We now define $b.t_{max}$ and $b.i_{max}$ for a state, b, in which $\text{TOT}(b) = \mathit{true}$. Consider the choice vector $(b.t_1 \ldots b.t_n)$. Since $\text{TOT}(b) = \mathit{true}$, there must exist $i \in \{1 \ldots n\}$ such that, for all $j \neq i$ and $j \in \{1 \ldots n\}$, $b.t_j \preceq b.t_i$. Let $b.t_{max} = b.t_i$. Let $b.i_{max}$ be the largest index j such that $b.t_j = b.t_{max}$.

The final difference between BCTSS and UCTSS is in the code for MAKELABEL_i. Recall that in UCTSS, MAKELABEL_i nondeterministically picks a real number that is larger than t_{max}. In BCTSS, MAKELABEL_i also picks the new label based on t_{max}. In states in which $\text{TOT}(b) = \mathit{true}$, $b.t_{max}$ and $b.i_{max}$ are defined. We let MAKELABEL_i be a no-op for states in which $\text{TOT}(b) = \mathit{false}$. In Section 5 we will show that $\text{TOT}(b) = \mathit{true}$ for all reachable states. When i_{max} is defined and $i \neq i_{max}$, MAKELABEL_i finds the minimum h such that at least $n - h$ t-labels, excluding t_i, agree with the prefix of t_{max} up to and including the hth digit. Then the new label is the same as t_{max} for the first $h - 1$ digits, it differs from t_{max} at the hth digit based on the function NEXT, and its remaining digits are equal to 1. The code for MAKELABEL_i of BCTSS is given in Figure 4.

```
FULL_i(h), h ∈ {1...n − 1}
   if NUM_i(t_max, h) ≥ n − h
      then return (true)
      else return (false)

MAKELABEL_i(t_1 ... t_n)
   if i ≠ i_max
      then h' := minimum h ∈ {1...n − 1} such that FULL_i(h) = true
           nt_i := NEXTLABEL(t_max, h')
```

Fig. 4. Code for MAKELABEL_i of BCTSS

MAKELABEL_i finds the minimum integer h such that $\text{FULL}_i(h)$ returns *true*. We now show that such an h exists in $\{1 \ldots n-1\}$. The code that finds h is executed only when $i \neq i_{max}$. Notice that $\text{NUM}_i(t_{max}, n-1) \geq 1$ when $i \neq i_{max}$, hence $\text{FULL}_i(n-1) = true$.

The initial values for the labels in BCTSS are: $t_i = nt_i = 1^{n-1}$ for all $i \in \{1 \ldots n\}$. Furthermore, $\bar{o}_i = (1 \ldots n)$, $\bar{v}_i = (0 \ldots 0)$, $v_i = nv_i = 0$, and $pc_i = \{\text{BeginScan}_i, \text{BeginLabel}_i(nv_i)\}$.

5 Invariants

For use in the simulation proof we define the following invariants:

Theorem 12. *If b is a reachable state of* BCTSS *then, for all $i \in \{1 \ldots n\}$:*

I: $\text{TOT}(b) = \text{true}$.
II: *If $i = b.i_{max}$ then $b.t_i = b.nt_i$.*
III: *If $b.t_{max} \prec b.nt_i$ then there exists $h \in \{1 \ldots n-1\}$ such that $b.nt_i = \text{NEXTLABEL}(b.t_{max}, h)$.*
IV: *If $b.nt_i \preceq b.t_{max}$ then for any $h \in \{1 \ldots n-1\}$, $b.t_i \overset{h}{=} b.t_{max}$ implies that $b.nt_i \overset{h}{=} b.t_{max}$.*
V: *For any $h \in \{1 \ldots n-1\}$, if $b.nt_i \in \text{CYCLE}(b.t_{max}, h)$ then $b.t_i \overset{h-1}{=} b.t_{max}$.*
VI: *For any $h \in \{1 \ldots n-1\}$:*
a: if $b.nt_i = \text{NEXTLABEL}(b.t_{max}, h)$ then $\text{NUM}_i(b.t_{max}, h-1) \geq n-h$.
b: if $b.t_{max}[h] \neq 1$ then $\text{NUM}(b.t_{max}, h-1) \geq n-h+1$.

I, II, and III are used in the simulation proof. We use an inductive argument to show that all reachable states of BCTSS satisfy these invariants. The purpose of invariants IV–VI is to strengthen the induction hypothesis enough so that I can be proven. The only action that can cause I to be violated is MAKELABEL_i. Specifically, we must show that the new nt_i picked by MAKELABEL_i does not introduce any cycles in the $\prec$ ordering of the labels in any choice vector. Since the MAKELABEL_i code can examine all of the t-labels, the code can be written to avoid any cycles involving nt_i and the t-labels. However, the MAKELABEL_i code cannot examine the local nt-labels of the other processes. In order to show that cycles that include nt_i and other nt-labels are avoided, invariants IV and V are used to limit the possible values of the nt-labels based on the corresponding t-labels. Finally, invariant VIb is used to prove invariant V, and invariant VIa is used to prove VIb.

Proof. The initial case follows from the fact that $b.t_i = b.nt_i = 1^{n-1}$ for all $i \in \{1 \ldots n\}$. For the induction step we assume that I–VI hold for state b and that the step (b, π, b') is taken. We wish to show that I–VI hold for state b'. The only actions that modify any of the labels are UPDATE_i and MAKELABEL_i. We consider each separately.

Case UPDATE_k:

Although the details are quite involved, this case is intuitively easy. Notice that no new labels are picked in this step. Hence, it is easy to show that invariant I holds for b'. Therefore $b'.t_{max}$ and $b'.i_{max}$ are defined. Furthermore, we can use transitivity in the $\prec$ ordering of the labels in any choice vector. We give a short sketch of the argument for the remaining invariants. By invariant II, the state does not change when $k = b.i_{max}$, hence we assume that $k \neq b.i_{max}$. The proof of invariants II–VI, for the case where $k \neq b.i_{max}$, is divided into two cases: $b.nt_k \preceq b.t_{max}$ and $b.t_{max} \prec b.nt_k$. When $b.nt_k \preceq b.t_{max}$, t_{max} does not change. Using this fact it is straightforward to show that invariants II–VI hold in state b'. When $b.t_{max} \prec b.nt_k$, the new maximum label $b't_{max} = b'.t_k$. By invariant III and the fact that $b'.t_k = b.nt_k$, $b'.t_{max} = \text{NEXTLABEL}(b.t_{max}, h)$ for some h. Thus $b'.t_{max}$ has a very specific structure. This structure is heavily exploited to show that invariants II–VI hold in state b'.

Case MAKELABEL_k:

From the induction hypothesis we know that $\text{TOT}(b) = true$. Hence MAKELABEL_k is not a no–op. Furthermore, since no t-labels change, $b'.t_{max}$ and $b'.i_{max}$ are defined and $b'.t_{max} = b.t_{max}$ and $b'.i_{max} = b.i_{max}$. When $k = b.i_{max}$ the state does not change, so assume that $k \neq b.i_{max}$. Now, by definition of MAKELABEL_k, $b'.nt_k = \text{NEXTLABEL}(b.t_{max}, h')$ for some h'.

We now show an important property that is maintained by the MAKELABEL_k code. Specifically, $\text{NUM}_k(b.t_{max}, h') = \text{NUM}_k(b.t_{max}, h'-1) = n - h'$. By definition of MAKELABEL_k, $\text{FULL}_k(h')$ returns *true* in state b, so $\text{NUM}_k(b.t_{max}, h') \geq n - h'$. Moreover, $\text{FULL}_k(h'-1)$ returns *false* in state b so $\text{NUM}_k(b.t_{max}, h'-1) < n-(h'-1)$. But by definition, $\text{NUM}_k(b.t_{max}, h'-1) \geq \text{NUM}_k(b.t_{max}, h')$ so $\text{NUM}_k(b.t_{max}, h'-1) = \text{NUM}_k(b.t_{max}, h') = n - h'$.

We now show by contradiction that I holds in state b'. Assume that $\text{TOT}(b') = false$. Then there must exist a choice vector such that its values are not totally ordered. Since nt_k is the only label that changes, the choice vector must involve $b'.nt_k$. Now we can use Lemma 6 and a lengthy but straightforward argument to show that there must exist a non–transitive ordering between $b.\ell_i$, where $b.\ell_i \in \{b.nt_i, b.t_i\}$ and $i \neq k$, $b.t_{max}$, and $b'.nt_k$ that looks as follows: $b.\ell_i \overset{h'-1}{=} b.t_{max} \overset{h'-1}{=} b'.nt_k$ and $b.\ell_i[h'] \prec_A b.t_{max}[h'] \prec_A b'.nt_k[h'] \prec_A b.\ell_i[h']$. Furthermore, $\{b.\ell_i, b.t_{max}, b'.nt_k\} \subseteq \text{CYCLE}(b.t_{max}, h')$. We now consider the cases $b.\ell_i = b.nt_i$ and $b.\ell_i = b.t_i$ separately:

$b.nt_i$: Since $b.nt_i \in \text{CYCLE}(b.t_{max}, h')$, V for state b shows that $b.t_i \overset{h'-1}{=} b.t_{max}$. Recall that $\text{NUM}_k(b.t_{max}, h'-1) = \text{NUM}_k(b.t_{max}, h')$. Therefore, $b.t_i \overset{h'-1}{=} b.t_{max}$ implies that $b.t_i \overset{h'}{=} b.t_{max}$. Now, from IV for state b and the fact that $b.nt_i \prec b.t_{max}$, it follows that $b.nt_i \overset{h'}{=} b.t_{max}$, a contradiction to the fact that $b.nt_i[h'] \prec_A b.t_{max}[h']$.

$b.t_i$: Recall that $\text{NUM}_k(b.t_{max}, h'-1) = \text{NUM}_k(b.t_{max}, h')$. Therefore, $b.t_i \overset{h'-1}{=} b.t_{max}$ implies that $b.t_i \overset{h'}{=} b.t_{max}$. Now, $b.t_i \overset{h'}{=} b.t_{max}$ contradicts the fact that $b.t_i[h'] \prec_A b.t_{max}[h']$.

The proof for invariants II–IV is straightforward and therefore omitted. Now consider invariant V. Suppose that $b'.nt_k \in \text{CYCLE}(b'.t_{max}, h)$ where $h \in \{1 \ldots n-1\}$. The interesting case is $h \leq h'$. First consider the case $h = h'$. Since $\text{NEXT}(1) \notin \{3, 4, 5\}$, and $\text{NEXT}(b.t_{max}[h]) = b'.nt_k[h] \in \{3, 4, 5\}$, $b.t_{max}[h] \neq 1$. Now VIb for state b shows that $\text{NUM}(b.t_{max}, h-1) \geq n-h+1$. Recall that $\text{NUM}_k(b.t_{max}, h-1) =$

$n - h < n - h + 1$. Since $\text{NUM}(b.t_{max}, h-1) \geq n - h + 1$ and $\text{NUM}_k(b.t_{max}, h-1) < n - h + 1$, $k \in \text{AGREE}(b.t_{max}, h-1)$. Thus $b.t_k \overset{h-1}{=} b.t_{max}$. Since t_k and t_{max} do not change, $b'.t_k \overset{h-1}{=} b'.t_{max}$. The argument for $h < h'$ is analogous.

The proof for invariant VI is straightforward and therefore omitted. □

By Theorem 12, invariant I holds for all reachable states. Therefore, we can conclude that t_{max} and i_{max} are defined for all reachable states of BCTSS and that MAKELABEL_k is never a no–op.

6 Simulation Proof

In this section we prove that BCTSS is a correct CTSS. Specifically, we use Theorem 1 to show that *behaviors*(BCTSS) ⊆ *behaviors*(UCTSS). In order to use Theorem 1, we define the relation R between the states of BCTSS and the states of UCTSS as follows:

Definition 13. If b is a state of BCTSS and u is a state of UCTSS then $(b, u) \in \text{R}$ iff for all $i, j \in \{1 \ldots n\}$, $i \neq j$:

1. $b.\bar{o}_i = u.\bar{o}_i$.
2. $b.t_j \prec b.t_i$ iff $u.t_j < u.t_i$,
   $b.nt_j \prec b.t_i$ iff $u.nt_j < u.t_i$,
   $b.t_j \prec b.nt_i$ iff $u.t_j < u.nt_i$,
   $b.nt_j \prec b.nt_i$ iff $u.nt_j < u.nt_i$.
3. $b.v_i = u.v_i$.
4. $b.nv_i = u.nv_i$.
5. $b.\bar{v}_i = u.\bar{v}_i$.
6. $b.pc_i = u.pc_i$.

Parts 1 and 5 ensures that a process p_i returns the same response to a SCAN_i request in BCTSS and in UCTSS. Recall that $\bar{o}_i$ contains the order of the labels that was last observed by p_i. Part 2 states that the $\prec$ ordering of the labels in any choice vector from BCTSS is the same as the $<$ ordering of the corresponding labels from UCTSS. Notice that part 2 gives no information about the relation between t_i and nt_i. Parts 3 and 4 ensure that BCTSS and UCTSS associate values with labels in the same manner. Finally, part 6 ensures that UCTSS and BCTSS will be able to execute the corresponding action during each state transition.

Lemma 14. *For the initial state b of* BCTSS, *there exists an initial state u of* UCTSS *such that $(b, u) \in \text{R}$.*

Proof. This follows directly from the definition of the initial states for UCTSS and BCTSS given in Section 3 and Section 4 respectively. □

Lemma 15. *Let b be a reachable state of* BCTSS *and u be a reachable state of* UCTSS *such that $(b, u) \in \text{R}$. If (b, π, b') is a step of* BCTSS, *then there exists u' such that (u, π, u') is a step of* UCTSS *and $(b', u') \in \text{R}$.*

Proof. We proceed by case analysis on π. The cases where $\pi \in \{\text{BeginScan}_k, \text{EndScan}_k(\bar{o_k}, \bar{v_k}), \text{EndLabel}_k, \text{BeginLabel}_k(nv_k), \text{ORDER}_k\}$ are straightforward and therefore not included.

Case $\pi = \text{UPDATE}_k$:

Since $(b, u) \in \text{R}$, $b.pc_k = u.pc_k$. Hence, π is enabled in u. Let u' be the unique state such that (u, π, u') is a step of UCTSS. We will only consider parts 2 and 3 of R.

For part 2 of R there are four cases to consider. All other cases are immediate since they do not involve t_k, and since t_k is the only label that changes as a result of the action. Let $i \in \{1 \ldots n\}$ and $i \neq k$:

1. $b'.t_k \prec b'.t_i$ iff $u'.t_k < u'.t_i$:
   Since $(b, u) \in \text{R}$ and t_k is the only label that changes, $b.nt_k \prec b'.t_i$ iff $u.nt_k < u'.t_i$. As a result of the action, $b'.t_k = b.nt_k$ and $u'.t_k = u.nt_k$. Hence $b'.t_k \prec b'.t_i$ iff $u'.t_k < u'.t_i$.
2. $b'.t_i \prec b'.t_k$ iff $u'.t_i < u'.t_k$,
   $b'.nt_i \prec b'.t_k$ iff $u'.nt_i < u'.t_k$,
   $b'.t_k \prec b'.nt_i$ iff $u'.t_k < u'.nt_i$:
   For all three statements, the reasoning is similar to that of case 1.

Since $(b, u) \in \text{R}$, part 4 of R shows that $b.nv_k = u.nv_k$. Thus, $b'.v_k = u'.v_k$. For $i \neq k$, v_i does not change, hence part 3 is satisfied.

Case $\pi = \text{MAKELABEL}_k$:

Since $(b, u) \in \text{R}$, $b.pc_k = u.pc_k$. Hence, π is enabled in u. There are two cases: $k = b.i_{max}$ and $k \neq b.i_{max}$.

The case $k = b.i_{max}$ is straightforward, thus we only consider the case $k \neq b.i_{max}$. Since $(b, u) \in \text{R}$, part 2 of R implies that $b.i_{max} = u.i_{max}$. Hence, $k \neq u.i_{max}$. In this case there are many states u' such that (u, π, u') is a step of UCTSS; these states differ only by the value of $u'.nt_k$. We now define a particular value $u'.nt_k$ and hence a particular state u'.

Define $S = \{i | i \neq k \text{ and } b.t_{max} \prec b.nt_i\}$. Let $z = b.i_{max}$, then $b.t_z = b.t_{max}$. Invariant II shows that $b.nt_z = b.t_z$. Hence, $b.nt_z = b.t_{max}$. This implies that $z \notin S$. Consequently, $b.i_{max} \notin S$. For all $i \in S$, III for state b shows that $b.nt_i = \text{NEXTLABEL}(b.t_{max}, h_i)$ for some $h_i \in \{1 \ldots n-1\}$. Furthermore, the definition of MAKELABEL_k implies that $b'.nt_k = \text{NEXTLABEL}(b.t_{max}, h_k)$ for some $h_k \in \{1 \ldots n-1\}$. Define $S_1 = \{i | i \in S, h_i > h_k\}$, $S_2 = \{i | i \in S, h_i = h_k\}$, and $S_3 = \{i | i \in S, h_i < h_k\}$. Note that $S_1 \cap S_2 = S_2 \cap S_3 = S_1 \cap S_3 = \emptyset$ and $S_1 \cup S_2 \cup S_3 = S$. Since $\prec$ is a lexicographical order, the order between any two labels in BCTSS is determined by the first digit at which they differ. Therefore, for any $i_1 \in S_1$, $i_2 \in S_2$, and $i_3 \in S_3$, it is the case that $b.t_{max} \prec b.nt_{i_1} \prec b.nt_{i_2} = b'.nt_k \prec b.nt_{i_3}$. Recall $z = b.i_{max}$. Then, $b.t_z \prec b.nt_{i_1} \prec b.nt_{i_2} = b'.nt_k \prec b.nt_{i_3}$. Since $z \notin S$ and $(b, u) \in \text{R}$, part 2 of R shows that $u.t_z < u.nt_{i_1} < u.nt_{i_2} < u.nt_{i_3}$. Since $b.i_{max} = u.i_{max}$, $z = u.i_{max}$ and $u.t_z = u.t_{max}$. This shows that $u.t_{max} < u.nt_{i_1} < u.nt_{i_2} < u.nt_{i_3}$.

We use the following rules for picking $u'.nt_k$. If $S_2 \neq \emptyset$, let $u'.nt_k = u.nt_i$ for any $i \in S_2$. If on the other hand $S_2 = \emptyset$, let $u.nt_{max} = \max(u.nt_i | i \in S_1)$ if $S_1 \neq \emptyset$, otherwise let $u.nt_{max} = u.t_{max}$. Let $u.nt_{min} = \min(u.nt_i | i \in S_3)$ if $S_3 \neq \emptyset$, otherwise let $u.nt_{min} = \infty$. Choose any $u'.nt_k$ such that $u.nt_{max} < u'.nt_k < u.nt_{min}$. With either rule for choosing $u'.nt_k$, $u.t_{max} < u'.nt_k$. Hence, there exists an $X \in \Re^{>0}$ such that $u'.nt_k = u.t_{max} + X$.

We now show that $(b', u') \in$ R. We only consider part 2 of R. There are four cases to consider. All other cases do not involve $b'.nt_k$. Let $i \in \{1 \ldots n\}$ and $i \neq k$:

1. $b'.nt_k \prec b'.t_i$ iff $u'.nt_k < u'.t_i$,
$b'.t_i \prec b'.nt_k$ iff $u'.t_i < u'.nt_k$:
Since no t-labels change, $b'.t_{max} = b.t_{max}$ and $b'.i_{max} = b.i_{max}$. Recall that $k \neq b.i_{max}$, hence $b'.nt_k = \text{NEXTLABEL}(b.t_{max}, h_k)$ and $b'.t_{max} = b.t_{max} \prec b'.nt_k$. Furthermore, $b'.t_i = b.t_i$. Therefore, $b'.t_i \preceq b'.t_{max} \prec b'.nt_k$. Let $z = b'.i_{max}$. In this case $z \neq k$ and $b'.t_z = b'.t_{max}$. Since $i \neq k$, $z \neq k$ and $b'.t_z = b'.t_{max}$, there exists a choice vector that includes $b'.t_i, b'.t_{max}$, and $b'.nt_k$. By invariant I the values of this choice vector are totally ordered by $\prec$. Therefore, $b'.t_i \preceq b'.t_{max} \prec b'.nt_k$ implies that $b'.t_i \prec b'.nt_k$.
Similarly, since $k \neq u.i_{max}$, $u'.t_{max} = u.t_{max} < u'.nt_k$ as a result of the action. Furthermore, $u'.t_i = u.t_i$. Therefore, $u'.t_i \leq u'.t_{max} < u'.nt_k$. This implies that $u'.t_i < u'.nt_k$.
2. $b'.nt_i \prec b'.nt_k$ iff $u'.nt_i < u'.nt_k$,
$b'.nt_k \prec b'.nt_i$ iff $u'.nt_k < u'.nt_i$:
The statements consider $b'.nt_k$'s ordering with respect to the other nt-labels. We can divide the nt-labels, other than nt_k, into two disjoint sets. Recall that $S = \{j | j \neq k \text{ and } b.t_{max} \prec b.nt_j\}$. Define $T = \{j | j \neq k \text{ and } b.nt_j \preceq b.t_{max}\}$. Similarly, define $S_u = \{j | j \neq k \text{ and } u.t_{max} < u.nt_j\}$. Define $T_u = \{j | j \neq k$ and $u.nt_j \leq u.t_{max}\}$. By part 2 of R and the fact that $(b, u) \in$ R, $S = S_u$ and $T = T_u$. Suppose $i \in T$. Since $i \neq k$, $b'.nt_i = b.nt_i$. Furthermore, $b'.t_{max} = b.t_{max}$ and $b'.i_{max} = b.i_{max}$. Therefore, $b'.nt_i \preceq b'.t_{max} \prec b'.nt_k$. Let $z = b'.i_{max}$. In this case $z \neq k$ and $b'.t_z = b'.t_{max}$. Since $i \neq k$, $z \neq k$ and $b'.t_z = b'.t_{max}$, there exists a choice vector that includes $b'.nt_i, b'.t_{max}$, and $b'.nt_k$. By invariant I the values of this choice vector are totally ordered by $\prec$. Therefore, $b'.nt_i \preceq b'.t_{max} \prec b'.nt_k$ implies that $b'.nt_i \prec b'.nt_k$. Similarly, $u'.nt_i = u.nt_i$ since $i \neq k$. Therefore, $u'.nt_i \leq u'.t_{max} < u'.nt_k$. This implies that $u'.nt_i < u'.nt_k$.
Now suppose $i \in S$. Recall that, $S_1 \cup S_2 \cup S_3 = S$ and that S_1, S_2, and S_3 are disjoint. Consider any $i_1 \in S_1$, $i_2 \in S_2$, and $i_3 \in S_3$. Recall that $b.t_{max} \prec b.nt_{i_1} \prec b.nt_{i_2} = b'.nt_k \prec b.nt_{i_3}$ and $u.t_{max} < u.nt_{i_1} < u.nt_{i_2} < u.nt_{i_3}$. Using a simple case analysis it is possible to show the following. If $i \in S_1$, then $b'.nt_i \prec b'.nt_k$ and $u'.nt_i < u'.nt_k$. If $i \in S_2$, then $b'.nt_i = b'.nt_k$ and $u'.nt_i = u'.nt_k$. If $i \in S_3$, then $b'.nt_k \prec b'.nt_i$ and $u'.nt_k < u'.nt_i$.

□

We can now conclude that BCTSS correctly implements the properties of a CTSS since Lemma 14 and Lemma 15 show that the two assumptions required by Theorem 1 are true.

Theorem 16. *behaviors*(BCTSS) $\subseteq$ *behaviors*(UCTSS).

Proof. This follows directly from Theorem 1, Lemma 14, and Lemma 15. □

7 Discussion

We believe that the modular construction of our bounded timestamping system, which combines the atomic snapshot of Afek et al. with the labeling methodology of Dolev and Shavit, yields a simple, understandable, bounded timestamp system. Furthermore, the simulation techniques of the I/O Automata model allow us to give a formal yet intuitive proof for the correctness of our algorithm.

We see two directions for future work. The complexity of our algorithm is the complexity of the underlying snapshot algorithm. Currently the best snapshot algorithm has a complexity of $O(n\sqrt{n})$ for the SNAP and the UPDATE action. Improvements to the complexity of the snapshot algorithm would benefit our bounded timestamping system as well as other algorithms that use the snapshot primitive.

Large parts of the proof of the invariants are essentially extensive case analyses. Each case rests on a very simple, yet at times technically involved, argument. Therefore, we believe that our bounded timestamping algorithm would be a good test case for the automatic theorem provers that are currently being developed.

References

1. Y. Afek, H. Attiya, D. Dolev, E. Gafni, M. Merritt, and N. Shavit. Atomic Snapshots of Shared Memory. In *Proc. 9th ACM Symp. on Principles of Distributed Computing*, 1990, pp. 1–14.
2. H. Attiya and M. P. Herlihy. Private Communication, 1991.
3. B. Chor, A. Israeli, and M. Li. On process coordination using asynchronous hardware. In *Proceedings of the* 6th *Annual ACM Symposium on Principles of Distributed Computing*, August 1987.
4. D. Dolev and N. Shavit. Bounded concurrent time-stamps are constructible. *SIAM Journal on Computing*, to appear. Also in *Proceedings of the* 21st *Annual ACM Symposium on Theory of Computing, Seattle, Washington*, pages 454–465, 1989.
5. C. Dwork and O. Waarts. Simple and Efficient Bounded Concurrent timestamping – or – Bounded concurrent time-stamps are comprehensible. Unpublished Manuscript, Stanford University, 1991.
6. M. P. Herlihy. Wait-free synchronization. In *ACM TOPLAS*, 13(1), pages 124–149, January 1991.
7. A. Israeli and M. Li. Bounded time stamps. In 28th *Annual Symposium on Foundations of Computer Science, White Plains, New York*, pages 371–382, 1987.
8. A. Israeli and M. Pinchasov. A linear time bounded concurrent timestamp scheme. Technical Report, Technion, Haifa, Israel, March 1991.
9. L. Lamport A new solution of *Dijkstra's* concurrent programming problem. *Communications of the ACM*, 78(8):453–455, 1974.
10. L. Lamport The mutual exclusion problem. part I: a theory of interprocess communication. *J. ACM*, 33(2):313-326, 1986.
11. L. Lamport On interprocess communication. parts I and II. *Distributed Computing, 1*, 1 (1986) 77–101.
12. M. Li and P. Vitanyi. A Very Simple Construction for Atomic Multiwriter Registers. Report, Aiken Computation Laboratory, Harvard University, 1987.

Distributed Evaluation: a Tool for Constructing Distributed Detection Programs*

Jean-Michel Hélary and Michel Raynal

IRISA , Campus de Beaulieu, 35042 RENNES CEDEX, FRANCE
FAX 99 383832, Telex UNIRISA 950 473F
e-mail helary@irisa.fr,raynal@irisa.fr

Abstract. Methodological design of distributed programs is of major concern to master parallelism. Due to their role in distributed systems, the class of observation or detection programs, whose aim is to observe or detect properties of an observed program, is very important. The detection of a property generally rests upon consistent evaluations of a predicate; such a predicate can be global, i.e. involve states of several processes and channels of the observed program. Unfortunately, in a distributed system, the consistency of an evaluation cannot be trivially obtained. This is a central problem in distributed evaluations. This paper addresses the problem of distributed evaluation, as a basic tool for the design of a general distributed detection program.

1 Introduction

Studying a program can be made by analyzing the set of its possible runs. These runs can be characterized by properties, defined over their states. In an asynchronous distributed context, programs are composed of processes and channels, and it may be very difficult to detect such properties since it is impossible to observe at the same time all the components of a program. It is well-known that this impossibility is the core of the difficulties encountered in the control of distributed programs. Specific solutions have been formulated for particuliar properties, specially in the case of stable ones, e.g. termination or deadlock detection [4, 5, 7, 10, 11], or for properties whose detection lie over the record of a global snapshot [2, 6].

In this paper, we are primarly interested in the problem of evaluating a predicate, defined over the states of a distributed program, whether this predicate is stable or not. Informally, we have a distributed predicate (or even a distributed function of a more general type) whose values depend on variables belonging to different processes sharing no common memory. Each component of the predicate, depending on a single process, can be evaluated by that process in a single state; however, each process having its own control flow, all these partial evaluations cannot be performed in the same state: that's why a global evaluation is necessarily *non-simultaneous*. Moreover, values obtained on each process have to be collected, in order to get complete evaluation. Since this collect is not instantaneous, the final result of the

* This work was supported by French Research Program C^3 on Parallelism and Distributed Computing

evaluation is *delayed*. These informal notions are formalized with the important paradigm of *Non Simultaneous Delayed Evaluation* (NSDE). This concept catches the notion of ***distributed snapshot of local evaluations***. Such a NSDE is worked out by a control program: the notion of ***superimposition***, previously made clear by several authors [1, 3], is a useful tool to modelize this task.

The second goal of this paper is to contribute to the development of methods for distributed detection of properties, expressed by a predicates over the states of a distributed program. An iterative scheme, based upon a sequence of NSDEs, is well suited to this development. We generalize to the distributed context the usual iteration derivation techniques known in a sequential context, namely the expression of a result as the conjunction of an invariant and a stop condition. Invariant condition is expressed as a conjunction of local predicates (***guards***), and can be insured by subjecting the progression of each NSDE to the satisfaction of these guards. On the other hand, the stop condition is evaluated by each NSDE: the value returned determines whether another round has to be performed, or whether the expected result has been obtained. This leads to the second original concept put forward in this paper, namely the ***guarded waves sequence***. Together with this construction, safety and liveness properties are addressed very carefully.

The rest of the paper is organized as follows: in §2, we present the computational model, based upon interleaving semantics, and making use of what we call ***behaviour rules*** for events. Evaluation problems are addressed in §3, details of construction for the detection method are in §4. The interested reader will find more developments in [9] which applies this systematic distributed detection method to the particular case of termination.

2 The Computationnal Model

A distributed program is made of a network of n processes $P_1, P_2, \dots, P_n$, sharing no common memory. They communicate only by exchanging messages through communication channels. Let $X = \{1, \dots, n\}$ be the set of process identifiers, and $\Gamma \subseteq X \times X$ the set of channels. Each channel is an ordered pair $c_{ij} = (i, j)$ carrying messages from P_i to P_j. The directed graph $G = (X, \Gamma)$, modelizing the network, is supposed to be ***strongly connected***: there is a directed path from any i to any j ($i \in X, j \in X$). Each process is a sequential program, with its own context. Messages carry values, since they are used to exchange information between processes. Thus a message is made of two parts: a ***header***, containing such informations as message identification, sender and/or receiver identities, etc. and a ***value*** (of a certain type). The two parts of a message m will be denoted respectively by $m.id$ and $m.v$. For the ease of exposition, we will suppose that each message is uniquely identified.

To a distributed program is associated a set of ***events***, which correspond to the executions of atomic operations performed by the processes. There are three types of events: ***sends***, ***receipts*** and ***internal events***. Each send or receive event is parameterized by a single message. We will denote by

$E_{ij}(m)$ the event "P_i sends message m on channel c_{ij}",
$R_{ij}(m)$ the event "P_j receives message m on channel c_{ij}",
INT_i an internal event of P_i.

To each message m sent over a channel c_{ij} are associated the two predicates $sent(i,j,m)$ and $rec(i,j,m)$ expressing respectively the facts that m has been sent by P_i on c_{ij} (resp. received by P_j on c_{ij}). When a process P_i performs a send event $E_{ij}(m)$, it assigns a value to $m.v$. On the other hand, when a process P_j performs a receive event $R_{ij}(m)$, the value $m.v$ is assigned to a local variable of P_j.

To represent a *run* of a distributed program, we use the well-known *event-state interleaving* model. The run proceeds in a sequence of steps. Each step is a *triple* (s,e,s') where s ans s' belong to a set of *states* and e is an event: when the program is in state s and the event e occurs, the next state is s'. Recall that the state of the program is the set of values of all variables (including those representing channels). A step (s,e,s') is called a *transition* from state s to state s'. Moreover, to each event e is associated an *enabling condition* $en(e)$, which is a state assertion. The notation $\{p\}\ e\ \{q\}$, where p and q are state assertions, means, on the one hand, that $en(e) \Rightarrow p$ and, on the other hand, that for the step (s,e,s'), if p holds in state s, then q holds in state s'. Such a notation will be called a *behaviour rule*.

For instance, $\forall m,\ \forall (i,j) \in \Gamma$:

$\{\neg sent(i,j,m)\}\ E_{ij}(m)\ \{sent(i,j,m)\}$
$\{\neg rec(i,j,m)\}\ R_{ij}(m)\ \{rec(i,j,m)\}$

When assertion $en(e)$ is true in a state s and remains true as long as e doesn't occur, we say that e is *forever enabled from the state s.*

A run of a distributed program is thus a *sequence* of steps $s_0\ e_0\ s_1 \ldots s_k\ e_k\ s_{k+1} \ldots$ such that, for all $k \geq 0$, s_k is a state, e_k is enabled in state s_k and s_{k+1} is the state resulting when e_k occurs in state s_k. It will be assumed that distinct events are never simultaneous, so that each run corresponds to a totally ordered list of states. We will use the following notations: in a given run,

- $s < s'$ iff state s is before state s' in the run (s is earlier than s')
- given a finite set of states $\mathcal{S} = \{s^{(1)}, \ldots, s^{(p)}\}$ belonging to a run, $\max(s^{(1)}, \ldots, s^{(p)})$ (resp. min) is the latest (resp. earliest) state from this set:

$$\max(s^{(1)}, \ldots, s^{(p)}) \in \mathcal{S} \text{ and } 1 \leq j \leq p \Rightarrow s^{(j)} \leq \max(s^{(1)}, \ldots, s^{(p)})$$

To each event e can be associated an *occurrence predicate* $p(e)$ defined in the following way: if e occurs in a step (s,e,s'), then $p(e)$ holds in a state σ if, and only if, $s' \leq \sigma$. Finally, following Lamport, we will say that event e *leads to* event e' if any occurrence of e is necessarily followed by an occurrence of e' after a finite number of steps (denoted by $e \overset{*}{\Rightarrow} e'$).

This model allows us to give a precise meaning to the notions of *progress, non-determinism* and *fairness*, and to the hypotheses of *asynchronous* and *reliable* communications. For a given run, the following properties can be defined:

progress : when at least one event is enabled in state s, one of these events occurs in state s,

non-determinism : when several events are enabled in state s, any one of them may occur in state s,

fairness : when an event is forever enabled from a state s, it will eventually occur (after a finite number of steps).

Also, we will say that communication is ***asynchronous*** if, for any channel c_{ij} and any message m on c_{ij}, the number of steps between the two events $E_{ij}(m)$ and $R_{ij}(m)$ is unpredictable. Thus, in any run of an asynchronous program, we have:

$$\forall m,\ \forall(i,j) \in \Gamma :\ en(R_{ij}(m)) \Rightarrow sent(i,j,m) \wedge \neg rec(i,j,m)$$

We say that a channel is *reliable* iff, for any message m on channel c_{ij}:

1. $sent(i,j,m)$ is the occurrence predicate of $E_{ij}(m)$ and $rec(m,i,j)$ is the occurrence predicate of $R_{ij}(m)$. This implies:
   (a) channel c_{ij} cannot spontaneously create messages ($sent(i,j,m)$ cannot hold unless event $E_{ij}(m)$ occurred),
   (b) channel c_{ij} cannot duplicate messages ($rec(i,j,m)$ remains true forever after $R_{ij}(m)$ occurred),
   (c) channel c_{ij} cannot loose messages ($sent(i,j,m)$ remains true forever after $E_{ij}(m)$ occurred and $rec(i,j,m)$ cannot hold unless event $R_{ij}(m)$ occurred)).
2. $R_{ij}(m)$ is forever enabled after a finite number of state transitions after the occurrence of $E_{ij}(m)$.

From this it follows that, if channels are reliable and run is fair, every send event $E_{ij}(m)$ leads to the corresponding receipt $R_{ij}(m)$, and no receipt $R_{ij}(m)$ can occur unless a corresponding $E_{ij}(m)$ occurred before (recall that we assume messages are uniquely identified).

From now on, we will restrict ourselves to this model of computation, with asynchronous and reliable communications. We will consider only distributed programs whose runs verify progress, non-determinism and fairness assumptions. All subsequent notions will be relative to an arbitrary run of a distributed program, unless otherwise stated by the use of quantifiers over the set of possible runs, such as *for any run ...* or *there exists a run such that...*

3 Evaluating Predicates

3.1 Some Concepts about Distributed Evaluation

Consider a function F defined over the set of states of a distributed program. The value of F in state s will be denoted by $F[s]$.The evaluation of F by a process P in a state s is an operation which allows this process to compute $F[s]$.

The evaluation of F by a process P is *atomic* (or instantaneous) if no state transition occurs during this evaluation. In an asynchronous distributed model, atomic evaluation of F by P is possible if, and only if, F depends only of P's local context since, in such a computation model, no process can have an immediate access to other processes context: this is inherent to the model.

For example, any predicate $sent(i,j,m)$ can be atomically evaluated by P_i but not by P_j. Similarly, $rec(i,j,m)$ can be atomically evaluated by P_j but not by P_i.

Several functions $F_1,\ldots,F_k$ can be ***simultaneously evaluated*** by a process P if there exists a state s such that P can atomically evaluate $F_1[s],\ldots,F_k[s]$. Like in the case of atomic evaluation, simultaneous evaluation is possible in asynchronous distributed model if, and only if, functions to be evaluated depend only of variables all belonging to the same process.

Let $\mathcal{F} = f(F_1, F_2, \ldots, F_n)$ be a function such that F_i is a function atomically evaluable by P_i.

Definition 3.1 *A non-simultaneous evaluation of $\mathcal{F}$ is an evaluation $f(F_1[s^{(1)}], \ldots, F_n[s^{(n)}])$, where $s^{(i)}$ denotes the state in which P_i evaluates F_i.*

Definition 3.2 *A non-simultaneous delayed evaluation (NSDE) of $\mathcal{F}$ by process P is a non simultaneous evaluation whose result is recorded in P's local context in a state $s \geq \max(s^{(1)}, \ldots, s^{(n)})$. Such an evaluation will be denoted by*

$$\mathcal{F}[s^{(1)}, \ldots, s^{(n)} \mid s]$$

This concept captures the essence of "global" function evaluation in asynchronous distributed systems. The following definitions give a more precise meaning to the quality of such evaluations in the case of boolean functions (predicates).

Definition 3.3 *A NSDE of $\mathcal{F}$ is said to be safe with regard to a predicate $\mathcal{T}$ whenever*

$$\mathcal{F}[s^{(1)}, \ldots, s^{(n)} \mid s] \Rightarrow \mathcal{T}[s]$$

Definition 3.4 *A predicate $\mathcal{F}$ is said to be live with regard to predicate $\mathcal{T}$ whenever, in any run,*

$$\mathcal{T}[s] \Rightarrow \exists(s^{(1)}, \ldots, s^{(n)}, s') \text{ with}$$

$$\left(s \leq \min(s^{(1)}, \ldots, s^{(n)}) \leq \max(s^{(1)}, \ldots, s^{(n)}) \leq s'\right) \wedge \mathcal{F}[s^{(1)}, \ldots, s^{(n)} \mid s']$$

Note Definition 3.3 is weaker than the assertion $\mathcal{F} \Rightarrow \mathcal{T}$ since the latter means that implication holds in all states of the program, while our definition is related to a particuliar NSDE. Similarly, if we consider, as in [3], the relation (over predicates) $\mathcal{T}$ *ensures* $\mathcal{F}$, which means that, if $\mathcal{T}[s]$ holds, then $\mathcal{F}$ will eventually hold in a state $\sigma \geq s$, liveness definition 3.4 is weaker, since it doesn't assert the existence of a state σ in which an atomic evaluation $\mathcal{F}[\sigma]$ would give the result *true*, but only the existence of a NSDE whose result is *true*. The safety and liveness notions stated here are thus closely related to the concept of NSDE. In that sense, they are different, for instance, from the *detects* relation in UNITY [3].

3.2 Control Program for Evaluation: the Superimposition Model

Consider a distributed program, called *underlying program*, and a predicate $\mathcal{F}$ defined over the states of this program. Performing a NSDE of $\mathcal{F}$ is a task which may involve some messages, variables, and thus events, not belonging to the underlying program. This task is thus worked out by a program different from the underlying program, which is called a *control program* (relative to the underlying program). This notion is well-known; a formal framework well-suited to its expression is the *superimposition model* [1, 3], which can be described as follows:

- To each proces P_i of the underlying program is associated a process C_i (controller) of the control program,
- A non-empty subset of the local context of each P_i can be atomically "observed" by the corresponding controller C_i: this means that all functions defined over this subset can be atomically evaluated by C_i,
- To each event of the underlying program corresponds an event of the control program. In particular, the control program simulates emission and receipt of the underlying program messages: to each *send* and *receive* event of the underlying program corresponds a *send* and *receive* event of the control program, with the same message parameter.
- In addition to underlying events, the control program has specific events (*control events*). For instance, sends or receipts of messages not belonging to the underlying program, called *control messages*, are such control events.

Thus, any run of the superimposed control program is partially dependant of a run of the underlying program. The local context of each controller C_i comprises:

1. P_i's variables atomically observable by C_i: their value depend only of the run of the underlying program (P_i can read and write it, but C_i can only *read* them)
2. perhaps some other variables (control variables), specific to the control program (they can be *read* and *written* by C_i, and are hidden to P_i).

Processes C_i can communicate through a set of channels including Γ (the underlying program set of channels) and possibly extra channels (which can be used only by control messages). Finally, to each state of the underlying program corresponds a state of the control program: a run of the underlying program is a subsequence of the corresponding run of the control program. Designing a superimposed control program consists in specifying control events and their associated behaviour rules.

In what follows, UM will denote the set of underlying messages.

3.3 Designing a Control Program for NSDE

Recall that a NSDE of predicate $\mathcal{F} = f(F_1, \ldots, F_n)$ by a process C is obtained when a set of values $F_1[s^{(1)}], \ldots, F_n[s^{(n)}]$ has been recorded (in a state s) in the context of C. Two events, *start* and *return* correspond to the beginning and the end of the NSDE program. To which process belongs *start* is not specified at this level of abstraction, whereas *return* belongs to the process recording the result of NSDE. For each $i \in X$ let *collected*(i) be a predicate, expressing the fact that process C_i has participated in the NSDE of $\mathcal{F}$, in other words, has evaluated F_i. The NSDE is specified by the following behaviour rules:

$$\begin{array}{lll} \{en(start)\} & start & \{\bigwedge_{i \in X} (\neg collected(i))\} \\ \{\bigwedge_{i \in X} (collected(i))\} & return & \{a = \mathcal{F}[s^{(1)}, \ldots, s^{(n)} \mid s]\} \end{array}$$

where a denotes the value returned by NSDE.

In order to progress from the post-condition of *start* to the precondition of *return*, each process C_i must perform an atomic evaluation of F_i in a state $s^{(i)}$.

This evaluation corresponds to an event, namely $visit_i$. This event must occur once and only once during the step, so we obtain the following behaviour rules:

$$\begin{array}{llll} & \{en(start)\} & start & \{\bigwedge_{i\in X}(\neg collected(i))\} \\ \forall i \in X & \{\neg collected(i)\} & visit_i & \{collected(i)\} \\ & \{\bigwedge_{i\in X}(collected(i))\} & return & \{a = \mathcal{F}[s^{(1)}, \ldots, s^{(n)} \mid s]\} \end{array}$$

Finally, we will say that NSDE program is *live* whenever, in any run, $start \overset{*}{\Rightarrow} return$.

This set of behaviour rules is an abstract specification of the now classical tool known as a *wave* [8, 12]. In the next section, we use and generalize this tool in order to obtain a detection control program.

4 Detection Problems

Let $\mathcal{T}$ be a predicate defined over the states of a distributed program. We want to solve the following problem: *detect a state s of the distributed program such that $\mathcal{T}[s] = true$.*

We don't assume that $\mathcal{T}$ is stable (recall that a predicate $\mathcal{P}$ is said to be *stable* if, and only if: $(\mathcal{P}[s] \wedge s' \geq s) \Rightarrow \mathcal{P}[s']$).

4.1 Derivation of a Detection Control Program

Let $\mathcal{F}$ be a predicate such that it is possible to perform a sequence ($k = 1, 2, \ldots$) of NSDEs

$$\mathcal{F}[s_k^{(1)}, \ldots, s_k^{(n)} \mid s_k] \text{ with :}$$

$$\forall k \geq 0 \; : \; \max(s_k^{(1)}, \ldots, s_k^{(n)}) \leq s_k \leq \min(s_{k+1}^{(1)}, \ldots, s_{k+1}^{(n)}) \qquad (SC)$$

The predicate $\mathcal{F}$ will solve the detection problem stated above if it meets the two requirements:

1. detection must be safe, that is to say:
   $\forall k \geq 0$, the kth NSDE is safe with respect to $\mathcal{T}$. This insures that, whenever exists k such that $\mathcal{F}[s_k^{(1)}, \ldots, s_k^{(n)} \mid s_k]$ is true, we can conclude $\mathcal{T}[s_k]$ is also true.
2. The detection must be live, that is to say:

   $$\mathcal{T}[s] \Rightarrow \exists k \; : \; s_k \geq s \wedge \mathcal{F}[s_k^{(1)}, \ldots, s_k^{(n)} \mid s_k]$$

   This insures that, whenever exists s such that $\mathcal{T}[s]$ is true, then it exists k such that the kth NSDE will return true.

Now, suppose we can separate $\mathcal{F}$ into two parts $I, \mathcal{A}$ verifying

$$\forall k \geq 0 \; : \; I \equiv \bigwedge_{i \in X} I_i[s_k^{(i)}]$$

where I_i is a predicate atomically evaluable by C_i ($i \in X$), and $\mathcal{A} = f(A_1, \ldots, A_n)$ (each A_i atomically evaluable by C_i), such that

$$I \wedge \mathcal{A}[s_k^{(1)}, \ldots, s_k^{(n)} \mid s_k] \equiv \mathcal{F}[s_k^{(1)}, \ldots, s_k^{(n)} \mid s_k]$$

I is a *loop invariant* and $\mathcal{A}$ is the associated *stop condition*. The sequence of NSDEs must be designed in order that, for all $k \geq 0$, states $s_k^{(i)}, i \in X$ and s_k verify:

(1) $\mathcal{A}[s_k^{(1)}, \ldots, s_k^{(n)} \mid s_k]$ is evaluated (let a_k denote this value),
(2) $\bigwedge_{i \in X} I_i[s_k^{(i)}]$ is true,

These two conditions are relative to each iteration step. We omit subscript k, since we refer to a single iteration step. Condition **(1)** is realized with a ***wave*** as seen in §3.3. But we must also insure the loop invariant **(2)**. To this end, each state $s^{(i)}$ must be such that $I_i[s^{(i)}]$ be true. In fact, it may happen that, according to the underlying program and to the implementation of the wave, some i exist for which I_i is false in the state where visit_i occurs. To overcome this, each event visit_i is no longer considered as atomic: it is split into two distinct events, namely $\mathit{beg\_visit}_i, \mathit{end\_visit}_i$. The former corresponds to the occurrence of C_i's visit, according to the wave, the latter is enabled as soon as I_i becomes true: I_i is the ***guard*** of the event $\mathit{end\_visit}_i$. For each $i \in X$, the predicate $wh(i)$ expresses the fact that event $\mathit{beg\_visit}_i$ occurred, but event $\mathit{end\_visit}_i$ didn't yet occur (for the current step). Denoting by ss, $sb^{(i)}$, $se^{(i)}$, sr the states in which events start, $\mathit{beg\_visit}_i$, $\mathit{end\_visit}_i$, return respectively occur (indexed by the number k of the current wave if necessary), we obtain the behaviour rules:

$$
\begin{array}{lll}
\{en(start)\} & start & \{\bigwedge_{i\in X} (\neg collected(i))\} \\
\{\neg wh(i) \wedge \neg collected(i)\} & beg\_visit_i & \{wh(i) \wedge \neg collected(i)\} \\
\{wh(i) \wedge \neg collected(i) \wedge I_i\} & end\_visit_i & \{\neg wh(i) \wedge collected(i)\} \\
\{\bigwedge_{i\in X} (I_i[se^{(i)}] \wedge collected(i))\} & return & \{a = \mathcal{A}[se^{(1)}, \ldots, se^{(n)} \mid sr]\}
\end{array}
$$

Hence, the loop invariant (or wave guard) $I \equiv \bigwedge_{i \in X} I_i[se^{(i)}]$ holds.

Now, the sequentiality condition (SC) has to be satisfied. For that purpose, we define $en(start)$ and strenghten the postcondition of return; a predicate $\mathit{new\_step}$ expresses the fact that a new step can start ($en(start) \equiv new\_step$):

$$
\begin{array}{lll}
\{new\_step\} & start & \{\neg new\_step \wedge \bigwedge_{i\in X} (\neg collected(i))\} \\
\{\neg wh(i) \wedge \neg collected(i)\} & beg\_visit_i & \{wh(i) \wedge \neg collected(i)\} \\
\{wh(i) \wedge \neg collected(i) \wedge I_i\} & end\_visit_i & \{\neg wh(i) \wedge collected(i)\} \\
\{\bigwedge_{i\in X} (I_i[se^{(i)}] \wedge collected(i))\} & return & \\
 & & \{a = \mathcal{A}[se^{(1)}, \ldots, se^{(n)} \mid sr] \wedge new\_step = \neg a\}
\end{array}
$$

This set of behaviour rules corresponds to what can be called a ***sequence of guarded waves***. It generalizes the well-known "sequence of waves" scheme, in the sense that, for each wave, each event $\mathit{end\_visit}_i$ is preconditionned (guarded) by an assertion I_i.

4.2 Safety and Liveness

Let's address the question of how to meet safety and liveness requirements.

Safety. To meet this requirement, it is sufficient to find guards I_i and stop condition $\mathcal{A}$ such that, in any run,

$$\bigwedge_{i \in X} \left(I_i[se^{(i)}]\right) \wedge \mathcal{A}[se^{(1)}, \ldots, se^{(n)} \mid sr] \Rightarrow \mathcal{T}[sr]$$

Liveness. This point is not so obvious. First, it is necessary that waves themselves are live, that is to say, in any run:

$$(l1) \qquad \forall i \in X \; : \; start \overset{*}{\Rightarrow} beg\_visit_i$$
$$(l2) \; (\forall i \in X \; : \; end\_visit_i) \overset{*}{\Rightarrow} return$$

These requirements depend only on the implementation of waves, which is a part of the control program design, and not of the underlying program.

If waves are live, we can assert that, in any state of the control program, either there is a "current wave" or the stop condition has been met in a preceeding state. More precisely, in any state s of the control program, there is an integer $k \geq 1$ such that, one and only one of the three situations holds:

either $ss_k \leq s \leq sr_k$ (wave k is currently run in state s),
or $sr_{k-1} \leq s \leq ss_k \wedge new\_step[sr_{k-1}]$ (wave $k-1$ has returned and wave k is enabled but not yet started. Event $start_k$ will eventually occur),
or $sr_{k-1} \leq s \wedge \mathcal{A}[se_{k-1}^{(1)}, \ldots, se_{k-1}^{(n)} \mid sr_{k-1}]$ (Wave $k-1$ has returned and stop condition holds. This wave was the last one).

In the first two cases, wave k is the *current* one, and $s \leq sr_k$ holds.

However, waves liveness properties ($l1$) and ($l2$) are not sufficient to insure that a wave will eventually return. The following property:

($l3$) : "in any run of the control program, $\forall i \in X \; : \; beg\_visit_i \overset{*}{\Rightarrow} end\_visit_i$" must also be verified. But ($l3$) depends on the guards I_i which, in turn, depend on events belonging to the underlying program. Thus, the event end_visit_i might be not forever enabled: even in a fair run, it might happen that beg_visit_i doesn't lead to end_visit_i, and consequently that the current wave never returns. So, in the context of detection, ensuring liveness requires that, if $\mathcal{T}[s]$ is true, then $\exists k$ such that:

1. wave k eventually returns, and
2. $\mathcal{A}[se_k^{(1)}, \ldots, se_k^{(n)} \mid sr_k] \wedge \bigwedge_{i \in X} I_i[se_k^{(i)}]$, with $s \leq \min\left(se_k^{(1)}, \ldots, se_k^{(n)}, sr_k\right)$.

The following lemma gives a sufficient condition, depending on the underlying program behaviour, to obtain a live detection.

Lemma 4.1 *If waves are live, and if guards I_i and stop condition $\mathcal{A}$ verify, in any run of the control program:*

i) $\mathcal{T}[s] \Rightarrow \left(\forall i \in X \; \exists \sigma^{(i)} \; : \; \left(\sigma \geq \sigma^{(i)} \Rightarrow I_i[\sigma]\right)\right)$
ii) $\forall s^{(1)}, \ldots, s^{(n)}, \overline{s}$ such that $s \leq \min(s^{(1)}, \ldots, s^{(n)}) \leq \max(s^{(1)}, \ldots, s^{(n)}) \leq \overline{s}$ *the assertion* $\mathcal{T}[s] \Rightarrow \mathcal{A}[s^{(1)}, \ldots, s^{(n)} \mid \overline{s}]$ *holds*

then the detection is live.

Unformally, assumption i) means that, if $\mathcal{T}$ holds in a state s, all the guards I_i eventually hold and are stable. This assumption is used to prove that the current wave eventually returns. Assumption ii) means that every NSDE of the stop predicate $\mathcal{A}$, performed after s, will return the value *true*. This assumption is used to prove that there will be a "last" wave.

The proof is omitted here. It can be found in the full paper [9].

5 Conclusion

Methodological design of distributed programs is of major concern to master parallelism. Distributed detection problems are important, due to their role in distributed systems. Since their solution essentially involve predicate evaluations, we have put forward the difficulties inherent to distributed evaluation. After recalling that, in asynchronous distributed context, such evaluations can be only non-simultaneous and delayed, we have formalized this concept as the NSDE paradigm, and we have given precise definitions of its associated safety and liveness properties. The detection problem itself has been set in its generality such that, whatever the predicate to detect, the solution is expressed by an iterative NSDE scheme. The well-known technique used in centralized context, which consists in decomposition of a goal specification into an invariant and a stop condition, has been extended to the asynchronous distributed context: this leads to a "two-level" iterative scheme, namely a spatial iteration (*for all processes do ...*), which is a NSDE implemented by a wave, and a temporal iteration (*while* $\neg$ *stop do* NSDE *done*), implemented by a sequence of waves. The systematic design of the wave (a step of the temporal iteration) is deduced from its specification: the concept of guarded wave is introduced, in order to insure the desired invariant (the guards control the wave progression), and the stop condition is evaluated by the non simultaneous delayed evaluation scheme realized by the spatial iteration. This is the general part. There is a particular part when concerned with a particular detection problem: it remains to obtain a NSD-evaluable predicate $\mathcal{F}$ associated to the particular predicate $\mathcal{T}$ we want to detect, insuring safety and liveness requirements. In the full paper [9], this problem is solved for the particular case of distributed termination detection; moreover an insight is put on how this could be generalized to the detection of other kinds of stable predicates, namely the computation of monotonic functions on the state of underlying programs.

References

1. L. Bougé and N. Francez. A Compositional Approach to Superimposition. in *Proc. ACM Symposium on POPL*, San Diego, 1988.
2. K.M. Chandy and L. Lamport. Distributed Snapshots : Determining Global States of Distributed Systems. *ACM TOCS*, 3(1):63–75, Feb. 1985.
3. K.M. Chandy and J. Misra. *Parallel Program Design: a Foundation.* Addison Wesley, 1988.
4. E.W. Dijkstra and C.S. Scholten. Termination Detection for Diffusing Computations. *Inf. Proccessing Letters*, Vol. 11:1–4, 1980.
5. N. Francez. Distributed Termination. *ACM Toplas*, 2-1, 1980.
6. J.M. Hélary. Observing Global States of Asynchronous Distributed Computations. in *Proc. 3rd Int. Workshop on Distributed Algorithms*, Nice, sept. 1989. Springer-Verlag LNCS 392:124-135.
7. J. M Hélary, C. Jard, N. Plouzeau, and M. Raynal. Detection of Stable Properties in Distributed Applications. in *Proc. 6th annual ACM Symposium on Principles of Distributed Computing*, pages 125–136, Vancouver, August 1987.
8. J. M. Hélary, M. Raynal. *Control and Synchronisation of Distributed Systems and Programs.* Wiley Series in Parallel Computing, August 1990.

9. J. M. Hélary, M. Raynal. Towards the Construction of Distributed Detection Programs, with an Application to Distributed Termination. *Res. Rep.* IRISA, University of Rennes 1, june 1991.
10. F. Mattern. Algorithms for Distributed Termination Detection. *Distributed Computing*, 2:161–175, 1987.
11. J. Misra. Detecting Termination of Distributed Computation Using Markers. in *Proc. 2d ACM Symp. on PODC*, Montreal, 1983, pp 290-294.
12. F.P. Schneider. Paradigms for Distributed Programs. In *Distributed Systems*, LNCS 190: 431-480, Springer-Verlag Ed., 1985.

This article was processed using the LaTeX macro package with LLNCS style

FOUNDATIONS OF ASYMPTOTICAL THEORY OF DETERMINATE COMPACT TESTING

Evgeny V. Luk-Zilberman

Abstract

It is considered the main problem of Determinate Compact Testing (DCT): the problem of selecting of function that compresses output sequences of Tested Discrete Device (TDD). The problem of adequate probability model selection describing TDD output error is discussed and the nonhomogeneous Markov chain of arbitrary order is considered. Within this model frame the criteria of quality of realized by finite automata (FA) compressing functions is introduced. The class of asymptotical optimal FA is singled out. It is shown that probability of errors detection by belonging to this class FA tends to (M-1)/M exponentially with t, where M is number of FA states.

Description of the class of asymptotical optimal FA is also given in terms of permutation groups and it is shown that, in general, this class places strictly "between" the transitive and primitive groups.

Class of asymptotical optimal FA realizing Checksums to Modulo M is singled out. Class of asymptotical optimal signature analyzers defined over field GF(2) is singled out. The simple sufficient conditions describing the class of asymptotical optimal signature analyzers defined over field GF(k) (k is a prime number) are also given here.

1. Introduction

The procedure shown in Fig.1 is called Determinate Compact Testing (DCT). The determinate (predetermined) sequence is supplied to the inputs of the Tested Discrete Device (TDD).The TDD output sequence with length t is mapped by a compressing function into a sequence with length m , $m < t$. The obtained sequence is compared with the correct reference sequence (with length m) which has been obtained by applying this procedure to a fixed TDD. If these sequences coincide then it is submitted that the TDD is fixed, otherwise is faulted.

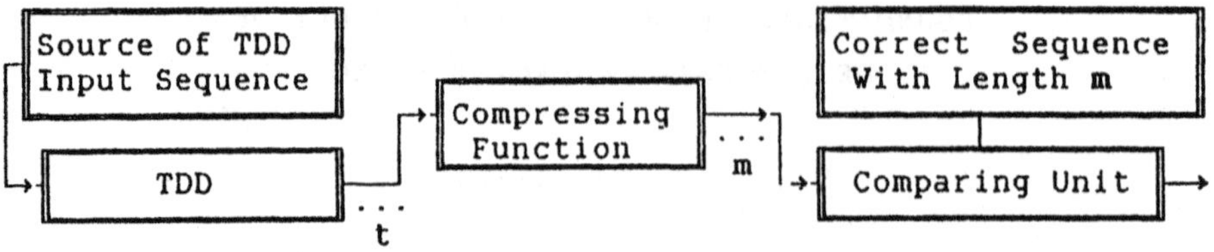

Fig.1

If m << t, then the correctness of the TDD can be determined by comparing the sequences smaller than t in length. This is the sense of the application of DCT .

Well known methods of DCT are Checksums Modulo M [1] and Signature Analyses [2].

In this paper the main problem of DCT theory is considered: the selection of a function that compresses TDD output sequence. TDD is supposed to be completely tested; if there is a fault in it then an error in TDD output sequence will surely appear.

The quality of the compressing function is determined by the probability of error detection in the TDD output sequence. To estimate this probability it is necessary to define a model of output sequence distortion of TDD. The need to be within the limits of some distortion model is specified by the fact that the mapping done by the function is not one-to-one and at m < t it can not detect all errors in input information. It is obvious that in addition, the model must be adequate (i.e. match real output errors of TDD). Otherwise the arguments for quality of test results will only be of a speculative character.

The selection of an adequate model is a very complicated matter because it must provide a good description of output errors of most of the TDD. In consequence, restrictions imposed by the model should be minimized, taking into account only the most general rules of TDD output errors. This is the essence of the difference between the DCT theory and the Coding Theory. The conventional Coding Theory approach consists of error statistics research (in our case in the TDD output sequence) and then finding their detecting compressing function (i.e. decoder). Such an approach cannot be applied to the DCT. This is because we have to select a compressing function before actually knowing nothing about the Discrete Device which will be tested or about the test sequences which will test them. Therefore there is nothing known about probabilistic distribution of the TDD output errors. Hence, the main property that a compressing function must have is universality. It must minimize loss of information in the results of compressing for almost any TDD and therefore for almost any probabilistic distribution of TDD output errors.

As known a common way of testing a microcomputer system consists of the separation and sequential examination of different units of the system (see [3], for example). Thus, we shall assume that the appearance of faults in different units of tested microcomputer system is independent. Then, the erroneous bits in this system output sequence are dependent on each other's and this dependence is restricted within some vicinity (the distance between the dependent erroneous bits does not exceed the length of the sequence testing given unit). In this case errors in output signals form a Markov chain (in general nonhomogeneous one) of some ν order. These arguments are the basis for the next, main assumption for the present work: distortion of output signals of TDD form a nonhomogeneous Markov chain of arbitrary ν order. No restrictions are imposed on the value of ν and on probabilities of distortions of the output signals . There is only one condition - these probabilities must not be equal to zero. If this condition is not satisfied then the output sequence is error-free and testing is pointless.

The present work generalizes results obtained in the papers [4 - 6] and singles out the class of functions realized by finite automata (FA) which:

a) in cases when output signal distortions of the TDD form nonhomogeneous Markov chain of arbitrary order are asymptotical optimal;

b) detect any single error .

The requirement to detect any single error for compressed TDD output sequence by FA is present in almost all the works done on DCT and is conventional. The restriction of compressing function selection by FA set is not essential because FA is an abstract model of any Discrete Device.

2. Asymptotically optimal analyzers

In this section we shall introduce the model of distortion of output sequences of TDD and quality criterion for compressing information analyzers in this model. Class of asymptotically optimal analyzers (AOA) is singled out from the set of FA.

Definition. A finite automaton is a set consisting of five items (X, S, Y, φ, f): sets of input and output signals $X = \{X_1, \dots, X_N\}$, $Y = \{Y_1, \dots, Y_K\}$, a set of states $S = \{S_1, \dots, S_M\}$ and functions of transitions and output $S^t = \varphi(X^t, S^{t-1})$, $Y^t = f(S^t)$, where $t = 1,2,3,\dots$ are discrete moments during which automaton functionates.

For simplicity of notation we shall assume that $S_q = q$, $q = 1,\dots,M$. As it will be seen later this does not restrict the generality of our discussion.

Let initial state of FA be $S^0 = q_0$ for some $q_0 \in \{1,\dots,M\}$ and some sequence $v^t = X_{i_1} \dots X_{i_t}$ be supplied to FA input. We shall assume that events of the distortions of i-th input signal into j-th one in different moment of time form nonhomogeneous Markov chain of order ν $(\nu \geq 0)$ and that their probabilistic distribution is given:

$$P(X^t = X_{i_t}, X_{j_t} \mid X^{t-1} = X_{i_{t-1}}, X_{j_{t-1}}; \dots; X^1 = X_{i_1}, X_{j_1}) =$$

$$= \begin{cases} P(X^t = X_{i_t}, X_{j_t} \mid X^{t-1} = X_{i_{t-1}}, X_{j_{t-1}}; \dots; X^1 = X_{i_1}, X_{j_1}) & \text{at } t<\nu \\ P(X^t = X_{i_t}, X_{j_t} \mid X^{t-1} = X_{i_{t-1}}, X_{j_{t-1}}; \dots; X^{t-\nu} = X_{i_{t-\nu}}, X_{j_{t-\nu}}) & \text{at } t\geq\nu \end{cases} \qquad (1)$$

for any $j_1, \dots, j_t \in \{1,\dots,N\}$.

We shall say that input sequence v^t =

$X_{i_1} \ldots X_{i_t}$ transforms FA from state q_o to state q, and designate $v^t(q_o) = q$ or $X_{i_1} \ldots X_{i_t}(q_o) = q$ if $S^o = q_o$ and after supplying this sequence to FA input $S^t = q$. Under these conditions probability of FA output distortion at t moment is equal to

$$P(Y^t | S^o = q_o, v^t) = \sum_{q: f(q) \neq f(v^t(q_o))} W(S^t = q | S^o = q_o)$$

where $W(S^t = q | S^o = q_o)$ is the probability of that $S^t = q$ at $S^o = q_o$ with allowance for distortions in input sequence.

Probability $P(Y^t | S^o = q, v^t)$ characterizes quality of the realized by a given FA analyzer at given S^o, v^t and distribution (1): the higher the probability of FA output distortion the better the analyzer detects errors in the input sequence.

It is also obvious that $P(Y^t | S^o = q_o, v^t) \leq P(S^t = v^t(q_o) | S^o = q_o)$ where

$$P(S^t = v^t(q_o) | S^o = q_o) = \sum_{q:\ q \neq v^t(q_o)} W(S^t = q | S^o = q_o) \qquad (2)$$

for any S^o, v^t and distribution (1); that is why without any restrictions for discussion generality we may (and we shall) assume that $Y = S$ and $Y^t = S^t$, $t = 1,2,3,\ldots$, i.e. FA is considered to be a set consisting of three items (X, S, φ).

Let us introduce quality criterion for analyzers:

$$P_M(t) = \max_{\mathscr{A}_M} \min_{S^o,\, v^t,\, \text{distribution (1)},\, T} P(S^t = v^t(q_o) | S^o = q_o) \qquad (3)$$

where $\mathscr{A}_M$ is the set of all FA with a fixed number of states: $|S| = M$ and T is some subset of indexes of input signals ($T \subseteq \{1,\ldots,N\}$) at the following restrictions:

$$P(X^\tau = X_{i_\tau}, X_{j_\tau} | X^{\tau-1} = X_{i_{\tau-1}}, X_{j_{\tau-1}}; \ldots; X^1 = X_{i_1}, X_{j_1}) \geq \sigma \qquad (4)$$

for any $j_1, \ldots, j_\tau \in T$, $\tau = 1,2,\ldots,t$ and some $\sigma > 0$

$$|T| \geq 2 \qquad (5)$$

Criterion (3) specifies requirements to an analyzer. They all together require the highest level of analyzer universality. An analyzer which satisfies by these requirements must detect output errors of TDD with high probability for:

a) any initial state of analyzer. This demand comes out from the minimization $P(S^t = v^t(q_0) | S^0 = q_0)$ with S^0 in (3). This demand is required because an initial state of the analyzer may be arbitrary. For example, if Signature Analysis [2] is used, the initial state is defined by reference signature;

b) any input sequence of analyzer. This demand comes out from minimization in (3) with v^t. This demand is required because the input sequence of an analyzer is dependent on test sequence of TDD and may be arbitrary;

c) any distribution (1) (within the framework of model of distortion and with accuracy to restrictions (4), (5)). This demand comes out from minimization in (3) with distribution (1) and T. Restrictions (4), (5) require that an input signal could distort at any moment with nonzero probability at least into one another. This condition is satisfied for any faulty TDD and hence is a rather weak restriction.

The next statement gives an upper bound of $P_M(t)$.

Statement 1. For any t:

$$P_M(t) \leq (M-1)/M.$$

Thus, value of (M-1)/M is the upper bound for analyzer quality and analyzers for which

$$\lim_{t \to \infty} \min P(S^t) = (M-1)/M \tag{7}$$

are asymptotically optimal.

Let us single out the class of FA which are AOA and which detect any single error in input sequences.

Definition. The set of FA states S is called regular with regard to T, $T \subseteq \{1,...,N\}$ if at some t all equations $X_{i_1} \ldots X_{i_t}(q_0) = q$ for any $q, q_0 \in S$ have solutions in $X_T = \{X_i | i \in T\}$.

Definition of S regularity with regard to T is equivalent to t-controllability of FA [7] under condition that the set of input signals is equal to X_T.

A single error in the sequence $X_{i_1} \dots X_{i_t}$ is its distortion into one of sequences $X_{j_1} \dots X_{j_t}$ which is such that $X_{j_\tau} \neq X_{i_t}$ for some one $\tau \in \{1, \dots, t\}$ and $X_{j_l} = X_{i_l}$ for any $l \neq \tau$.

We shall say that FA detect any distortion in input sequence v_1^τ if for any sequence v^l, v_2^τ and for any $q_0 \in \{1, \dots, M\}$ the inequality $v^l v_1^\tau (q_0) \neq v^l v_2^\tau (q_0)$ is satisfied.

Theorem 1. For finite automaton to be AOA and to be able to detect any single error in arbitrary input sequence, it is necessary and sufficient that for any $T \subseteq \{1, \dots, N\}$, $|T| \geq 2$ its states be regular with regard to T and cardinality of every set $\{q | \varphi(X_i, q) = q_1\}$ for any $i \in \{1, \dots, N\}$, $q \in \{1, \dots, M\}$ and $\{X_i | \varphi(X_i, q) = q_1\}$ for any $q, q_1 \in \{1, \dots, M\}$ be not greater than one. When it takes place $\min P(S^t)$ tends to $(M-1)/M$ exponentially with t.

Theorem 1 solves the general problem that states in the present work: optimal analyzers are singled out from entire class of FA. However, the check of regularity of FA states with regard to any T in general case is rather complex. In other words, we check whether FA is controllable in any pair of input signals, and this problem is known to be a complex one. The next sections present the research of the conditions which can be easily checked and which allow to single out asymptotically optimal analyzers realizing Checksums Modulo M and asymptotically optimal signature analyzers.

3. Optimal Checksums Modulo M

Let us say that FA $A = (X, S, \varphi)$ realizes a permutation group $G = \langle \Pi_1, \dots, \Pi_N \rangle$, if input signal X_i realizes the permutation Π_i on S, $i = 1, \dots, N$. It is easy to note that the second condition of theorem 1 is equivalent to the following: each input signal X_i realizes some permutation on S. Thus, any FA from AOA class realizes some permutation group on S. This fact permits to use the results of the group theory to obtain easily tested conditions describing AOA class. However, the mathematics body of the group theory can not be used directly for these purposes in a general case . Let us illustrate this by the following example.

<u>Example 1</u>. Let us consider automata $A = (X, S, \varphi)$ and $A' = (X', S, \varphi)$ where $X = \{0,1\}$, $X' = \{1\}$, $S = \{0,1,\dots,M-1\}$ and $S^t = = X^t + S^{t-1} \pmod M$. Their transition diagrams are shown in Fig.2 a), b) respectively.

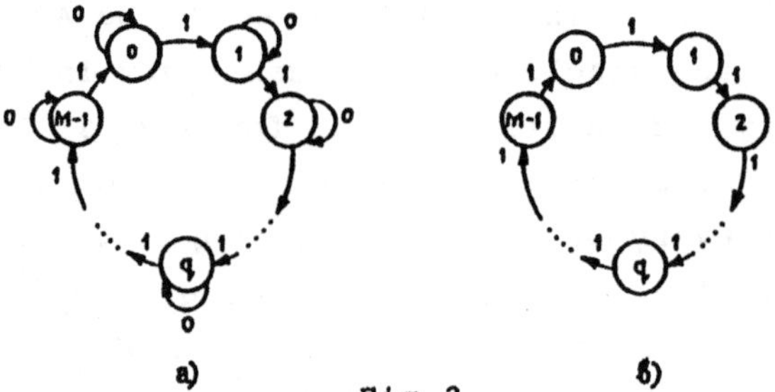

Fig.2

Automaton A realizes $G = \langle e, \Pi \rangle$ and A' realizes $G' = \langle \Pi \rangle$ where e is a single permutation and $\Pi = (012\dots M)$. At the same time the states set of A is regular (the presence of at least one "loop" in a strongly connected set provides its regularity) and the states set of A' is not regular (for any t from any (one) state it is possible to come only to one another).

Thus the automata can realize isomorphic permutation groups but the sets of their states can be either regular or not. The following lemma gives a classification of FA states according to the connectivity in this case.

Let a set of integers be designated as $\mathbb{Z}$. The definitions of strongly connected sets and cyclic classes is given in [8].

<u>Lemma 1</u>. Let FA $A = (X, S, \varphi)$, $|X| = N$, $|S| = M$ realizes a permutation group $G = \langle \Pi_1, \dots, \Pi_N \rangle$ so that $\Pi_i = \Pi^{r_i}$, $r_i \in \mathbb{Z}$, $i = = 1,\dots,N$, for some permutation Π consisting of k independent cycles with the length of $M_1, M_2, \dots, M_k$ respectively. Then S consists of l strongly connected sets every one of which is divided into d_j of cyclic classes, $j = 1,\dots,l$ where $l = \sum_{i=1}^{k} l_i$, $l_i = GCD(M_i, r_1, \dots, r_N)$ and $d_j = GCD(M_i, r_1 - r_2, \dots, r_1 - r_N, \dots, r_{N-1} - r_N)/l_i$ for any $j \in \{$

$\sum_{n=1}^{i-1} l_n + 1, \ldots, \sum_{n=1}^{i} l_n\}$, $i = 1, \ldots, k$.

Theorem 2. In order for the finite automaton $A = (X, S, \varphi)$, $|X| = N$, $|S| = M$ were AOA and to be able to detect any single error, it is necessary that:

a) $N \geq 2$ at $M \geq 2$;

b) it realizes the permutation group $G = \langle \Pi_1, \ldots, \Pi_N \rangle$;

c) $\Pi_i(q) \neq \Pi_j(q)$ for any $i \neq j$, $i, j = 1, \ldots, N$, $q \in S$;

d) if $\Pi_i = \Pi^{r_i}$ and $\Pi_j = \Pi^{r_j}$ for some permutations of Π, Π_i, Π_j, $i \neq j$, $i, j \in \{1, \ldots, N\}$ and n umbers r_i, $r_j \in \mathbb{Z}$ then $\Pi = (q_1 q_2 \ldots q_M)$, $q_i \in S$, $i = 1, \ldots, M$ and $GCD(M, r_i, r_j) = GCD(M, r_i - r_j) = 1$;

e) subgroups $G_{ij} = \langle \Pi_i, \Pi_j \rangle$ of the group G are transitive for any $i \neq j$, $i, j = 1, \ldots, N$.

Theorem 3. In order for the finite automaton $A = (X, S, \varphi)$, $|X| = N$, $|S| = M$ were AOA and to be able to detect any single error it is sufficient to fulfill the conditions a) - d) of the theorem 2 and the subgroups $G_{ij} = \langle \Pi_i, \Pi_j \rangle$ of the group G to be primitive for any $i \neq j$, $i, j = 1, \ldots, N$.

Theorem 4. If M is a prime number, then the conditions of the theorems 2, 3 coincide and are necessary and sufficient. In the opposite case the conditions of the theorems 2 and 3 are strictly necessary and strictly sufficient respectively.

Theorem 4 shows that the group classification according to connectivity (transitive, primitive, doubly transitive, etc.) accepted in the group theory is not sufficient to describe the permutation groups which provide the regularity of sets on which they have an effect. In general these groups are somewhere "between" the transitive and primitive groups.

Automaton realizing Checksums Modulo M can be described the next way: $A = (X, S, \varphi)$ where $X = \{0, 1, \ldots, N-1\}$, $N \geq 2$, $S = \{0, 1, \ldots, M-1\}$, $M \geq 2$ and $S^t = X^t + S^{t-1} (\bmod M)$. The subset of AOA class realizing the given method of DCT is singled out by the following statement.

Consequence 1. For FA realizing Checksums Modulo M to be AOA and to be able to detect any single error it is necessary and sufficient that M be mutually prime with all numbers 2,3,...,N-1.

Thus at N = 2, i.e. when binary bits are added in each step, there are not any limits for M. The validity of the error detection probability in this case will be asymptotically equal to (M-1)/M. While N increases the selection of M becomes more and more restricted. These results correspond to the intuitive representation about "compression" of the diagnostic information. The increase of N means that for one step the automaton processes more information and hence, the testing time decreases. To obtain the same value of error detection probability should be somehow "repaid". In our case,"the payment" is expressed in the increase of limitations for the selecting of the number M.

3. Linear finite sequential machines that belong to the class AOA

In keeping with the work of [7] we shall designate the set of linear finite sequential machines (LFSMs) signals and states by $X = (x_1 \ldots x_n)^T$ and $S = (s_1 \ldots s_m)^T$ respectively (letter T over the vector means transposition), $A = (a_{ij})_{m\times m}$ will denote the characteristic matrix of LFSM, $B = (b_{ij})_{m\times n}$ is matrix characterizing the paths in LFSM from input to states and $L_r = (A^{r-1}B,\ A^{r-2}B, \ldots, B)$ where $m = \log_k M$, $n = \log_k N$ and k is a prime number, characteristic of the Galois field GF(k) over which LFSM is defined.

Let L_{mr} denote sub matrix of L_m matrix consisting of columns with $r + l \cdot n$, $l = 0,\ldots,m-1$, $r \in \{1,\ldots,n\}$ numbers. Then from theorem 1 we have

Consequence 2. For LFSM to be AOA and detect any single error it is necessary that $\mathrm{rank}(L_{mr}) = m$ for any $r \in \{1,\ldots,n\}$, $\mathrm{rank}(A) = m$ and $\mathrm{rank}(B) = n$. If LFSM is defined over the field GF(2) then this conditions are also sufficient.

Consequence 3. Let LFSM is defined over GF(2) field , matrix A is fixed and n and matrix B are arbitrary such that rank(B) = n. Then for LFSM to be AOA and detect any single error it is necessary and sufficient that characteristic polynomial of matrix A to be irreducible.

Easy checkable sufficient conditions for LFSM defined over an arbitrary field GF(k) and belonged to AOA class are given by the following statement.

Consequence 4. If characteristic polynomial of matrix A is primitive then for LFSM to be AOA and detect any single error it is necessary and sufficient that rank(B) = n.

The example of signature analyzer (SA) which is AOA and detects any single error is conventional SA [2] because its characteristic polynomial of matrix A is primitive, $B = (10...0)^T$ and rank(B) = n = 1. The example of optimal SA with many inputs can be SA implementing parallel signature analyzers (see [9] and references in it) with irreducible characteristic polynomial of matrix A and unitary matrix B: in this case rank(B) = n at $n \leq m$.

References

1. T.R.N.Rao , Fujiwara E. Error-control coding for computer systems. USA: Prentice-Hall, 1989, 524p.
2. R.A.Frohwerk, "Signature Analysis: A new digital field service method", Hewlett-Packard J., 1977, vol 28, No 9, pp.2-8.
3. Hewlett-Packard Corp."A Designs Guide to Signature Analysis". Appl. 222, 1978.
4. A.N.Efimov, E.V.Luk-Zilberman,"Signature Analyzers", Avtomatika i telemekhanika, 1988, No 1, pp. 90 - 97.
5. A.N.Efimov, E.V.Luk-Zilberman, "The sensitive finite automata to distortions of input signals and signature analysis", Itogi nauki i tekhniki. Ser. Tekhn. kibern., 1988, 25, pp. 135 - 168.
6. E.V.Luk-Zilberman, "Theory of Determinate Compact Testing". Proc. 11th All-Union Conf. on Problems of Control, 1989, pp. 247-248.
7. A.Gill,. Linear Sequential Circuits. New York: McGraw-Hill, 1966, 215p.

8. J.G.Kemeny, J.L.Snell, Finite Markov Chains. Princeton: VanNostrand, 1960, 210p.

9. M.Yinghua, K.M.Yashwant, J.Boping, "Analysis of Detection Capability of Parallel Signature Analyzers", IEEE Trans. Comput., 1991, vol 40, No 9, pp. 1075-1081.

Optimal k-colouring and k-nesting of intervals

Irith Ben-Arroyo Hartman

Mathematics Faculty
Technion - Israel Institute of Technology,
Technion City, Haifa, Israel 32000
MAR4037 @ TECHNION.BITNET

Abstract: We describe and solve two problems motivated from routing in CMOS cells layed out in the style of one-dimensional transistor arrays, as well as from channel routing. In the first problem we find an optimal subset of intervals to be layed out on k tracks, for any given k. In the second problem we find an optimal set of nested intervals, to be layed out on any given number of tracks. Both solutions are polynomial time, and have applications in many routing problems.

1.Introduction

We discuss and solve two graph theoretical problems. These problems are are strongly related to routing polysilicon nets in CMOS cells, in the one-dimensional transistor array style as was suggested by Uehara and vanCleemput. Another application of these problems is to channel routing.

We open with graph theoretical definitions, and precise formulations of the problems. In section 2 we describe the motivations to these problems, and their applications to routing in CMOS standard cells, as well as to channel routing. We note that these theoretical problems may be essential to many other applications in routing problems. Finally, in sections 3 and 4 we present optimal polynomial time solutions to the problems defined in the introduction.

Definitions 1.1: Let $\mathcal{I}$ be a set of intervals on the real line. A set of intervals is *independent* if all the intervals in the set are pairwise non-intersecting. Let k be a positive integer. A *partial k-colouring* of $\mathcal{I}$ is a collection $T = \{T_1, T_2, \ldots, T_k\}$, of disjoint subsets of $\mathcal{I}$, where each subset T_i is an independent set of intervals. We note that some of the subsets may be empty.
Denote by $\mathcal{I}(T)$ the set of intervals covered by T. ($\mathcal{I}(T) = \bigcup T_i$). Note that $\mathcal{I}(T)$ is a subset of $\mathcal{I}$. Assume that each inteval $I \in \mathcal{I}$ has a weight defined by a weight function $w(I)$.
A partial k-colouring is *optimal* if $\sum_{I \in \mathcal{I}(T)} w(I)$ is maximum. For example, if $w(I) = 1$ for each $I \in \mathcal{I}$ then an optimal partial k-colouring contains as many intervals as possible.

Problem 1.1: Given a set of intervals $\mathcal{I}$, a weight function w, and an integer k, find an optimal partial k-colouring of $\mathcal{I}$.

Figure 1 (a),(b) depicts a set of intervals $\mathcal{I}$, and an optimal partial k-colouring of $\mathcal{I}$ for $k = 2$, and weight function which is identically one.

An optimal polynomial tim. solution to this problem will be discussed in section 3.

Given a set of intervals, each pair of intervals will satisfy exactly one of the following properties:

Containment. One of the intervals is contained in the other.

Overlap. The intervals intersect but neither contains the other.

Disjointedness. The intervals have an empty intersection.

Definitions 1.2: Let $\mathcal{I}$ be a set of intervals, $w(I)$ a weight function on $\mathcal{I}$, and k a positive integer. A *partial k-nesting* is a partial k-colouring $\mathbb{N} = \{T_1, T_2, \dots, T_k\}$, with the property that no two intervals in $\mathcal{I}(\mathbb{N})$ overlap.
In other words, any two intervals in a partial k-nesting are either disjoint, or one is contained in the other.
A partial k-nesting $\mathbb{N}$ is *optimal* if $\sum_{I \in \mathcal{I}(\mathbb{N})} w(I)$ is maximum.

Problem 1.2: Let $\mathcal{I}$ be a set of intervals with weight function w, and let k be a positive integer. Find an optimal partial k -nesting of $\mathcal{I}$.

Figure 1(a),(c) depicts an optimal partial 2-nesting for $w = 1$ and interval set $\mathcal{I}$.

An optimal polynomial time solution to this problem will be described in section 4.

Figure 1. . (a) A set of intervals $\mathcal{I}$. (b) Optimal partial 2-colouring. (c) Optimal partial 2-nesting.

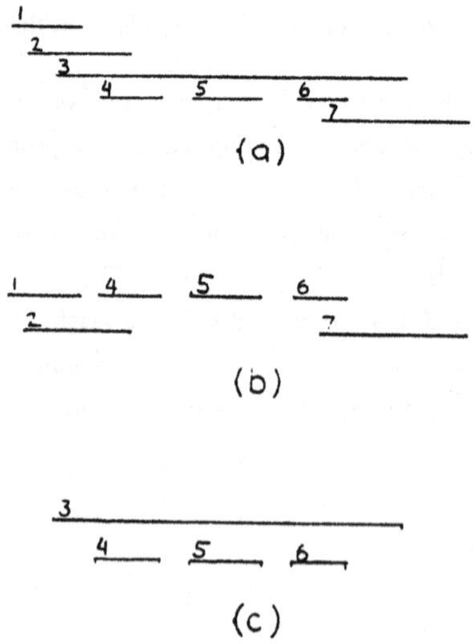

2. Applications and motivations

2.1 Routing polysilicon nets in CMOS cells

Problems 1.1 and 1.2 are strongly motivated from the problems of routing in CMOS standard cells, laid out in a one-dimensional array style suggested by Uehara and vanCleemput [16]. We make the following assumptions on the layout: (see Figure 2)

All transistors are arranged on two parallel horizontal rows. One row for the P-type transistors, and one for the N-type transistors.

Assume that the transistors are arranged in pairs of N and P types.

Gates are implemented by vertical polysilicon strips, where pairs which share a common gate, share the same vertical polysilicon strip.

Power supplies are metal strips which run horizontally along the p-transistors, and n-transistors.

Wiring is done either in metal (no assumption on the number of layers used is made) or in polysilicon.

There is a restricted number of wiring tracks above the diffusion, and a restricted number of wiring tracks off the diffusion (outside the diffusion). Routing off the diffusion can be done either on the top or bottom sides of the cell, or between the two rows of the transistors.

Figure 2. A CMOS cell. Shaded area-diffusion. Black squares-contacts. Wide stripes-polysilicon. Narrow stripes-metal. Notice the routing in polysilicon off the diffusion area.

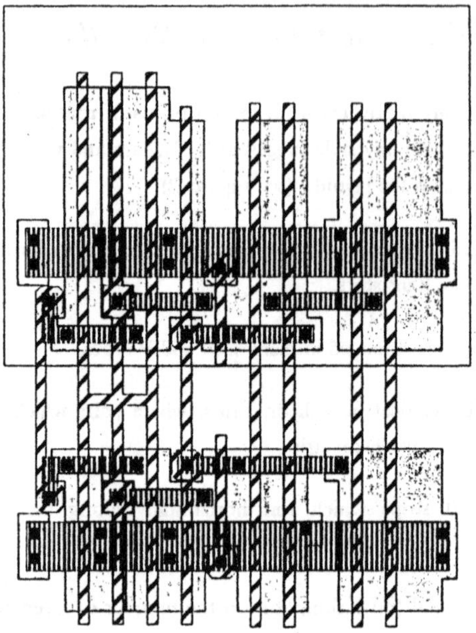

A *feasible routing* is a routing of the nets which does not violate the restrictions on the number of wiring tracks. Wiring over the diffusion can be, obviously, done only in metal (a polysilicon wire would create a new transistor), and it requires the use of contacts. Adjacent contacts over the diffusion often require more space, thus expanding the area of the cell. Hence, a good strategy is to wire, initially, as many nets (or parts of nets) as possible outside the diffusion area, and then wire the rest of the nets (using a greedy interval graph colouring algorithm) over the diffusion.

A *poly-net* is a net all of which ports are on gates. Each poly-net is a candidate to be wired off the diffusion area. We represent each such net by a *poly-interval,* whose endpoints are the x coordinates of the leftmost and rightmost ports of the net, (see Figure 3). We remark that some 'mixed' nets, consisting of ports on gates and on diffusion, can be broken down into poly-intervals and *diffusion intervals* . Let k be the number of wiring tracks off the diffusion area. Our aim is to wire as many of the poly-intervals on the given k tracks. Problem 1.1 is a formal description of this problem, where $\mathcal{I}$ is the set of candidate poly-intervals. The weight function w can be defined according to our desirability for a specific net to be routed off the diffusion. For example, nets with many ports, or nets which span long intervals may receive a heavier weight.

Figure 3. Nets, and their corresponding intervals.

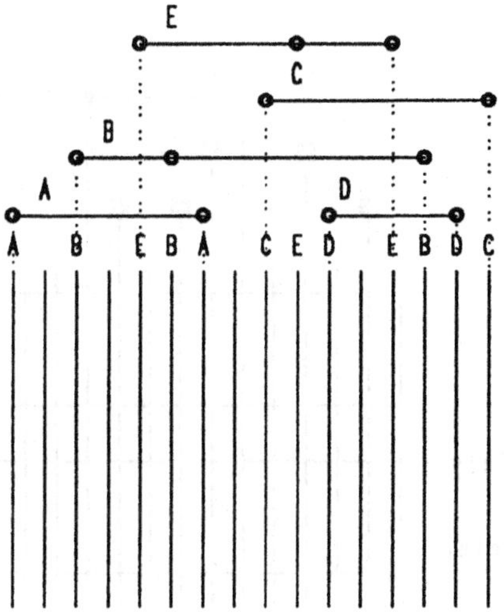

Given a solution $T = \{T_1, T_2, \dots, T_k\}$ to Problem 1.1, then the routing can be done using polysilicon wires, as well as metal wires according to the following guidelines:

All poly-nets in the channel can be routed in polysilicon, unless the poly-interval crosses a vertical polysilicon line belonging to a different net. In this case metal must be used.

If there is a single track above (or below) the cell, then the nets assigned to it are wired in poly.

If there are more than two tracks above (or below) the cell, then it is possible to wire the horizontal intervals on the furthest track from the cell in poly, and intervals on other tracks in metal. Vertical wires are wired in poly. (see Figure 4 for example.) The connection between poly and metal uses contacts. In [4] there is an efficient solution to a related problem of minimizing the number of necessary poly-metal contacts.

The rest of the poly-nets which are not covered by any independent set are routed in metal over the diffusion.

Figure 4. Routing poly-nets above the cell.

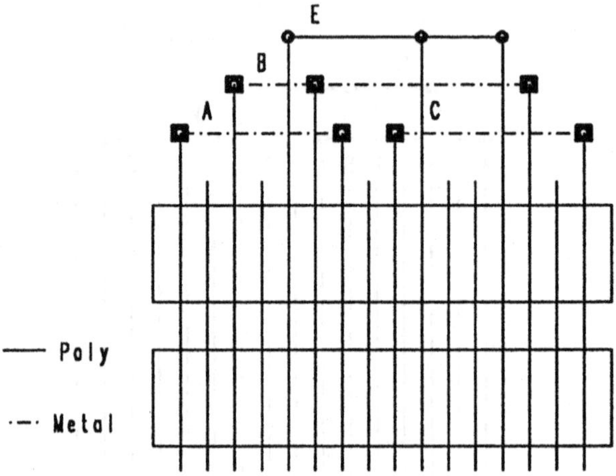

Suppose now, that we have a set of poly-nets, all of which are candidates for routing off the diffusion in one region, say above the cell, and we insist that the routing is done in polysilicon, and not in metal. This gives us the advantage of not using contacts for these nets. As can be seen in Figure 5, any two poly-intervals routed in polysilicon are either disjoint, or one is contained in the other. We claim that the problem of routing in polysilicon as many poly-nets as possible off the diffusion, is equivalent to Problem 1.2:

Let k denote the number of available intervals off the diffusion area in one region, say above the cell. The set $\mathcal{I}$ will be defined now slightly differently than above: For any pair of consecutive gate ports P_1, P_2 on a net, define an open interval (x_1, x_2), where x_i, $i = 1,2$, is the $x-$ coordinate of P_i. For example, if we have a net with gate ports at positions x_1, x_2, and x_3, the corresponding poly intervals are (x_1, x_2) and (x_2, x_3). Since, by definition, all intervals corresponding to a unique net are disjoint, they may be assigned to the same track in an optimal partial k-nesting.

Finally, given an optimal solution to Problem 1.2, $\mathbb{N} = \{T_1, T_2, \dots, T_k\}$, the intervals in each set T_i are assigned to track i and routed in polysilicon.

Figure 5. . (a)$\mathcal{J}$ (b)$T = \{T_1, \ldots, T_4\}$

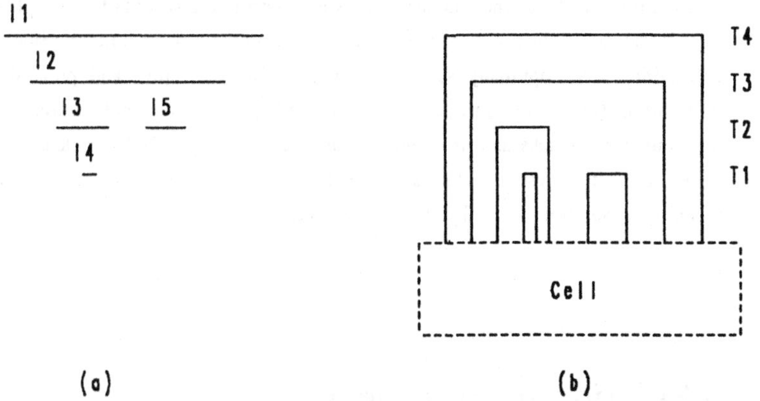

2.2 Channel Routing

A channel routing problem is described by two parallel rows of terminals. The rectangular area between the rows is called a *channel*. The channel routing problem is to connect all terminals of each net using the area in the channel, such that no two nets are electrically shorted. Alternatively, the problem is to find a solution which requires the minimum number of tracks used in the channel. Channel routing problem is NP-complete, and it is known to be NP-complete under various models and restrictions [15]. (For a survey on the subject see also [13].) Among the many heuristic algorithms to the problem, the approach known as the "left edge algorithm" suggested by Hashimoto and Stevens [9] is widely used, and is a basis for further improvements (see [20], [19] and [18]). According to this heuristic, the horizontal tracks are processed sequentially, starting from the tracks closest to the channel, and finishing at the inner ones. At each iteration, (say, for track i) a choice of the nets to be placed in track i is made. The choice is made by taking into consideration vertical constraints [1] , and other considerations which arise from the specific channel routing problem. When no additional nets can be placed on track i, the next track is processed.

---

[1] *vertical constraints* occur when two distinct nets have ports which share a column.

A new improvement on this heuristic can be gotten by processing a given number of tracks simultaneously. For example, if we would like to minimize the total length of vertical wires used (total length of "legs"), we define the set $\mathcal{I}$ as the set of all nets containing a large number of ports on the top (or bottom) side which are good candidates to be wired on the k topmost (or bottommost) tracks in the channel. We assign appropriate weights to the nets in $\mathcal{I}$ by taking into consideration the number of ports in each net on the top (or bottom) side, and the vertical constraints. We optimally solve Problem 1.1 for this input, and proceed to the next k bottommost (or topmost) tracks, etc. Using this heuristic, we cannot ensure, of-course, that the total number of tracks used is minimum (since the problem is NP-complete), but we are likely to get satisfactory results as far as the total vertical wire length. We remark that this solution includes the solutions in [19] and [18] as a special case for $k = 1$.

3.Solution to Problem 1.1

In [17] the authors propose a linear algorithm to Problem 1.1 for $k = 1$, and suggest that the problem is intractable for $k > 1$. We present here a polynomial solution for this problem for all k.

Let $\mathcal{I} = \{I_1, I_2, \dots, I_n\}$ be the given set of intervals. We define a directed graph $G = (V,E)$ where V corresponds to the set of intervals. Label V with $\{1,2, \dots, n\}$. The arcs of G are defined by:

$(i,j) \in E$ if and only if I_i is disjoint from I_j and is on its left.

The weight w_i of vertex i is the weight of the corresponding interval I_i. If we wish to optimize the number of intervals in T then we set $w_i = 1$ for all i.
The following facts are easy to see:

Fact 1: G is acyclic and transitive.

Fact 2: Any set of pairwise non-intersecting intervals corresponds to an acyclic tournament [2] in G, and vice versa.

Since an acyclic tournament contains a unique spanning path (also known as a *Hamilton path* or a *total order*) we have an obvious 1-1 correspondence between sets of pairwise non-intersecting intervals, and directed paths in G.
Thus, Problem 1.1 is equivalent to the following:

---

[2] A *tournament* is a directed graph where any two vertices are connected by an arc.

Problem 3.1: Let G be a directed acyclic graph with weights on its vertices, and let k be a positive integer. Find a set of k disjoint directed paths of maximum weight. (The weight of a path is the sum of the weights of the vertices on the path.)

Remarks:

1. The unweighted version of Problem 3.1 was optimally solved by Hoffman [10] . See also [1] .

2. If the graph G is not acyclic, then Problem 3.1 is NP-complete for any constant k. This can be shown by reducing the directed Hamilton path problem to Problem 3.1.

3. For $k = 1$, Problem 3.1 is equivalent to the problem of finding a longest path in an acyclic digraph, for which a simple linear algorithm exists. (see for example [5] .) For $k > 1$, no linear or 'greedy' algorithm is known and more powerful tools are needed.

4. Figure 6 below demonstrates that for $k = 2$, and $w = 1$ any greedy algorithm which finds a longest path P_1 in G, and then finds another longest path P_2 in $G - P_1$, fails to find an optimal set of two paths. The graph G in Figure 6(b) is the acyclic digraph as defined above, corresponding to $\mathcal{I}$. Clearly, the paths $P_1 = (1,2,3,4)$ and $P_2 = (1', 2', 3', 4')$ form an optimal set of paths, since they cover $V(G)$. Now, consider all the longest paths in G. There are two such paths: $Q_1 = (1,2,3,3', 4')$ and $Q_2 = (1',2,3,3', 4')$. In either case, the remaining graph, $G - Q_i$, $i = 1,2$ cannot be covered by a single path. Hence, the greedy algorithm of picking consecutive longest paths fails to find an optimal solution.

Figure 6. . (a) An interval set $\mathcal{I}$. (b) The corresponding graph G.

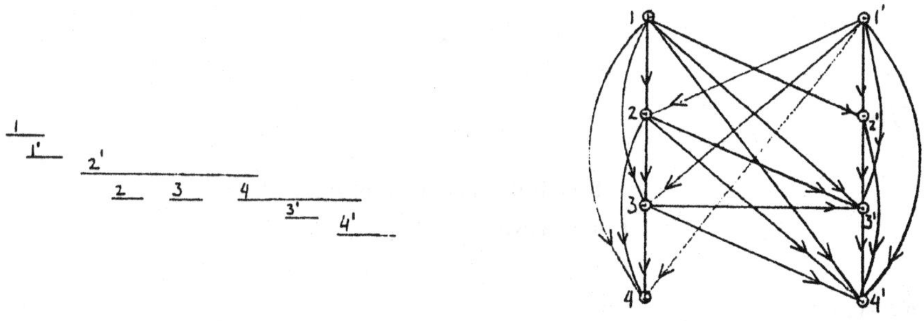

(a) (b)

Solution to Problem 3.1: Define a linear program similar to [10] and [1] .

Let $C = (c_{ij})$, $i,j = 0,1, \dots, n$ be defined by
$c_{i0} = 0$ for all i ; $c_{0j} = w_j$ for all $j > 0$
$c_{ii} = 0$ for all i

$$\text{if } i>0, j>0, \text{ and } i \neq j, \text{ then } c_{ij} = \begin{cases} w_j & \text{if } (i,j) \in E \\ \text{not defined if } (i,j) \notin E. \end{cases}$$

Consider the transportation problem:

$$\text{maximize} \sum_{i,j=0}^{n} c_{ij} x_{ij} \tag{3.1}$$

where

$$\sum_{j=0}^{n} x_{0j} = \sum_{i=0}^{n} x_{i0} = k \tag{3.2}$$

$$\sum_{j=0}^{n} x_{ij} = 1 \text{ for } i>0; \quad \sum_{i=0}^{n} x_{ij} = 1 \text{ for } j>0 \tag{3.3}$$

and $x_{ij} \geq 0$ for all i, j, except that x_{ij} is not defined if $i > 0, j > 0, i \neq j$ and $(i,j) \notin E$. (3.4)

Every set of t disjoint paths $\{P_1, P_2, \dots, P_t\}$, $t \leq k$, corresponds to a feasible solution x, of (3.1) - (3.4) defined in the following way:

$$x_{00} = k - t$$

if $j > 0$,

$$x_{0j} = \begin{cases} 1 & \text{if } j \text{ is the start of one of } P_1, \dots, P_t \\ 0 & \text{otherwise .} \end{cases}$$

if $i > 0$,

$$x_{i0} = \begin{cases} 1 & \text{if } i \text{ is the end of one of } P_1, \dots, P_t \\ 0 & \text{otherwise .} \end{cases}$$

if $i > 0$,

$$x_{ii} = \begin{cases} 1 & \text{if } i \notin V(P_1) \cup \cdots \cup V(P_t) \\ 0 & \text{if } i \in V(P_1) \cup \cdots \cup V(P_t) \end{cases}$$

if $i > 0, j > 0, i \neq j$, then

$$x_{ij} = \begin{cases} 1 & \text{if } (i,j) \text{ is an edge of } P_r \text{ for some } r = 1, \dots, t \\ 0 & \text{otherwise} . \end{cases}$$

Conversely, we shall show that any integral feasible solution of (3.1)-(3.4) above corresponds to a set of at most k disjoint paths. (alternatively, a set of exactly k disjoint paths, where some of the paths are allowed to be empty, as in the case of $k > n$.) Since the coefficient matrix of equations (3.2)-(3.3) is totally unimodular [11] there exists an integral optimal solution X^0 for this problem. Furthermore, any known algorithm for solving a linear program (such as the 'simplex method') will terminate with an integral optimal solution. By Khachian's algorithm [12] , it follows that there exists a polynomial time algorithm to the linear program.
Now let X be a feasible solution of the LP. Each x_{ij} in X must be 0 or 1 , except for perhaps x_{00} which may be larger. Now let X^0 be a feasible integral solution. Each $i > 0$ such that $x^0_{0i} = 1$ is the beginning of a path. The edges of the paths are all (i,j) such that $x^0_{ij} = 1$ and $i \neq j$. Similarly, each $i > 0$ such that $x_{i0} = 1$ is the end of a path. Since G is acyclic, the edges defined above form a collection of exactly t disjoint paths, where $t = k - x_{00}$.

Since the objective function (3.1) measures the total weight of these paths, an optimal solution to the linear program corresponds to an optimal solution to Problem 3.1. ∎

4.Solution to Problem 1.2

Let $\mathcal{I} = \{I_1, I_2, \dots, I_n\}$ be the set of given intervals. We define the *overlap graph* $G = (V,E)$ of $\mathcal{I}$ as follows:

> $V = \{1, 2, \dots, n\}$ corresponds to the intervals $I_1, I_2, \dots, I_n$, and
> $(x,y) \in E$ if and only if the corresponding intervals I_x and I_y overlap.

In [8] an algorithm is presented for finding a maximum independent set in an overlap graph. This corresponds to finding a maximum k-nesting where k is unrestricted (say, $k \geq n$), and all the intervals have weights one. Here we introduce the restriction of k, and assume that the intervals have weights given by the weight function w.

As in [8], we define two more directed graphs $G_C = (V,C)$ and $G_F = (V,F)$ defined on the same vertex set V. Let $G_C = (V,C)$ be the *containment digraph* of $\mathcal{I}$ where $(x,y) \in C$ if and only if I_x is contained in I_y.
Let $G_F = (V,F)$ be the *disjointness digraph* of $\mathcal{I}$ where $(x,y) \in F$ if and only if I_x and I_y are disjoint, and I_x is entirely to the left of I_y.

For all $x \in V$, let $U(x) = \{v \in V | vx \in C\}$ be the set of indices whose corresponding intervals are contained in I_x. The algorithm is as follows:

Input:

A collection $\mathcal{I}$ of intervals whose overlap graph is $G = (V, A)$.

A weight function $w(x)$.

The graphs G_C and G_F.

An integer k.

Output:

An optimal partial k nesting of $\mathcal{I}$.

Method:

We assign, to each vertex $x \in V$ a cost $c(x)$ and a maximum i-nesting $S(x)$ contained in x, where $c(x)$ is the total weight of the set $S(x)$. This is done recursively in such a way that the vertices are assigned weights according to their order with respect to G_C. At every recursive call i is increased by 1 from 1 to k. The algorithm uses a subroutine MAXWEIGHT CLIQUE, which finds a maximum weight clique in a transitive graph $G_F[X] = (X, F[X])$, the graph induced by the vertex set X. (See [8] for such a subroutine.) This optimal clique corresponds to a set of pairwise disjoint intervals $\{I_v\}_{v \in T}$ that generates in line 6 of MAXSTABLE the best possible i-nesting. The entire algorithm is as follows:

```
   Procedure MAXSTABLE(X,k ):
   begin
1.   If X=φ then return φ;;
2.   while ∃x∈X with w(x) undefined do
     begin
3.        if k=1 then s(x) ← {x};
          else
4.        s(x) ← {x} ∪ MAXSTABLE(U(x),k-1);;
5.        w(x) ←   Σ    c(x);
               x∈S(x)
     end
6.   T ← MAXWEIGHT CLIQUE ( X,F[X] );
7.   return ∪ s(v);
   end     v∈T
```

It can be shown, by induction on k, that MAXSTABLE (X,k) correctly finds an optimal partial k-nesting. We omit the proof since it is similar to the proof presented in [8].

Acknowledgements: I thank my colleague R. Aharoni for improving the solution to Problem 1.2, and also my colleagues at IBM, J. Feldman, M.C. Golumbic, A. Turgeman, I.A. Wagner, and S. Wimer for fruitful discussions.

Note Added in Proof: I recently learned that M. C. Carlisle and E. L. Lloyd have solved Problem 1.1 with an $O(kn\log n)$ algorithm. Their result appears in Lecture Notes in Computer Science: Advances in Computing and Information - ICCI '91, Springer-Verlag, May 1991, 90-101.

References

[1] R.Aharoni, I.B-A. Hartman, and A.J.Hoffman, **Path Partitions and Packs of Acyclic Digraphs,** *Pacific Journal of Mathematics,118(2)* (1985), 249-259.

[2] R.Bar-Yehuda, J.A.Feldman, R.Y.Pinter, and S.Wimer, **Depth First Search and Dynamic Programming Algorithms for Efficient CMOS Cell Generation** *IEEE Trans. on CAD, 8(7),* (1989),737-743.

[3] J.A.Bondy and U.S.R.Murty, **Graph Theory with Applications** *Macmillan, London, and American Elsevier,New York* 1976.

[4] H.Edelsbrunner, M.Overmars, and E.Welzl, I.B-A.Hartman, and J.A.Feldman, **Ranking Intervals Under Visibility Constraints,** *Intern. J.Computer Math. 34,* (1990), 129-144.

[5] S. Even, **Graph Algorithms,** *Computer Science Press,* 1979.

[6] J.C.Fournier, **Une Characterization des graphes de cordes,** *C.R.Acad.Sci.Paris 286A,* (1978), 811-813.

[7] F.Gavril, **Algorithms for a maximum clique and a minimum independent set of a circle graph,** *Networks 3,* (1973), 261-273.

[8] M.C.Golumbic, **Algorithmic Graph Theory and Perfect Graphs,** *Academic Press,* 1980.

[9] A.Hashimoto and J.Stevens, **Wire Routing by Optimizing Channel Assignment,** *Proc. 8th DA Conference,* (1971), 214-224.

[10] A.J.Hoffman, **Extending Greene's Theorem to Directed Graphs,** *J. Combinatorial Theory, Ser.A, 34* (1983), 102-107.

[11] A.J.Hoffman and J.B.Kruskal, **Integral boundary points of convex polyhedra,** in *Linear inequalities and related systems, Annals of Mathematics Study 8,* (1956), 223-246.

[12] L.G.Khachian, **A Polynomial algorithm for linear programming,** *Doclady Akad. Nauk USSR, 244, no.5* 7 (1979), 1093-96.

[13] A.S.LaPaugh and R.Y.Pinter, **Channel Routing for Integrated Circuits,** *Annual Review of Computer Science 4,* (1989).

[14] L.Redei, **Ein Kombinatorischer Satz,** *Acta Litt. Sci. Szeged* 7 (1934), 39-43.

[15] T.G.Szymanski, **Dogleg Channel Routing is NP-Complete,** *IEEE Trans. on Computer-Aided Design CAD-4,* (Jan. 1985), 31-41.

[16] T. Uehara and W. M. vanCleemput, **Optimal Layout of CMOS Functional Arrays,** *IEEE Trans. on Comput., C-30,* (1981), 305-312.

[17] S. Wimer, R. Y. Pinter, and J. A. Feldman, **Optimal Chaining of CMOS Transistors in a Functional Cell,** *IEEE Trans. on CAD of Integrated Circuits and Systems, CAD-6,* (1987), 795-801.

[18] U. Yoeli, **A Robust Channel Router,** *IEEE Trans. on Computer-Aided Design CAD-10(2),* (February 1991), 212-219.

[19] T.Yoshimura, **An Efficient Channel Router**, *Proc. 21st Design Automation Conference,* (June 1984), 38-44.

[20] T.Yoshimura and E.S.Kuh, **Efficient Algorithms for Channel Routing**, *IEEE Trans. on Computer-Aided Design, CAD-1(1),* (Jan. 1982), 25-35.

Lecture Notes in Computer Science

For information about Vols. 1–515
please contact your bookseller or Springer-Verlag

Vol. 516: S. Kaplan, M. Okada (Eds.), Conditional and Typed Rewriting Systems. Proceedings, 1990. IX, 461 pages. 1991.

Vol. 517: K. Nökel, Temporally Distributed Symptoms in Technical Diagnosis. IX, 164 pages. 1991. (Subseries LNAI).

Vol. 518: J. G. Williams, Instantiation Theory. VIII, 133 pages. 1991. (Subseries LNAI).

Vol. 519: F. Dehne, J.-R. Sack, N. Santoro (Eds.), Algorithms and Data Structures. Proceedings, 1991. X, 496 pages. 1991.

Vol. 520: A. Tarlecki (Ed.), Mathematical Foundations of Computer Science 1991. Proceedings, 1991. XI, 435 pages. 1991.

Vol. 521: B. Bouchon-Meunier, R. R. Yager, L. A. Zadek (Eds.), Uncertainty in Knowledge-Bases. Proceedings, 1990. X, 609 pages. 1991.

Vol. 522: J. Hertzberg (Ed.), European Workshop on Planning. Proceedings, 1991. VII, 121 pages. 1991. (Subseries LNAI).

Vol. 523: J. Hughes (Ed.), Functional Programming Languages and Computer Architecture. Proceedings, 1991. VIII, 666 pages. 1991.

Vol. 524: G. Rozenberg (Ed.), Advances in Petri Nets 1991. VIII, 572 pages. 1991.

Vol. 525: O. Günther, H.-J. Schek (Eds.), Advances in Spatial Databases. Proceedings, 1991. XI, 471 pages. 1991.

Vol. 526: T. Ito, A. R. Meyer (Eds.), Theoretical Aspects of Computer Software. Proceedings, 1991. X, 772 pages. 1991.

Vol. 527: J.C.M. Baeten, J. F. Groote (Eds.), CONCUR '91. Proceedings, 1991. VIII, 541 pages. 1991.

Vol. 528: J. Maluszynski, M. Wirsing (Eds.), Programming Language Implementation and Logic Programming. Proceedings, 1991. XI, 433 pages. 1991.

Vol. 529: L. Budach (Ed.), Fundamentals of Computation Theory. Proceedings, 1991. XII, 426 pages. 1991.

Vol. 530: D. H. Pitt, P.-L. Curien, S. Abramsky, A. M. Pitts, A. Poigné, D. E. Rydeheard (Eds.), Category Theory and Computer Science. Proceedings, 1991. VII, 301 pages. 1991.

Vol. 531: E. M. Clarke, R. P. Kurshan (Eds.), Computer-Aided Verification. Proceedings, 1990. XIII, 372 pages. 1991.

Vol. 532: H. Ehrig, H.-J. Kreowski, G. Rozenberg (Eds.), Graph Grammars and Their Application to Computer Science. Proceedings, 1990. X, 703 pages. 1991.

Vol. 533: E. Börger, H. Kleine Büning, M. M. Richter, W. Schönfeld (Eds.), Computer Science Logic. Proceedings, 1990. VIII, 399 pages. 1991.

Vol. 534: H. Ehrig, K. P. Jantke, F. Orejas, H. Reichel (Eds.), Recent Trends in Data Type Specification. Proceedings, 1990. VIII, 379 pages. 1991.

Vol. 535: P. Jorrand, J. Kelemen (Eds.), Fundamentals of Artificial Intelligence Research. Proceedings, 1991. VIII, 255 pages. 1991. (Subseries LNAI).

Vol. 536: J. E. Tomayko, Software Engineering Education. Proceedings, 1991. VIII, 296 pages. 1991.

Vol. 537: A. J. Menezes, S. A. Vanstone (Eds.), Advances in Cryptology – CRYPTO '90. Proceedings. XIII, 644 pages. 1991.

Vol. 538: M. Kojima, N. Megiddo, T. Noma, A. Yoshise, A Unified Approach to Interior Point Algorithms for Linear Complementarity Problems. VIII, 108 pages. 1991.

Vol. 539: H. F. Mattson, T. Mora, T. R. N. Rao (Eds.), Applied Algebra, Algebraic Algorithms and Error-Correcting Codes. Proceedings, 1991. XI, 489 pages. 1991.

Vol. 540: A. Prieto (Ed.), Artificial Neural Networks. Proceedings, 1991. XIII, 476 pages. 1991.

Vol. 541: P. Barahona, L. Moniz Pereira, A. Porto (Eds.), EPIA '91. Proceedings, 1991. VIII, 292 pages. 1991. (Subseries LNAI).

Vol. 542: Z. W. Ras, M. Zemankova (Eds.), Methodologies for Intelligent Systems. Proceedings, 1991. X, 644 pages. 1991. (Subseries LNAI).

Vol. 543: J. Dix, K. P. Jantke, P. H. Schmitt (Eds.), Nonmonotonic and Inductive Logic. Proceedings, 1990. X, 243 pages. 1991. (Subseries LNAI).

Vol. 544: M. Broy, M. Wirsing (Eds.), Methods of Programming. XII, 268 pages. 1991.

Vol. 545: H. Alblas, B. Melichar (Eds.), Attribute Grammars , Applications and Systems. Proceedings, 1991. IX, 513 pages. 1991.

Vol. 546: O. Herzog, C.-R. Rollinger (Eds.), Text Understanding in LILOG. XI, 738 pages. 1991. (Subseries LNAI).

Vol. 547: D. W. Davies (Ed.), Advances in Cryptology – EUROCRYPT '91. Proceedings, 1991. XII, 556 pages. 1991.

Vol. 548: R. Kruse, P. Siegel (Eds.), Symbolic and Quantitative Approaches to Uncertainty. Proceedings, 1991. XI, 362 pages. 1991.

Vol. 549: E. Ardizzone, S. Gaglio, F. Sorbello (Eds.), Trends in Artificial Intelligence. Proceedings, 1991. XIV, 479 pages. 1991. (Subseries LNAI).

Vol. 550: A. van Lamsweerde, A. Fugetta (Eds.), ESEC '91. Proceedings, 1991. XII, 515 pages. 1991.

Vol. 551:S. Prehn, W. J. Toetenel (Eds.), VDM '91. Formal Software Development Methods. Volume 1. Proceedings, 1991. XIII, 699 pages. 1991.

Vol. 552: S. Prehn, W. J. Toetenel (Eds.), VDM '91. Formal Software Development Methods. Volume 2. Proceedings, 1991. XIV, 430 pages. 1991.

Vol. 553: H. Bieri, H. Noltemeier (Eds.), Computational Geometry - Methods, Algorithms and Applications '91. Proceedings, 1991. VIII, 320 pages. 1991.

Vol. 554: G. Grahne, The Problem of Incomplete Information in Relational Databases. VIII, 156 pages. 1991.

Vol. 555: H. Maurer (Ed.), New Results and New Trends in Computer Science. Proceedings, 1991. VIII, 403 pages. 1991.

Vol. 556: J.-M. Jacquet, Conclog: A Methodological Approach to Concurrent Logic Programming. XII, 781 pages. 1991.

Vol. 557: W. L. Hsu, R. C. T. Lee (Eds.), ISA '91 Algorithms. Proceedings, 1991. X, 396 pages. 1991.

Vol. 558: J. Hooman, Specification and Compositional Verification of Real-Time Systems. VIII, 235 pages. 1991.

Vol. 559: G. Butler, Fundamental Algorithms for Permutation Groups. XII, 238 pages. 1991.

Vol. 560: S. Biswas, K. V. Nori (Eds.), Foundations of Software Technology and Theoretical Computer Science. Proceedings, 1991. X, 420 pages. 1991.

Vol. 561: C. Ding, G. Xiao, W. Shan, The Stability Theory of Stream Ciphers. IX, 187 pages. 1991.

Vol. 562: R. Breu, Algebraic Specification Techniques in Object Oriented Programming Environments. XI, 228 pages. 1991.

Vol. 563: A. Karshmer, J. Nehmer (Eds.), Operating Systems of the 90s and Beyond. Proceedings, 1991. X, 285 pages. 1991.

Vol. 564: I. Herman, The Use of Projective Geometry in Computer Graphics. VIII, 146 pages. 1992.

Vol. 565: J. D. Becker, I. Eisele, F. W. Mündemann (Eds.), Parallelism, Learning, Evolution. Proceedings, 1989. VIII, 525 pages. 1991. (Subseries LNAI).

Vol. 566: C. Delobel, M. Kifer, Y. Masunaga (Eds.), Deductive and Object-Oriented Databases. Proceedings, 1991. XV, 581 pages. 1991.

Vol. 567: H. Boley, M. M. Richter (Eds.), Processing Declarative Kowledge. Proceedings, 1991. XII, 427 pages. 1991. (Subseries LNAI).

Vol. 568: H.-J. Bürckert, A Resolution Principle for a Logic with Restricted Quantifiers. X, 116 pages. 1991. (Subseries LNAI).

Vol. 569: A. Beaumont, G. Gupta (Eds.), Parallel Execution of Logic Programs. Proceedings, 1991. VII, 195 pages. 1991.

Vol. 570: R. Berghammer, G. Schmidt (Eds.), Graph-Theoretic Concepts in Computer Science. Proceedings, 1991. VIII, 253 pages. 1992.

Vol. 571: J. Vytopil (Ed.), Formal Techniques in Real-Time and Fault-Tolerant Systems. Proceedings, 1992. IX, 620 pages. 1991.

Vol. 572: K. U. Schulz (Ed.), Word Equations and Related Topics. Proceedings, 1990. VII, 256 pages. 1992.

Vol. 573: G. Cohen, S. N. Litsyn, A. Lobstein, G. Zémor (Eds.), Algebraic Coding. Proceedings, 1991. X, 158 pages. 1992.

Vol. 574: J. P. Banâtre, D. Le Métayer (Eds.), Research Directions in High-Level Parallel Programming Languages. Proceedings, 1991. VIII, 387 pages. 1992.

Vol. 575: K. G. Larsen, A. Skou (Eds.), Computer Aided Verification. Proceedings, 1991. X, 487 pages. 1992.

Vol. 576: J. Feigenbaum (Ed.), Advances in Cryptology - CRYPTO '91. Proceedings. X, 485 pages. 1992.

Vol. 577: A. Finkel, M. Jantzen (Eds.), STACS 92. Proceedings, 1992. XIV, 621 pages. 1992.

Vol. 578: Th. Beth, M. Frisch, G. J. Simmons (Eds.), Public-Key Cryptography: State of the Art and Future Directions. XI, 97 pages. 1992.

Vol. 579: S. Toueg, P. G. Spirakis, L. Kirousis (Eds.), Distributed Algorithms. Proceedings, 1991. X, 319 pages. 1992.

Vol. 580: A. Pirotte, C. Delobel, G. Gottlob (Eds.), Advances in Database Technology – EDBT '92. Proceedings. XII, 551 pages. 1992.

Vol. 581: J.-C. Raoult (Ed.), CAAP '92. Proceedings. VIII, 361 pages. 1992.

Vol. 582: B. Krieg-Brückner (Ed.), ESOP '92. Proceedings. VIII, 491 pages. 1992.

Vol. 583: I. Simon (Ed.), LATIN '92. Proceedings. IX, 545 pages. 1992.

Vol. 584: R. E. Zippel (Ed.), Computer Algebra and Parallelism. Proceedings, 1990. IX, 114 pages. 1992.

Vol. 585: F. Pichler, R. Moreno Díaz (Eds.), Computer Aided System Theory – EUROCAST '91. Proceedings. X, 761 pages. 1992.

Vol. 586: A. Cheese, Parallel Execution of Parlog. IX, 184 pages. 1992.

Vol. 587: R. Dale, E. Hovy, D. Rösner, O. Stock (Eds.), Aspects of Automated Natural Language Generation. Proceedings, 1992. VIII, 311 pages. 1992. (Subseries LNAI).

Vol. 588: G. Sandini (Ed.), Computer Vision – ECCV '92. Proceedings. XV, 909 pages. 1992.

Vol. 589: U. Banerjee, D. Gelernter, A. Nicolau, D. Padua (Eds.), Languages and Compilers for Parallel Computing. Proceedings, 1991. IX, 419 pages. 1992.

Vol. 590: B. Fronhöfer, G. Wrightson (Eds.), Parallelization in Inference Systems. Proceedings, 1990. VIII, 372 pages. 1992. (Subseries LNAI).

Vol. 591: H. P. Zima (Ed.), Parallel Computation. Proceedings, 1991. IX, 451 pages. 1992.

Vol. 592: A. Voronkov (Ed.), Logic Programming. Proceedings, 1991. IX, 514 pages. 1992. (Subseries LNAI).

Vol. 593: P. Loucopoulos (Ed.), Advanced Information Systems Engineering. Proceedings. XI, 650 pages. 1992.

Vol. 594: B. Monien, Th. Ottmann (Eds.), Data Structures and Efficient Algorithms. VIII, 389 pages. 1992.

Vol. 595: M. Levene, The Nested Universal Relation Database Model. X, 177 pages. 1992.

Vol. 596: L.-H. Eriksson, L. Hallnäs, P. Schroeder-Heister (Eds.), Extensions of Logic Programming. Proceedings, 1991. VII, 369 pages. 1992. (Subseries LNAI).

Vol. 597: H. W. Guesgen, J. Hertzberg, A Perspective of Constraint-Based Reasoning. VIII, 123 pages. 1992. (Subseries LNAI).

Vol. 598: S. Brookes, M. Main, A. Melton, M. Mislove, D. Schmidt (Eds.), Mathematical Foundations of Programming Semantics. Proceedings, 1991. VIII, 506 pages. 1992.

Vol. 599: Th. Wetter, K.-D. Althoff, J. Boose, B. R. Gaines, M. Linster, F. Schmalhofer (Eds.), Current Developments in Knowledge Acquisition - EKAW '92. Proceedings. XIII, 444 pages. 1992. (Subseries LNAI).

Vol. 600: J. W. de Bakker, K. Huizing, W. P. de Roever, G. Rozenberg (Eds.), Real-Time: Theory in Practice. Proceedings, 1991. VIII, 723 pages. 1992.

Vol. 601: D. Dolev, Z. Galil, M. Rodeh (Eds.), Theory of Computing and Systems. Proceedings, 1992. VIII, 220 pages. 1992.